Microsoft® Exchange Server 2013

Design, Deploy, and Deliver an Enterprise Messaging Solution

Nathan Winters

Neil Johnson

Nicolas Blank

SYBEX®
A Wiley Brand

Acquisitions Editor: Mariann Barsolo

Development Editor: Gary Schwartz

Technical Editor: Henrik Walther

Production Editor: Liz Britten

Copy Editor: Linda Recktenwald

Editorial Manager: Pete Gaughan

Production Manager: Tim Tate

Vice President and Executive Group Publisher: Richard Swadley

Vice President and Publisher: Neil Edde

Book Designers: Maureen Forys, Happenstance Type-O-Rama; Judy Fung

Proofreader: Daniel Aull, Word One, New York

Indexer: Ted Laux

Project Coordinator, Cover: Katherine Crocker

Cover Designer: Ryan Sneed

Cover Image: ©iStockphoto.com/Kalawin

ISBN: 978-1-118-54190-6
ISBN: 978-1-118-75027-8 (ebk.)
ISBN: 978-1-118-77953-8 (ebk.)

For general information on our other products and services or to obtain technical support, please contact our Customer Care Department within the U.S. at (877) 762-2974, outside the U.S. at (317) 572-3993 or fax (317) 572-4002.

Wiley publishes in a variety of print and electronic formats and by print-on-demand. Some material included with standard print versions of this book may not be included in e-books or in print-on-demand. If this book refers to media such as a CD or DVD that is not included in the version you purchased, you may download this material at http://booksupport.wiley.com. For more information about Wiley products, visit www.wiley.com.

Library of Congress Control Number: 2013937651

10 9 8 7 6 5 4 3 2 1

Dear Reader,

Thank you for choosing *Microsoft Exchange Server 2013*. This book is part of a family of premium-quality Sybex books, all of which are written by outstanding authors who combine practical experience with a gift for teaching.

Sybex was founded in 1976. More than 30 years later, we're still committed to producing consistently exceptional books. With each of our titles, we're working hard to set a new standard for the industry. From the paper we print on, to the authors we work with, our goal is to bring you the best books available.

I hope you see all that reflected in these pages. I'd be very interested to hear your comments and get your feedback on how we're doing. Feel free to let me know what you think about this or any other Sybex book by sending me an email at nedde@wiley.com. If you think you've found a technical error in this book, please visit http://sybex.custhelp.com. Customer feedback is critical to our efforts at Sybex.

Best regards,

Neil Edde
Vice President and Publisher
Sybex, an Imprint of Wiley

To my wife, Elizabeth: You have supported, loved, and inspired me through so many challenges. Who would have thought having said "never again" after my first book that I would now have completed two more!
—Nathan Winters

I dedicate this book to the special ladies in my life: to my wife, Mandy, for standing by me while I sacrificed time to make this book happen, and to my daughters, Anna and Lisa. I would also like to thank God for the gift of communication that makes writing a book of this nature possible.
—Nicolas Blank

I would like to dedicate this book to my family, all of whom have supported me throughout the writing process in some way. I would especially like to thank Liz for her tolerance of me writing during the early hours and Leo for always being able to make me smile.
—Neil Johnson

Acknowledgments

As you can probably imagine, writing a book is a hefty task. It requires the inspiration and coordination of many different groups of people without whom it would not be possible. Therefore, I am very grateful for this opportunity to call them out for some well-earned recognition.

Throughout this book, we have worked to ensure that you get the very best advice. This has meant working with our accumulated network of friends and colleagues, calling in favors to ensure that we take advantage of the insights of the top experts in their fields.

I would like to start by thanking Neil Johnson and Nicolas Blank personally. Both fall into the friends and colleagues category. We have worked together in various capacities over the last several years, and without their knowledge, enthusiasm, and sheer hard work, this book would absolutely never have happened.

Of course, outside of the authors, the other major driver behind a book like this is the publisher. As always, Sybex has helped us at every stage of the process with a superb team, starting with Mariann Barsolo, our acquisitions editor, who helped us shape the book and hone in on the audience, Gary Schwartz, our development editor, who put up with the random formatting and grammar that we came up with and turned it into something resembling what you see now, and Liz Britten and the copy editing team who did a crack job in getting this polished for printing while accommodating some late changes! Over all, Pete Gaughan had the job of pushing us to keep at least within some semblance of a schedule!

That leaves one very important person in the team, our technical editor, Henrik Walther. Henrik had a big part to play in ensuring the technical accuracy of the examples throughout the book. As someone with huge experience in the Exchange world, he also provided useful guidance and thoughts on the project as a whole.

As previously mentioned, one of the things that made this book possible was our close network of colleagues who contributed. I would like to give special thanks to the following group of people who contributed significant chunks—up to and including whole chapters.

◆ Bhargav Shukla, Director of Product Research and Innovation at KEMP Technologies

◆ Ruth Bacci, Exchange Consultant at Microsoft UK

◆ Glen Scales, Exchange MVP who works as a freelance developer and engineer specializing in Exchange development

◆ Steve Goodman, Exchange MVP who works as a technical architect at one of the UK's leading IT services providers

◆ Nic Bishop, Exchange Technical Solution Professional at Microsoft UK

I would also like to call out specifically members of the Exchange product group who provided support, guidance, and material:

◆ Julie Xu, Principal Group Program Manager, and Thomson Qu, Program Manager

◆ Astrid McClean, Senior Program Manager, Quentin Christensen, Program Manager, and Ryan Wilhelm, SDE

◆ Greg Taylor, Principal Program Manager Lead

—*Nathan Winters*

There are many people who helped me form ideas or simply spent time with me talking about design and Exchange in general. Among these, I would most like to thank all of my colleagues and customers, without whom my contribution to this book would have been impossible.

I would also like to thank the following people specifically for their help:

◆ Matt Gossage for his help and insight on the storage and monitoring chapters

◆ Conrad Sidey for believing in me and making himself available to talk about pretty much anything that I needed to discuss

◆ Robert Gillies, Andrew Ehrensing, Ross Smith IV, Greg Taylor, Jeff Mealiffe, Ramon Infante, David Espinoza, John Rodriguez, Alexandre Costa, Michael Wilson, Brian Day, and Scott Schnoll, who all provided guidance to me about deploying or designing Exchange Server 2013

—Neil Johnson

I have many people to thank in writing this book, starting with the fine people at Wiley as well as my coauthors, Nathan Winters and Neil Johnson. I would like to extend my thanks to the following individuals:

◆ Joe Newbert for language and process in dissecting the finer points of requirements in Chapter 1

◆ Boris Lokhvitsky for your kindness and patience, making the mathematical world accessible to the common man in Chapter 13

—Nicolas Blank

About the Authors

Nathan Winters has worked in IT since graduating from the Royal College of Music (RCM) in 2003, where he studied the clarinet! His first job was at the RCM, migrating from Exchange 5.5 and Windows NT4 to Exchange and Windows Server 2003. Nathan has since worked in a variety of roles for Microsoft partners, including consultancy and practice management. He now works for Microsoft UK as a presales technical specialist. Throughout 2012 and 2013, Nathan has been a regular speaker at industry conferences, such as TechEd and Exchange Connections, both in Europe and in the United States. Before joining Microsoft, Nathan was active in the UK technical community, running the Exchange user group (MMMUG) and writing numerous articles for *Windows IT Pro* magazine and the MSExchange.org website, among others. He was awarded the distinction of Microsoft MVP between 2006 and 2011. In addition to this book, Nathan has recently completed *Mastering Microsoft Lync Server 2013*, also published by Sybex/Wiley. On the rare occasions when he is not working, he enjoys wildlife photography and badminton.

Nicolas Blank is a messaging architect, author, and speaker focused on all things Exchange at NB Consult in South Africa. With over 14 years of experience with Exchange, Nicolas consults with customers on cloud-based and on-premises Exchange projects, as well as companies building Exchange-focused products. Nicolas currently holds the status of Microsoft Certified Master, Exchange 2010 and Office 365, and has received the Microsoft MVP award for Microsoft Exchange every year since 2007. Nicolas blogs regularly on Exchange and messaging topics at blankmanblog.com as well as tweeting as @nicolasblank.

Neil Johnson has worked in IT since leaving Derby University, where he studied engineering. Initially, he worked with Novell Netware and Unix but then quickly moved on to Windows NT and Exchange Server. Neil worked in a number of roles, including third-line support, field engineer, technical design authority, and systems analyst before joining Microsoft in 2006. Since joining Microsoft, Neil has led some of the largest and most complex Exchange deployments in the United Kingdom. He can often be found speaking at Microsoft internal and public events about Exchange or Exchange Online, and he is also an instructor with the rank of Microsoft Certified Solutions Master: Messaging. Neil writes for the Microsoft Exchange Team Blog (EHLO) and maintains both the Jetstress Field Guide and Exchange Client Network Bandwidth Calculator. Neil has a passion for motorsport and is a lifelong Williams F1 team supporter. In his limited spare time, Neil is a keen photographer and loves to explore the national forest woodlands in the midlands where he lives with his son, Leo, and partner, Liz.

Contents at a Glance

Contents

Introduction

This book came about after several conversations among the authors that focused on the common problems we found in discussing Exchange architecture with clients. We all felt that while Exchange is a very mature product, many people, from small in-house shops to the largest consultancies, often fall into similar traps when designing, deploying, and delivering a new Exchange-based messaging platform. To this end, we wanted to capture our conversations and experiences with customers and share them more widely in the hope of helping others avoid the common pitfalls we've seen.

Who Should Read This Book

This book is aimed at those among you who are going to be, or are, working closely with Exchange in a design and deployment capacity. You could be working for an in-house IT department as the messaging lead or as part of the messaging team. You could equally be a consultant working for one of the myriad of Microsoft partners who specialize in Exchange. That doesn't necessarily mean that you have to consider yourself an Exchange specialist, however. The point of this book is to help you get it right when you come to run your Exchange project. We appreciate that you won't necessarily be doing this day in and day out, because we all know that IT departments do a messaging upgrade every two to five years. A secondary audience is the architect community: those of you who are supervising the Exchange project as a program of work but are not necessarily involved in every day-to-day aspect.

What You Will Learn

Instead of focusing, as so many books do, on the "click Next" type guidance, we felt it was far more important to teach how to think about an Exchange project. Of course, we have plenty of technical material in the book, and we've made a point to call out where to find more, whether it's on TechNet or on third-party sites. Likewise, we have called on colleagues in the Exchange product group on many occasions to help us give not only the view from the field but also the thought processes behind the creation of Exchange; that is, how it was envisioned.

What's Inside?

This book is very straightforward in structure. In essence, it was conceived as a series of essays on the topics outlined. As such, is it not necessary to read the book from cover to cover, though some may find that useful. We have tried to lay things out in a manner that would make the most sense.

Chapter 1: Business, Functional, and Technical Requirements   The goal of this chapter is to help you address and answer questions from the people around you in the form of a common language. *Requirements* are essential for implementing Exchange 2013 successfully. Exchange brings a huge number of features to the table. How do you choose which features to implement and how specifically should they be implemented? The answer is requirements!

Chapter 2: Exchange Design Fundamentals   In Chapter 1, we introduce requirements elicitation as we grapple with the nuances of the different types of requirements and how to distill those into a readable form. In this chapter, our goal is to transform those requirements into design decisions. We examine the structure of the design document and delve into the content that goes into each section, which includes a discussion of sizing Exchange. We cover the concept that a good design document is not a purely technical record, nor is it purely a business- or project-based one. A well-written design document is intended for many audiences, from the technical implementers on various teams right up to the CEO.

Chapter 3: Exchange Architectural Concepts   The aim of this chapter is to define the concepts upon which Exchange is built and then to extrapolate those concepts into the design choices that have resulted in the Exchange 2013 version. If you are a messaging consultant or administrator faced with upgrading from an earlier version of Exchange, then the history section in this chapter will help you address the architectural changes and features required to guide your customer through an upgrade to Exchange 2013. Knowing which features have changed, which have been discontinued, and which have been deemphasized is a critical skill for messaging administrators and consultants. We walk through each of the major functional areas of Exchange 2013 to get you up to speed with the latest in Exchange best practice.

Chapter 4: Defining a Highly Available Messaging Solution   When eliciting requirements, desired availability is often one of the first topics to be raised. This chapter first seeks to define high availability (HA). We then look at which components help provide an HA solution before getting into depth about the configuration-related and operational practices required to ensure a high level of uptime.

Chapter 5: Designing a Successful Exchange Storage Solution   Over the last 16 years, the adoption of Microsoft Exchange Server, which began in earnest with Exchange 5.5, has expanded dramatically. Email has become a pervasive application, and it is now a primary communication medium for most organizations. Over this time, Exchange storage has also undergone an evolution. Back in 1996, the focus was primarily on making the best use of costly hard disk capacity. In recent years, however, the focus has shifted toward being able to make use of larger and, most significantly, cheaper disks. This chapter covers the history of Exchange storage and then examines how to approach Exchange storage design in Exchange Server 2013, including the data you will need, the tools that are available, and how to validate the solution that you propose.

Chapter 6: Management   Some of the biggest elements to consider when planning a new system are the management and operation of that system. After all, it is these elements that together form the majority of the cost of ownership. In this chapter, we focus on the management tools that are available for Exchange. In particular, we cover concepts such as Role-Based Access Control, which enables granular delegation of permissions to administrators. We also address new Exchange features, such as the move to a web-based management interface.

Chapter 7: Exchange 2013 Hybrid Coexistence with Office 365 Exchange hybrid is the term used when an Exchange organization running in a customer or partner datacenter is connected to Microsoft's Office 365. This configuration can provide an extremely rich coexistence feature set that allows mailboxes to be hosted on-premises or in Office 365, and the end-user experience remains virtually the same. This chapter discusses why you may want to evaluate Exchange hybrid, identifies the design considerations, and provides some tips from real-world deployments to help make sure that your Exchange hybrid project is a success.

Chapter 8: Designing a Secure Exchange Solution As a messaging consultant, you'll find that some of the most complex areas in designing a Microsoft Exchange solution are those relating to security. This chapter provides you with useful insights to prepare you for the awkward questions from your security officer and enable you to elicit the security requirements in a concise manner, thus avoiding the lengthy and soul-destroying security workshops and the spectrum of confusion that will arise from that disparity between the vision and the reality!

Chapter 9: Compliance This chapter takes you through the discussions that are needed about compliance. We introduce the regulations that businesses face, cover the conversations you need to have with the legal representatives from your organization, discuss the resulting policies that should be set, and then examine what Exchange functionality is available to implement those polices.

Chapter 10: Collaborating with Exchange Exchange is often defined as a groupware product. From the outset, it was intended to be a collaborative software suite. Although it has evolved over time, the fundamental purpose of Exchange remains to help people work better together. In this chapter, we discuss exactly what makes Exchange a collaborative product; that is, what is in the current version of Exchange that helps users collaborate right out of the box? Moreover, when you add in the full suite of Office Server products, how does this improve the end-user experience and allow users to get better value out of Exchange and its related products?

Chapter 11: Extending Exchange As a messaging platform, Exchange has grown over the years into a highly competent and cohesive system with a vast range of functionality. Nevertheless, that doesn't preclude the possibility of extending Exchange's functionality or leveraging it through other systems. This chapter examines the use of Exchange as a messaging platform to build upon, and it touches on where it resides within the Microsoft catalog of products. We begin by investigating the concepts and capabilities Exchange provides to developers for creating custom solutions, and we discuss the thought processes behind integrating Exchange with other Microsoft and non-Microsoft systems.

Chapter 12: Exchange Clients One of the reasons behind the success of Exchange Server is that it supports many client types. It is possible to connect to an Exchange mailbox from pretty much any operating system. The experience provided by clients varies so dramatically that end users may not even realize that they are using Exchange Server. This chapter addresses ways in which clients differ and how they may impact your design and deployment approach for Exchange Server 2013. We also discuss some features enhanced in Exchange 2013 that help protect your Exchange 2013 servers from rogue clients.

Chapter 13: Planning Your Deployment Deploying any version of Exchange for the first time can be a daunting task. Each version of Exchange has architectural considerations that are different from previous versions. Prerequisites may even change between service packs as well as best practices relating to both the deployment and operation of Exchange. This chapter will help you to understand what makes Exchange 2013 different from other versions of Exchange, and it will help to ensure that you achieve a successful rollout.

Chapter 14: Migrating to Exchange 2013   Exchange migrations are just like any other type of solution deployment—they require practical planning to ensure success. This chapter outlines some of the more important aspects for migration planning and some common problems that you may experience in the field.

Chapter 15: Operating and Monitoring Exchange Server 2013   Why monitor and report on your Exchange service? Exchange monitoring, reporting, and alerting are fundamentally about one thing—keeping your messaging infrastructure running sufficiently to meet your service availability targets. Given this fact, it often surprises us that project teams will go to great lengths designing highly available clustered solutions, with overly complex redundant components, and then assume that installing an operations-monitoring product with its out-of-box configuration will be sufficient to keep things running. This chapter takes you through what you really must do to ensure successful monitoring and operations of Exchange.

Hardware and Software Requirements

You have a variety of options to test out the concepts in this book. You can go and start an Exchange deployment project—only kidding! Seriously, however, much of this book discusses concepts and thought processes rather than actual step-by-step technical procedures. Of course, those exist too. In order to immerse yourself into the actual technology, build a lab and get an Office 365 trial tenant. If you want to explore the basic functionality of Exchange, then an Office 365 tenant is one of the simplest ways to get up and running, because this allows you to test out the vast majority of client-side functionality and much of the administrative side without the need of servers. If the actual underlying workings of Exchange are important to you, then an on-premises lab is a necessity. In this case, much can be achieved on a single, well-specified machine. For example, a lot of the lab work for this book was created on a Dell T7500 workstation with five hard drives and 24 GB of RAM—a fairly lowly specified box these days!

How to Contact the Authors

We welcome feedback from you about this book. Obviously, it's always nice to get messages about what you liked about the book, but we also welcome suggestions for improvements that we could make in future editions. You can reach Nathan by writing to nathan@clarinathan .co.uk, Nicholas at nicholas@nbconsult.co.za, or Neil at neil.johnson@microsoft.com. If you are looking for information about Nathan's future articles or would like to discuss a speaking engagement, visit Nathan's blog at www.nathanwinters.co.uk.

Sybex strives to keep you supplied with the latest tools and information you need for your work. Please check www.sybex.com/go/exchangedesigndeploy, where we'll post additional content and updates that supplement this book should the need arise.

Chapter 1

Business, Functional, and Technical Requirements

The goal of this chapter is to help you address and answer questions from the people around you in the form of a common language. *Requirements* are essential for implementing Exchange 2013 successfully.

Exchange can be a daunting product to contemplate, with over 20 million lines of code. There are many, many features from which to choose, though some have not changed significantly between Exchange versions (address book generation, for example). Furthermore, there's a discussion of how these features are to be implemented and the entire best practices conversation, which comes with the territory. How do you choose which features to implement and which to leave behind? The answer is requirements. And how do you decide which best practice to apply? Again, the answer is requirements.

Building the Foundation for Requirements

Requirements elicitation can sometimes be seen as boring, tedious, and overly complex. This perception can often derail this most critical part of a new project. Requirements elicitation is traditionally associated with software engineering, which implies a long list of requirements to satisfy the discipline of creating or modifying software. With the exception of writing scripts, most administrators who wish to implement Exchange don't need to know or care about the difference between a functional and a business requirement, since they're not creating software from scratch. However, we still need to capture the essence of "why" we are taking certain actions, as well as the "what" and the "how" we are doing them.

This chapter is particularly important for the Exchange administrator or consultant who may have been tasked with installing, upgrading, or migrating to Exchange for the first time in a formal manner and who doesn't know where to start. Even if you have successfully implemented Exchange, this chapter will still be of tremendous value to you if this is the first time that you are the one documenting a design.

Requirements are the core of an Exchange project. Based on the requirements, a host of other documentation items can be affected. These may include the following:

- Vision and scope document
- The Exchange 2013 design
- Testing plan
- Migration plan
- The bill of materials required to implement Exchange

- Test case documentation

- Adjustments to the disaster recovery plan (DRP)

A good place to start is to learn how to identify and document requirements correctly and with enough detail to satisfy people from different parts of IT and within the business as a whole. A bad place to begin is by installing Exchange on the basis of a diagram only. Since we are in IT, we often start with a diagram of something and then wind up making design changes on the fly.

Documenting requirements is thus a critical part of the design process, as we will explore later in this chapter. In summary, this chapter will equip you with the tools to ensure that "why," "what," and "how" are addressed and documented adequately, without requiring a degree in software engineering in order to do so.

Establishing Project Roles

Establishing roles at the outset of a project of significant magnitude is critically important. Most of you reading this book fall into one of two camps:

Camp 1: You are a highly respected individual with demonstrated competence in your field. You tend to be external to the companies you consult with, even if you are part of a multi-year project or outsource contract.

Camp 2: You are responsible for messaging within your company, or you may be a project manager who needs background reading for your first Exchange project. You have just been tasked with delivering an implementation of the newest version of Exchange.

Whichever camp you fall into, either external or internal to the organization, your attitude about such a project determines its success or failure. Your mindset needs to be that of a consultant toward a client. If you work inside the company, this may be harder to adopt; however, the methods within this chapter work equally well with either camp.

Getting Started with the Exchange Design

Often we are asked to review a design, which may be technically brilliant, architecturally sound, and mindful of the newest features introduced in the latest service pack. However, designs are very often written without capturing the essence—or even the reason for the existence—of the design. The essence or the reason for existence for an Exchange design is documented by capturing the requirements.

Exchange designs and implementations are often driven by a version's new features list, as opposed to having captured and wrestled with requirements and extrapolated the features necessary to satisfy the needs of the business. Having a solid set of requirements to work against, among other reasons, makes your technology choices defensible, since designing or building Exchange without a solid set of requirements is like going food shopping without a list and putting anything that suits you into the shopping cart.

Documenting requirements also makes a document much easier to review. A structured document may have one section summarizing the security requirements and then a separate section encompassing the technical detail on how those security requirements are manifested as configuration detail or product features. This would allow the security or compliance officer to sign off on that portion of the document without having to wade through the storage design, unless of course the storage design captured a secure requirement.

When reviewing designs, we often see that the author has discussed the technology and then made a statement that a feature or technology should be implemented in a certain way. For example, the author may wish to implement Database Availability Groups (DAGs), which were introduced with Exchange 2010, and allow databases to be highly available. The author may say something like, "DAGs are great, so we're going to implement a DAG." However, the "why" of implementing a DAG is not captured. The question of why you are recommending the implementation of DAGs and which requirement you are fulfilling must be answered. Your reasons for choosing technology should always be clearly documented.

Most designs that we reviewed have little or no longevity. That is, if you were to review your own design in five years' time, would you understand the "why" of the design? Why did you choose to implement a DAG in the manner that you did, and so forth? Keep this in mind when eliciting requirements and as a continual thread throughout your document. When your design document is reviewed, arguing that the reasons behind the design were not enumerated because you didn't think it through or were ignorant of other options available at the time is not adequate for explaining why the "why" part of documentation is missing.

Requirements as Part of a Larger Framework

If you are a member of a consulting organization, then you will be quite familiar with the following. If you are doing this for the first time, then this section should be considered a primer as to where requirements fit into a larger framework.

There are several available methodologies from which to choose, including the Microsoft Solutions Framework. Irrespective of which methodology you choose, the steps are often quite similar:

Envisioning Phase   This is the "thinking phase" of the project where you and others work to blue sky the project. In its simplest form, this involves the critical people considering the version of Exchange to be implemented and addressing such issues as *how* things are being done today and *why* they need to be done differently.

Requirements Definition Phase   This phase captures the requirements, which is the focus of this chapter.

Design Phase   This phase molds the requirements into something deployable and practical.

Testing Phase   This is a standard phase of larger projects, and it is based entirely on the defined requirements. If the requirements are clear, the tests can be written well before the design is complete.

Deployment Phase   This phase implements the design.

The first three phases will naturally generate a document set, which at minimum is similar to the following:

Vision and Scope Document   This document captures the reason for the existence of the project, and it defines the business's vision of the technology to be implemented. It also defines what is in and out of scope.

Functional or Technical Specification Document   This can be separate from the design document. It defines the business requirements and lists the derived functional or technical requirements. Often, the consultant will use the scoping meeting to document the basic scope of the project and then try to derive the business and functional or technical requirements for further clarification. We will cover this process in much greater depth shortly.

Design Document   This document captures the resulting design.

Depending on the methodology selected, many other documents, such as testing plans, will also be expected.

If you are doing this for the first time, the level of detail required for a large project may overwhelm you. Nevertheless, as a consultant, it is likely that you are indeed working with this level of detail. While there is a wealth of material available about the available methodologies, the basic problem that requirements are often captured poorly, or not at all, remains.

Understanding the Types of Requirements

Classical requirements elicitation is a very deep and mysterious discipline, unless you're a business analyst, systems analyst, or the like. The aim of this chapter is not to address classical requirements elicitation from a systems analysis point of view, since that would only help you become a better systems analyst. The goal of this chapter is to determine what kinds of requirements are important for your Exchange design and to give you the ammunition you need to defend your technology choices.

You may be tempted to wrestle with the nuances among some of the more esoteric requirements. At minimum, however, you need to examine the business and technical requirements. We will take a moment to define each of these later.

The purists among you may question why we don't break technical requirements out into functional and nonfunctional requirements. *Functional requirements* describe what a system is required to do, while *nonfunctional requirements* describe how the system behaves. As mentioned at the beginning, this chapter is focused on eliciting the requirements necessary to implement existing software, not on writing software from the ground up.

If your project is small, the lines between functional, nonfunctional, and business and technical requirements may blur and add unnecessary complexity. Unless you find a compelling reason to include functional and nonfunctional requirements, we suggest that you focus exclusively on the business and technical requirements. Once your project reaches a certain level of complexity, however, you will need to define technical requirements in much more detail. Thus, you will then break out the functional and nonfunctional requirements aspects of the project.

Business requirements may also be captured separately in a vision document. Consulting organizations will be familiar with this procedure, and they will require completion of a specific document set in order to capture this level of detail.

You may argue that you have been given a requirement, and that sounds something like, "We need to upgrade." This statement is, in itself, only half a requirement, and it is an insufficient rationale for a business today to invest in your project. Now let's examine our two chosen requirements in more detail.

Business Requirements

In this section, we are going to discuss business requirements in the context of our upcoming Exchange implementation. This is the "why" part of your requirements. The project sponsor or management team member provides the business drivers for the project. You want to be sure that you don't get stuck in "analysis paralysis," since business requirements tend to be broad statements lacking the detail expected in technical requirements.

For our purposes, businesses tend to have a few simple drivers. These tend to fall into the category of decreasing costs, increasing/retaining revenue, or decreasing risk. A good set of business requirements should address all of these drivers if possible. You may not often be in the position of being able to drive sales up by, say, 40 percent, but you are certainly able to reduce risk by implementing a well-thought-out high-availability strategy for email, if email is a critical business function.

Let's look at a few examples of business requirements:

- Revenue requirement: A company may choose to implement a mobility app to increase productivity of its sales staff.

- Risk requirement: A company needs to protect itself from a failed audit because of a lack of support for its existing version of Exchange.

- Risk requirement: A company has made a strategic decision to migrate their technology base from Lotus Notes and Domino to Microsoft Exchange and Microsoft SharePoint due to in-house development moving to .NET based languages.

We will examine business requirements in the context of a sample customer, *XYZ Bank*.

BUSINESS REQUIREMENTS FOR A SAMPLE EXCHANGE UPGRADE

XYZ Bank has retained you to design and implement a replacement for its aging messaging system. XYZ's current messaging system is implemented in Exchange 2003, which was state of the art at the time. XYZ has an extensive branch network, with many individual Exchange 2003 servers across the country.

When it was implemented, email was not considered to be a critical application. XYZ is growing fast, adding a branch every two to three months. XYZ has also made it known that it intends to list itself on the stock exchange, which will subject XYZ to regular security and process audits.

The bank has recently decided to use email as one of the primary tools for communicating with its customers. XYZ currently limits mailboxes to a few hundred MBs. Because of this limit, employees are forced to move email data to PST files on desktops and file shares, exposing XYZ to risk from theft and corruption. Even with stringent restrictions, a number of branches are complaining that email performance is decreasing, even though the number of users on the respective servers remains the same.

Because of its critical nature, XYZ would like email to be centralized in a datacenter alongside its existing critical banking applications, with a similar level of redundancy and availability. Of course, XYZ is concerned about cost, and it wishes to explore a number of storage options before committing to purchasing a new Storage Area Network (SAN) solely for Exchange's use. Finally, XYZ has stated that it would like similar messaging functionality as provided by Exchange 2003 on day one of implementation while reserving the right to add features in the future.

This story is quite typical. It includes a mixture of requirements, including a clue that the bank is researching later versions of Exchange and that it is aware that several storage options are available. This is an indication that the bank has a number of well-defined feature-based requests.

We can discern a number of business-specific requests from this scenario:

◆ Replace the unsupported Microsoft Exchange 2003 platform with a currently supported Exchange 2013 environment.

◆ Increase the availability of the email environment to match the XYZ bank standard.

◆ Design for future growth.

◆ Allow for auditing administrative activity with the ability to demonstrate such processes.

Notice that the requirements are broad and contain little technical detail. The business requirements captured as part of a design along with an executive summary, for example, allow management and key staff to assimilate quickly the reasons why the Exchange upgrade is being deployed without getting bogged down in technical detail. In our example, XYZ concentrates on mitigating risk (support, availability, and auditing), while also supporting the stated goals of the business (expansion and increased communication).

Technical Requirements

Staying with the theme of combining technical requirements with functional and nonfunctional requirements, they are quite different from business requirements. Technical requirements are the "what" and "how" parts of requirements. Furthermore, business requirements are written as broad statements, while technical requirements are designed to be precise statements. Technical requirements should be simple lists that are both individual and granular. One of the biggest causes of confusion for implementers is ambiguity in technical specifications. Adding too much explanation within the requirements can cloud the specification.

When dealing with a product like Microsoft Exchange, we take a lot of functionality for granted, and so we should. However, there is a fine line to walk in terms of writing specifications. Let's take, for example, the last line from our XYZ Bank scenario:

> Finally, XYZ has stated that it would like similar messaging functionality as provided by Exchange 2003 on day one of implementation while reserving the right to add features in the future.

We could take for granted how to interpret this statement. However, it is actually quite subjective and needs clarification. For example, taken alone, we do not know who or what XYZ is, what "similar messaging functionality as provided by Exchange 2003" means, and what types of features could be added in the future. There are two possible paths of interpretations of this statement: One is broad interpretation based on our knowledge of Microsoft Exchange, and the other is "analysis paralysis."

An example of analysis paralysis would be to specify Exchange functionality as follows:

◆ A user must be able to generate an email.

◆ A user must be able to display the contents of an email.

◆ A user must be able to share their calendar with another user.

◆ Calendar sharing must support granular rights.

This would be a massive book on its own. What we want to do is to clarify what "similar messaging functionality" means and to specify it. This may include the following:

- Sending and receiving of email internal to the organization

- Sending and receiving of Internet mail

- Rich client access using Outlook 2013

- Thin client access using Outlook Web App (OWA)

- Mobile client access using Exchange ActiveSync (EAS)-based compatible devices

New systems require signoff or acceptance testing criteria to be fulfilled. Each technical specification should be capable of being tested and proved or disproved. Your technical and/or your functional specification should translate easily into testing criteria, which will allow for a relatively easy signoff. In other words, you should be able to write a test plan based on your technical or functional specifications.

If you need to break out technical requirements into a separate document listing functional and nonfunctional requirements, consider the following example.

Based on the following business requirement, we are able to infer these functional and non-functional requirements:

Design for future growth in mind

Functional Requirement

Hub transport server queues must be located in a separate storage area from the system volume so that growing mail flow volume will not overwhelm the OS drive. (We could list many other functional requirements that pertain to the scalability of the system.)

Nonfunctional Requirement

Infrastructure supporting email services should be designed to meet the XYZ Bank's fore-casted growth of 20 percent a year.

Constraints

A *constraint* in a design is a non-negotiable item, which has been specified in advance or required by the project. For example, you have a requirement to do X but are constrained by factor Y. Constraints have a direct bearing on the project and may have a significant impact on the final result. Constraints should be listed as a separate heading in the requirements section of your document.

Some constraints are economic, for example, when the customer has already purchased and installed the new hardware without knowing if it will fit the project's ultimate requirements. Another constraint can occur when the customer has specified that Exchange must utilize an existing investment in virtualization or storage. Other constraints may be time-based; that is, the project must be completed within the financial year, or before the change freeze period around a given holiday, and so forth.

Whatever the constraints, make sure that they are documented in your requirements so that you may reference them later in your design. Depending on the nature of the business, security, risk, and compliance may pose significant constraints for a new project.

Assumptions

We often see assumptions listed in documentation. However, assumptions have no place in your documentation. When you review the documentation, endeavor to clarify such assumptions as facts and then list them as either project requirements or constraints.

Requirements Elicitation

Now let's discuss how to get requirements and who creates them. Notice that we use the term *requirements elicitation* and not *requirements gathering*. Gathering implies that requirements are easy to find and include in your documentation. More often than not this is not the case. Requirements elicitation is a much clearer description of what you're trying to achieve. Elicit means "to draw out," which is much closer to how requirements are brought forth, that is, through interactions with teams and individuals.

During this phase, you need to manage constantly the fine balance between assumption and fact. This applies as much to you, the consultant, as to the rest of the project group. You may or may not have been briefed before you joined the project. However, more often than not, as the consultant you may have several assumptions that, if left unspoken, will filter into the design. Your assumptions, and the assumptions of the assembled group, must be verified as facts in order to be considered valid requirements.

High availability is a classic example of the difference between an assumption and a fact. Someone may state, "We want 99.9 percent availability." Your assumption might be 99.9 percent availability during work hours, not including scheduled downtimes. Their assumption might be 99.9 percent availability on a 24/7/365 scale. Your job is to take the "We want 99.9 percent availability" statement and eliminate any ambiguity immediately by eliciting how that availability is measured and then update the statement. For example, "We want 99.9 percent availability on a 24/7/365 basis, not to include any scheduled downtime." If this request sounds unreasonable or implausible, then part of your role is to educate the group as to why this is not feasible and drive consensus on what is stated in the final requirement.

REQUIREMENTS ELICITATION AND THE LONG TAIL OF OBSOLETE BEST PRACTICES

Exchange has many features that can be implemented in many ways. The subset of the best ways to implement Exchange is known as "best practice." Best practice may be specific to a particular version of Exchange. For example, Exchange 2003 and earlier mandated that data should be stored on tier one storage, that is, fast disks and a redundant storage array of some sort.

To this day, we must often begin a storage discussion by dispelling this notion and educating our audience about how dramatically Exchange has changed, often using the Mailbox Server Role Requirements Calculator spreadsheet. Storage best practices as well as many others have evolved, but it is very tempting to reference obsolete best practices as your base model when thinking about newer versions of Exchange. Best practices, obsolete or not, may fall into the category of assumptions, which must be transformed into facts before they can form part of a design.

Summary

As you read through the subsequent chapters in this book, you will be reminded that Exchange is a feature-rich and exciting product. However, without clearly defining the requirements—that is, the "what," "where," and "why"—your Exchange implementation will likely not deliver the results you hoped for. Learn to document the reasons for your choices at all times, make your designs defensible and justifiable, and know why you wrote what you did when you review your design document again in the future.

Chapter 2

Exchange Design Fundamentals

In Chapter 1, we introduced requirements elicitation as we grappled with the nuances of different types of requirements and how to distill those into a readable form. In this chapter, our goal is to transform those requirements into design decisions.

Before we delve into the meat of the design contents, let us examine the document structure. A good design document is not a purely technical record, nor is it purely a business or project-based one. A well-written design document is intended for many audiences, from the technical implementers on various teams right up to the CEO.

Introducing Design Documents

Let us take a moment to define what a design document is *not*. A design document is not written to *sell* Exchange 2013. That is, it is *not* a marketing document, and it should not be approached as such. It should not list every Exchange 2013 feature, and it should not ramble on about how wonderful a product it is or about the marvels of a given feature. The discussion of relevant features does have a valid place in the document; however, it should not bulk up the document unnecessarily with praise for the product and its features, or else it will alienate the vast majority of its intended consumers.

Ideally, this document should start with a structure in mind, which allows various teams to find the information that is most relevant to them without having to read through the entire document. You may choose to write this document in sections that pertain to various teams, for example, storage, security, and so on, or you may maintain a separate table of contents that calls out the sections pertinent to each team.

We prefer the second approach, because it allows us to design a document based on the major feature areas of Exchange and follow the natural flow of the product, rather than disassembling the product into the many disciplines for which Exchange offers support.

From Requirements to Design

A requirement is translated into many design decisions. Though it often may be difficult to defend a particular decision beyond that you believe it is "right," this belief is not nearly enough to justify technical decisions. Storage and availability are just two of many often contentious topics that may lead to emotionally charged discussions. Thus, the various chapters throughout this book, including those covering storage and availability, provide sufficient background as to how to make sound, justifiable technical decisions. Any documented design choice must be supported by solid reasoning, which can be clearly demonstrated in your design.

> ### PROCESS IS MORE IMPORTANT THAN TECHNOLOGY
>
> It is easy to be bedazzled by Exchange 2013 and its enhanced capabilities. Resist the temptation to design toward features, and concentrate on the "what" and "how" of the requirements. Without these, you'll have no substantive basis for your design.

No Single Way to Implement Exchange

A requirement may often be interpreted or implemented in any number of ways. Without deep product knowledge and extensive experience in a product, this may be difficult to accomplish, because the business for which you may be consulting or working is adequately unique such that it will not fit into a standardized approach.

When a requirement may be implemented in different ways, formalize the decision-making process using a number of test cases, each with a view to satisfying the unique conditions of the business or the design constraints within which you may have to work. Wherever possible, build a representative lab that includes the source environment and the Exchange 2013 target environment, and work through the test cases to determine which implementation path works best for a particular design decision.

How Much Detail Is Enough?

There is a fine line between providing sufficient detail to document the design principles and writing an implementation guide. How much detail is enough? If you are including the PowerShell scripts to set specific URLs, you're adding too much detail. A table of URLs is more appropriate. Remember that your design is intended for multiple audiences. As such, it should start out as broad as possible and narrow the focus going forward as required.

If you are doing this for the first time, consider reading the "Infrastructure Planning and Design Guides" available for free from Microsoft at

```
http://technet.microsoft.com/en-us/solutionaccelerators/ee382254.aspx
```

You may also want to check out "White Papers: Exchange 2010 Tested Solutions" from Microsoft TechNet at

```
http://technet.microsoft.com/en-us/library/gg513520(v=exchg.141).aspx
```

Both of these resources are great primers when pondering the amount of relevant detail necessary and how to document a design decision in light of the number of alternatives considered. You must demonstrate due care and consideration for alternative or competing choices. Doing so makes the choice of technology defensible in the context of the design.

Section Guide

Assuming that you have your requirements, assumptions, constraints, and scope and vision documented, you now need to apply these to a design in a logical manner that may be easily consumed. At minimum, we suggest that you consider the following sections for inclusion in your design:

Section Index

This section should be a catalog of lists grouped by discipline, thus allowing the relevant individual to find the sections they need to review or implement quickly, without having to dig through the entire design. The security team leader, for example, is not going to be interested in your storage design but will be very interested in how Exchange 2013 is published externally. We suggest that you take your lead from the requirements elicitation sections as to how to group these. At minimum, however, you can expect to be addressing messaging, infrastructure, networking, security, business, storage, compliance, and auditing.

Following is a sample grouping of design document sections:

Business

Executive Summary

Business Requirements

Summary of Vision and Scope

Functional Specification

Architecture Summary

Security

Compliance

External Publishing

Infrastructure Teams

Migration or Legacy Integration Requirements

Interoperation with Third-Party Applications

High-Availability Strategy and Requirements

Transport Design

Client Access Design

Mailbox Design

VM Requirements

Bandwidth Requirements

Executive Summary

The Executive Summary is your elevator pitch, your two minutes of time with someone extremely busy and influential. The real trick with this section is to keep it precise and focused toward a senior management audience; that is, focus on the benefit to the business and costs rather than technical details. Provide as much rich information as you can realistically cram in. Quite often, the data that you provide in this section will be presented again, so make sure that anything you put in here is accurate and relevant.

This section should be no longer than one page, summarizing the pertinent points of the project and its reason for existence.

Business Requirements

The Business Requirements are the reason for a design's existence. Failure to list actual business requirements in this section may cause the project sponsor or owner to dismiss the document and potentially the project outright.

As with the Executive Summary, this section needs to be precise and focused towards a senior management audience. This section must cover the business requirements which you would have gathered using the methods described in Chapter 1: "Business, Functional and Technical Requirements."

Summary of Vision and Scope

The *Vision and Scope document* contains essential inputs to the design. If the document is small enough, consider repeating or quoting the necessary sections in your design. This may provide direction for you as you craft the design. It will also help the reader understand the context without continually referring to an external document.

The best way to think about the Vision and Scope document is as a frame for the solution. The *vision* part is intended to define *what* the end goal looks like. The *scope* part is intended to define *how much* of that vision you need to solve in this particular design. It is worth remembering this when you create your Vision and Scope document. Try to avoid solving things at this point in the process. The Vision and Scope document should be written so that it rarely or never requires an update during the project. The key words are *high level*; this is not a design document.

Functional Specification

The Functional Specification is just a list of requirements. At its most basic, the Functional Specification defines precisely what the solution will provide. On large projects we typically like to see a separate Functional Specification document since it can get quite large and will often require significant effort to gain sign-off. From our perspective, this is probably the single most important document that will be created, because once it has been signed, it defines precisely what the final solution must do.

It is also worth mentioning here that the test process should be driven directly from the Functional Specification; that is, for each requirement that is defined and agreed on, there should be a matching test case in the test plan.

This approach supports two benefits:

1. The test plan can be created at the same time as the design.

2. The test plan and design are independent.

For smaller projects, it is quite acceptable and often beneficial to include the Functional Specification as a section within your design documentation; however, we still recommend that formal sign-off of the section be recorded before beginning solution design.

Architecture Summary

The *Architecture Summary* is a two-page summary of the entire design from a technical perspective. This includes diagrams representing the existing messaging, networking, and possible datacenter design, as well as the end state of the new Exchange 2013 design.

This section is useful for someone who is new to the project and should show visually what the solution design looks like and how it will integrate with any other systems. Ideally, it should be quite high level; however, it should use customer specific nomenclature for sites, servers, and projects where possible.

Compliance

This section captures the compliance-specific details of your Exchange 2013 design, and it should detail which feature or configuration is being used to meet a specific requirement. It is also useful to detail how a specific feature will meet the compliance requirement. Usually compliance requirements are also constraints, since they are mandatory and non-negotiable; that is, they must be met or the solution cannot be deployed. Make it clear wherever a constraint is met with a specific feature or configuration.

A compliance framework often requires a clear demonstration of a control being in place, such as the ability to perform a search. Depending on the specific requirements you receive from a business, you must show how each requirement is met by your recommended configuration. Journaling, archiving (both native and third-party), storage and retention policies, data leak prevention, integration with third-party compliance appliances, administrative logging, PowerShell, and command logging and search features are often listed in this section.

External Publishing

External publishing of Exchange services usually involves IT risk and security teams plus infrastructure and messaging. Where you have sections of your design document that many teams need to read, it pays to spend a little extra time to speak with them up front to find out what kind of information they would like to see in your design document. This section should include the basics, such as restating any requirements for external publishing of Exchange services and how you intend to provide them at a high level, for example, by reusing additional publishing infrastructure or deploying something entirely new for Exchange.

You should add in any additional information requested by the other team, such as firewall requirements, predicted network bandwidth, intrusion detection, certificate requirements, and so on. As a general rule, all of the teams involved with this section should already know what you are going to propose before they read it in your design document. Our recommendation is to involve key security stakeholders early in the design process.

The main aim of this section is to clearly specify the external publishing solution for Exchange 2013 and how Exchange 2013 service and data access will be secured.

Migration or Legacy Integration Requirements

The new design may reflect the first implementation of Exchange in the business. Novell GroupWise, Lotus Notes, Gmail, and other email systems have particular coexistence requirements in order to make the intended migration or end state as seamless and as painless as possible. This section should capture whether native or third-party tools will be used, the possible impacts on the business during the migration period, the risk-mitigation strategy, and roll-forward and roll-back plans, should they be required. If this includes too much detail, consider breaking this section out into a separate document called a migration design and referencing it in your design document.

Similarly, an upgrade from previous versions to Exchange 2013 in the same Exchange organization requires much thought and planning, and this section should list considerations for achieving a migration with as little impact on the business as possible. You may list interoperation requirements, such as the activation of Outlook Anywhere on all downstream versions of Exchange or the minimum Outlook versions required on the desktop, depending on the Exchange 2013 features implemented in the new end state.

Interoperation with Third-Party Applications

Very few Exchange 2013 implementations will never interoperate with other systems. You may need to list *Receive connectors* with defined scopes. These allow devices or other systems to relay email through Exchange. CRM and instant messaging systems, such as Lync, often require Exchange Web Services to be published without the use of a wildcard certificate, preferring SAN certificates instead. While this detail is often reflected in the pertinent section such as the Transport Design for the Receive connectors, this section follows the theme of making the information available without requiring a developer or administrator to mine the entire design.

You may find that the amount of detail required for a specific application or technology is too much to call out of a specific section, for example, listing a Receive connector for third-party use when the Transport Design features a table with many other Receive connectors. In this case, it is appropriate to summarize that there is a requirement to integrate with legacy SMTP systems and that the specific details may be found in the Transport Design section.

Legacy protocols that are no longer supported, such as WebDAV and other types of integration, may require significant re-architecting of the application requiring such integration. Applications requiring integration points that have been deprecated from previous versions of Exchange should be listed, as well as your mitigation strategy, which may include a replacement of the application or a rewrite of the integration points, for example, from WebDAV to Exchange Web Services. The lack of mitigation of legacy integration can pose a significant delay to your project if not quantified and addressed as early on in the project as possible.

Site mailboxes and the eDiscovery features in SharePoint as well as specific Lync compliance features may need to be referenced in separate documents. However, you need to decide how much detail to include in your design in order to list the appropriate amount of coverage for Exchange. In addition, hybrid deployments with Office 365 will require significant detail as you call out the dependencies with AD FS, directory synchronization, specific versions of Office, and so forth in your design.

High-Availability Strategy and Requirements

After listing the high-availability requirements, we like to address each requirement by major architecture feature as it affects Exchange (see Chapter 4, "Defining a Highly Available Messaging Solution"). Depending on the complexity of our design and the availability required, we like to take an outside-in approach as follows:

- Perimeter service availability
- Hybrid mode availability
- Datacenter availability
- Transport availability

- Frontend availability

- Backend availability

- Storage availability

Each section should discuss the features of Exchange in light of the business requirement it satisfies as well as detail how the requirement is to be met.

As an alternative to providing significant detail that may be repeated elsewhere in the design, you may also choose to point out that the high-availability features for transport, storage, and so on are detailed in their respective sections. However, you should only do this after addressing the requirements for availability adequately in this section by documenting that the requirement has been met through the features you have selected to implement.

Where a specific section has a different service-level target, you should mention this and the business justification of why the service level is different. For example, it is common for some organizations to have a lower target service level in the event of a datacenter failure.

Transport Design

As we pointed out in the interoperation section, Exchange 2013 nearly always integrates with the outside world in some way. This often begins with transport, because the default transport configuration will require some modification in order to send and receive email via the Internet, legacy systems, or third-party email systems.

As part of the design, you will need to specify any modifications made to the default state in order to allow Internet email to flow, detail any edge requirements, and specify how email hygiene is performed either on-premises or via a cloud-based service such as Exchange Online Protection. If you are using Exchange 2013 integration with Active Directory Rights Management Services (AD RMS) via transport rules or other transport rule-based software to implement compliance features, consider adding a note to point to the Compliance section. Exchange hybrid deployment-specific detail, such as the Receive connector detail required to implement secure messaging, should also be mentioned. Bear in mind that in Exchange 2013 the CAS role has changed considerably, and performs the function of an SMTP proxy; as such all incoming and potentially all outgoing SMTP mail flow integrates with this role. The Receive connector configuration is required to be detailed for the Exchange 2013 CAS role, as opposed to the Hub Transport roles of Exchange 2007 and Exchange 2010. Transport will be covered in significant detail in Chapter 3: "Exchange Architectural Concepts." The following list should be included at minimum:

- Transport name spaces

- Transport antispam and antimalware

- Internal transport configuration: topology, network configuration, and Receive connectors

- External transport configuration: Send connectors and remote domains

- Interoperation configuration: legacy device integration, migration-specific detail, or Exchange hybrid configuration with Office 365

- Global configuration: shadow redundancy, safety net, accepted domains, email address policy, transport settings, mail tips, data leak prevention, and journaling

- Database queue location

Client Access Design

Before we begin, it is worth explaining what has happened to the Client Access server (CAS) in Exchange Server 2013. In Exchange Server 2010, we also had a Client Access server role; however, its purpose was somewhat different from the CAS role in Exchange Server 2013. Fundamentally, most of what the Exchange 2010 CAS did is included in the Exchange 2013 Mailbox role, and Exchange 2013 CAS is a totally new role that acts as a front-end server and SMTP proxy for inbound email messages. Ideally, it would have been nice for it to have had a totally new name too, but I guess we can't have everything. The new CAS role will be covered in significant detail in Chapter 3: "Exchange Architectural Concepts"

Further detail should be supplied according to the following list:

- Client access name space
- DNS configuration
- Internal and external CAS URL configuration
- Internal and external autodiscover URL configuration
- Outlook Anywhere configuration
- SSL certificate configuration
- Client types
- Client access features
- Client access network configuration
- Client access network load balancing
- Client access array configuration (not to be confused with Exchange 2010 CAS arrays)
- External publishing configuration
- Office 365 hybrid configuration

For almost all deployments, it makes sense to collocate the CAS and Mailbox roles on the same server. The reasoning behind this decision is the same as it was for Exchange 2010 and fundamentally boils down to two benefits:

Makes Better Use of Hardware By running both roles on the server, you can make use of all available system resources and so require fewer servers overall.

Simplification Since your design includes only a single type of Exchange server with all roles installed, every single Exchange server will be the same; this greatly simplifies operating the environment.

Mailbox Design

The Mailbox role is the core of your hardware design. We suggest reviewing the architecture, storage, and availability chapters of this book as preliminary reading.

If you are implementing *database availability groups (DAGs)*, you will need to reflect the detail for each DAG, which includes the following in addition to other detail required for this role:

- ◆ DAG topology
- ◆ DAG network configuration
- ◆ Mailbox role storage configuration

MAILBOX STORAGE CONFIGURATION DETAIL

There are typically two approaches to storage design for Exchange. The first one is where the Exchange design team does the storage design itself; this is very common where direct attached storage and JBOD solutions are deployed. The second one is where the Exchange design team defines the storage requirements and then outsources the solution design to a hardware vendor.

The following must be reflected in this section:

- ◆ User mailbox profiles
- ◆ Database configuration
- ◆ Performance requirements and storage (disk) configuration

UNIFIED MESSAGING DESIGN

Exchange 2013 may need to integrate with a Session Initiation Protocol (SIP)-based telephony solution such as Lync 2013. This section should clearly specify the Unified Messaging endpoints provided by Exchange 2013.

In that the Unified Messaging role is included in the Mailbox role, there is sufficient detail possible in this unit to justify its own section. Reciprocally, if there is no Unified Messaging requirement, you may choose to state that you have disabled this role or that it will not be implemented.

VM Requirements

Virtualizing Exchange traditionally has been a contentious issue. Vendors often offer features or advertise capabilities that, if implemented, may cause your installation to become unsupportable by Microsoft support services or Microsoft partners. Because virtualization guidance may differ slightly between versions, and even between service packs or cumulative updates of Exchange, we like to list the pertinent information published by the product group at the time of writing in this section, in addition to how it applies to Exchange 2013 in the design.

In order for the design to be supported, the virtualization solution must be included in the Server Virtualization Validation Program (SVVP) and applied to the version of Exchange 2013 that you are implementing. The SVVP is found here:

```
http://www.windowsservercatalog.com/svvp.aspx
```

Detail those virtualization features that are included and excluded in your design in order to satisfy the requirements and make your solution supportable. More often, you may need to specify which virtualization features should be disabled as opposed to which features should be enabled.

Often, virtualization may carry a performance cost to the total system, including processor cycles, disk IOPS, and even memory. The Mailbox Server Role Requirements Calculator makes an allowance for this; however, you need to indicate your awareness as well as any mitigation steps required in the design.

One area that is often missed when considering virtualization is the concept of failure domains. A *failure domain* is a single point of failure that could affect multiple areas of your Exchange service. When considering virtualization it is crucial to consider each virtual host as a failure domain and avoid putting dependent Exchange servers on the same host; that is, do not store multiple database copies on separate virtual machines and then store both virtual machines on the same virtual host. Where you are mixing virtualization and Exchange high-availability features, your design document should clearly show how you are dealing with failure domains.

Bandwidth Requirements

This section should reflect any network bandwidth-specific details or the impact of your design on bandwidth. For example, you may need to calculate the amount of client bandwidth required for a centralized Exchange 2013 deployment for either WAN or Internet-based clients. You may need to reflect the SMTP traffic bandwidth requirements in order to journal to a central location or to distributed points.

Networking parameters that may need to be listed are current available bandwidth, projected bandwidth impact of the new solution, and amount of bandwidth required if the current infrastructure cannot cope with the new requirements.

A significant aid in establishing a bandwidth model is the Exchange Client Network Bandwidth Calculator, which was announced here:

```
http://blogs.technet.com/b/exchange/archive/2012/02/10/announcing-the-exchange-
client-network-bandwidth-calculator-beta.aspx
```

Another area of network bandwidth that often needs to be planned for is DAG replication traffic. This network traffic is caused by DAG nodes replicating data and maintaining a content index on passive copies. This is an extremely important metric to consider carefully because if your DAG spans multiple sites across a wide area network with limited network throughput, your choices for database copies in your DAG may be limited, not because of storage capacity or cost but because of a lack of network throughput. By far the best way to determine your DAG replication bandwidth requirements is by using the Exchange 2013 Server Role Requirements Calculator, which can be found here:

```
http://blogs.technet.com/b/exchange/archive/2013/05/14/released-exchange-2013-
server-role-requirements-calculator.aspx
```

Exchange Solution Sizing

Sizing Exchange solutions is as much art as it is science. This may come as a surprise to some of you, but the reality is that Exchange sizing is based on a series of approximations that try to map end-user activity to server resource usage. With the best of intentions, end users rarely do what you expect them to, and so one of the primary goals of sizing is to make your solution large enough to cope with all demands and peaks but no larger than it needs to be.

This section will take a brief look at how to approach Exchange server sizing.

SIZING REQUIREMENTS

All sizing exercises begin by analyzing the identified requirements and defining the user profile. The user profile is the cornerstone of all Exchange sizing calculations. If you get your user profile wrong, you will get your Exchange sizing wrong. The user profile is defined as the average number of email messages that a user sends and receives within a working day, plus the average size of email messages sent by the users. This value is generally expressed as a value between 50 and 500 messages per day, and the average message size is in kilobytes.

WHAT TO DO WITH VERY SMALL OR VERY LARGE USER PROFILE NUMBERS

Profile values that are above 500 or below 50 are not recommended for use with Exchange sizing calculations. If your profile is below 50, then round up to 50. If it is above 500, then you will need to perform your own load testing with LoadGen. This is expected to be released for Exchange Server 2013 in July 2013.

Your requirements will also define what target service availability metrics your solution will need to reach. The higher the service availability, the more database copies and servers you will require. It is difficult to provide precise guidance on the quantity of database copies or servers required to reach a specific service level since the single most important aspect to service quality is how you operate your Exchange solution. As a rule of thumb, 99.9 percent availability requires three isolated database copies and 99.95 percent availability requires four or more.

STORAGE SIZING

There are two aspects to storage sizing:

- Storage capacity
- Storage performance

Capacity sizing is fundamentally the process of determining how many mailboxes of a specific quota size can fit on a disk volume. This isn't quite as simple as it sounds since the capacity that a mailbox takes up on disk is made up of the message contents, mailbox white space, and recoverable items, plus you need to take into account the content index database and the database transaction logs. As a general rule, the following approximations can be made on a per-mailbox basis:

- Mailbox size on disk is ~7 percent larger than the mailbox quota size.
- Content index is ~20 percent of the mailbox size.
- Transaction log space required in MB = user profile × 20 percent.

To calculate the maximum number of mailboxes per volume by capacity, you would perform the following tasks:

1. Calculate the formatted capacity of the volume. To do this, multiply the raw size by 0.9313; for example, a 3 TB drive would be 3000 × 0.9313 = 2794 GB.

2. Calculate the maximum capacity that you want to use. Typically, on drives larger than 2 TB you want to leave around 5 percent free. To do this, multiply the formatted capacity by 0.95; for example, 2794 × 0.95 = 2654 GB.

3. Allocate 25 percent of the volume for content index (20 percent) and transaction logs (5 percent). For example, multiply 2654 GB × 0.75 = 1990 GB.

4. Divide available volume space by size of mailbox on disk. To do this, calculate size of mailbox on disk; let's assume a 5 GB quota, so the size on disk will be 5 × 1.07 = 5.35 GB. Your available capacity for the 3 TB volume works out to be 1990 GB after taking all other factors into account, so 1990 GB / 5.35 GB = 372 5 GB mailboxes per 3 TB volume from a capacity perspective.

Now that you know that you can store 372 5 GB mailboxes on a 3 TB volume, you need to consider the performance of that volume and check to see if it will be sufficient for your users. To do this, you need to look at the random Input/Output Operations Per Second (IOPS) for both the volume and the mailboxes. Most manufacturers will provide random IOPS data for their disk spindles, but for the most part Exchange 2013 should be deployed on 7.2K RPM 3.5" SAS midline storage, and these spindles usually provide around 55 IOPS.

The next step is to determine how many IOPS your mailboxes will require. To do this, you multiply the user profile by 0.00067. Let's assume a user profile of 200 email messages per day. This gives you 200 × 0.00067 = 0.134 IOPS per mailbox. You can then divide the IOPS provided by your volume by the IOPS per mailbox, which in this case would be 55 / 0.134 = 410 mailboxes per volume from a performance perspective.

This very rough storage sizing exercise shows that you can fit 372 5 GB mailboxes on your 3 TB volume from a capacity perspective and 410 mailboxes from a performance perspective. You would therefore take the lower of these numbers when you size the solution and put no more than 372 mailboxes on each 3 TB disk drive.

This logic applies even if there are multiple databases per volume. In this instance, if you had two databases on your 3 TB volume, you would still store 372 mailboxes in total, but during normal operation 186 of the mailboxes would be active and 186 would be passive.

Let's assume that you're using 12 3 TB volumes within your server. Out of these 12, 2 are required for the host operating system and transport, which leaves 10 for mailbox database volumes. Let's leave one to function as an auto-reseed spare, which leaves 9 3 TB JBOD volumes for your databases. This means that your server could support 9 × 372 = 3348 mailboxes from a storage perspective.

PROCESSOR SIZING

Processor sizing is based on the same approach as storage. First, you need to know what your user profile is, and then you use that to determine your processor requirements per mailbox. Next, you calculate the processor capacity of your potential server and how many mailboxes it can support.

One of the first things you need to understand for processor scaling is the concept of megacycles. A *megacycle* is a processor term used to define the amount of work that a processor can complete in one million clock cycles. The first problem is that the amount of work that a processor can do in one clock cycle varies between processor types. To counter this you use a comparison benchmark called SPECint to help you compare workloads between different processor types.

However, you first need to determine your processor megacycles requirements per mailbox. To do this, multiply the user profile by 0.0425. If you stick with your profile of 200, this becomes $200 \times 0.0425 = 8.5$ megacycles/mailbox for the Mailbox role only. We will discuss processor requirements for CAS later on.

The next step is to calculate how many megacycles your server has available. For this example, let's assume that you're going to be using a server with two Intel XEON E5-2660 CPUs. According to the www.spec.org website, the SPECint2006 CINT2006 rate score for a system with two of these processors is 591. This system has 16 processor cores and so each one has a SPECint2006 rate score of $591 / 16 = 36.93$. The base system used for all Exchange 2013 processor size calculations has a SPECint2006 rate score per core of 33.75. To estimate the available Exchange workload megacycles on the target server, you can use the following formula:

(Target platform per-core value x MHz per-core of baseline platform)/(Baseline per-score value)

In this case this becomes $(36.93 \times 2000 \text{ MHz}) / 33.75 = 2188$ megacycles/core. The system has 16 processor cores, and so the total available megacycles is $2188 \times 16 = 35{,}015$ megacycles.

The next step is to determine how many mailboxes you can support with your 35,015 megacycles of processing power. But before we dive in, you need to adjust your capacity a little since it is generally never a good idea to run your processors at 100 percent capacity. As a general rule, it is a good idea to aim for 80 percent utilization in the worst-case scenario, so immediately you know that each of your 200 user-profile mailboxes requires 8.5 megacycles, so to determine how many mailboxes your server can handle safely, you must divide 28,012 by $8.5 = 3295$ mailboxes per server.

If you are planning to collocate mailbox and client access on this server, the formula changes slightly. A Client Access server requires roughly 20 percent of the processor power that is required for the Mailbox role. To approximate this, if you are sizing for a multirole server, you would take your system megacycles target of 28,012 and take off 25 percent for CAS, which would leave $28{,}012 \times 0.75 = 21{,}009$ megacycles. This means that your two-socket XEON E5-2660 server would support $21{,}009 / 8.5 = 2471$ mailboxes on a multirole server.

MEMORY SIZING

Memory sizing follows a similar path to both disk and processor sizing. The amount of memory required is primarily based on the user profile. If you take our example profile of 200 messages per user per day, this would end up being $200 \times 0.24 = 48$ MB of RAM per mailbox.

Given our previous calculations,

- Max mailboxes supported by storage = 3348 (5 GB quota)

- Max mailboxes supported by processor = 2471 (multirole)

You are essentially limited by your processor in this example, and so you need to provide sufficient memory for 2471 mailboxes with a 200-message profile. You know that each mailbox requires 48 MB of RAM, so your requirement becomes 48 × 2471 = 115 GB. However, this only considers the Mailbox role. You also need to consider the requirements for CAS, which requires 2 GB RAM per CPU core used. As a rough approximation, CAS requires 25 percent of the peak worst-case processor capacity on a multirole system, and so your calculation becomes 16 × 80% × 25% × 2 GB = 6.4 GB. When you add this to the 115 GB required for the Mailbox server role, you get a total Exchange Server RAM requirement of 115 GB + 6.4 GB = 121.4 GB. The only remaining thing you need to account for is the Windows operating system itself, which requires a further 2 GB, so your total system requirement becomes 121.4 GB + 2 GB = 123.4 GB.

SIZING SUMMARY

We hope that this brief overview of Exchange sizing has been useful. It is not intended to provide a detailed set of instructions to help you to perform sizing; it is meant more to highlight some of the things that go into a successful sizing calculation.

For almost all scenarios, we recommend using the Exchange 2013 Server Role Requirements Calculator, which is discussed more in Chapter 5, "Designing a Successful Exchange Storage Solution." The calculator can be found here:

```
http://blogs.technet.com/b/exchange/archive/2013/05/14/released-exchange-2013-
server-role-requirements-calculator.aspx
```

If you are curious as to just what the calculator is doing, then we strongly advise that you pour yourself a large version of your favorite drink and spend some time reading Jeff Mealiffe's blog post about Exchange Server 2013 sizing, which can be found here:

```
http://aka.ms/Exchange2013SizingGuidanceBlog
```

Moving Forward

You may be tempted to launch into documenting your new design immediately and use the lists provided in this chapter as your own design document headings. Before doing that, consider the following topics:

A Living Document

Design documents are considered to be "living documents" while they being are written. In other words, they are subject to change and may iterate through a number of versions before the final published report is released. Bear this in mind as you craft your design. Design documents are not considered set in stone until they are accepted as final via a formal sign-off mechanism.

How Do You Know When to Finish Designing?

Designs go through a number of iterations, and your customer may request various features at a late stage in the design process that they would like to include. The solution to this is to require a formal handover procedure. The key is identifying the stakeholders and gaining their approval of the requirements before the design is issued. Design approval then becomes a straightforward task of demonstrating that the proposed design meets the previously identified requirements.

If new requirements are added as the design progresses, then these must be identified as a clear change, and they are subject to change control and potential redesign.

Overengineering

Be careful not to overengineer a solution. Try to address each requirement as simply as possible without excessively complicating the solution. For example, external publishing and security may be achieved using a single service or appliance, or you may choose to implement multilayer security, using layers of network zones, routers, and software. The latter example may represent massive overengineering of the customer's actual needs.

Keep It Simple

Simple is relative in design terms. Essentially, you want to be careful not to design something that the final customer is unable to implement or operate. Complexity often increases total cost of ownership and can lead to lower service availability. As a design approach, try to identity the "total cost" in each of your decisions. That is, don't just concentrate on capital expense; consider what the impact of your decision will be on the operations teams. Typically, the capital expenditure for hardware on an Exchange project is small compared to the total cost of running the service for many years.

Future Proofing

Don't design yourself into a corner. Remember that one day, your customer may need to migrate away from this shiny new platform to a newer platform. The more complicated you make things now, the harder it will be for your customer to migrate in the future. The best approach to this is to try to adopt recommended practices within your design wherever possible and only change default values or deploy third-party software as required.

The Microsoft Way

You may decide to look at how Microsoft has implemented Exchange internally and want to implement Exchange 2013 in a similar fashion. You should bear in mind, however, that Microsoft is a unique organization, subject to compliance laws unlike those of your organization or client. Microsoft will also have particular business requirements that may be significantly different than those of your organization or client. For example, Microsoft IT has not implemented Exchange 2013 on-premises in any significant numbers outside of their own dog-food environment but has elected to move virtually all mailboxes to Exchange Online.

Looking at how other organizations have implemented Exchange 2013 is certainly interesting. However, just because a design solution works for another organization doesn't necessarily mean it is the ideal solution for you or your customer.

Chapter 3

Exchange Architectural Concepts

In Chapter 1, "Business, Functional, and Technical Requirements," we spoke about the best practices that we tend to take for granted: that storage should be built in a certain way, that roles should be allocated in a certain ratio, and so forth. To this day, we often come across Exchange 2010 implementations that clearly reflect Exchange 2007 and even Exchange 2003 thinking. Exchange 2013 is a completely new version and, as such, the best ways for implementing it will develop as the product is deployed and it matures through various cycles of cumulative updates.

Exchange 2010 went through a similar cycle. The recommendations for implementation at RTM were very different than those made at SP2. These kinds of changes in guidance are natural for Exchange. Nevertheless, it means that those who don't keep up with the changes in guidance will implement Exchange according to some old guidance, and they will not be able to take advantage of the full capabilities, either of Exchange or the hardware platform on which it is deployed. Significant savings can also be achieved by deploying Exchange according to new guidance, because it takes advantage of the latest storage and application replication capabilities, which may be lost if deploying Exchange using outdated guidance.

The aim of this chapter is to define the concepts on which Exchange is built and then to extrapolate those concepts into the design choices that have resulted in the Exchange 2013 version.

If you are a messaging consultant or administrator faced with upgrading from an earlier version of Exchange, then the history section in this chapter will help you address the architectural changes and features required to guide your customer through an upgrade to Exchange 2013. Knowing which features have changed, which have been discontinued, and which have been de-emphasized is a critical skill for messaging administrators and consultants. Consider the example where significant applications have been developed to take advantage of WebDAV. As a consultant, you must be able to point out that this mechanism is no longer available to access mailbox contents and what the available alternatives are.

We will explore both the history of the product and specific areas that pertain to Exchange 2013. This chapter is built on the concepts and vocabulary for Exchange to increase your *understanding* of the product. Understanding Exchange fully will help you choose features and build a messaging system that meets the requirements put forth by a business. Understanding what and where Exchange starts and ends and what it does not do may also arm you with the necessary appreciation of how to choose products and features from the third-party ecosystem.

The Evolution of Exchange 2013

NOTE   As a messaging professional, we assume that you have a basic understanding of email systems such as Exchange. If your background is Novel GroupWise, Lotus Notes, or another mail system—or even previous versions of Exchange—this chapter will provide the basic architectural concepts of Exchange 2013 without exploring every specific feature of Exchange in detail.

To appreciate fully where Exchange 2013 is today, it helps to examine where Exchange 2013 came from. As we explore the previous versions of Exchange, we can identify the best practices of yesteryear and how those practices no longer apply to Exchange 2013. In Chapter 1, we explored that the "long trail of obsolete best practices" is still being applied to current-day products such as Exchange 2013 through storage and other best practices that originated in earlier versions of Exchange. As a consultant, you must be able to understand and identify which best practices no longer apply and why when faced with the inevitable discussions surrounding best practices, including topics such as storage, security, high availability, and so forth.

Exchange started as Microsoft Mail in 1991. Microsoft Mail reflected the thinking of the day in terms of storing email in a post office and interoperating via a Message Transfer Agent (MTA) and connectors. Exchange 4.0 was released in April 1996 followed by Exchange 4.0 (a) in August of the same year. Five service packs later, Exchange 5.0 was released in March 1997 and Exchange 5.5 SP4 in November 2000. Though Exchange 5.5 scaled well as a departmental messaging solution, it did not scale well at all as a global enterprise solution by today's standards.

The most important piece of technology for our purposes was the birth of the *Extensible Storage Engine (ESE)*. It is the only architectural concept that has been carried forward—in a vastly optimized version—from Exchange 5.5 and below to Exchange 2013.

ESE is the database engine used in Microsoft Exchange, Microsoft Active Directory, and a number of other Microsoft products. It was built as a non-hierarchical database so that it could store unstructured data. ESE was designed to survive system crashes and to cache data intelligently in order to provide high-speed access to data when required. These tenets of ESE design have been carried through its various offspring released with different versions of Exchange.

ESE was initially optimized for the scenario when disk speeds were very slow and disk storage was very expensive. Emails were *single instanced* wherever possible. This meant that an email received for several recipients was stored only once but referred to as many times as necessary, eliminating the need to write disparate copies for every recipient into the same database. Because of the single-instance scenario, ESE was also highly optimized for random access in its read/write profile.

Exchange 2000/2003

Exchange 2000/2003 and later versions introduced a number of concepts that are carried forward into the current product in one form or another. We will briefly introduce each concept in order to add context to the overall architectural view of Exchange 2013. Unless otherwise noted as discontinued, the features discussed in previous versions of Exchange continue into Exchange 2013. These versions of Exchange moved the product out of the departmental email space and firmly into a datacenter-based enterprise-messaging solution. They supported high availability and a scale that was impressive for their time. Exchange had moved from a "garage" mentality to a datacenter approach.

ACTIVE DIRECTORY INTEGRATION

We will consider Exchange 2000 and Exchange 2003 together, because these versions introduced one of the key features of Exchange to this day: Active Directory integration. Exchange 2000 was the first product to integrate directly into Active Directory. Previous versions of Exchange, including version 5.5, maintained a separate directory that defined configuration data, recipient data, and authentication data for recipients. With Active Directory integration, Exchange 2000 natively integrated recipient and authentication information so that virtually all pertinent recipient information and configuration data resided in one place. This was a huge leap forward, and it allowed Exchange to scale to the limits of Active Directory. We are aware of Exchange implementations within the confines of a single forest that number into the millions of mailboxes. Moving forward in time, Exchange is now able to take advantage of the authentication mechanisms provided by Active Directory, including NTLM and Kerberos.

Exchange 2000/2003 used administrative and routing groups as administrative and message routing boundaries, respectively. Administrators were required to plan both the administrative layout of Exchange servers as well as the message routing topology. Limited delegation of responsibilities could be achieved using administrative groups and Exchange-specific groups.

Transport

Exchange incorporated message transport standards early on using the dominant standards of the day to route mail. Exchange 2000 was no exception, introducing SMTP as the standard for message routing.

Management

Exchange 2003 had limited management capability, with only three roles available for delegation via a Microsoft Management Console (MMC)-based administration console. No granular delegation models existed via the Exchange management utilities, and Exchange administrators tended to set very high levels of rights in Active Directory. Significant management overhead existed in order to build and maintain a granular delegation structure.

Role Separation

Exchange 2000/2003 could achieve *role separation*. Servers had differing functions, such as email storage, email routing, public folder storage, and client access for some client protocols. The drawback in this version of Exchange, however, was that it achieved role separation via configuration, not via a dedicated role. Administrators needed to enable specific features or configurations in order for a server to be a dedicated client access endpoint, which in Exchange 2000/2003 terminology was called a *front-end server*.

High Availability

Exchange 2000/2003 could be clustered in order to archive *high availability*. That is, a component could fail, but the availability of email remained unaffected. Clustering was dependent on expensive SAN-based storage that introduced a high level of complexity. Often, clustered implementations had lower uptime numbers when compared to standalone implementations. These solutions had no awareness of the nature of the data that they attempted to safeguard, and administrators needed to be highly proficient with both clustering and SAN technologies in order to maintain good uptime figures.

Storage

Storage groups are Exchange mailbox and public folder databases with a shared asynchronous database-logging mechanism per group. Exchange 2003 raised the limit of the number of databases to 20 to be contained in a maximum of four storage groups in the Enterprise version.

To this day, Exchange 2000/2003 storage recommendations surface incorrectly as "best practices," specifically:

◆ Exchange databases require super-fast disks because of the high amount of Input/Output Operations Per Second (IOPS) required.

◆ Logs need to be written to the fastest disks available because of the sequential nature of log writing.

◆ Exchange performance is directly related to the speed of the log drives, because transactions cached in memory cannot complete until they are committed to disk. Thus, transactions are queued in memory until they can be committed, directly relating to the speed of the entire system.

◆ Exchange logs must be placed on separate disks from Exchange databases.

Sacrificial spindles were often needed, which allowed extra disks to be used in order to achieve the needed IOPS. This was accomplished at the expense of unused disk capacity.

Very few choices existed to the messaging administrator in terms of how to create storage solutions. RAID 5/10/50 for database volumes and RAID 1/10 for log volumes prevailed, both as SAN-attached volumes as well as locally attached volumes in the case of smaller implementations.

Exchange 2007

Exchange 2007 was a major milestone that introduced several new concepts while improving on others. Exchange 2007 was the first version of Exchange that mandated a 64-bit architecture, albeit with a limit of 32 GB of usable memory. Technically, more memory was addressable, although it was cheaper to add more servers than to double the memory from 32 GB to 64 GB. Exchange 2003 had significant scalability limitations, due to a 32-bit memory model, which severely restricted how many mailboxes a given server could serve. Exchange 2007 discontinued a number of features, including routing groups, administrative groups, support for network-attached storage, and the Exchange Installable File System (ExIFS), among others. Nonetheless, these features were still available for the Exchange 2003 server hosting a desired feature or connector, for example, GroupWise. Exchange 2007 was the first version of Exchange to move from a centralized storage model to an application-based replication model, and it introduced the replication concepts that led to the model available via Exchange 2013.

ACTIVE DIRECTORY INTEGRATION

Exchange 2007 built on the model of using Active Directory by not only storing Exchange data in Active Directory but also through leveraging the Active Directory topology for message routing instead of using Exchange 2003 routing groups.

TRANSPORT

Exchange 2007 built on the foundation provided by Exchange 2003 and introduced new features that directly related to the scalability and availability of the platform:

Self-Signed Certificates   Exchange 2007 introduced self-signed certificates, which were those certificates created by the Exchange server in order to bootstrap a secure configuration for Exchange. The Exchange 2007 Transport service made extensive use of certificates to secure mail flow so that message transfer between Exchange servers was encrypted by default.

Back Pressure   This feature protects the message-transfer capabilities of Exchange by monitoring free disk space and memory. If thresholds are exceeded, Exchange throttles connections and eventually stops accepting messages. Once the monitored thresholds return to normal, Exchange accepts new messages.

Active Directory Site-Based Routing   This feature leverages the Active Directory concepts of sites and Active Directory IP site links to route mail. Routing was configured automatically based on the Active Directory topology. However, administrators were still able to define additional routing information to specific Active Directory sites and Active Directory site links.

Least-Cost Routing   This concept uses an algorithm that uses Active Directory site-based routing to determine the path a message should follow. Active Directory link costs are used to calculate the path with the lowest cost and the fewest message hops. An Exchange administrator may have configured a different Exchange cost to an Active Directory link. This would impact the resulting least-cost path directly and thereby define a different message route.

Receive Connectors   These are server-based, dedicated configuration items that allow as many Receive connectors as necessary to be constructed. These connectors specify items such as source, authentication parameters, and IP address to receive email on, among others. Receive connectors introduced a new level of granularity in the ability to configure connections to receive email.

Send Connectors   These are organization-wide configuration items that can be scoped to a specific Active Directory site and route messages to specific address spaces. Send connectors allow specific parameters to be defined per address space, such as whether a smart host or DNS should be used, what authentication parameters should be specified, whether secure message transfer via TLS is to be used, and other parameters.

Transport Rules   These run on the Hub Transport or Edge Transport server role. They allow the administrator to create actions affecting mail in transit without writing any code. Transport rules can be defined via the Exchange Management Console or the Exchange Management Shell.

Transport Dumpster   The transport dumpster is hosted by the Hub Transport role, and it defines an area to retain email messages that have already been delivered to mailboxes hosted on a CCR cluster participating in the same Active Directory site as the Hub Transport server. Messages are retained in transport queues for a stated period of time, along with defined storage limits, which may be adjusted by the administrator. Messages are replayed to mailboxes stored on the participating CCR cluster should a failover occur in which the passive node is not 100 percent in sync with the active node. The transport dumpster is not a guarantee against data loss in a failover scenario, because it is only able to protect email that has already been transmitted, as opposed to email still in transit or changes made to a mailbox using Outlook in online mode.

MANAGEMENT

Exchange 2007 introduced a new management paradigm with the use of PowerShell. Management capabilities were implemented via PowerShell first and afterward through the

GUI. Just as Exchange 2000 was a trendsetter for its use of Active Directory, Exchange 2007 set the standard for future products in how PowerShell was used for administration.

Administrative roles were improved over Exchange 2003. However, granular delegation capabilities still did not exist natively. Split-permission models were available so that Exchange administrators had limited permissions in Active Directory. However, this required the implementation of custom access control lists at an Active Directory object and attribute level using tools such as ADSI Edit and DSACLS. Split-permission models were difficult to create and maintain, and they were by no means self-documenting.

Whereas Exchange 2000/2003 forced administrators to become storage experts, Exchange 2007 required administrators to learn new skills, specifically how to create and maintain X509 certificates. The following Exchange 2007 management features were significantly changed or introduced:

Autodiscover   The introduction of Autodiscover, that is, the ability for an Outlook or ActiveSync client to query Exchange for configuration information based on an email address and credentials and to receive the connection parameters required to configure itself, was a major step forward. Autodiscover forms the basis not only of client configuration but also of high availability in this and future versions of Exchange.

Public Folders   These were announced as deprecated in Exchange 2007, which initially did not even ship with a public folder management console. Recanting the preliminary announcement, Microsoft shipped service packs that introduced a new management console with limited capabilities. However, administrators soon learned that, beyond the basic tasks represented by the GUI, PowerShell was needed for day-to-day administration.

Exchange Web Services   Exchange Web Services (EWS) provided a SOAP-based protocol via a web services interface to access mailbox and public folder data. It replaced WebDAV, CDOEX, and ExOLEDB, which prevailed as the dominant access mechanisms in Exchange 2003. These mechanisms were still available in Exchange 2007, but they were de-emphasized in favor of EWS.

Role Separation

Exchange 2007 reintroduced role separation via the concept of Exchange roles, which could be deployed together on a single server, by themselves on dedicated servers, or a combination of the two models. Exchange 2007 introduced five roles:

Client Access Server (CAS)   This was used for handling most client access protocols, with the exception of MAPI.

Hub Transport Server (Hub/HT)   This was used for handling all mail flow, as well as message delivery, journaling, and application of transport rules.

Mailbox Server   This was used for hosting mailbox and public folder databases.

Unified Messaging Server   This was used to integrate Exchange 2007 into telephone/SIP networks and for facilitating voicemail and fax integration into a unified inbox.

Edge Transport Server   This was used as a standalone SMTP Transport server, designed to be deployed in perimeter networks.

The primary reason for role separation was that servers were "CPU bound," such that CPU resources were exhausted first. Role separation allowed CAS to be separated from Hub and Mailbox roles, facilitating a scaling out of Exchange functions. An Exchange 2007 CAS server and Exchange 2007 Hub server were required in every Active Directory site hosting an Exchange 2007 Mailbox server.

Roles could be deployed autonomously from each other and thus facilitated flexibility in deployment, management, and engineering. Administrators no longer needed to deploy a full server and then disable the features that they did not want to use. Management tasks could now be grouped around a set of roles as opposed to a group of servers. An extra role could be deployed if required to bolster specific capacity that might be required. For example, if the existing CAS server could not handle all incoming HTTP client traffic, then another CAS role could be deployed. Although the roles could be split out, they still needed to be updated in sequence, specifically CAS, Hub, and then Mailbox roles.

In Exchange 2007, databases were grouped together via storage groups that contained the databases and the transaction logs. Single instance storage was available for databases within a storage group.

HIGH AVAILABILITY

In Exchange 2007, roles could be combined such that CAS, Hub, and Mailbox roles could coexist, although if the Mailbox role was clustered in any way, then the CAS and Hub roles could no longer be combined with the clustered Mailbox role. A resulting role combination that became quite popular was combining CAS and Hub roles over two or more machines that were highly available, using either Windows Network Load Balancing or another load-balancing mechanism and clustered mailboxes on other machines.

Exchange 2007 introduced several mechanisms for ensuring that stored mail was highly available via the Mailbox role using either traditional shared storage clustering similar in nature to Exchange 2003 or log shipping. *Log shipping* allows an Exchange database to be replicated from one location to another by copying the transaction logs asynchronously generated by the primary database to another location. There the logs are replayed to construct another database. Exchange 2007 supported the following cluster or log shipping-based features:

Local Continuous Replication (LCR)   This is a single-server solution that used log shipping to create and maintain a copy of a storage group in another location, normally another set of disks. The administrator drove the switchover; that is, it was a manual process.

Cluster Continuous Replication (CCR)   CCR paired clustered Exchange 2007 servers using non-shared storage in an active-passive arrangement. Storage groups containing mailbox databases were made highly available using log shipping on the passive node. Failover was automatic or administrator driven. However, upon failover, all databases needed to failover from the primary node to the secondary node. If bandwidth allowed, the nodes of the CCR cluster could be deployed in different datacenters. Because of the shared-nothing clustering model of CCR and the less stringent requirements, CCR nodes could be dissimilar, as long as the storage paths were identical. CCR rapidly became the most adopted high-availability mechanism.

Standby Continuous Replication (SCR)   This feature was introduced in Exchange 2007 SP1, and it allowed the administrator to create a copy of a storage group on another machine, irrespective of whether the source was a clustered or standalone instance, normally in another location. SCR required a manual switchover to activate a storage group in another location, and it was considered a disaster recovery solution.

Single Copy Clusters (SCC)   These were a natural evolution of the traditional shared-storage clustering mechanism introduced in Exchange 2000/2003. Storage tended to be

SAN-based in order to provide storage resilience, which allowed one of the hosts to suffer a failure so that the responsibilities of that node could be moved to another node, either manually or automatically. SCC supported a maximum of eight active and passive nodes combined. Similar to clustering in previous versions of Exchange, it was highly complex and had a stringent list of requirements. Nodes needed to be identical in terms of hardware, software, and, often, firmware levels.

Transport Dumpster   This concept was introduced with CCR clusters, and it allowed received messages to be retained for a configurable period of time. In the event of a lossy CCR failover, messages retained in the transport dumpster would be retransmitted in order to negate possible data loss.

STORAGE

Exchange 2007 Enterprise increased the number of databases to a maximum of 50 contained within 50 storage groups. Even though a storage group could contain up to five databases each, Microsoft recommended the use of one database per storage group.

Improvements in the ESE database in Exchange 2007 gave the administrator more storage choices. Specifically, it provided the administrator with the ability to choose between SAN-based storage or Direct Attached Storage (DAS) shelves. Because of the introduction of roles as well as the CCR HA model, Exchange could scale up and out as required. Flexibility in storage choices made both scaling up and out cheaper than ever before, since DAS storage is far cheaper than SAN-based storage.

Exchange 2010

Building on the success of Exchange 2007, Exchange 2010 introduced many new features that form the basis of our understanding of Exchange 2013. Exchange 2003 and Exchange 2007 could still be upgraded from within the organization. While Exchange 2010 deprecated a number of features from both Exchange 2003 and Exchange 2007, such as Lotus Notes migration, by retaining the Exchange 2007 server hosting of the Microsoft Transporter Suite as part of the organization, these features can still be accessed. Exchange 2010 deprecated non-GUI features in the replication model, such as SCR, and it consolidated the various high-availability models available into one model. It also became the easiest version of Exchange ever to achieve a multiple-copy, highly available Exchange installation. It did so without having to reinstall Exchange (unlike every previous version of Exchange).

DISCONTINUED FEATURES

Exchange 2013 requires Exchange 2003 to be removed completely from the organization as an installation prerequisite. This means that a "double-hop" migration from Exchange 2003 to Exchange 2007/2010 and then from Exchange 2007/2010 to Exchange 2013 is the most natural upgrade path. As mentioned in the introduction, a consultant must be able to identify which features or product capabilities will be left behind during such an upgrade.

Exchange 2010 discontinued a number of features and concepts from Exchange 2007, some of which had been in place as far back as Exchange 2003. Thus, a number of features stand out architecturally from those that were deprecated, discontinued, or replaced:

◆ Exchange WebDAV, ExCDO, MAPI32, CDOEX, and ExOLEDB were deprecated and replaced by EWS.

◆ Storage groups were replaced by a new database architecture.

- CCR, LCR, SCR, and SCC were replaced by a new high-availability architecture.

- Recovery databases replaced recovery storage groups.

- Mailbox databases were no longer connected to servers.

- Single-instance storage was discontinued in order to optimize ESE for slow storage.

- The Streaming Backup API was no longer accessible to back up applications. However, it could still be used within the product for database seeding operations within a DAG.

Every version of Exchange has brought with it new features while discontinuing others. The lack of single-instance storage is still mourned by the storage community to this day. Nevertheless, this concern is only valid when thinking about high-cost storage. Single-instancing messages made a lot of sense when storage was expensive and needed to be very fast. Exchange 2010 introduced a new storage paradigm, which administrators still struggle with to this day—the ability to place databases on relatively slow and cheap disks. In Chapter 5, "Designing a Successful Exchange Storage Solution," we will cover what changed and why, in order to leave single instancing behind and why it is no longer desirable.

Active Directory Integration

Exchange 2010's use of Active Directory to store configuration and directory information is similar to that of Exchange 2007. Every subsequent version of Exchange continued extending the Active Directory schema as features were added to Exchange.

Transport

Exchange 2010 introduced a number of new features designed to prevent a particular service from abuse or from becoming overwhelmed to the point of failure:

Message Throttling This protects the Transport service by implementing limits on message processing rates, SMTP connection rates, and SMTP session timeout values. These limits are adjustable to suit the messaging requirements of an organization, assuming that the rates defined at shipping time are insufficient.

Transport Agents These permit extensibility of the transport stack by allowing the administrator to install custom software that may access and act on messages while they are being transported via SMTP. A classic example of a transport agent is antivirus software, which inspects a message item in transit, before it reaches the intended destination.

Version-Based Routing Because of the differences between the API versions used to deliver messages to an Exchange store, Exchange 2010 introduced version-based routing, which prevents an Exchange 2007 Hub Transport server from delivering a message to an Exchange 2010 message store and vice versa.

Integrating transport rules with an Active Directory Rights Management server allowed the administrator to encrypt messages in transit, even after they had left the user's mailbox, if defined conditions were met.

Management

Exchange 2010 delivered a new set of management tools built on the remote PowerShell features introduced with PowerShell 2.0. The GUI capabilities were enhanced via the new *Exchange*

Management Console with greater capabilities in the MMC-based tools and a new web-based administration portal, the *Exchange Control Panel.*

Similar to Exchange 2007, the Exchange 2010 Exchange Management Console was built on a PowerShell-based foundation in that it executed PowerShell in order to manage Exchange. However, the 2010 version of the Exchange Management Console exposed PowerShell, which it would execute via the properties dialog box via these features. Exchange 2010 introduced a number of new management features or improvements over Exchange 2007. A description of these features follows:

Administrator Audit Login This allowed actions performed in the Exchange Management Console, Exchange Admin Center, and PowerShell to be logged.

Role-Based Access Control Exchange 2010 introduced Role-Based Access Control (RBAC), which provided a new paradigm of granular control to Exchange administrators. Role-Based Access Control allows for the definition of roles, which define with exacting granularity *who* can do *what* and *where* can they do it. RBAC no longer relied on access control lists as did Exchange 2007, and, by the introduction of roles, it eliminated the management challenges caused by the use of access control lists. We will deal with RBAC in detail in Chapter 6, "Management."

Split Permission Model A split permission model was introduced in Exchange 2010, which separated Exchange management and Active Directory management. If it was implemented while running setup, Exchange administrators could no longer create users, groups, or other security principals in Active Directory, but they could perform tasks pertaining to the management of servers and existing recipients. Choosing this model also meant that RBAC was not going to be used to delegate permissions.

Client Throttling Policies These policies defined a set of wide-ranging client access parameters to ensure that, irrespective of client access method, an individual or a few abusive clients would not affect Exchange Client Access server performance.

Multi-Tenant Model This was introduced in Exchange 2010 Service Pack 1. It allowed enterprises to host multiple Exchange customers in a single organization, with a logical separation between customers. This feature, known as *hosting mode*, replaced solutions such as Microsoft Hosted Messaging and Collaboration from Exchange 2007. However, it was deprecated with the release of Exchange 2010 Service Pack 2. Hosting mode provided no management GUI with the exception of ECP, which permitted limited management, and it did not see mass adoption. Exchange 2010 Service Pack 2 also introduced hosting guidance and *Address Book Policies (ABP)*, which allowed hosting partners and customers to achieve global address list (GAL) separation, that is, the creation of multiple GALs within a single organization, for a hosted solution or an on-premises organization.

Archive Mailboxes These were introduced in Exchange 2010 as a concept for a secondary mailbox that could be stored in another database. Retention policies initiated via Messaging Records Management (MRM) or user interaction could cause mail to be moved from the primary mailbox to the archive mailbox. Users could interact with messages in the archive mailbox in a manner identical to the primary mailbox.

Retention and Litigation Holds These holds were introduced in Exchange 2010 and created a copy of items modified in the primary mailbox or the archive and stored them in a non-client-accessible area, specifically the mailbox dumpster. These changes could then be surfaced via another feature introduced in Exchange 2010, Discovery Search.

Discovery Search   This feature of the Exchange Control Panel allowed users who had been given the required rights via RBAC to perform discovery searches against Exchange 2010 mailboxes and to store the results in a Discovery mailbox for further examination.

ROLE SEPARATION

The role separation concepts introduced in Exchange 2007 were maintained in Exchange 2010. However, a new high-availability model meant that the Exchange 2010 CAS, Hub, and Mailbox roles could now be combined, even if the Mailbox role was highly available. The combination of these roles onto one machine became the default guidance for Exchange 2010 in order to maximize hardware utilization. It should be noted that this guidance evolved over the life cycle of Exchange 2010 as hardware became more powerful.

Technically, the Unified Messaging role could also be combined with the CAS, Hub, and Mailbox roles, although it was not best practice to do so. An Exchange 2010 CAS server and Exchange 2010 Hub server were still required in every Active Directory site hosting an Exchange 2010 Mailbox server.

Deployment guidance has evolved significantly over the life cycle of Exchange 2010. However, there are still a significant number of deployments based on Exchange 2010 RTM or Exchange 2007 guidance. Old guidance is reflected in how roles are either fully split out to individual machines or combined so that the CAS and Hub roles share a server, while Mailbox roles that are part of a DAG are deployed separately. While the latter instance does make sense when Windows NLB is the load-balancing mechanism, since two types of clustering cannot coexist within the same OS, it should not be the default deployment option for an enterprise.

Client Access servers gained a new service, the *RPC Client Access service*, which allowed users to connect to their mailboxes, regardless of the location of their active database. Since databases were no longer connected to specific servers (more on this later in this section), CAS servers now acted as the MAPI endpoint, introducing near-seamless database failover.

HIGH AVAILABILITY

Exchange 2010 changed the high-availability model used in previous versions of Exchange from a server-based availability model to a database-based availability model. Database availability groups (DAGs) replaced all other continuous log-based shipping mechanisms and became the most flexible database high-availability model to date, with up to 100 databases potentially participating in a 16-node DAG.

Database Availability Groups   DAGs superseded all other database, high-availability mechanisms in Exchange 2007, including high availability across sites. They incorporated the log-shipping technology of CCR clusters; however, they expanded the boundary to 16 servers and introduced failover at a database level, as opposed to the server level in Exchange 2007. Because of failover at the database level, different database copies could now be activated across nodes in the DAG cluster, thereby introducing load distribution and granular failover as high-availability concepts while still maintaining a single master architecture for database updates. The active database copy's log stream would be replicated to all other passive copies. Significant improvements were made from Exchange 2007, however, if databases or log streams diverged. Database copies could be seeded either from an active or a passive copy, allowing secondary copies to be created from passive copies within a site, as opposed to a potentially active copy in another site.

Datacenter Activation Coordination   DAC mode was introduced as a DAG feature that acted as extra level of *quorum*, a clustering concept based on counting the active/remaining nodes in a cluster and making majority-based decisions to activate failover or deactivate technology as a result. DAC mode caused all databases participating in a DAG to dismount in the event of DAG quorum loss in order to prevent *split brain*, a condition that results when databases activate in two datacenters simultaneously.

Client Access Server Arrays   CAS arrays represented a highly available MAPI (RPC over TCP) connection point per Active Directory site. CAS arrays had a logical name that was defined in DNS, and they required a persistent load-balancing mechanism that persisted connection states, such as a hardware load balancer. Clients would connect to the CAS array, as opposed to individual CAS servers, and would not reconnect semi-transparently in the event of a single CAS server failure.

CAS arrays introduced a MAPI-based name space alongside the other HTTP-based workloads, each having their own name space. This meant that, with only two datacenters participating in a site-resilient design, Exchange 2010 administrators could define up to nine disparate types of name spaces, specifically:

- Autodiscover name space
- Legacy name space for legacy Exchange or mail systems
- Internet protocol name space: primary datacenter (EWS, OWA, Active Sync, Outlook Anywhere, or POP/IMAP)
- Internet protocol name space: secondary datacenter (EWS, OWA, Active Sync, Outlook Anywhere, or POP/IMAP)
- Outlook Web App failback name space: primary datacenter
- Outlook Web App failback name space: secondary datacenter
- RPC client access name space: primary datacenter (MAPI)
- RPC client access name space: secondary datacenter (MAPI)
- Transport name space (encrypted SMTP)

The MAPI name spaces did not need to be secured via a certificate.

Shadow Redundancy   This is one of the features that made Exchange 2010 Transport highly available by design. It did so by retaining a copy of a message on the server responsible for initiating the transmission until the next hop had acknowledged successful transmission of the message. Shadow redundancy allows Hub Transport servers to be taken out of service with no data loss, as long as more than one Hub Transport server exists in an Active Directory site and the next message hop consists of another Exchange 2010 Hub Transport server or Exchange 2010 Edge Transport server.

STORAGE

Exchange 2010 Enterprise increased the number of databases to a maximum of 100. Improvements in the ESE database in Exchange 2010 gave the administrator even more storage choices, specifically the ability to choose between SAN-based storage, direct-attached storage (DAS) shelves, near-line SAS, and SATA drives. Low-cost disks could now be attached in a JBOD (just a bunch of disks) configuration.

EXCHANGE ONLINE INTEGRATION

Exchange 2010 Service Pack 1 introduced features that could integrate an on-premises Exchange deployment into Office 365 Exchange organizations. These hybrid deployments achieved a level of integration that provided a seamless experience for users. The introduction of Exchange 2010 CAS and Hub servers into an existing Exchange 2003 or Exchange 2007 organization meant that older Exchange versions could participate in, and migrate to, Office 365 Exchange.

The hybrid model required extensive configuration of both the CAS and Hub roles. However, the effort required to achieve this was massively reduced by the introduction of the *Hybrid Configuration Wizard* in Exchange 2010 Service Pack 2.

Exchange 2013

Exchange 2013 introduces some of the most significant changes to date in Exchange, including a single code base for customer, Office 365, or partner-hosted deployments. Quarterly cumulative updates, as opposed to service packs, allow customers and hosting partners to take advantage of new fixes and features as they become available in Office 365.

Architecturally, Exchange 2013 shares many concepts and features with previous versions of Exchange, especially Exchange 2010. While the Exchange server role functionality is present as in Exchange 2010, its implementation in Exchange 2013 is different.

Even though Exchange 2010 guidance recommended multi-role servers, many deployments still used individual physical or virtual servers per role, causing massive underutilization of CPU and memory resources on many of these servers. (See the sidebar in Chapter 1 called "Requirements Elicitation and the Long Trail of Obsolete Best Practices.")

We hope that as we reviewed the history of Exchange, you gained an understanding of why role separation was introduced and where it and role amalgamation made sense. Exchange 2013 introduces a set of new paradigms, while a vast amount of functionality from previous versions of Exchange is retained or improved.

Exchange 2013 ships with the following design goals in mind:

- ◆ Simplify Exchange 2013 implementations at a large scale.

- ◆ Balance hardware utilization across all server roles to take advantage of modern hardware.

- ◆ Improve failure isolation as much as possible, irrespective of where the failure occurs.

- ◆ Integrate high availability for all server roles.

- ◆ Simplify dependence on network architecture, and lower the requirements for high-end load balancers.

◆ Lower the amount of effort and complexity required to interoperate with previous versions of Exchange.

The following list summarizes the major areas of change to Exchange 2013 architecture from Exchange 2010, which will be addressed in greater detail throughout the rest of this chapter:

Role Separation

◆ Exchange 2013 ships with a new evolution of the Exchange server roles effectively implemented in a front-end and back-end configuration, that is, the Exchange 2013 CAS and Exchange 2013 Mailbox roles.

◆ RPC protocol use has been banned for Exchange server role-based communication and for client-to-server communication.

◆ Two Exchange 2010 name space types have been discontinued: primary and secondary datacenter RPC client access.

◆ RPC over HTTP has been retained, while RPC over TCP has been discontinued as a client access protocol.

◆ The Exchange 2013 CAS server role acts as a front-end stateless protocol proxy, requiring layer 4 routing only.

◆ The Exchange 2013 Mailbox server role is an amalgamation of Exchange 2010 server roles, specifically CAS, Hub, Mailbox, and UM.

Transport

◆ The Exchange 2013 CAS server role is a protocol endpoint for incoming and outgoing SMTP traffic while storing nothing on the CAS role.

◆ The Exchange 2013 Mailbox role performs the Exchange 2010 Hub Transport function, and it can be configured to send mail itself, thereby bypassing the protocol proxy functionality of the Exchange 2013 CAS role.

◆ DAGs are able to function as routing boundaries for message delivery.

◆ Optional antivirus scanning is included with Exchange Transport.

Management

◆ The Exchange Management Console and Exchange Control Panel have been discontinued and replaced by the Exchange Admin Center (EAC).

◆ The Hybrid Configuration Wizard has been improved and simplified.

◆ SharePoint and Lync integration are significantly improved, especially in the areas of search and discovery.

◆ Reporting has been added to the EAC for new features, such as Data Leak Prevention.

High Availability

◆ Safety Net has been introduced to improve Transport resilience.

◆ CAS arrays have changed to become a unit of HTTP-based CAS arrays as opposed to MAPI-based arrays in Exchange 2010.

- Public folder replication has been deprecated in favor of storing Exchange 2013 public folder mailboxes in databases that are members of a DAG.

- Managed Availability has been introduced as a self-healing capability.

Storage

- Public folder databases have been discontinued and replaced by Exchange 2013 public folder mailboxes.

- Exchange 2013 improves IOPS performance by another 50 percent compared to Exchange 2010, allowing four 2 TB databases to share a single volume.

- Site mailboxes have been introduced to allow deeper integration with SharePoint team sites.

Exchange 2013 also ships with new logic, which has been rewritten so that RPC calls between functionality tiers, such as Transport submitting email directly to the store via MAPI, and so forth, have been eliminated. This level of isolation builds on the design goal of failure isolation, since every server becomes an island.

Furthermore, moving away from five roles, each representing a potential building block in Exchange 2010, Exchange 2013 introduces a new model comprised of only two: the Client Access server and the Mailbox server roles.

Exchange 2013 offers a number of architectural benefits over previous versions of Exchange. These will be explored in greater detail throughout this chapter:

Deployment　Exchange 2013 simplifies name space management dramatically, allows for transparent deployment with up- and down-level versions of Exchange, and introduces Layer 4 routing compared with Layer 7 routing required by Exchange 2010.

Client Connectivity　Existing Exchange 2010 client protocols are supported with the exception of TCP-based protocols.

Client Protocol Offloading　Exchange 2013 CAS servers are able to offload all client connections and authentication functions from the Mailbox server role, increasing scalability and failure isolation of the platform.

Exchange 2013 server roles overcome a number of boundaries introduced by Exchange 2007/2010 server roles. The following new capabilities are also introduced:

Functionality　Interdependent functionality in Exchange 2010 was scattered among CAS, Hub, and Mailbox server roles, requiring these roles to be upgraded as a unit, even if they were not deployed as such. Exchange 2013 CAS versions may be deployed and upgraded independently of the Exchange 2013 mailbox role.

Geographic Affinity　The CAS and Hub roles had very tight RPC-based integration, requiring the roles to be deployed on low-latency, LAN-type conditions. Exchange 2013 CAS uses WAN-resilient protocols (HTTP, SMTP), which are tolerant of tighter latencies, to communicate with Exchange 2013 Mailbox.

Versioning　Exchange 2007 roles could not service Exchange 2010 roles and vice versa. Exchange 2013 CAS is able to integrate downstream with Exchange 2010 and upstream with newer versions of Exchange.

User Partitioning　Generally speaking, a set of users served by a given Exchange 2010 Mailbox role was also served by a given set of Exchange 2010 CAS/Hub server roles.

Exchange 2013 eliminates session affinity from the CAS server role, because the Exchange 2013 Mailbox server role now maintains session affinity. Users are able to move transparently among a pool of 2013 CAS servers, which are load balanced at Layer 4 as opposed to Layer 7.

Throughout the rest of this chapter, we will explore the new architecture of Exchange 2013.

Discontinued Features

Exchange 2013 discontinued a number of features and concepts from Exchange 2010. While a number of individual features were deprecated, discontinued, or replaced, those that stand out architecturally are as follows:

◆ The Hub Transport and Unified Messaging server roles are discontinued. The functionality for both roles is now integrated with the Exchange 2013 Mailbox role.

◆ Antispam features have been discontinued.

◆ The Exchange Management Console and the Exchange Control Panel have been replaced by the Exchange Admin Center.

◆ Outlook 2003 is no longer supported due to its lack of Autodiscover support.

◆ RPC over TCP has been discontinued in favor of using RPC over HTTP (Outlook Anywhere).

◆ Linked connectors have been deprecated.

◆ Managed folders have been deprecated in favor of retention policies.

While the loss of some features has been mourned more than others, the new GUI has been met with some criticism and disapproval. The Exchange 2010 MMC-based GUI relied on remote PowerShell, which massively increased its management and RBAC capabilities, while sacrificing speed. Exchange 2013 introduces a web-based GUI, which is fast and feature rich, giving the administrator more configurability than in any previous version of Exchange since Exchange 2007. However, the new GUI caused the loss of the ability to show the PowerShell-generated management operations, arguably one of the most popular management features of Exchange 2010. This feature is expected to return via a later service pack.

Exchange 2013 Editions

Exchange 2013 is available in two editions: Standard and Enterprise. These editions are limited to 5 and 50 databases, respectively. As with Exchange 2010, specific functionality is determined by the product key used to license the Exchange server. Standard and Enterprise editions can both take advantage of high-availability features such as DAGs, limited only by the number of databases available per edition.

The Exchange Hybrid edition is available for hybrid deployments, and while its name indicates that it could be could be considered a separate edition from the Standard or Enterprise editions, the license model by which it operates is its only distinguishing factor. Introduced with Exchange 2010, this edition is available for free when used as part of an Office 365 hybrid deployment. To obtain a Hybrid edition product key, contact Office 365 support.

Transport

Transport in Exchange 2013 has changed from Exchange 2010. Here is a brief summary of the changes and benefits in Exchange 2013:

Transport Pipeline   The transport pipeline is split between the Front End Transport service on Client Access servers and the Transport service on Mailbox servers.

Routing   Active Directory sites are still recognized as routing boundaries. However, database availability group boundaries have been introduced.

Connectors   The default maximum message size of Send and Receive connectors has been increased from 10 MB to 25 MB.

Edge Transport   Exchange 2013 does not ship with an Edge Transport server, and it requires the use of either an Exchange 2007 or Exchange 2010 Edge Transport server.

For an examination of the Exchange 2013 transport pipeline and the transport components, please review the Exchange 2013 Client Access server and Mailbox server sections of this chapter. The following section examines the next-largest change in Exchange 2013: transport mail flow.

MAIL FLOW

Earlier, we stated that messages, which originate externally to the organization, are handled by the Front End Transport service on the Client Access server role and proxied to the Transport service on the Mailbox server role. Messages from within the Exchange organization are received by the Transport service on the Mailbox server role via one of the following methods:

◆   Receive connector

◆   Pickup or replay directories

◆   Mailbox Transport service

◆   Agent submission

Similar to Exchange 2010, all messages sent or received must be categorized by the Transport service on the Mailbox server role in order to be routed or delivered. Mail routing is achieved using the same least-cost routing algorithm used in Exchange 2010. Exchange 2013 defines a *delivery group* as a collection of transport servers responsible for delivering messages to a routing destination. Post categorization, messages are placed in a delivery queue for one of the following delivery groups:

Active Directory Site   This can be either as a hub site or an Edge Transport server subscribed to the Active Directory site.

Mailbox Delivery Group   This a collection of Exchange servers in the same Active Directory site separated by Exchange version.

Connector Source Servers   This is a collection of Exchange 2007, 2010, or 2013 servers, in the same or different Active Directory sites, which share a defined scope for a Send connector, a Delivery Agent connector, or a Foreign connector.

Server List   This consists of Exchange 2007, 2010 Hub Transport, or Exchange 2013 Mailbox servers configured as distribution group expansion servers.

Destination Database Availability Group   This is also known as the routable DAG.

The *routable DAG* is a new routing destination, which is defined simply as a group of Exchange 2013 Mailbox servers that belong to the same DAG. Routable DAGs may span Active Directory sites as a routing destination. Messages will be delivered to the closest DAG member.

The final delivery location within the routable DAG will be the server hosting the active database copy.

Management

Exchange 2013 introduces a number of new management features or improvements over Exchange 2010. A description of these features follows.

EXCHANGE ADMINISTRATION CENTER

The *Exchange Administration Center (EAC)* is a complete replacement for the MMC-based Exchange Management Console in Exchange 2010. With a few exceptions, all Exchange 2013 management operations can be performed via this new web-based GUI. PowerShell is required for those operations that cannot be performed within the GUI. The Exchange Administration Center presents a single, unified interface for Exchange Online and Exchange on-premises when operating in Hybrid mode.

OUTLOOK WEB APP

The Outlook Web App has been completely rewritten to look and feel like a tablet-optimized application. It supports the Office Web App extensibility model so that it may be extended using web-based applications via the Office Marketplace or an on-premises equivalent. As with Exchange 2010, the Office Web App ships with support for multiple browsers. However, because of the capabilities of HTML5 and offline browser databases, the Office Web App ships with an offline mode, similar in concept to Outlook's cached mode.

DATA LEAK PREVENTION

Exchange 2013 introduced a new set of features based on improved transport rules, including prebuilt Data Leak Prevention (DLP) templates for common scenarios. DLP integrates with both Outlook MailTips and Transport Rules to offer a configurable experience to the end user. A range of actions may be chosen by the administrator, which range from a Non Delivery Report (NDR) of the message down to a MailTip, warning the user about sensitive information contained in the message body.

SHAREPOINT INTEGRATION VIA SITE MAILBOXES

Site mailboxes have been introduced in Exchange 2013. They offer a way to share data between Exchange mailboxes and SharePoint team sites via a shared mailbox. Exchange 2013 and SharePoint 2013 have become aware of each other along this integration point. Documents submitted via Outlook into the site mailbox are uploaded to the correct SharePoint document library. Reciprocally, SharePoint users are able to view the shared email via OWA without requiring Outlook, while users who prefer to use Outlook may consume the relevant SharePoint documents without leaving the application. Outlook 2013 is required to participate in a site mailbox.

LYNC INTEGRATION

Lync 2013 is able to store compliance information into the Exchange mailbox dumpster as opposed to using SQL servers to store data. If a user is placed on hold in Exchange 2013, they are automatically placed on hold in Lync 2013, as long as Exchange and Lync are configured accordingly.

SHAREPOINT INTEGRATION VIA THE EDISCOVERY PORTAL

SharePoint is able to search and locate Exchange and Lync discovery data via a single integrated eDiscovery portal. Discovery capabilities in Exchange have been retained using the EAC. However, the eDiscovery portal introduces significant added functionality, such as real-time searching.

HOSTING

The hosting model based on Address Book Policies introduced in Exchange 2010 SP2 persists in Exchange 2013. Hosting in Exchange 2013 is based on one of a number of certified control panels, which are available along with published guidance at the following link:

```
http://technet.microsoft.com/en-us/exchange/jj720331.aspx
```

Role Separation

Role separation in Exchange 2013 still exists, but the architecture is quite different from Exchange 2010. Exchange 2013 has simplified the number of roles from five down to two in Exchange 2013: Client Access server and Mailbox server roles.

EVERY SERVER IS AN ISLAND

A significant change in Exchange 2013 over Exchange 2007 and Exchange 2010 is the banning of RPC for inter-role communications. This includes the RPC functionality used in what used to be Exchange 2010 CAS and Hub roles when communicating with the Exchange 2010 Mailbox role. In Exchange 2013, WAN-friendly protocols such as SMTP and HTTP are used for inter-server role communication, even if the servers are adjacent to each other within the same Active Directory site. For example, the Transport service in Exchange 2013 no longer uses RPC to write an email to the destination mailbox database on a mailbox server within the same Active Directory site. If an email needs to be submitted to an adjacent server, it will be done via SMTP. RPC is still used, but only within a Mailbox server role and no longer between servers.

CLIENT ACCESS SERVERS

Client Access servers in Exchange 2013 are quite different than the functionality rich, code-laden CAS role in Exchange 2010. The Exchange 2013 Client Access server role (CAS 2013) is a thin, stateless Layer 7 protocol proxy that requires very few server resources and may be deployed together with the Exchange 2013 Mailbox role or by itself. No files or data will ever be written or stored on the CAS 2013 role. Similar to Exchange 2010, CAS 2013 must be deployed on a domain-joined machine and not placed in a DMZ.

By itself, CAS 2013 without a Mailbox role is unable to service requests of any sort, because the Client Access server logic now resides on the Exchange 2013 Mailbox server role. CAS 2013 performs three major functions:

Authentication   CAS 2013 authenticates the connection in order to establish who is the incoming user.

Location   CAS 2013 locates the user's mailbox on the mailbox server on which it is currently active.

Proxy/Redirect   CAS 2013 proxies the connection to the Mailbox server, and it either maintains the connection or redirects it to another Mailbox server.

These three functions are performed for the two components hosted by CAS 2013: client protocols (HTTP, POP, IMAP, or SIP) and SMTP.

A fundamental concept for CAS 2013 and Mailbox 2013 is that the Mailbox server hosting the active database copy for a given mailbox is always the connection endpoint. CAS 2013 determines the correct endpoint for all incoming protocols, and it proxies traffic to the same Mailbox server that is hosting the active copy, irrespective of which CAS 2013 server the session originated, and it will do that for Mailbox servers inside or outside its own Active Directory site. The Exchange 2013 Mailbox server hosts the logic, and it is the endpoint for all protocols, including client and transport traffic. These concepts are illustrated in Figure 3.1, which shows client traffic passing through a Layer 4 load-balancing device before reaching the Exchange 2013 CAS server role.

FIGURE 3.1
Client traffic and
Layer 4 distribution

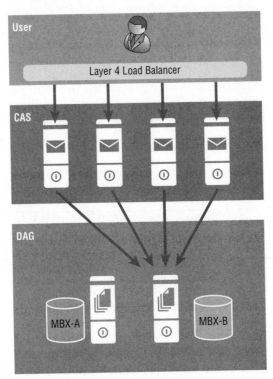

The Mailbox server hosting the active database copy, as opposed to the Client Access server, now maintains affinity and persistence for a user's session. In this model, CAS servers are loosely coupled to Mailbox servers. The same Mailbox server is responsive to the user's requests, irrespective of which CAS server the request originates from. Effectively, this means that as long as traffic can reach the Exchange 2013 CAS server at a Layer 4 level, it will make the networking decisions previously required by a Layer 7 load balancer. The advantage of this model is that a number of Layer 4 load-balancing mechanisms become available, including the following:

◆ Round robin DNS

◆ Windows network load balancing

◆ Hardware load balancers

The available range of load-balancing mechanisms as well as how to make a choice for your organization will be discussed in Chapter 4, "Defining a Highly Available Messaging Solution."

MAPI IN EXCHANGE 2013

Earlier in this chapter, we stated that Exchange 2013 has reduced the potential number of name spaces required by two: the RPC client access name space for the primary and secondary datacenters. This does not mean that client-side MAPI has been discontinued as a protocol. Rather, it means that MAPI over TCP has been discontinued and that RPC over HTTP (Outlook Anywhere) is the only remaining connectivity option. Clients have had the option of using MAPI via either TCP or HTTP since Exchange 2003. Exchange 2013 reduces the available transport mechanisms for MAPI down to TCP.

An Outlook client connecting to Exchange for the first time is supplied with several connection endpoints that appear to be quite similar to an Exchange 2010 Autodiscover request. The connection endpoint, however, is no longer an Exchange server's name. It is now in the form of a GUID and a UPN suffix, for instance, GUID@UPN similar to b0f54714-5af0-4564-a71b-ebe8b780f0ca@exchange-D3.com. Autodiscover will also supply the HTTP connection endpoints required for Outlook.

Once Outlook is configured, it will connect to the Exchange 2013 CAS via HTTP, supplying the GUID@UPN endpoint with which it has been configured. Remember that CAS is loosely coupled to Mailbox. Using the supplied endpoint, CAS will query Active Directory for location information as well as the Active Manager component to determine which Mailbox server is currently hosting the active database copy. Once CAS has the required information, it is able to proxy the request to the correct Mailbox server or redirect it to another CAS server in the same forest.

A significant advantage to using the GUID@UPN endpoint as opposed to an Exchange server name is realized during a switchover or a failover event. If the connection to the Mailbox server is lost due to a switchover or a failover event, and Outlook is reconnected via CAS to the new active database copy, the connection endpoint remains the same, that is, GUID@UPN as opposed to a new RPC connection endpoint. Outlook no longer displays the "The administrator has made a change which requires you to restart Outlook" message since, as far is it is concerned, no change has occurred.

MAPI-BASED APPLICATIONS

Third-party products using MAPI need to use RPC over HTTP to connect to CAS 2013 via the updated MAPI.CDO download. These applications may require reconfiguration in order not to default to RPC over TCP, either by programmatically editing the MAPI profile or by setting a registry key value.

Note that Exchange 2013 is advertised as the last version of Exchange to support MAPI/CDO, and that future applications will need to move to Exchange Web Services. We will discuss how to access Exchange programmatically as well as how to port your old code in Chapter 11, "Extending Exchange."

NAME SPACE REDUCTION

Exchange 2013 reduces the number of name spaces required for a two-datacenter scenario by two name spaces: the primary and secondary client RPC name spaces. This also means that the minimum number of name spaces required for a given Exchange 2013 deployment is two: the Autodiscover name space and the Internet Protocol name space.

For example, in a single datacenter using the `Exchange-D3.com` name space, we need the following:

```
autodisover.exchange-D3.com
mail.exchange-D3.com
```

A graphical representation of the minimum number of name spaces required is shown in Figure 3.2. The details of each potential protocol are found in Table 3.1.

FIGURE 3.2

Single name space

autodiscover.exchange-d3.com
mail.exchange-d3.com

TABLE 3.1: Name spaces and protocols—single name space

NAME	PROTOCOL
`Autodisover.Exchange-D3.com`	Autodiscover
`Mail.Exchange-D3.com`	SMTP
`Mail.Exchange-D3.com`	Outlook Anywhere
`Mail.Exchange-D3.com`	EWS
`Mail.Exchange-D3.com`	EAS
`Mail.Exchange-D3.com`	OWA
`Mail.Exchange-D3.com`	ECP
`Mail.Exchange-D3.com`	POP/IMAP

We previously stated that the Mailbox server hosting the active database copy for a given mailbox is always the connection endpoint. The Exchange 2013 Client Access server will proxy traffic to the active database copy even if it is in another Active Directory site. Understanding this logic allows us to build a single global Internet Protocol name space using a mechanism as simple as DNS round robin or a more advanced mechanism, such as a global load balancer. Assuming that connectivity from any point around the globe is roughly equal, and that connectivity between datacenters is high speed with acceptable latency in order to guarantee a positive user experience, we are able to build a two-datacenter scenario using the same two name spaces. This is illustrated in Figure 3.3 for a similar protocol breakdown as detailed in Table 3.1.

FIGURE 3.3
Single name space
with global load
balancer

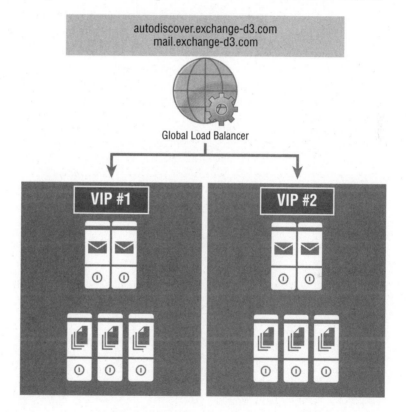

AUTODISCOVER

Autodiscover is a major component of Outlook connectivity because, without it, Outlook would require manual configuration to connect to a mailbox. Outlook will perform an autodiscover under the following circumstances:

◆   New profile configuration

◆   Regular discovery of EWS URLs

◆   When Outlook is disconnected from an endpoint

When planning Exchange name spaces, Autodiscover is the only name that needs to follow a number of potential conventions. You need to consider it if you are planning for external or internal Autodiscover.

External Autodiscover behavior will see Outlook attempt to connect to the following URLs in order, based on the SMTP domain specified in the user's email address:

```
https://<smtpdomain>/Autodiscover/Autodiscover.xml
```

```
https://autodiscover.<smtpdomain>/Autodiscover/Autodiscover.xml
```

```
http://autodiscover.<smtpdomain>/Autodiscover/Autodiscover.xml
```

If any of these fail, Outlook will perform a DNS SRV record lookup or a local registry query.

If Outlook manages to connect to Autodiscover, Autodiscover will supply the rest of the connection information required in order to connect to the user's mailbox. One aspect of using Autodiscover is that only one name space needs to be named in a predictable manner. The naming convention for other name spaces is largely open ended, as long as Autodiscover is able to reveal their location.

Internal Autodiscover behavior will see an authenticated Outlook client query Active Directory for service connection point (SCP) records pointing to Exchange CAS servers, filtering those SCP records for a well-known GUID. Every CAS server publishes an SCP record with Autodiscover information, which results in a list of available SCP records. Once a list of SCP records has been returned, Outlook will choose the *oldest* record and the following attributes:

serviceBindingInformation This attribute contains a URL in the form of `https://caas-server.exchange-D3.com/autodiscover/autodiscover.xml`.

keywords This attribute contains the Active Directory site name in which the CAS server is located.

Using the URL contained in `serviceBindingInformation`, Outlook will connect to Autodiscover and obtain the rest of its profile information to connect to the given mailbox.

UNDERSTANDING AND MANAGING SCP RECORDS

Outlook sorts the list of SCPs by date and binds to the oldest (first created) SCP in the list. If the SCP record points to an Exchange 2007 or Exchange 2010 CAS server, it will then query a downstream version for Exchange 2013 information. SCP records may be updated using a command similar to the following via Exchange Management Shell:

```
Set-ClientAccessServer -AutodiscoverUri https://cas2013.exchange-D3.com/
autodiscover/autodiscover.xml -AutodiscoverSiteScope ActiveDirectorySite
```

The `-AutodiscoverUri` parameter sets the URL used in the `serviceBindingInformation` attribute. It should point to an Exchange 2013 load-balanced name space, as opposed to an individual server name, wherever possible.

Autodiscover returns the information required to configure the profile including EXCH and EXPR nodes, which point to internal and external configuration items, respectively.

Traditionally EXPR points to the protocol used to connect a client to Exchange via RPC over HTTP. Exchange 2013 Autodiscover includes a new node type, EXHTTP, for Outlook 2013 clients. Autodiscover will return two EXHTTP nodes: an internal Outlook Anywhere URL (HTTP URL) and an external Outlook Anywhere URL (HTTPS URL).

Outlook 2013 will attempt to bind to each URL, running from the first to the last one. If it manages to bind via the HTTP URL, then it will establish an HTTP-based Outlook Anywhere session (as opposed to an HTTPS session). While you may be tempted to think that this eliminates certificate planning, you should note that the other services that Outlook requires, such as Exchange Web Services and the Offline Address Book among others, still require certificates.

TRANSPORT ON THE EXCHANGE 2013 CLIENT ACCESS SERVER ROLE

As with the client protocol components, the SMTP component of CAS functions as a Layer 7 proxy. Since the Exchange 2013 Mailbox server role houses the equivalent of the Exchange 2010 Hub Transport role, a new component emerges on the CAS 2013 server role: the *Front End Transport service*. Similar to the client protocol components, all inbound and outbound SMTP protocol traffic passes through CAS 2013 for the Exchange organization and, if desired, all client SMTP traffic. The Front End Transport service is completely stateless. As a Layer 7 protocol proxy with full access to the conversation occurring within the SMTP protocol, it does not store any data on the server role, nor does it perform any sort of message bifurcation. The Front End Transport service can filter messages based on connections, domains, senders, and recipients.

The Front End Transport service listens for SMTP traffic on the following three ports:

TCP 25   Similar to previous versions of Exchange, this port is used for external SMTP into the Front End Transport service, SMTP traffic with Exchange 2007 and Exchange 2010 Hub Transport server roles, and SMTP traffic between Exchange 2013 Mailbox server roles. This port matches up with a Receive connector named Default Frontend ServerName.

TCP 587   Similar to Exchange 2007 and Exchange 2010, this port is used for POP and IMAP clients requiring SMTP services. This port matches up with a Receive connector named Client Frontend ServerName.

TCP 717   This port is used to proxy connections from the transport service on the Mailbox server role to the Front End Transport service. Send connectors that have the FrontEndProxyEnabled property enabled can use the CAS 2013 server role as the outbound connection point, as opposed to the Transport service on the Mailbox server role, so that messages appear to have originated from the CAS server role. This port matches up with a Receive connector named Outbound Proxy Frontend ServerName.

The Front End Transport service receives an inbound message and locates a single destination, which is a healthy transport service on a Mailbox server role. Based on a number of rules in the Transport section of Exchange 2013 that will be discussed later in this chapter, it proxies the connection to the Transport service.

MAILBOX SERVERS

Exchange 2010 guidance recommended deploying CAS, Hub, and Mailbox server roles on the same Exchange server, as a multi-role or "brick" configuration. The term *brick* implies a standardized unit or building block, which may be replicated inexpensively. This model is used quite successfully in large datacenter or cloud-based configurations. Thus, the benefits of a brick or standardized configuration hold true with three or three hundred servers. The Exchange 2013

Mailbox role installed as a multirole server includes the following equivalent Exchange 2010 server roles:

- Client Access server role
- Hub Transport server role
- Mailbox server role
- Unified Messaging server role

No Exchange 2013 components may be deployed separately; that is, the Client Access, Hub, Mailbox, or Unified Messaging server roles cannot be installed on their own. However, additional Exchange 2013 Mailbox server roles can be deployed and used purely as Unified Messaging servers if required, or more servers can be added for the sake of additional capacity if additional roles are required.

Exchange 2013 Mailbox Database Improvements: Managed Store

The Information Store process has been completely rewritten in C# (a .NET-based language) from C and C++, thereby moving it to what is known as managed code as opposed to unmanaged code. As part of the rewrite, the Information Store service has been split into two processes: `Microsoft.Exchange.Store.Service.exe` and `Microsoft.Exchange.Store.Worker.exe`. Instead of having only one Information Store process responsible for all of the mounted databases as in previous versions of Exchange, the Worker process spawns a new Store service for every mounted database. If a store process were to suffer a catastrophic failure of some kind, only one database would be affected at any one time. Another effect of process isolation is that database failover times have been reduced.

Due to the rewrite and further optimization of the Mailbox database structure, a 50 percent drop in IOPS has been achieved over Exchange 2010. We will cover this in depth in Chapter 5, "Designing a Successful Exchange Storage Solution."

Modern Public Folders

Public folder databases have been discontinued in favor of storing public folders in public folder mailboxes. If these mailboxes participate in a database availability group, then public folders are as highly available as any other mailbox. All public folder PowerShell cmdlets are still available, but the public folder database cmdlets have been discontinued.

The first public folder mailbox contains the public folder hierarchy; successive public folder mailboxes contain a read-only copy of the hierarchy and the public folder contents. Administrators have the option of choosing the public folder mailboxes when creating or moving public folders. Public folder mailboxes are subject to the same management requirements as other mailboxes in terms of size and quota management.

A major shift for administrators is that public folders have moved to a single-master model. Previous versions of Exchange employed a multi-master model, where every instance of a public folder was writable and would replicate changes to all other public folder instances. In Exchange 2013, a public folder is writable to one network location only. Specifically, it will only be writeable in the mailbox database containing the public folder mailbox.

TRANSPORT ON THE EXCHANGE 2013 CLIENT ACCESS SERVER ROLE

The Transport service on the Exchange 2013 Mailbox server role is similar to the Exchange 2010 Hub Transport server role, hosting both Send and Receive connectors, as well as the queuing and routing of the logic required to process messages. The Transport service listens for SMTP traffic on the following ports:

TCP 25   This port is used by the Transport service to receive SMTP connections. This port matches up with a Receive connector named Default ServerName.

TCP 465   This port accepts the proxied connections, which were accepted by the Front End Transport service on port TCP 587 for POP and IMAP clients requiring SMTP service. This port matches up with a Receive connector named Client Proxy ServerName.

TCP 476   This port is used by the Mailbox Transport Delivery service to listen for connections from either the Transport service SMTP Send connector or the Transport service on other Mailbox server roles attempting to route mail for users located on this role.

TCP 2525   This port is used by the Transport service to receive connections in the event that the CAS 2013 and Mailbox 2013 server roles are collocated on the same machine. In this case, the Front End Transport service will listen on port TCP 25 and the Transport service will listen on port TCP 2525. This port matches up with a Receive connector named Default ServerName.

Typically, messages that originate from outside the Exchange organization are handled by the Front End Transport service and then proxied by the Front End Transport service to the Transport service on the Mailbox role. The Transport service is one of a number of transport-related services on this role that help process incoming and outgoing messages as follows:

Transport Service

The *Transport service* is included with every Mailbox server role and, for all intents, is a duplicate of the Hub Transport server role in Exchange 2007 and Exchange 2010. All SMTP mail flow for the Exchange organization is processed by the service, which includes message categorization and message content inspection. Reenforcing the concept that every server is an island, the Transport server no longer delivers email directly to mailbox databases via RPC. This task is now completed by the Mailbox Transport service. The Transport service is responsible for overall message routing among the Mailbox Transport service, the Front End Transport service, and itself.

Mailbox Transport Service

The *Mailbox Transport service* is another service that is included with every Mailbox server. This service comprises two different services: the Mailbox Transport Submission service and the Mailbox Transport Delivery service. The *Mailbox Transport Submission service* builds on the concept that every server is an island by using RPC calls to retrieve messages from *local* mailbox databases, and it submits these messages via SMTP to the Transport service. It does this without queuing any messages in a local queue. The *Mailbox Transport Delivery service* receives SMTP messages from the Transport service and again, building on the concept that every Exchange 2013 server is an island, uses RPC to perform a delivery to a *local* mailbox database.

UNIFIED MESSAGING

Unified Messaging is a standard feature of Exchange 2013. This functionality is split between the Exchange 2013 Client Access and Mailbox server roles. The Exchange 2013 Client Access server role includes the Microsoft Exchange Unified Messaging Call Router service, while the Exchange 2013 Mailbox server role includes the Microsoft Exchange Unified Messaging service. Neither of these services can be uninstalled. They may be disabled, however, if desired.

Unified Messaging ships with the following enhancements:

◆ The dependency on the Unified Communications Managed API (UCMA) has changed from version 2.0 in Exchange 2010 to version 4.0 in Exchange 2013.

◆ UCMA 4.0 and Speech Engine 11.0 allow for better grammar and language generation during text-to-speech operations as well as improvements in accuracy during voicemail preview.

◆ IPv6 support has improved and includes IPv6 support for dial plans as well as Lync integration.

◆ Caller ID integrates with the social media connectors in Exchange 2013, allowing caller ID to take advantage of a much larger pool of contacts for caller recognition.

High Availability

Exchange 2013 continues the trend that began with Exchange 2010 of a database-based availability model as opposed to the server-based availability models that were used in previous versions of Exchange. Along with the simplification of Exchange server roles, Exchange 2013 simplifies high availability planning down to two building blocks: the client access array and the database availability group.

CLIENT ACCESS ARRAYS

Client access arrays are different than those in Exchange 2010 in that they do not represent RPC or MAPI endpoints. Exchange 2013 *Client Access server arrays (CAS arrays)* are a grouping of Exchange 2013 Client Access servers, represented by a single DNS-based name. In Exchange 2013, CAS arrays are no longer RPC endpoints. Rather, they are HTTP-based endpoints for all client protocols. CAS arrays are grouped behind a single DNS name and load-balanced using any of the supported Exchange 2013 load-balancing methods.

DATABASE AVAILABILITY GROUPS

Database availability groups (DAGs) are the basis for all storage-based high availability in Exchange 2013. Though similar to DAGs in Exchange 2010, they offer some significant improvements:

◆ The reduction in IOPS allows for multiple databases to be located on the same volume. Assuming the availability of an 8-terabyte disk, a maximum of four 2-terabyte databases may be located on the same volume, with one active and the rest passive.

◆ Automatic reseed restores the redundancy of a database automatically by using a spare disk designated by the administrator for automatic reseeds, should a disk or volume containing a database participating in a DAG fail.

These improvements will be covered further in Chapter 5.

DAG Networks Autoconfiguration

DAG networks in Exchange 2010 required administrators to collapse the networks created by deploying DAG members in multiple subnets with multiple network interfaces. These would be created automatically as DagNetwork01, DagNetwork02, and so on. Exchange 2013 requires the administrator to mark those networks that are used for MAPI and those that are used for replication. It then automatically collapses the DAG networks into their appropriate MAPI and replication networks. This behavior is enabled by default, and it may be configured using the EAC or using the `Set-DatabaseAvailabilityGroup` cmdlet and setting the `ManualDagNetworkConfiguration` parameter to `$TRUE`.

Best Copy Selection and Best Copy and Server Selection

Best copy selection (BCS) is the algorithm used in Exchange 2010 to determine the best available mailbox database copy to activate based on copy queue length, replay queue length, database status, and content index status.

Best copy and server selection (BCSS) is the Exchange 2013 version of BCS, and it is still performed by the Active Manager component. Now, however, it includes four indicators of Exchange 2013 health status supplied by Managed Availability as part of the selection status. If BCSS detects that is was invoked as a result of Managed Availability, then an additional rule is added to BCSS, which mandates that the components that failed in the server that are currently holding the active copy (for example, OWA) must be healthy on the target server.

The four new status indicators are evaluated as part of database selection in the following order:

1. All Healthy—All monitoring components report a healthy state.

2. Up to Normal Healthy—All monitoring components report a healthy state with Normal priority.

3. All Better than Source—Monitoring components report a better healthy state than the server currently hosting the affected copy.

4. Same as Source—Monitoring components report the same state as the server currently hosting the affected copy.

MANAGED AVAILABILITY

Exchange 2013 ships with the capability to monitor health and, based on the health of specific components, take remedial action. Health is monitored using several probes that inspect the health of Exchange at multiple levels. If a component is degraded or deemed unhealthy, then Managed Availability will attempt to recover the component via one or more actions. These actions may include a service restart, a server restart, or even marking the server as unavailable.

If OWA or other components fail on one of the nodes within a DAG, and Managed Availability is unable to restart OWA via recycling the OWA application pool, or it is unable to restart the affected services and return it to a healthy state, then it will select a node within the DAG and failover the databases affected by the OWA failure to the next available node where OWA is healthy.

Managed Availability runs on both the Client Access server and Mailbox server roles. Managed Availability comprises the following components:

Probe Engine   This component is responsible for measuring and collecting data.

Monitor   The monitor contains the business logic required to make the decisions to determine if a component is healthy or if action is required.

Responder   This component is responsible for initiating and managing recovery actions.

Managed Availability manifests itself as two services: Exchange Health Manager Service (MSExchangeHMHost.exe) and Exchange Health Manager Worker process (MSExchangeHMWorker.exe), which are the controller and worker processes, respectively. The controller process builds, executes, starts, and stops the worker process so that, in the case of a worker process crash, no single worker process becomes a distinct point of failure. The worker process, as the name implies, performs the unit of work selected by the controller process.

Managed Availability health checks span the entire Exchange 2013 spectrum of workloads. They include the functionality that shipped as scripts in Exchange 2010, for example, the Exchange 2010 CheckDatabaseRedundancy.ps1 script, which checks that at least two healthy copies of a replicated database exist and generates an event log if they do not. As in Exchange 2010, Managed Availability still performs the same checks, and it alerts administrators using event log notifications. However, in Exchange 2013, it now includes the ability to generate an appropriate action.

TRANSPORT HIGH AVAILABILITY

Exchange 2013 builds on the Exchange 2010 concepts of shadow redundancy and the transport dumpster to ensure that messages are successfully delivered by keeping redundant copies of messages. *Shadow redundancy* is now aware of both Active Directory sites and DAGs as transport high-availability boundaries. The transport dumpster concept has been retained, improved, and renamed to Safety Net.

Safety Net stores messages that have been successfully processed by the server in a Transport service queue on a Mailbox server for a default period of two days. However, when compared with the Exchange 2010 transport dumpster, Safety Net does not require a DAG, and it will also function for individual Mailbox servers in the same Active Directory site.

The key differentiator for Safety Net is *guaranteed* mail delivery compared to *best effort* mail delivery for the transport dumpster. Thus, the only configurable parameter for Safety Net is the retention period of messages. Messages are stored on the destination Mailbox server as well as Mailbox servers that participated in shadow transport. These are known as the *Primary* and *Shadow Safety Nets*.

If required, messages are resubmitted from Safety Net automatically after a mailbox database failover within a DAG or a lagged mailbox database copy is activated. Message resubmission is initiated by the Active Manager component of the Replication service, and it requests message resubmission over a specific time period for a specific mailbox database. If the Primary Safety Net becomes unresponsive, or if it is unavailable within 12 hours, Active Manager will revert to the Shadow Safety Net.

We will discuss the implications of these features and how to apply them in Chapter 4.

STORAGE

Exchange 2010 Enterprise reduced the number of databases to a maximum of 50. Improvements in the ESE database in Exchange 2013 allow the administrator to retain the storage choices from Exchange 2010. Additional details on these improvements will be addressed in Chapter 5.

Exchange Online Integration

Building on the success of Exchange 2010, Exchange 2013 continues integration with Office 365, known as *hybrid deployments,* such that the on-premises organization and the Office 365 tenant appear to be a single Exchange organization. Exchange 2007 and Exchange 2010 organizations may also benefit from an Exchange 2013 hybrid configuration. In order to be deployed, however, it requires at least one Exchange 2013 CAS and Mailbox role running Exchange 2013 Cumulative Update 1 or later. A number of improvements and new configurations exist. These will be covered in Chapter 7, "Hybrid Configuration."

Summary

Exchange 2013 is the newest messaging platform to be released by Microsoft, and it forms the basis for new enterprise as well as ongoing Office 365 deployments.

We started this chapter by noting that the history of Exchange is relevant in order to appreciate the feature set of Exchange 2013. We also made the point of stating that the features that were introduced and later deprecated in previous versions of Exchange have driven certain deployment patterns, which may no longer be relevant.

It is worth restating that, as a consultant, you should know which new and which deprecated features are relevant to your customer. If you're facing an Exchange 2000/2003/2007/2010 upgrade, or even an Exchange 5.5 upgrade, you should be able to articulate the gains and losses of moving to the newer platform.

If you are reading this chapter as background for building an Exchange organization using a structured approach, then we suggest that you review both Chapter 1 and Chapter 2 in this book to consolidate your approach. As the newest version of the Exchange platform, Exchange 2013 is feature and functionality rich. However, we suggest that you take the time to understand the deployment choices that are available and implement according to requirements and not features. Armed with the information provided in this book, you will be able to design and deploy a successful messaging solution.

Chapter 4

Defining a Highly Available Messaging Solution

As you saw in Chapter 1, "Business, Functional, and Technical Requirements," when eliciting requirements, desired availability is often one of the first topics to be raised. It is important to note that one of your functions as a consultant or implementer is to make the businesses aware that raising the availability of any system has a direct cost implication.

With quality cloud-based solutions, messaging systems are no longer shackled to the limits of on-premises capabilities. Keep cloud-based solutions in mind as a possible fit for some of your highly available messaging solution requirements.

If you have deployed Exchange Online in conjunction with on-premise solutions, and you are running in Hybrid mode, then you need to consider how the Exchange Online service-level agreement dovetails with your on-premise service-level agreement. In traditional on-premise systems, the more available a system becomes, the more expensive it is to operate. The price of increasing availability, however, is often offset by the cost of an outage. For a large company or well-known brand, an email outage may become a visible public failure with an associated loss of confidence.

Defining Availability

The definition of availability and how that availability is measured is one of the key factors in the choice of technology you will use to implement in your design. One of the critical factors to establish is how the availability of the system will be measured and what the context for that measurement will be. We will use the following formula to calculate availability levels:

$$\text{percentage availability} = (\text{total elapsed time} - \text{sum of downtime}) / \text{total elapsed time}$$

Using the example of 99.9 percent availability, which is often noted as "three nines" availability, this translates to the system suffering downtime of 8.76 hours on an annual basis. That may not sound like a lot; if the measure is changed to three nines *per day*, this translates to 1.44 minutes of downtime, which may or may not be enough time for a reboot to occur.

If you calculate the permutations from one nine to five nines, you will understand why you don't often hear of systems that are available beyond five nines, as shown in from Table 4.1. This depends, however, entirely on how the availability is measured.

TABLE 4.1: Availability by the nines

		DOWNTIME BY TIME PERIOD			
NINES	AVAILABILITY	YEAR	MONTH	WEEK	DAY
One nine	90%	36.5 days	3 days	16.8 hrs.	2.4 hrs.
Two nines	99%	3.65 days	7.2 hrs.	1.68 hrs.	14.4 mins.
Three nines	99.9%	8.76 hrs.	43.2 mins.	10.08 min	1.44 mins.
Four nines	99.99%	52.56 mins.	4.32 mins.	60.48 secs.	8.64 secs.
Five nines	99.999%	5.256 mins.	25.92 secs.	6.048 secs.	864 ms
Six nines	99.9999%	31.536 secs.	2.592 secs.	604.8 ms	86.4 ms

Defining Availability Components

One of the many things you'll do during requirement elicitation is to help the business define and understand the services that Exchange delivers in terms of Exchange availability. At minimum, Exchange availability is a superset of dependency services. These services may be classified as follows:

◆ Client access

◆ Email transport

◆ Email storage

For the sake of clarity, we will not define auxiliary services such as message hygiene third-party application integration, or the many other examples that come to mind. Assuming you are satisfied to continue with the three basic services listed, your criteria may also include that availability could be measured per service. The availability of a system consisting of several independent critical components is a *product* of the availabilities of each individual component. The product is calculated by multiplying together the availabilities of each individual component in the following manner:

$$A(n) = A_1 \times A_2 \times \ldots \times A_n$$

In the case of three components, our equation becomes

$$A(3) = A_1 \times A_2 \times A_3$$

Let us examine a hypothetical example of three nines availability across three hypothetical components, as shown in Table 4.2. Using Excel, you would list the three availability components and use the PRODUCT function to multiply the three numbers together. Or, you could simply multiply the first number by the second number and then by the third number to obtain the fourth number, or result. Since we have multiplied three numbers together to obtain a fourth number, we need to move our decimal to the left by four places, or divide by 10,000 (four zeroes), to obtain a number that may be expressed as a percentage availability. The result will look similar to Table 4.2.

TABLE 4.2: Component availability

COMPONENT	PERCENT AVAILABILITY
Client access	99.9
Email transport	99.9
Email storage	99.9
Total availability	99.7

Notice that the total availability is lower than the availability of any of the component pieces. In order to build a system with a particular stated resilience, the components' availability requires examination. This may include network, power, chassis, and storage availability to name just a few, because these are all dependent features in larger systems.

Figure 4.1 illustrates the interdependency of component systems. Note that each one of the boxes of components can carry its own availability measurement when calculating total system availability.

FIGURE 4.1
Interdependent
systems
Credit: Boris Lokhvitsky

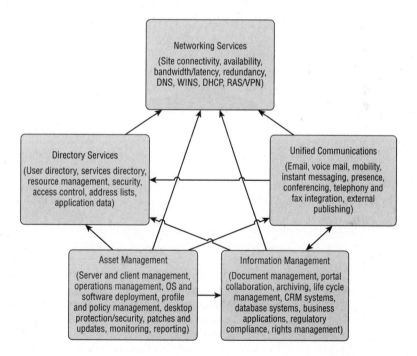

Figure 4.1 clearly illustrates that it is extremely difficult to establish even theoretical total system availability when so many systems are interrelated. When agreeing on the resulting availability of the desired system, clarify the definition of availability, downtime, and scheduled downtime as it pertains to the business.

Scheduled system downtime classically is not included in how availability is measured—in our three nines example, 1.44 minutes per day does not allow for much action to be taken. However, if the measure is adjusted to per year, then 8.76 hours becomes much more plausible for system maintenance.

Defining the Cost of Downtime

Defining the cost of downtime may appear to be an emotional measure, and it may seem somewhat intangible. In this section, we will look at turning some of the intangibles back into definable measures.

Often the actual cost of downtime may be difficult to measure without an understanding of the business in question and how the services provided by Exchange fit into the processes deemed mission critical. We will examine a number of examples of businesses in different vertical markets:

◆ A financial brokerage may email customers throughout the day about stock evaluations. Customers may then interact with brokers, giving instructions to buy or sell.

◆ A law firm may use email to receive instructions from its clients, send and receive documents for approval, and store and file email. While legal representatives are in court, they may call on their colleagues to forward urgent documentation or correspondence via email to their phones, tablets, or laptops.

◆ Retailers nowadays conduct much of their business online. Customers order products online and are notified via email about the progress of their shipments. If the products ordered are perishable, deliveries may be time-critical.

Each of these businesses has a critical path enabled by email and an average cost or value associated with it. For example, if an average day's worth of transactions is $500,000, and this amount represents 1,000 transactions, the average transaction value is easily calculated as $500. The financial transaction may have multiple email interactions associated with it, so there is little point in trying to calculate the average cost of an email. If the bulk of the transactions are occurring over a 10-hour period, and assuming that customers' transactions occur evenly throughout the day, then each hour's transactions may be worth $50,000.

Continuing with our example, assuming a two-hour outage during which email-based transactions cannot occur, the business may face a loss of at least $100,000. Very often, however, this represents only the tip of the iceberg in terms of financial losses, because the damage to the business's reputation may multiply this number in terms of transactions that will not occur in the future. That is, customers may elect to move their business to another company that they deem is more reliable. This is particularly prevalent in the retail, online, and premium brand segments.

If email is part of the critical transaction path, then the hourly cost of the workers who are attempting to facilitate the transaction, as well as in-house or third-party personnel who are endeavoring to rectify the failure, are added to the cost of the downtime. With this in mind, we are able to measure in part some of the more tangible losses accrued to downtime. We say "in part" because reputational and confidence losses may cascade for months or even years to come.

In the following equation, we include the percentage impact, since rarely is the outage 100 percent, with the exception of an actual disaster, of course.

lost revenue = (gross revenue/business hours) × percentage impact × hours of outage

cost of the outage = personnel costs + lost revenue + new equipment

From these equations, we are able to compute a value. It is worth restating, however, that this value may represent only a portion of the total attributable loss due to confidence and reputational loss.

A bank may argue that email is a non-mission-critical system, since the equipment and software required to process transactions during the day are represented via mainframes and traditional banking systems. Nonetheless, confidence loss comes into play here as well. Since email is ubiquitous, no bank is immune from the confidence loss, which may occur if its customers or partners are unable to email for two or three days at a time. This time frame is quite realistic when faced with even a small outage without redundancy in place.

Planning for Failure

Failure of systems or components is inevitable. However, you will be better able to plan for failure as you come to understand that failure is not a random event by which to be taken by surprise. Rather, it should be a carefully planned scenario. We will use drives as our topic for discussion of failure, because there will be more drives in your deployment than there are servers, racks, or cooling units. Nevertheless, the logic presented here applies equally to all of these components.

Hardware components have a published *annual failure rate (AFR)*, which is simply the rate at which the component is expected to fail. One hundred SATA drives assembled in a system will suffer an approximate failure rate of 5 percent. Does that mean that for every 100 drives, we need to keep 5 spares available on a shelf? Not quite. It does, however, lead us down the road of planning for failure, as we consider factors such as database distribution within a database availability group (DAG) or how many servers to deploy in order to satisfy a services dependency.

Earlier, we defined total availability as the product of component availability. However, you will recall that the three components with an availability of 99.9 percent had a total availability of only 99.7 percent. A similar mathematical model is available when we add multiple components to a given system.

The logic used for calculating the probability of failure when using identical components is to take the probability of failure of the component and calculate to the *power*, as opposed to the product. The probability of failure of a system consisting of several identical redundant components is a product of the probabilities of failure of each component. Because all probabilities are identical, the product becomes a power:

$$P(n) = P \times P \times \ldots \times P = P^n$$

The difference between the availability and probability of failure is that in the first case, each component must be available in order for the entire system to be available, whereas in the second case, each component must fail in order for the entire system to fail. We will use probability of failure of identical SATA drives to demonstrate this principle.

Remembering that SATA drives have an expected failure rate of 5 percent, the first drive has a probability of failure of 5 percent, $P_1 = P = 5\%$. In other words, the probability of one drive failing (P1) is the same as the overall probability of failure ($P_1 = P$), which we know is 5 percent, thus $P_1 = P = 5\%$.

Things become more interesting as soon as we add a second identical component into the same system. For two identical drives, we will use the notation of P_2, three identical drives P_3, and so on. Assuming up to four components in a system, you will note that the probability of failure drops considerably.

$$P_1 = P = 5\%$$

$$P_2 = P^2 = 0.25\%$$

$$P_3 = P^3 = 0.0125\%$$

$$P_4 = P^4 = 0.000625\%$$

As the probability of failure becomes smaller, the availability value of the system increases. Availability (A) is calculated as An = 1 – Pn. Using our one-drive example, this becomes $A_1 = 1 - 5\% = 95\%$. As we add multiple drives or identical components to a system, system availability increases radically:

$$A_1 = 1 - 5\% = 95\%.$$

$$A_2 = 1 - 0.25\% = 99.75\%$$

$$A_3 = 1 - 0.0125\% = 99.9875\%$$

$$A_4 = 1 - 0.000625\% = 99.9994\%$$

While we have used this logic to demonstrate failure rates with drives, we can also apply the identical logic to calculate the probability and possible availability of individual systems or system components such as switches, servers, datacenters, and so forth.

When thinking about Exchange 2013, however, the logic is even simpler. Two CAS servers per location are better than one, and four database copies on SATA drives have a probability of failure of 0.000625 percent and, reciprocally, an availability of 99.9994 percent.

Taking it as a given that failures are an event for which you must plan, you can look for and mitigate failure domains. *Failure domains* are service interdependencies or shared components of a system that are able to reduce the overall availability of the system, or they may introduce a significant impact to the overall system should a failure occur.

An obvious example of a failure domain in a datacenter is a single power source. Should that power source fail, then the entire datacenter fails. Similarly, we can think of power to a rack, shared-blade chassis, non-redundant switches, and cooling systems as other obvious examples. A not-so-obvious example might be a *storage area network (SAN)*. SANs tend to be designed with redundancy in mind. However, as we observed when we calculated the probability of failure of a single component, it makes sense to use multiple database copies. The benefit of those multiple database copies is nonetheless negated if they are stored on the same SAN, because the probability of failure is now identical to that of the SAN itself, as opposed to a fraction of what it could be, even when choosing multiple, identical, cheap drives.

Virtualization introduces similar failure domains. If you elect to virtualize, then know that each host represents a failure domain. It makes sense to distribute your Exchange components over different hosts, as opposed to centralizing them onto a single host.

When planning for failure, isolation and separation are great concepts to use in your datacenters. Isolation of components—for example, using multiple cheap drives as opposed to shared storage—increases availability considerably. Separation significantly reduces the number of shared failure domains. When Exchange servers are distributed across multiple racks, servers, or even virtualization hosts, the probability of overall failure increases dramatically as the number of service interdependencies, or possible failure domains, decrease dramatically.

Well-publicized failures of public cloud-based services have taught us that as systems scale, complexity and interdependencies increase and failure becomes inevitable. Operational efficiency is a significant factor in maintaining availability. How you respond to a failure can significantly increase or decrease outage times.

Defining Terms for Availability

Service-level agreement, recovery point objective, recovery time objective, high availability, and *disaster recovery* are common terms used when discussing availability. In this section, we will discuss each of these terms with regard to a messaging system, which is part of a larger IT ecosystem.

Service-Level Agreements

A *service-level agreement (SLA)* is an agreement between a business and an IT vendor, which defines the services that the IT vendor will deliver to the business, as well as the uptime, or availability, of each service. The SLA must include how availability will be measured. This could be a complex exercise, depending on the constituent pieces of each service. As an example, for which of the following is the Exchange storage tier considered available?

◆ The information service is started and/or the database is mounted.

◆ Monitoring software can retrieve an item from a nominated mailbox.

◆ Only 10 percent of the end users are suffering from a degraded Outlook experience when opening a mail item.

How SLAs are measured and reported is an important matter when documenting requirements. It is one of the items that you must clarify, turning assumptions into documented facts, using the skills you learned in Chapter 1.

RPO and RTO

Recovery point objective (RPO) and recovery time objective (RTO) factor strongly in SLA definitions. Figure 4.2 represents an example of a very simple system or non-highly-available server. It is worth starting with a simple example in order to baseline your understanding of these concepts. Just be aware that the example shown in Figure 4.2 is not representative of all the possible highly available configurations that are achievable using Exchange 2013.

Recovery Point Objective   The *recovery point objective (RPO)* is the allowable period for which data can be lost due to an incident. For example, a backup is normally completed at 4 a.m. and the next backup is scheduled for 24 hours later. The RPO is considered to be 24 hours. If a 24-hour RPO is unacceptable, then another backup method is required that is able to deliver a lower RPO.

Recovery Time Objective The *recovery time objective (RTO)* is the allowable period in which the service is restored without data ($T_2 - T_1$) or the service is restored with data ($T_3 - T_1$).

FIGURE 4.2
Interdependent
systems
Credit: Boris Lokhvitsky

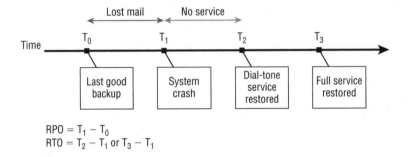

$$RPO = T_1 - T_0$$
$$RTO = T_2 - T_1 \text{ or } T_3 - T_1$$

Defining High Availability and Disaster Recovery

High availability (HA) and disaster recovery (DR) are sometimes incorrectly used interchangeably when, in fact, they are quite different from each other. The one thing that they do have in common is that because of some level of duplication of hardware, software, networks, storage, or other components, the overall cost of the system goes up, commensurate with the level of redundancy required.

HIGH AVAILABILITY

A *high availability (HA)* system is defined as a system that includes redundant components that increase the availability or fault tolerance of the overall system in a near-transparent manner and confined within a defined geography. It is also important to note that HA is a technology-driven function; that is, the technology used in making the system highly available is often the same one that initiates a failover to another available system or component of that system. In other words, IT is responsible as the initiator of the failover as well as being the decision maker to fail a system over.

DISASTER RECOVERY

Disaster recovery (DR) is defined as the restoration of an IT-based service. It includes the use of a separate site or geography, and it addresses the failure of an entire system or datacenter containing that system. It includes the use of people and processes to make DR possible. Lastly, DR is hardly ever seamless or swift.

FAILOVER VS. SWITCHOVER

Failover is a term that denotes the automatic nature of highly available systems moving from one state to another, or switching over components, in order to remain available.

Switchover, in contrast, is the equivalent of having to pull a big, old-fashioned high-current switch, which initiates the set of processes that move the service(s) from one datacenter location to another.

Consider this example: Datacenter A houses multiple copies of data within a highly resilient cluster representing the implementation of an email service. Datacenter B has a single server with a near-identical specification as one of the servers in Datacenter A, except that it has a tape drive attached. If Datacenter A is lost, a restore of the last-known good backup will occur in Datacenter B—however long it takes. From that point forward, the single server in Datacenter B represents the restoration of the service that used to live in Datacenter A. There may be a significant gap in the data restored in Datacenter B, depending on when the outage occurred, as well as the point in time of the last known good backup. If no good backup can be found, then Datacenter B will offer a "dial tone" service for email, which means that customers may send and receive email. However, no historical mail, contacts, or calendar information will be present in their mailboxes. There is a sharp contrast between what was implemented in Datacenter A versus what was implemented in Datacenter B.

This kind of dramatic contrast between locations can be expected as companies figure out how to balance the cost of a DR facility with the stated RPO and RTO. The lower the RPO and RTO, the higher the cost of the overall solution.

Achieving High Availability

As stated at the beginning of the chapter, raising the availability of any system has a direct cost implication. Exchange is in a league of its own in terms of interdependency with other systems, as illustrated in Figure 4.1. Following are a number of factors to consider that will dramatically influence both cost and complexity when planning for high availability:

Process Existing processes for a decentralized, non-highly available system will not suffice when considering a move to a highly centralized or a higher level of availability. Increased hardware cost is only one of the factors to consider with high availability. Another is the cost of a larger number of processes, often interdependent with each other.

User Locations Users may be centralized in one well-connected campus or located in many different geographies across the globe, all with varying connectivity and power, which may or may not be guaranteed.

Servers Server construction may or may not have its own availability factors to consider. Memory bank redundancy, power supply redundancy, processor redundancy, and backplane failure in the case of blade servers are some of the factors that influence total server availability.

Network End users may have varying amounts of bandwidth available to access email as well as different network topologies, which themselves may present points of failure. Do the datacenters hosting the Exchange servers have multiple connection points to the Internet as well as redundant routes to the rest of the network? Are the routing and the switch fabric redundant? Are firewalls and reverse proxy/hygiene solutions redundant?

Power to the Datacenter Power availability is often taken for granted. Events have shown, however, that power may be compromised during extreme weather or may not be guaranteed in some parts of the world at all.

Power to the Racks Is the power to the racks themselves wired so that loss of any one power source or power distribution point within a rack does not affect the entire contents of the rack?

Cooling Cooling is another critical measure of datacenter availability. Do the datacenters housing your servers have redundant cooling available in the event of an outage?

Cloud Solutions You may rely on an external cloud solution for some of the availability of your infrastructure. Does your vendor have a published availability strategy, and does that strategy map to your desired availability goals in a compatible manner?

Virtualization While virtualization carries with it the promise of on-demand capacity and higher levels of availability, Exchange may not fit into your current virtualization strategy. You may be increasing risk and lowering availability by virtualizing Exchange, as opposed to deploying on physical hardware.

Capacity All of the points mentioned thus far have a measure of available capacity that may be overwhelmed or compromised during an outage or a denial-of-service attack.

Single Points of Failure When increasing availability, redundancy of components is a given. However, one not so obvious factor is a single point of failure or, as you learned earlier, a failure domain. A failure domain could include an individual server, power supply, the network, the rack itself, or any datacenter component, including the datacenter itself.

This is not meant as an exhaustive list of all possible factors. Your own analysis of your environment may yield a number of other factors that may be relevant.

Once you identify the factors influencing availability, you can evaluate each in an attempt to mitigate them. For example, let's say your analysis has shown that cooling and the centralization of all IT into a single datacenter represent a single point of failure. The business will remedy the lack of cooling redundancy, but it will not build or rent another datacenter. You may want to capture this and other potential factors as demonstrated in Table 4.3.

TABLE 4.3: Availability factors and mitigation

FACTOR	DETAIL	MITIGATION
Datacenter	Only one datacenter exists currently, which makes it impossible to achieve the stated disaster recovery goals.	The customer has been advised of the risk and has chosen to not invest in another datacenter. The stated disaster recovery goals have been adjusted accordingly to reflect a longer time to recover.
Cooling	Two cooling units service the datacenter with insufficient individual capacity to assume the full cooling requirement in the event of failure.	The customer has elected to upgrade the cooling units.
Virtualization	The customer has deployed a virtualization solution on shared storage SAN, which automatically moves guests to the least-busy node. Customer wishes to deploy a DAG.	After reviewing the Exchange support statement and possible storage models, the customer has decided to deploy on physical hardware.
Network/mail flow	The customer has deployed a point solution for branding and hygiene in the DMZ. No redundancy exists.	The customer has elected to replace a point solution with a cloud-based equivalent. This equivalent presents an SLA with 99.99 percent availability.

When calculating availability (remember that total availability is a product of all the availability factors), the biggest factor influencing total availability is the component(s) in the entire chain that is most likely to fail. As you saw in Table 4.2, when calculating total availability, a single machine is not very redundant, and it is able to drop the total availability of a single factor, such as networking or mail flow, quite significantly.

Building an Available Messaging System

In order to tie the concepts in this chapter together, let us consider the concepts introduced here as well as the high-availability features built into Exchange that were presented in Chapter 3, "Exchange Architectural Concepts."

When setting a high-availability goal, consider your recovery priorities; that is, do you want to recover quickly? Do you want to recover to the exact point of failure? Or do you want to do both? Also consider which services are critical and require a level(s) of redundancy or higher availability. Finally, you also need to decide which of the features introduced in Chapter 3 make sense in terms of your high-availability requirement versus those that are just nice to have.

The following sections examine major Exchange concepts or features in the light of high availability.

Transport

Transport is the superset of features and functions of the Hub Transport role, including the sending and receiving of messages via SMTP as well as the redundancy features included in Exchange 2013, such as shadow redundancy and shadow transport.

In Chapter 3, you learned that Safety Net is an improved version of the transport dumpster in Exchange 2010. Shadow redundancy was similarly introduced in Chapter 3. Due to the automation capabilities in Safety Net and shadow redundancy, very little else needs to be considered—except for the location of the transport queue. If you are planning for an outage of any sort that may cause email to queue or to be deferred, as in the case of Safety Net, make sure that you allocate enough storage on the volume containing the storage queues. Safety Net and shadow redundancy both transport lower RPO. Transport itself, however, may cause an outage if the queue location has not been taken into account.

During an outage, email queues may grow considerably. If Exchange is installed on the system volume, or the queues are not located on a dedicated volume, then an outage may be exacerbated considerably by a disk-full condition on an Exchange server.

Your availability concerns for transport will include:

◆ Transport queue location

◆ Transport queue volume sizing

Namespace Planning

Namespace planning is often a misunderstood topic. The impactions for high availability, however, are substantial. The cheaper side of misunderstanding this topic is an incorrect set of names on a *Subject Alternate Name (SAN)* certificate. The more expensive side is a total lack of system availability after a failover event has occurred.

As presented in Chapter 3, the minimum number of name spaces we need for Exchange 2013 has fallen to two. For example, using our Exchange-D3.com name space in a single datacenter scenario, we need the following:

◆ autodisover.exchange-D3.com

◆ mail.exchange-D3.com

A graphical representation of the minimum number of name spaces required including a single internet protocol name space is shown in Figure 4.3. The details of each protocol may be found in Table 4.4.

FIGURE 4.3
Single name space

autodiscover.exchange-d3.com
mail.exchange-d3.com

TABLE 4.4:   Name spaces and protocols—single name space

NAME	PROTOCOL
Autodisover.Exchange-D3.com	Autodiscover
Mail.Exchange-D3.com	SMTP
Mail.Exchange-D3.com	Outlook Anywhere
Mail.Exchange-D3.com	EWS
Mail.Exchange-D3.com	EAS
Mail.Exchange-D3.com	OWA
Mail.Exchange-D3.com	ECP
Mail.Exchange-D3.com	POP/IMAP

Similarly, if we use a global load balancer or even Round Robin DNS, we are able to utilize a single name space. Table 4.4 is still valid in this scenario, because two virtual IPs representing each datacenter are stored in the global load balancer and presented to the external client simultaneously. The client will then attempt to access each datacenter's IP address as shown in Figure 4-4.

FIGURE 4.4

Single name space with global load balancer

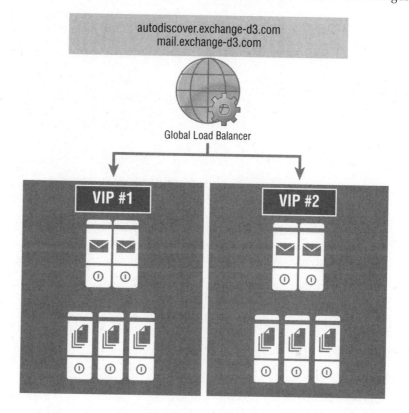

We could quite easily extrapolate this example out to three, four, or more datacenters within a single name space. However, this assumes that connectivity from any point around the globe is roughly equal and that connectivity between datacenters is high speed in order to guarantee a good user experience.

For both of these examples, our SAN certificate entries remain simple:

♦ `autodisover.Exchange-D3.com`

♦ `mail.Exchange-D3.com`

Assuming, however, that you would like to present a different name space for Exchange housed in different datacenters, as shown Figure 4.5, the entries on your SAN certificate would read as follows:

♦ `autodisover.Exchange-D3.com`

♦ `uk.Exchange-D3.com`

♦ `us.Exchange-D3.com`

FIGURE 4.5
Single name
space across two
datacenters

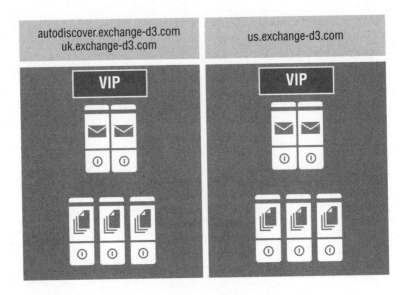

Remember from Chapter 3 that endpoint URL names are not important, since the autodiscover service is responsible for servicing endpoints to any requesting client. This implies that the URL endpoints may be named anything at all, as long as there is a valid path for the client to bind to the autodiscover endpoint.

You may choose to forego SAN certificates altogether and choose to implement a wildcard certificate; however, you are still required to plan your name spaces and define these in DNS.

Availability concerns for name space planning include:

◆   Internal and external DNS

◆   Networking (reverse proxy, firewall)

◆   Load balancer

◆   Exchange Client Access Servers (CAS)

Exchange Hybrid Deployment

Exchange Online presents its own set of SLAs, and it is of interest to us in terms of its interactions with on-premises Exchange. Assuming that your organization is running in Hybrid mode, there will be three on-premises points of interaction with Exchange Online. Specifically, these interaction points are as follows:

◆   Exchange CAS servers

◆   Directory synchronization

◆   Active Directory Federation Services 2.x

Each of these is not highly available by default because each is deployed on a single server. The only possible exception for keeping a single server may be directory synchronization, since it is built as a no-touch software appliance by default, unless deployed using the full-featured Forefront Identity Manager using a highly available SQL instance.

Exchange Client Access Servers providing Exchange Hybrid mode integration may be a subset of the total number of Client Access Servers contained in your organization. If more than one of these exists, they will be load-balanced via some sort of load-balancing mechanism. Client Access Servers facilitating Exchange Hybrid mode are responsible for the interaction between Exchange Online and on-premises Exchange and directly facilitate the features required, which makes the on-premises system and Office 365 appear as a single organization. With this in mind, you will do well to ensure that sufficient redundancy exists to guarantee availability during a server outage, as well as during periods of high server load.

Active Directory Federation Services (AFDS) enable external authentication to an on-premises Active Directory by validating credentials against Active Directory and returning a token that is consumed by Office 365, thereby facilitating one set of Active Directory credentials to be used against both on-premises services as well as Office 365. ADFS servers may have a DMZ-based component (ADFS Proxy servers) alongside the LAN-based ADFS server. *ADFS Proxy servers* are a version of ADFS that is specifically designed to be deployed in the *DMZ*, a secure network location, disconnected from a production network via additional layers of firewalls. Since all that these Proxy servers do is to intercept credentials securely and pass them onto LAN-based ADFS instances, they may not be required if an equivalent service is available via Microsoft TMG/UAG or similar.

These types of servers are great virtualization targets because of their light load. Depending on load, you will require a minimum of two ADFS servers and two ADFS Proxy servers.

Your availability concerns for Exchange Online/Hybrid mode include the following:

◆ Internet connectivity.

◆ Sufficient ADFS servers.

◆ Sufficient ADFS Proxy servers (if required).

◆ Networking (Reverse Proxy, firewall).

◆ Load balancer.

◆ Validity of certificates: A server certificate issued by a third-party certificate provider, which should not be expired. The certificate may be a SAN certificate or a wildcard certificate.

Database Availability Group Planning

Database availability group (DAG) planning requires you to balance a number of factors. Most of these are interdependent and require significant thought and planning.

DATABASE SIZING

The theoretical maximum database size should not be based purely on the maximum database size supported by Exchange 2013. Large databases require longer backup/restore and reseed times, especially when over the 1 TB mark. Databases size of 1 TB and upward are impractical to back up, and they should only be considered if enough database copies exist in order not to require a traditional backup, specifically three or more copies. You need to strike a balance between fewer nodes and larger databases versus more nodes and smaller databases.

Database Copies

The number of database copies required in order to meet availability targets is a relatively simple determination. Early on, we discussed the number of disks or databases required in order to calculate a specific availability. If we have been given a stated availability target of 99.99 percent, then we will not be able to achieve such a target with a single database copy. Four copies within a datacenter is the minimum number required for a 99.99 percent availability target. Taking into account the number of databases is just one of the factors in our availability calculation.

In multi-datacenter scenarios, datacenter activation is a manual step, as opposed to the automatic failover provided by high availability. Therefore, switchover requires more time and incurs more downtime that an automatic failover. While Exchange 2013 is able to automate a switchover event, we would argue that the business via the administrator initiating the event should wield that level of control, so that the state of Exchange is always known and understood.

When the second datacenter uses RAID to protect volumes on a single server, as opposed to individual servers with isolated storage, this slightly increases the availability of each individual volume and therefore slightly increases overall availability. In the case of three or more database copies, however, the additional gain will hardly justify the additional costs of doubling the disk spindles (depending on the RAID model) and the additional RAID controllers. Applying the principle of failure domains, it may be cheaper to deploy extra servers with isolated storage, as opposed to deploying the extra disks and RAID controller per RAID volume required to achieve higher availability.

Database Availability Group Nodes

The number of DAG nodes is driven not only by the number of copies required but also by how many nodes are required in a database availability group in order to maintain quorum. *Quorum* is the number of votes required to establish if the cluster has enough votes to stay up or to make a voting decision, such as mounting databases. Quorum is calculated as the number of nodes/2 + 1. A three-node cluster can therefore suffer a single failure and still maintain quorum. Odd-numbered node sets easily maintain this mathematical relationship; however, even-numbered node sets require the addition of a file share witness.

File Share Witness Location

The *file share witness* is an empty file share on a nominated server that acts as an extra vote to establish cluster quorum. Whichever datacenter in which the file share witness is located may be considered the primary datacenter. In Exchange 2013, the file share witness may be located in a third datacenter from the primary and secondary location, thereby eliminating the risk of *split brain*, which is a condition that occurs when two datacenters become active for the same database copy. Changes are now written to different instances of the same database, which requires considerable effort to undo should the WAN link between the primary and secondary datacentre break. This change, while not recommended, is now supported in Exchange 2013, and it is the first version of Exchange to support the separation of the file share witness into a third datacenter.

Database Distribution

The distribution of databases on database availability group nodes has a direct impact on performance and availability. In order to demonstrate this concept, consider a four-node DAG with four database copies and with all databases active on Server 1, as shown in Figure 4.6.

FIGURE 4.6
Uneven database distribution

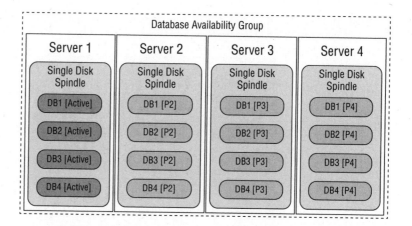

Server 1 will serve all of the required client interactions, while Servers 2, 3, and 4 remain idle, with the exception of logging replay activity. Assuming Server 1 fails, all active copies fail with the server and, depending on the health of the remaining copies, may all activate on Server 2. This is a highly inefficient distribution structure.

Figure 4.7 shows how databases are distributed in a manner such that client and server load is balanced and failure domains are minimized (assuming the storage is not shared). Note that this symmetry is precalculated on a current version of the Exchange calculator.

FIGURE 4.7
Balanced database distribution

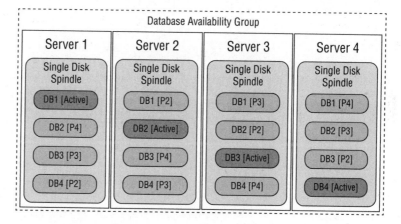

DETERMINING QUORUM AND DAC

In Chapter 3, we discussed how quorum is established and how Database Activation Coordination (DAC) mode affects DAG uptime. Remember that if you have DAC mode enabled on your DAG and a WAN failure occurs, both datacenters will dismount databases in order to prevent split brain. By design, DAC mode may be the cause of an outage if it is not implemented correctly. If properly implemented, however, it will act as an extra layer of quorum against split brain.

If WAN links are unreliable, and your DAG appears similar to Figure 4.8, consider planning your DAGs without DAC mode, as per Figure 4.9.

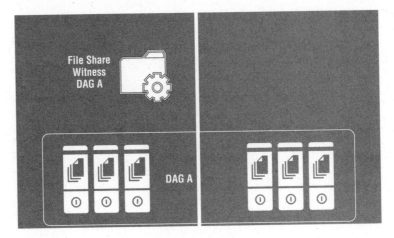

DAGs may be split into two or more DAGs with either datacenter maintaining quorum if a WAN failure occurs, similar to what appears in Figure 4.9.

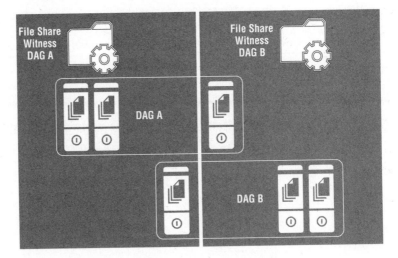

INTERSITE REPLICATION BANDWIDTH

The bandwidth required for intersite replication may be considerable. Let's consider an example of a four-node DAG, with the first node containing all database copies, as shown in Figure 4.10.

As the first database copy is added, we have a replication unit of traffic, as shown in Figure 4.11.

As copies 3 and 4 are added, we have a multiple of this traffic, that is, replication traffic × 3, as shown in Figure 4.12.

FIGURE 4.10
DB1 before seeding

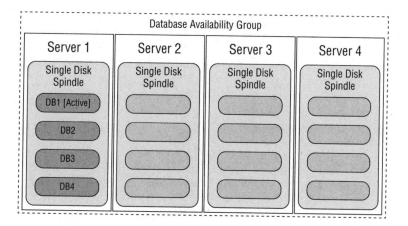

FIGURE 4.11
DB1 with one copy

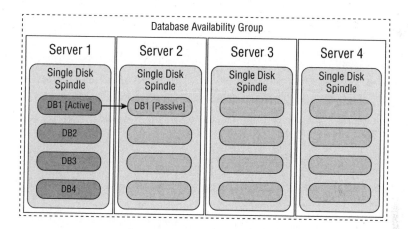

FIGURE 4.12
DB1 with three
copies

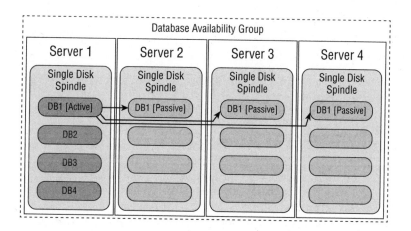

Exchange 2013 database replication is quite similar to that of Exchange 2010 in that it uses a single source as its replication master. Note that we are able to seed from any active or passive node in the DAG. This means that Server 3 can seed from Server 2. Likewise, Server 4 can seed from Server 3, all while Server 1 contains the active copy. If Server 3 and Server 4 are in different datacenters, then the replication traffic for all databases may outweigh the cost of placing two additional servers in the DR site.

RESEED PLANNING

Database sizing is critical, because reseed times are directly related to database sizes, especially if reseeds occur via WAN connections.

Assuming that you have established the AFR for your disks at 5 percent, you now have a potential number of reseed events that require planning. In Chapter 6, we will also discuss the automatic reseed capability of Exchange 2013. This capability is based on the forethought and planning required to ensure that the additional disks or LUNs have been allocated to each server so that Exchange may execute the automatic reseed.

Reseed times vary greatly across different networks. Therefore, it is vital to benchmark the time required to reseed a database under different conditions, because the reseed time factors directly into RPO and RTO times. Note that disks that are allocated as spares for automatic reseed targets suffer the same rate of failure as live production disks.

Your availability concerns for database availability group planning include the following:

◆ Correct database sizing, which may be an iterative process

◆ Calculating the appropriate number of database copies

◆ Calculating the appropriate number of database availability group nodes

◆ Placing the file share witness

◆ Distributing the databases to achieve optimum availability and load distribution as well as maintain quorum in case of an outage

◆ Deciding whether to use DAC mode

◆ Having sufficient bandwidth to support the number of copies required

◆ Planning for spare disks or LUNs to archive automatic reseeds

◆ Understanding reseed times and managing reseed expectations

◆ Understanding log replication requirements, so that RPO is not affected by a log replication build up

Summary

There is no single way to achieve high availability. However, after working through the first few chapters in this book and armed with a set of requirements, you'll be able to build an availability model based on a solid set of requirements and the methodology needed to defend your design choices.

Chapter 5

Designing a Successful Exchange Storage Solution

Over the last 16 years, the adoption of Microsoft Exchange Server, which began in earnest with Exchange 5.5, has expanded dramatically. In the beginning, email was not a critical service for all organizations, and web access and email were sometimes reserved for those at higher levels in the organization who were trusted not to misuse it. Over time, email has become a pervasive application, and it is now a primary communication medium for most organizations.

Exchange storage has undergone a similar evolution. Back in 1996, the focus was primarily on making the best use of costly hard disk capacity. In recent years, however, the focus has shifted toward being able to make use of larger and, most significantly, cheaper disks.

Before diving into the process of Exchange Server storage design, we will spend some time discussing the history of the product and why storage has been the subject of such intense focus from both the Exchange product group and the IT community. We will then examine how to approach Exchange storage design in Exchange Server 2013, including the data you will need, the tools that are available, and how to validate the solution that you propose.

A Brief History of Exchange Storage

As mentioned, Exchange has been around for quite a while, and it has been adapted to the changing landscape of email. Quite often, especially if they have skipped a few versions of Exchange, people are shocked at how the storage recommendations for the latest version have evolved. We find the best way to remedy this situation is a brief walkthrough of the history of Exchange and how it has evolved to meet changing demands. This helps us identify trends in email usage and understand why Exchange has progressed as it has.

Exchange 4.0–5.5

These versions represented the very early days of Exchange Server outside of Microsoft. Usage increased rapidly with the release of Exchange Server 5.5, and many IT shops struggled to deal with Exchange storage for the very first time. The most common approach to Exchange storage design during this time frame was to fill the server chassis with hard disk drives and then to create a RAID 5 array for the large Exchange databases and a RAID 1 mirror to hold the log files. If a performance bottleneck occurred, more Exchange 5.5 servers were deployed and the workload was shared among the servers until the end-user experience became acceptable.

The Exchange database schema in this time frame was optimized to make extremely efficient use of free space on hard disk drives because of their small capacity and very high cost. The primary goal for Exchange versions 2000 and beyond was to improve the performance of Exchange in order to take better advantage of hardware and to better utilize the new clustering technology to provide higher availability with fewer servers.

Exchange 2000–2003

Exchange 2000 allowed more and larger databases on each server, but it retained the goal of making the best use of available hard disk space. The enhancements brought with them new challenges for Exchange storage design, such as having to provide a backup solution for the additional data that Exchange could now store and meeting the increased storage *Input/Output Operations Per Second (IOPS)* performance requirements that were the result of being able to store more mailboxes in each database on each Exchange server or cluster.

Microsoft also began to encourage clustered high availability with Exchange 2000 and Windows 2000. This brought with it the additional requirement for shared storage that often resulted in a complex storage area network (SAN).

Exchange 2000 caused design teams and storage vendors to deal with storage complexity for the very first time, and many service delivery managers were forced to address the inevitable consequences of operating a complex infrastructure—even one that was allegedly highly available and that could never fail. When things did go wrong, they typically did so with exquisite complexity.

Shared storage clustering required a precise recipe of a particular Windows version, host bus adapter (HBA) device drivers, HBA firmware, SAN fabric switch firmware, and SAN storage firmware to remain even vaguely reliable in the early days. Embarrassingly, it was not unheard of that customers would attempt to implement such solutions in order to increase their Exchange service availability, only to discover that they had actually made things worse than with their previous Exchange Server 5.5 installations, and they did so at great cost.

Exchange 2007

Exchange 2007 provided a solution that materially improved service availability and performance at a much lower cost. It was also capable of meeting the growing need for much larger mailbox sizes.

Exchange 2007 brought about a radical change in storage technology. *Continuous cluster replication (CCR)* was a new high-availability model that did not require a shared storage solution. Combined with an I/O reduction of up to 70 percent (when compared to Exchange Server 2003) and site resiliency technology, this enhancement produced a paradigm shift in Exchange storage design.

The reduction in I/O and the introduction of CCR meant that it was no longer necessary to deploy a shared storage solution to achieve high availability. This allowed Exchange to make use of less complex and, more crucially, less expensive storage solutions than in previous Exchange versions. This not only reduced the capital expenditure required for Exchange 2007 hardware, but it also reduced deployment and operational costs due to the reduction in storage complexity.

CCR also brought with it support for up to 200 GB databases. It also provided for two copies of each database plus a third copy maintained by *standby continuous replication (SCR)* in a secondary site. The introduction of multiple database copies stored on physically independent storage resulted in a measurable increase in Exchange service availability for most customers plus the ability to provide end users with much larger mailboxes.

The downside of CCR was that design teams that stuck with their expensive storage infrastructure often could not justify the extra costs of deploying a CCR/SCR solution, or they had to limit the size of mailboxes to keep storage costs down. In many cases, customers kept using their SAN storage to take advantage of their enterprise backup infrastructure and to get the ever-growing amount of Exchange data backed up in an acceptable time frame.

For the first time, storage choice was significantly affected by the type and success of Exchange high-availability solutions. Customers staying with SAN storage were mostly using the legacy *single copy cluster (SCC)* that was available in previous versions of Exchange, while customers using cheaper directly attached storage were generally adopting the new CCR/SCR technology and benefitting from improved availability and reduced costs. In extreme cases, customers who had chosen expensive SAN storage, but who still wanted to use CCR, would store both the active and passive copies on the same storage array. This added both cost and complexity, but did not improve service availability.

Even though IOPS had been reduced by 70 percent from Exchange 2003, the IOPS requirements for Exchange Server 2007 were still relatively high and most deployments were still using 10K rpm disk spindles in RAID 10 to meet the combination of performance and capacity.

Exchange 2010

Exchange Server 2010 made better use of cheap, directly attached storage in order to entice more enterprise customers into using the new continuous replication cluster technology. Exchange Server 2010 matured the CCR/SCR model in *database availability groups (DAGs)*. A DAG allowed up to 16 copies of each database and enabled each database to have multiple database copies. IOPS requirements were reduced an additional 70 percent, and the I/O profile for Exchange was modified to make much better use of cheaper 7.2K rpm hard disk drives.

With Exchange Server 2010, for the first time customers could also choose to design Exchange storage to use 7.2K rpm SAS hard drives with no RAID *JBOD* (just a bunch of disks). They also could now rely entirely on the Exchange continuous replication solution (DAG) to provide database availability.

Being able to use cheaper and slower 7.2K rpm hard disk drives came at a cost. The database schema and internal tables within the database were optimized to improve I/O performance by organizing items in a sequential manner. This change caused single-instance storage to be lost and Exchange to prefer sequential positioning of data to making use of every tiny morsel of free space within the database. The impact of this change was that Exchange databases were now larger than in previous versions despite the Exchange product group having introduced database compression that was intended to compensate for the growth.

COMPRESSION

It is worth noting that in the absence of compression, the database sizes increased by around 25 percent.

Design teams now had more flexibility than ever before because SAN, DAS, and JBOD were all viable options depending on the solution requirements. The storage and database copy layout flexibility provided by Exchange DAGs complicated the Exchange storage design process. Design teams began to ask the obvious questions:

◆ Is JBOD viable for enterprise?

◆ How many copies are needed?

◆ Are backups necessary?

◆ Can we use cheap SATA disks?

The increased flexibility provided by the database availability group model placed increasing importance on a good design process and requirements definition. With Exchange Server 5.5, storage choices were limited, and thus it was difficult to get it wrong. With Exchange Server 2010, the available storage choices ranged from expensive SAN storage arrays with multiple parity, right down to cheap, locally attached JBOD 7.2K SAS spindles.

For customers who did adopt the simple and cheap JBOD model, one problem became increasingly apparent. JBOD disk spindles were increasing in size, with some manufacturers listing 3 TB–4 TB disk spindles in 2012. Yet the maximum recommended Exchange 2010 database size was 2 TB.

The IEEE suggests that mechanical disk platter areal density will increase 20 percent per year for the rest of the decade. Both Hitachi and IBM are predicting that 6 TB hard disks will be commonly available during 2013. In contrast, random IOPS performance for mechanical hard disks has remained almost static over the last 10 years. Random IOPS performance is mostly governed by hard drive rotation speed; however, increases in rotational speed also bring with them large increases in cost and power. The most common format for capacity and performance in Exchange 2010 storage is 7.2K rpm 3.5". These disk drives vary in performance from 50–65 random IOPS per spindle depending on the manufacturer. There is no expectation that IOPS per-spindle performance will increase in the near future, and so Exchange Server 2013 must be able to make use of these larger capacity disk spindles.

Storage Changes in Exchange 2013

Exchange Server 2013 is a major new release and, as such, the Exchange product group invested in the key development areas that were projected to yield the largest benefits to both customers and the teams that run Exchange Online. A number of the product revisions centered on database and storage issues, many of which were needed to address problems in Exchange Server 2010, while others were added to deal with trends within the industry that Exchange 2013 would need during its 10-year life cycle. For example, the following issues existed in Exchange Server 2010 and needed to be resolved.

Issue 1: Storage Capacity Increasing

As shown in Figure 5.1, magnetic disk areal density has been increasing dramatically. This directly affects how much capacity each drive platter can store and thus how much capacity a drive of each form factor can provide. Historically, areal density increased by 40 percent a year. In 2010, however, the IEEE suggested that this increase had slowed to 20 percent a year.

Exchange Server 2010 had started to make better use of larger capacity disks. However, trying to use a spindle much larger than 2 TB JBOD was problematic because of Microsoft's recommendation not to exceed a 2 TB mailbox database and not to store multiple mailbox databases on a single spindle.

During the life cycle of Exchange Server 2013, most storage vendors are predicting that they will be making 6 TB–8 TB 3.5" 7.2K rpm disk drives. Ideally, this means that Exchange Server 2013 should be able to use an 8 TB 7.2K rpm spindle.

FIGURE 5.1
Areal density
increase over time

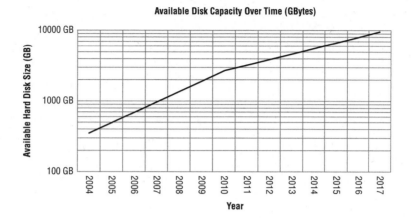

Issue 2: Mechanical Disk IOPS Performance Not Increasing

Despite constant increases in areal density and storage capacity, the random IOPS performance for mechanical disk drives has remained fairly static. This is largely due to the physics involved in mechanical hard drive I/O performance. The obvious question is, why don't we use *solid-state (SSD)* technology, which can provide extremely high IOPS for each device? Not surprisingly, the answer is cost, as shown in Table 5.1.

TABLE 5.1:   SSD vs. mechanical hard drive cost (at time of writing)

DRIVE TYPE	CAPACITY GB	COST ($)	$/GB
HP 2 TB 3G SATA 7.2K rpm LFF (3.5-inch) Midline hard drive (507632-B21)	2,000	479	0.2395
HP 300 GB SATA X25-M solid-state drive (LZ069AA)	300	1050	3.5

The prices in Table 5.1 show that solid-state drives are almost 15 times more expensive than mechanical hard disk drives when compared on a price-per-GB rating. Additionally, there are concerns about the longevity of solid-state memory for use with enterprise database workloads such as Exchange Server. There are storage solutions where a small number of high-speed SSD devices can be used as a form of secondary disk cache that provides higher performance without the high cost. In most cases, however, these solutions are extremely expensive when compared with an equal-size, directly attached storage solution. They may also result in unpredictable performance for random workloads. We will compare storage solutions later in this chapter.

Given this difference in cost between SSD and mechanical hard disk drives, SSDs are not recommended for Exchange Server storage. This leaves design teams with a common problem, that is, how to calculate the random IOPS capability for a mechanical hard disk drive. As a matter of fact, there is a relatively simple method for deriving random IOPS per spindle given two commonly available metrics.

Average Seek Time This is the average time for the disk head to reach its required position on the disk platter.

Rotational Speed in rpm This is the speed at which the disk platters spin.

Once these values are known, it is possible to determine how many random IOPS the disk spindle can accommodate. Review the following example:

Manufacturer Supplied Information

♦ Spindle speed: 7,200 rpm

♦ Average random seek time: 8ms

CALCULATING IOPS PER SPINDLE

The number of random read and write operations that a hard disk drive can complete is a function of how fast the disk spins and how quickly the head can move around. Given a few metrics about the disk drive, we can calculate the theoretical maximum random IOPS as follows:

Time for One Rotation This involves converting rpm into seconds per rotation in order to determine how long the platter takes to spin through 360°.

$$\frac{60,000}{7,200\,rpm} = \textbf{8.33ms}$$

Rotational Latency This value is the time that the platter takes to rotate through 180°. This is caused by the head moving to the track and then waiting for the right part of the platter to pass under it before it can read the data. On average, the platter will have to complete 180° of rotation before it can perform each I/O.

$$\frac{8.33ms}{2} = \textbf{4.167ms}$$

Rotational Latency + Average Seek Time This value is the sum of rotational latency, which is the amount of time we must wait after the head has reached the right track before it can read the bit of data that we want, plus average seek time, which is the time we have to wait to position the head in the first place. The combination of the two values is the average delay before we can get the head to the right bit of the disk platter.

$$4.15 + 8\,ms = \textbf{12.15ms}$$

Predicted Random IOPS This value is a theoretical prediction of the maximum random IOPS of which the spindle is capable. This formula calculates how many operations we can do per ms (1/Rotational Latency + Seek Time) and then converting that into operations per second (×1,000).

$$\left(\frac{1}{12.15}\right) \times 1{,}000 = \textbf{82.189 IOPS/spindle}$$

Why is this important? We are mainly interested in this because the two factors that govern random disk IOPS for mechanical disk drives are rotation speed and seek time. Neither of these factors is likely to improve dramatically in the near future. Disks have been available at up to 15K rpm spindle speeds for the last five years or more. Nonetheless, these high-speed spindles are very costly, and they require more power and generate more heat (thus requiring additional cooling) than slower spindle speeds. It is also difficult to spin a large disk platter at such high speeds, and so most manufacturers only offer high spindle speed drives in smaller capacities, because they require a smaller platter diameter to maintain the high spindle speed. Minor improvements in average seek time have been achieved as manufacturing and engineering processes have matured. However, most storage vendors report that they do not expect to see any significant improvements in this area.

This leaves Exchange design teams with a problem. Disk capacities are increasing and costs per megabyte are declining, but random IOPS performance is relatively static. This means that we are unable to take advantage of these newer, high-capacity hard disk drives effectively. Thus, Exchange 2013 must be able to make better use of 7.2K rpm mechanical disk drives with greater than 2 TB capacities.

Issue 3: JBOD Solutions Require Operational Maturity

Exchange 2010 allowed the use of JBOD. Though initially this term was confusing within the Exchange community, for our discussion the term JBOD will refer to the presentation of a single disk spindle to the operating system as an available *volume*.

JBOD represents a very cheap and simple way to provide Exchange storage. Ideally the JBOD spindles will be slow, cheap disks and directly attached to each DAG node to provide the best-cost model. The JBOD model requires three or more copies of each database to ensure sufficient data availability in the event that a disk spindle fails.

The most common problem area for JBOD is not in the technology. Rather, it is what has to occur operationally when a disk spindle inevitably fails. Since there is no RAID array, every single disk spindle failure will result in a predictable series of events:

1. Disk failure

2. Active workload moved to another spindle if the failed spindle was hosting an active copy

3. Physical disk spindle replacement

4. New disk brought online

5. New disk partitioned

6. New volume formatted

7. Database reseeded

8. Active workload moved back to the replaced disk if it was active in the first place

If the failed spindle was hosting the active copy of the database at the time of failure, there may be a minor interruption in service to the end user. However, typically the failover times are brief enough so that Outlook clients in cached mode will not notice this kind of failure.

Dealing with disk spindle failures in a JBOD deployment can be largely automated via a combination of PowerShell scripts and monitoring software. However, it does require a level of operational maturity both to capture the alerts and to execute the correct remediation processes once the alert is received. Compared to a RAID based solution where a disk must be replaced, the level of involvement, resource skills, and access requirements necessary to repair a JBOD spindle failure is high.

Exchange Server 2013 must provide an easier way to deal with JBOD disk spindle failures and to reduce the operational maturity and process required to recover from such failures. We will discuss how the product group achieved this later in this chapter.

Issue 4: Mailbox Capacity Requirements Increasing

If there is one thing that is common to every release of Exchange Server, it is the expectation that the latest version will be able to support ever-larger mailbox sizes. In recent times, this expectation has also grown to include mailbox item counts.

With Exchange Server 2010, the ability to store ever more data in the Exchange database via features such as In-Place Hold and single-item recovery meant that mailbox sizes increased dramatically.

IN-PLACE HOLD

In-Place Hold is a mechanism whereby an administrator can retain all contents in a mailbox, even if the end user deletes them. This is extremely useful in scenarios such as litigation or where organizations need to persist end-user data for internal review.

Many customers want to store all mailbox data within Exchange for both the real-time message service and compliance. Exchange Server 2013 must be able to maintain performance when clients are connected to these extremely large mailboxes.

Issue 5: Everything Needs to Be Cheaper

A common thread in Exchange projects is cost reduction. This encompasses not only the cost of the hardware but also running costs, datacenter costs, and network, power, cooling, and migration costs as well. As customer requirements have increased, Exchange has had to meet these needs and do so without spiraling costs upward. This is particularly evident with storage, where the requirements for capacity and performance have expanded dramatically while the demands for cost reduction have been equally dramatic.

Recent trends have placed an increasing focus on power, heating, cooling, and datacenter space. Organizations are looking for new ways to reduce their operating costs. Exchange infrastructure can often contribute significantly in large deployments, especially when the storage and supporting functions are considered, such as backup, monitoring, publishing, and so on.

Consolidation of roles was a common theme for Exchange 2010 projects, with many customers taking advantage of high-density locally attached storage, such as the HP MDS 600, which could provide 70 × 3.5" SAS disks in 5U of rack space. Additionally, customers could take advantage of multi-role Exchange deployments to reduce the server footprint. This was a substantial improvement over previous versions of Exchange, and it allowed large-scale consolidation of servers and storage into fewer, more easily managed datacenters. However, power, cooling, and datacenter space costs are increasing. Exchange Server 2013 must continue this trend of consolidation while meeting the increasing business and operational demands for a robust enterprise-messaging product.

Storage Improvements in Exchange Server 2013

Table 5.2 outlines some of the most interesting changes in Exchange 2013 that have an impact on storage.

TABLE 5.2: Storage enhancements in Exchange Server 2013

CHANGE	DESCRIPTION	BENEFITS
Store rewritten in managed code	Store.exe is the Exchange Information Store. It was rewritten in managed code to provide efficiencies and allow developers to concentrate on logical data flow rather than code challenges.	◆ Reduction in IOPS from being able to use binary large objects for storing data ◆ Easier to check for bugs ◆ Easier to maintain and secure ◆ Improved availability
Improved Extensible Storage Engine (ESE) cache allocation	This change allocates more ESE cache for active databases over passive databases. It makes better use of available memory in the server for servicing end users.	◆ Improves use of available resources ◆ Improves end-user performance
Database schema further improved	Further reduces random I/Os by storing more items within the database sequentially or on the same database page.	◆ Reduces IOPS ◆ Makes better use of newer, larger disks
Multiple DB copies per disk spindle	I/O profile improved to make better use of cheaper SAS 3.5" spindles. This allows multiple databases to be hosted on a single spindle.	◆ Makes better use of newer, larger disks
Automatic database reseed	Allows spare JBOD spindles to be prepared and used automatically in the event of a disk spindle failure.	◆ Reduces operational maturity requirements to make use of JBOD ◆ Makes better use of newer, larger disks

One of the interesting trends in Exchange Server 2010 and Exchange Server 2013 is that the Exchange product group will trade CPU utilization if it buys a reduction or smoothes out random disk I/O. This approach makes sense as we consider the hardware growth prediction during the Exchange Server 2013 life cycle. Moore's Law states that transistor densities double about every two years. This growth rate is expected to taper off to a doubling of transistor density every three years starting at the end of 2013. Regardless, the industry expects that available processor power will continue to rise, whereas mechanical disk random IOPS performance is expected to remain static. Exchange Server 2013 is designed to take best advantage of both the hardware resources currently available and those that are projected to be available during the life cycle of the product.

Exchange 2013 reduces IOPS by roughly 45 percent over Exchange Server 2010. If we consider active mailboxes only, Exchange Server 2010 required 0.0012 × user profile compared to Exchange Server 2013 requiring 0.00067 × user profile. If we plug in numbers for 100 messages sent and received per mailbox/per day/per user profile, this means that if the mailbox was hosted on Exchange Server 2010, it would require 0.12 IOPS/mailbox. But on Exchange Server 2013, it would need only 0.067 IOPS/mailbox.

Automatic Database Reseed

This is the single most important change in Exchange Server 2013. Quite simply, automatic database reseed makes deploying a JBOD storage solution viable for many organizations that found JBOD too difficult to manage in Exchange Server 2010.

The fundamental idea behind *automatic database reseed* is that you allocate more disk spindles to each DAG node than you require for your active and passive databases. The additional spindles are formatted and mounted, but they are not used to store database or logs. In the event of the failure of a disk spindle that is being used for an active or passive database copy, Exchange will make use of the "spare" disk spindles and automatically perform the necessary database reseed operation.

So why is automatic database reseed better than RAID? JBOD plus AutoReseed requires fewer disks than RAID 10 and does not suffer from the same level of performance degradation inherent in RAID 5 during rebuild. It also doesn't require the same level of operational maturity to maintain data availability.

Multiple Databases for Each JBOD Disk Spindle

The change allowing multiple databases for each JBOD disk spindle was necessary to permit the use of larger disk capacities without increasing the maximum mailbox database size above 2 TB. This change is often confused with storing multiple databases per volume but it is subtly different. What this change actually means is that in Exchange Server 2013, there exists the ability to store multiple mailbox databases on a single JBOD spindle, that is, a single disk spindle presented to the server. We have always been able to store multiple databases on a RAID array, but storing multiple databases on a JBOD spindle was previously not supported.

Seemingly, this change is simple to understand since it gives us the ability to store multiple databases on each spindle. This lets us retain the 2 TB maximum recommended mailbox database limit yet still takes advantage of larger-capacity disk spindles. However, this represents only half of the benefit of this change. The other half is that, when we reseed the disk spindle, we may potentially have multiple JBOD disk spindles participating in the reseed operation. Testing so far with Exchange Server 2013 suggests that a single spindle reseed operation, like those that already exist in Exchange Server 2010, runs at around 20 MB/sec. Testing with Exchange Server 2013 and multiple databases for each spindle shows that the reseed operation runs at around 20 MB/sec per spindle used in the reseed operation. For example, if a spindle stored two database copies and the alternate copies of those databases were on different spindles, the reseed operation would take place at around 2 × 20 MB/sec = 40 MB/sec. Figure 5.2 shows you potentially how to store four databases for each disk spindle with a JBOD deployment in Exchange Server 2013.

FIGURE 5.2
Multiple databases for each JBOD spindle layout

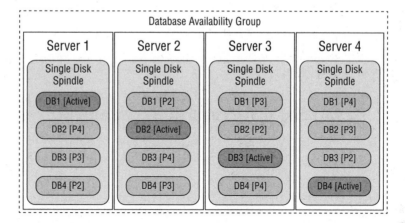

Now let's examine the reseed scenario where we have lost the JBOD disk spindle in Server 1. In this case, active workload for DB1, as shown in Figure 5.2, has been moved to Server 2. All of the remaining workload has stayed in place. The disk in Server 1 has been replaced, and all databases are now being reseeded from the active copy, as shown in Figure 5.3.

FIGURE 5.3
Multiple databases for each JBOD spindle reseed

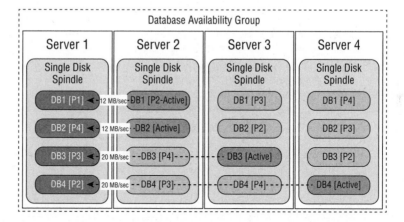

Testing shows that, for each reseed operation per source spindle, we can expect around 20 MB/sec performance. Where we have multiple reseed operations for each spindle, we can get around 24 MB/sec performance in total for that spindle. Let's see what this data yields for approximate reseed times.

Exchange Server 2010 (single DB/spindle)

◆ 2 TB data = ~29 hours

◆ 8 TB data = ~116 hours

Exchange Server 2013 (four DBs/spindle)

◆   2 TB data = ~9.1 hours

◆   8 TB data = ~36 hours

When we combine the reseed performance benefit with being able to make use of larger disk spindle capacities and automatic database reseed, it makes JBOD in Exchange Server 2013 a compelling proposition from a cost/simplicity perspective and also from an operational perspective. Thus, it is a win/win scenario.

Designing a Successful Exchange Storage Solution

The fundamental design process for an Exchange storage solution normally follows these steps:

1. Define requirements (functional specification).

2. Perform user profile analysis.

3. Complete the Exchange 2013 Server Role Requirements Calculator.

4. Select appropriate storage hardware.

5. Validate with Jetstress.

6. Document proposed solution.

In the early days of Exchange design, it was rare to see anything other than step 4 and perhaps step 6 practiced, largely because the Exchange 2013 Server Role Requirements Calculator didn't exist and we didn't have a way to validate the solution. As Exchange has matured, so too has the design process. More recently, it is expected that a storage solution is designed to meet requirements and to avoid overdeploying and operating unnecessary storage hardware.

Over-deploying storage was a common practice with Exchange Server 2003 as design teams tried to make up for performance and architectural limitations within the product. Generally, this proved unsuccessful since Exchange 2003 was limited by its underlying 32-bit architecture and the resulting memory fragmentation that it caused. However, it didn't stop IT departments trying to make it go faster by using very expensive, high-performance storage.

The golden rule of Exchange storage design is first to understand the user profile requirements, which we will discuss later in this chapter. The goal is then to design a solution that will meet those requirements adequately.

Good quality user-profile analysis is vital to the design process. Attempting to perform Exchange storage design without having good quality user-profile data and clearly defined requirements is just costly guesswork. We will discuss the importance of this concept in further detail in the validation section of this chapter.

Requirements Gathering

Every project should have a requirements-gathering phase, as we discussed in Chapter 1, "Business, Functional, and Technical Requirements." However, it's worth examining which specific requirements are important for Exchange storage design and why we need them.

Service Level   The *service-level agreement (SLA)* is a contract between two parties that sets out things like how a specific service will be operated, who is responsible for its maintenance, what level of performance it will provide, and what level of availability it will achieve.

From an Exchange storage design perspective, we are mainly interested in the service level because it drives our high-availability decisions. If the SLA dictates a high-availability solution, then it opens up some design choices for storage that we may not have had otherwise, such as JBOD. JBOD requires a high-availability deployment, since we must have multiple copies of each database to be able to recover in a timely fashion once a disk spindle fails. We may also consider running an *Exchange native data protection (backupless)* solution. Exchange native data protection makes use of native Exchange features, such as multiple database copies within a DAG and lagged copies, to provide resistance against corruption and component failure without needing to take point-in-time backups.

If the service level does not require a high-availability solution, and Exchange will be deployed without a DAG, then our storage is likely to be based on a RAID solution that can tolerate disk spindle failure. In addition, we will probably also need to consider a backup solution, since backupless solutions require multiple database copies.

The important thing to note here is that simply deploying a massive DAG with JBOD storage is not *always* the right thing to do. Consider the system requirements carefully, and be sure that you understand the impact of your storage design choices on the rest of the Exchange infrastructure.

User Profile Analysis   User profile analysis is an area of developing design requirements that is too often rushed and completed poorly. Frequently, this leads to problems later on in the deployment phase. Fundamentally, *user profile analysis* is the way to quantify the system workload required for each mailbox user. Without good user profile data, you cannot complete any of the Exchange planning calculators effectively. The common phrase "Garbage in, Garbage out" fits well here. If you guess at the user profile values in the Exchange 2013 Server Role Requirements Calculator, then you might as well guess the predictions too.

Given that we now understand that user profile data is vital to a quality storage design, what exactly do we need and how can we get it? Following are the most commonly requested core user profile metrics for designing Exchange storage:

Average Message Size in KB   This is the average size of items in the user's mailbox. It is used to predict storage capacity growth, transaction log file generation, dumpster size, DAG replication bandwidth, and so forth.

Messages Sent per Mailbox per Day   This is an average value of the number of messages sent by an average user on a daily basis. This value is used to predict workload; that is, how much are end users actually doing within the Exchange service?

Messages Received per Mailbox per Day   This is basically the same as the previous item, except it is for messages received. Typically, users will receive many more messages than they send.

Average Mailbox Size   Normally, this is the anticipated average quota size of the deployment. It is used to determine storage capacity requirements.

Third-Party Devices   The most common example of a third-party device that has an impact on Exchange storage is BlackBerry. These devices can have a significant impact on your Exchange database I/O, and so it is vital that you speak to your device vendor to understand the extent of this overhead. Make sure that you check this for each and every deployment because it changes from version to version. We often see designs based on the old 3.64 multiplier value for BlackBerry Enterprise Server (BES) that was specific to Exchange 2003. Exchange 2010 reduced this multiplier to 2; that is the same as another Outlook client. Exchange 2013 is anticipated to require roughly the same IOPS multiplier as Exchange 2010. However, at the time of this writing, there is no specific BES sizing data available for Exchange Server 2013.

It is also vital that you understand what percentage of your users will have BlackBerry devices and the percentage of expected growth. In many cases, the root cause of reduced performance is directly related to an increase in BlackBerry use, which can easily increase I/O requirements beyond original design targets.

Interestingly, you do not need to scale for most ActiveSync devices, such as Apple iOS and Windows Phone, since this IO workload is included in the Exchange 2013 Server Role Requirements Calculator prediction base formula.

When discussing Exchange storage design, we are often asked how to obtain user profile values. For Exchange Server 2003 and Exchange Server 2007, the *Exchange Server Profile Analyzer (EPA)* will provide most of this information. However, this tool requires WebDAV, which was dropped in Exchange Server 2010 and so it will not work in later versions. Fear not; there is an alternative that is addressed in this article:

```
http://blogs.technet.com/b/neiljohn/archive/2011/08/09/user-profile-analysis-for-
exchange-server-2010.aspx
```

This article explains how to use a script to parse message-tracking log data in Exchange Server 2010 and Exchange Server 2013 to derive the important user profile metrics. Nevertheless, for Exchange Server 2003 or Exchange Server 2007, we still prefer the data from the Exchange Server Profile Analyzer rather than the message-tracking log analysis script since experience shows that EPA provides more accurate user profile values.

The bottom line for user profile metrics is to understand exactly what the metric is and then figure out a way to obtain that information in the best and most practical way possible. This is particularly applicable when migrating from foreign messaging systems, such as *Lotus Domino*. There is no easy way to obtain user profile data from Domino, but it is possible to calculate most items by estimation. For example, you could use the following formula:

$$\frac{\text{Messages Received per Server One Day}}{\text{Mail Files Stored on That Server}} = \textit{Messages Received per Mailbox per Day}$$

Where user profile data is concerned, anything is better than making a random guess; that is, never guess your user profile information without some evidence to back it up. Always base user profile information on observed data, and record the process you used to derive it in your design documentation. This is especially important when you wish to engage in a design review cycle with a third-party consulting organization, because any good consultant will want to understand where the numbers came from that you put into the calculator. If the original source of data for those numbers is not recorded, it becomes impossible to provide any form of performance validation for your design.

Making Sense of the Exchange Mailbox Server Role Requirements Calculator

The Exchange 2013 Server Role Requirements Calculator, or storage calculator as it used to be known, is basically a complicated Excel spreadsheet that contains the calculations necessary to take your design requirements, as discussed in Chapter 1, and turn them into some storage-specific requirements. In this book, we will concentrate on the interesting prediction values that emerge from the calculator rather than on how to use it. Ross Smith IV has written many articles on the Exchange Team Blog about using the calculator. We strongly recommend reading some of these posts before attempting to work with the calculator:

http://blogs.technet.com/b/exchange/archive/2010/01/22/updates-to-the-exchange-2010-mailbox-server-role-requirements-calculator.aspx

The Exchange 2013 Server Role Requirements Calculator can be downloaded here:

http://blogs.technet.com/b/exchange/archive/2013/05/14/released-exchange-2013-server-role-requirements-calculator.aspx

Let's begin by examining the Disk Space Requirements table, which is on the Role Requirements tab. The Disk Space Requirements table shows how much disk capacity the solution will require in the database, server, DAG, and the total environment (see Figure 5.4). This is very useful, since it shows us the capacity requirements for each database plus transaction log combination for the specific user profile and high-availability configuration specified.

In this example, you can see that for each volume used to store a mailbox database, its transaction logs and content index database needs to be at least 2264 GB in size to avoid running out of disk space. This amount comprises 1510 GB for the mailbox database and 37 GB for the transaction logs, and the rest is needed to account for content index and sufficient volume free space to avoid filling up the disk.

FIGURE 5.4

Disk Space Requirements table in the Exchange 2013 Server Role Requirements Calculator

Disk Space Requirements	/ Database	/ Server	/ DAG	/ Environment
Database Space Required	1510 GB	12076 GB	193219 GB	193219 GB
Log Space Required	37 GB	297 GB	4745 GB	4745 GB
Database+Log Volume Space Required	2264 GB	18426 GB	289738 GB	289738 GB
Log Volume Space Required	0 GB	0 GB	0 GB	0 GB
Restore Volume Space Required	--	1628 GB	26048 GB	26048 GB

If we move to the Host IO and Throughput Requirements table, as shown in Figure 5.5, there is another deluge of interesting information. This table is of interest to us in understanding the IOPS requirements for our storage and the throughput requirements for *background database maintenance (BDM)*.

FIGURE 5.5

Exchange 2013 Server Role Requirements Calculator IOPS and BDM requirements

Host IO and Throughput Requirements	/ Database	/ Server	/ DAG	/ Environment
Total Database Required IOPS	6	302	4824	4824
Total Log Required IOPS	1	64	1017	1017
Database Read I/O Percentage	60%	--	--	--
Background Database Maintenance Throughput Requirements	1.0 MB/s	48 MB/s	768 MB/s	768 MB/s

The values in this table map directly to the target values that will be required when you learn about storage performance validation with Jetstress. Jetstress is the tool we use to simulate an Exchange storage I/O workload to prove that our solution is capable of meeting the demands predicted using the Exchange 2013 Server Role Requirements Calculator.

The most important bits of information from the Host IO and Throughput Requirements table are the Total Database Required IOPS per database and per server plus the Background Database Maintenance Throughput Requirements.

The *Background Database Maintenance Throughput Requirements value* defines how much sequential read-only I/O will be required to support the background checksum process. Generally speaking, if you are deploying to direct attached storage (DAS), you do not need to consider BDM. However, if you are deploying on SAN or iSCSI, BDM throughput may be an issue. There are many cases where SAN storage, especially iSCSI, can be performance-limited by the throughput requirements of BDM on Exchange Server 2010. Exchange Server 2013 has dramatically reduced the throughput requirements for BDM down to 1 MB/sec from 7.5 MB/sec because of observations from the Office 365 service and the number of CRC errors that were detected during the process. Total Database Required IOPS per database and per server refer to the random IOPS required for the mailbox database. It is important to note that we do not usually consider Log IOPS when planning Exchange storage performance, since it is entirely sequential and easy on the disk. As a caveat to this, it is recommended that you speak with your storage vendor, since this approach may not apply to some SAN technologies and you will need to take their advice on IOPS performance scaling. Nonetheless, the approach is well proven for directly attached storage deployments.

If we look at the Volume Requirements tab, we can see additional information about our storage requirements. This table shows the maximum number of mailboxes per DB, DB size, DB size plus overhead, and log size plus overhead (see Figure 5.6). This is useful for determining how many mailboxes can be stored for each database before it is considered full. It also shows how much space should be allocated for transaction log data.

FIGURE 5.6
Database and
LOG Configuration/
Server table

Database and Log Configuration / Server				
Database Copy	Max Mailboxes / DB	DB Size	DB Size + Overhead	Log Size + Overhead
DB-x	313	1258 GB	1510 GB	37 GB
DB-x	313	1258 GB	1510 GB	37 GB
DB-x	313	1258 GB	1510 GB	37 GB
DB-x	313	1258 GB	1510 GB	37 GB
DB-x	313	1258 GB	1510 GB	37 GB
DB-x	313	1258 GB	1510 GB	37 GB
DB-x	313	1258 GB	1510 GB	37 GB
DB-x	313	1258 GB	1510 GB	37 GB

On the same tab, we can see the calculator's recommended volume layout. This shows how many databases are recommended per volume and the capacity requirements for each (see Figure 5.7).

The calculator provides a recommended layout. However, you should just view this as a starting point. The problem with all of the values that we have accumulated up to this point is that they are theoretical minimum values, and we need to map them to actual physical hardware that we can buy and deploy in real places. In most cases, the calculator does a very good job of getting you into the right ballpark, but you will need to apply common sense to turn the recommendation into something practical to deploy.

FIGURE 5.7
DB and Log Volume
Design / Server
table

DB and Log Volume Design / Server		
Database Copy	DB+Log Volume Size Required	
DB1	2264 GB	0 GB
DB2	2264 GB	0 GB
DB3	2264 GB	0 GB
DB4	2264 GB	0 GB
DB5	2264 GB	0 GB
DB6	2264 GB	0 GB
DB7	2264 GB	0 GB
DB8	2264 GB	0 GB
DB9	318 GB	0 GB

Selecting the Right Storage Hardware

Now we can move on to selecting appropriate hardware for our requirements. There are many aspects to this decision, and the requirements that we have identified so far represent only a few of them. Often there may be a hardware constraint in your requirements, which mandates that you use a specific storage technology or vendor. This technology may not be ideal for use with Exchange but may align with the organization's overall storage strategy. In some cases, this strategy has been mandated for all services, regardless of their requirements or function, and it will be necessary to use a particular storage platform. The other scenario is that you have free choice regarding the storage platform for Exchange, but then you will need to narrow down your choices. How do you narrow down your options? This section will discuss both scenarios and how to deal with them.

COMPANY-MANDATED STORAGE PLATFORM

First, let's take on the scenario where your storage platform choice is fixed. Even though this decision has been made for you, you still have work to do. To start, you need to research the platform that has been designated. Begin this process by looking at the *Exchange Solution Reviewed Program (ESRP) - Storage*. Search for a submission from the same storage vendor and, hopefully, for the same platform that is to be used.

ESRP submissions vary in quality and the usefulness of the information provided, but they are almost always a great place to find specific configuration details for running Exchange on a particular platform. ESRP is grouped into versions that relate to the Exchange platform to which they apply:

◆ Exchange Server 2007: ESRP - Storage v2.1

◆ Exchange Server 2010: ESRP - Storage v3.0

◆ Exchange Server 2013: ESRP - Storage v4.0

If you cannot find an ESRP submission, look on the manufacturer's website for Exchange-specific configuration recommendations.

Next, evaluate your disk type options and RAID group configurations. Not all storage platforms allow all configurations, and so it is vital that you understand what you can and cannot do. Then try to map the data that you obtained from the Exchange 2013 Server Role Requirements Calculator, and try to make it fit the platform. Often, the best way to do this is to run a combined storage design workshop with the storage team, in order to evaluate the options, and then try to tweak the calculator accordingly.

Once this process is complete, try to define a validation approach. This is generally a small deployment of servers and storage on representative hardware that can be used for Jetstress testing. The goal of the Jetstress testing will be to validate that the proposed solution is capable of meeting the requirements identified by the calculator. This is where the marketing nonsense stops and the fun begins! We will discuss this process later in this chapter.

FREE CHOICE OF STORAGE PLATFORM

Recall that, in the second scenario, you have full control over the storage platform. This is often more challenging for a design team. Now you have to come up with a process for evaluating storage platforms and their ability to meet your requirements. To this end, the first things to define are your specification requirements. These are common areas of comparison; the aim for most team members is to grade the platform from 1 to 10 (where 1 is very poor and 10 is perfect for the task).

Cost   This is obviously a key aspect. However, it is vital to consider the total cost of the platform and not just the purchase price. What are the support costs? What about operator training expenses? What about installation and configuration costs? If possible, calculate the total cost of the platform over a period of time, for example, two or three years, and use this to compare the real costs of each platform.

Operations   How easy or difficult is this platform going to be to operate? Can it be easily upgraded? Can parts be swapped out without affecting service? Try to determine a common set of operational processes that will be required, and grade each platform on a 1 to 10 scale for the ease with which these tasks can be completed.

Space   Datacenter space is a primary concern for many customers. Space is an expensive commodity in most datacenters, and it should be taken into consideration for any new platform. Try to determine the rack space required per GB or per mailbox for each platform to aid in making a comparison.

Power   This is another area of increasing concern for recent deployments. The more power that a device draws, the more heat it usually generates. This leads to more demand for datacenter cooling. When possible, calculate the power in kWh per mailbox or per GB for comparison.

Performance   From an Exchange perspective, your performance requirements are defined in the Exchange 2013 Server Role Requirements Calculator. Can the platform meet your IOPS, throughput, and capacity requirements while remaining under your recommended I/O latency thresholds when tested with Jetstress? We generally suggest that you record a pass/ fail for each platform here, where failed systems are either redesigned and retested or discarded in the process.

Storage Validation Using Jetstress

What is *storage validation*? Simply put, the goal of this process is to ensure that the storage platform is capable of meeting the demands of Exchange Server to service end-user requests in a timely manner. If the storage platform is incapable of meeting these demands, then the end-user experience will suffer. We know this from experience in the early days with Exchange Server 2003, where poor storage performance equaled poor Exchange Server performance.

There is an important aspect to the validation process that is rarely discussed, however, and that is that it must take place with a calibrated workload. A *calibrated workload* means that the test workload applied should be approved (calibrated) by the Exchange product group as not only being a representative one but also equal to the workload generated by Exchange Server. This point is important because it separates out tools that generate workload, such as Iometer and LoadGen, from tools that generate a defined and calibrated workload, such as Jetstress.

Sometimes, in a project where the design has been completed and the storage is failing to pass the Jetstress test, a storage team member will insist that Jetstress is not a good test because the requirements can be met with Iometer, and that's proof that Jetstress is broken. A slight variation on this occurs when a team will use LoadGen to simulate the expected production workload and find that it passes whereas Jetstress fails and thus will come to the same conclusion; that is, LoadGen passes where Jetstress fails and so Jetstress must be broken. Both situations are equally difficult to address since the explanation of the results is complex. By far the most compelling explanation is that Jetstress is a calibrated workload, and when used with the values derived from the Exchange 2013 Server Role Requirements Calculator, it represents the peak two hours of a working day as accurately as possible.

When it comes to storage validation, Jetstress is the only real tool for the job. Now let's see how it works.

JETSTRESS TEST PROCESS

The Jetstress test process itself is documented in the *Jetstress Field Guide*. This does not yet exist for Jetstress 2013; however, the general process outlined for Jetstress 2010 still applies. The test must be conducted as follows if it to be considered successful:

- ◆ Meets or exceeds the database IOPS requirements identified within the calculator in normal conditions

- ◆ Meets or exceeds the database IOPS requirements identified within the calculator in degraded (rebuild) conditions

- ◆ Runs for a duration of two hours (strict mode test)

- ◆ Runs for a duration of 24 hours (lenient mode test)

- ◆ Completes all test runs with a status of Passed

A common area of confusion about these tests is the 2-hour vs. 24-hour test recommendation. Jetstress runs in strict mode when the duration is less than six hours. A completed test run in strict mode is required to be sure that the storage is meeting the performance requirements. The lenient mode relaxes some of the peak latency spike requirements, and it is intended for longer duration testing. The 24-hour test is recommended to ensure that the storage platform is capable of operating at peak workload for an extended duration, since several cases have been logged where performance deteriorates over time when a storage platform is operating at or near its limits. If a storage platform passes all of these Jetstress tests, experience shows that the design is then good to go.

BUILD-TIME VALIDATION

There is one more aspect to Jetstress validation work that is sometimes disregarded or over-looked, and that is build-time validation testing. Build-time validation testing involves running a Jetstress test on each production Mailbox server before it is accepted into production. When discussing this type of testing, the question often asked is, why bother with this test when we have already tested an identical solution in the test lab and it has passed? The answer is that, although the tests are the same, the purpose is different. Validation tests in the lab were designed to corroborate design assumptions and decisions about the storage platform. The build-time validation is designed to ensure that the hardware has been deployed and config-ured appropriately to meet the requirements, and it is operating according to expectations; that is, it is not faulty.

It is not unheard of for a storage platform to pass Jetstress with flying colors in the test lab, where it receives TLC from the vendor presales team, only to find out that it fails to pass the same Jetstress test in a production environment, where it has been deployed and configured by a completely different team. This can be addressed by adopting build and configuration stan-dards. However, these are still not foolproof, and so adopting an automated Jetstress validation test prior to installing Exchange Server into a production environment is highly recommended. This recommendation is even stronger when a complex storage solution has been deployed. One thing to remember is that it is much easier to fix a problem when Jetstress is the only user of the service. If you first become aware of a problem when an end user reports it, your job becomes significantly harder.

Summary

Storage design has been a part of creating Exchange solutions since the very beginning. Although Exchange Server is a messaging application, at its heart it is actually a database of email messages. The increase in requirements to store more and perpetually larger messages for an ever-increasing amount of time means that storage design remains at the heart of designing a successful messaging solution on Exchange Server 2013.

The trend over the last five years has been toward increasing system availability by stor-ing multiple, isolated copies of each mailbox database. This process enhances availability by being able to switch over to a virtually identical mailbox database in a matter of seconds. Nevertheless, it also increases the quantity of disks that a solution requires. Each copy that you add will increase your system availability but will also double your storage capacity require-ments. This means that the type, and more important the cost factors, of the storage platform that you choose will impact the number of database copies that you can provide. Remember that Exchange Server 2013 was designed to make great use of cheap, locally attached disk spindles. As of June 2013, the Exchange Product Group at Microsoft is recommending 4 TB 3.5" 7.2K rpm disk spindles to provide the best capacity vs. cost ratio.

Exchange storage design should also begin with an accurate requirements definition. Once the requirements are understood, the single most important part of any storage design is per-forming good quality user-profile analysis. The user profile defines how many IOPS each mail-box will require, and so it is a fundamental part of your design. Even a relatively small change in the user profile can result in significant redesign.

If it is available, use the Exchange 2013 Server Role Requirements Calculator to help you with your storage sizing and design. If not, use the details provided in the following post by Jeff Mealiffe on the Exchange Team Blog:

```
http://blogs.technet.com/b/exchange/archive/2013/05/06/ask-the-perf-guy-sizing-
exchange-2013-deployments.aspx
```

Once you have your completed storage design, it is vital that you validate it with Jetstress. Jetstress simulates Exchange database I/O very closely, and it is the only recommended way to test that your storage solution will provide sufficient performance to meet your calculated demand.

The single most important piece of advice for Exchange storage design is to keep things simple. If there is one area that has historically been overdesigned and made overly complicated, it is Exchange storage design. Exchange Server 2013 thrives on cheap, local, directly attached storage. Go down this path for the simplest and most cost-effective experience.

Chapter 6

Management

The management and operation of any system are some of the biggest elements to consider when planning for that new system. After all, it is these elements that together form the majority of the cost of ownership. In this chapter, we will focus on the management tools available. In particular, we will cover concepts such as Role-Based Access Control, which enables granular delegation of permissions to administrators. We will also address features, such as the move to a web-based management interface, in this chapter. Later in this book, we will discuss the day-to-day operations of Exchange.

Trends in Management of Platforms

When we look back at the early days of our IT careers in the late 1990s, the authors of this book remember how management of any given product was comparatively simple. Products were not designed with scale in mind. Neither were they designed to incorporate the idea of automation. It was just a bit early for those concepts to take hold within IT environments.

As time went by, technology became more complex. Components that enabled the creation of larger environments with thousands of users became cheaper and more readily available. Connectivity between locations became more reliable and affordable as both carriers and bandwidth providers invested in this infrastructure. Such advancements allowed businesses to create larger, more complex networks and systems that served a company's employees worldwide without having multiple, fragmented, and individualized systems serving this purpose.

In 1998, a cellular network provider with multiple offices in Southeast Asia was running Exchange 4.x. When we first visited them, they had Exchange systems implemented at each location. They also had separate Windows NT domains for each location. However, we were surprised to see that none of the systems installed at each location were connected with each other. They used Exchange to communicate internally in a given office but used Hotmail for communicating between offices!

While this setup seems unimaginable today, it was difficult back then to install a single system that served all of the disparate offices. This was due to the complexity involved, the bandwidth cost to connect each office, the lack of necessary telecommunications infrastructure, and the lack of automation for effectively managing such a system.

Fast-forward to today: Computing infrastructure and systems have advanced greatly. As we touched on at the beginning of this chapter, management and automation should be at the center of a system's design. Having the operational agility to manage such complex and advanced systems is a requirement of today's IT departments. Customers deploying such systems not only demand high levels of uptime, but they also want to ensure a quality end-user experience.

In order to achieve this, you need the ability to automate the simple processes, such as moving mailboxes or failing over servers to maintain availability. Thankfully, Microsoft Exchange leads the field in the trend toward ever-greater automation. If you are an IT professional who is designing, implementing, and/or maintaining a Microsoft Exchange Server infrastructure, it is highly likely that you have used some form of script, whether written by you or someone else, to automate a given Exchange-related task, big or small. These days, it is not enough just to rely on graphical user interface (GUI)-based tools.

Of course, it is not only the need for high uptime and a good user experience that drives the changes that management requires. In recent years, the global economic slowdown has put even more emphasis on increasing efficiency and reducing the staff-to-user population ratio. Microsoft and other software manufacturers have responded to such demands by making systems more intelligent using self-healing technology—generally simpler to manage and friendlier to automation. What once seemed like a highly complex task to automate a process in Exchange Server 2003 has now been reduced to only a few lines of PowerShell script, taking mere minutes to write for Exchange Server 2013.

Another trend in recent years that is impossible to ignore is the introduction of cloud-based offerings. More and more companies today are catering to some form of cloud-based system or, at the extreme end, becoming entirely cloud-based. Examples include a private cloud managed by the IT department for different groups within a company; a host, such as Rackspace (http://www.rackspace.com), offering outsourced services to its customers; or a public cloud, such as Microsoft Office 365, offering a solution to customers worldwide.

The introduction of cloud-based platforms to your existing infrastructure may mean that you will operate a *hybrid deployment* where cloud and on-premises systems coexist. Having an efficient means of managing both systems seamlessly becomes even more important than when simply operating an on-premises solution only.

What does all this mean to Microsoft Exchange Server 2013? Microsoft design teams have anticipated the challenges and have incorporated features that help you manage Exchange more efficiently by allowing the potential for automation, empowerment of users, and seamless management of hybrid deployments from within a toolset made up of Exchange Administration Center (EAC) and Exchange Management Shell (EMS).

NOTE   While we will touch on EMS in this chapter, using it to demonstrate configuration steps, this is not a book on PowerShell. There are, however, many excellent PowerShell books out there. Some good examples include

Windows PowerShell in Action, Second Edition, by Bruce Payette (Manning Publications, 2011)

Microsoft Exchange 2010 PowerShell Cookbook, by Mike Pfeiffer (Packt Publishing, 2011)

Having established the trend toward automation of systems and unification of cloud-based and on-premises management in the world of managing enterprise systems, let's move on and examine the capabilities of Exchange. In particular, let's walk through and design a solution suitable for your environment or one of your customers' environments. We will start by looking at Role-Based Access Control (RBAC), which underpins access to Exchange. We will examine RBAC both as an administrator and a user.

Role-Based Access Control

The concept of *Role-Based Access Control (RBAC)* has been around for a long time. Different systems implement access controls in their own ways, but ultimately they all address a single goal: to provide an individual with only the specific access that they require to carry out their *roles* and no more.

RBAC Overview

When we look at the history of Exchange Server systems, the introduction of Exchange Server 2000 was a watershed event. It marked the time when Active Directory (AD) became a requirement and the separate directory used for Exchange 5.5 objects went away. As Exchange Server became reliant on Active Directory infrastructure, it also became dependent on access control lists (ACLs) containing access control entries (ACEs) to provide administrators with the access they needed to manage the Exchange environment.

As previously stated, around the turn of the millennium, systems were becoming more complex and distributed. If you were the only administrator in a small IT shop, then administering permissions was simple. You had permissions to everything! However, if you wanted to delegate permissions to someone to perform certain administrative tasks, the Exchange Administration Delegation Wizard was at your disposal. The wizard was designed to ease the painful process of understanding the required permissions, translating them to appropriate ACEs/ACLs, and implementing them in Active Directory. All you had to do was run the delegation wizard and select one of the available roles. Depending on the version of Exchange Server, you had anywhere from three (Exchange Server 2000 and Exchange Server 2003) to five (Exchange Server 2007) predefined management roles available, as shown in Table 6.1.

TABLE 6.1:   Roles available for delegation in early versions of Exchange Server

EXCHANGE SERVER VERSION	BUILT-IN MANAGEMENT ROLES
Exchange Server 2000 & Exchange Server 2003	Exchange Full Administrator
	Exchange Administrator
	Exchange View-Only Administrator
Exchange Server 2007	Exchange Organization Administrator
	Exchange Recipient Administrator
	Exchange View-Only Administrator
	Exchange Public Folder Administrator
	Exchange Server Administrator

Each of the roles that were predefined in Exchange Server 2000, 2003, and 2007 addressed certain job roles and provided prescribed configuration of permissions within Active Directory. While this was a good solution, it had its limits. It was constrained in such a way that if you ever wanted to provide permissions that were different from the preconfigured roles, you had to determine the corresponding Active Directory permissions and how to configure them properly so as not to break the existing functionality of the product. Since the product itself wasn't built to provide such granularity, it made it very challenging to implement the granular permissions required for job roles that didn't map to predefined roles.

Dependency on Active Directory also meant that auditing of access for compliance or forensic analysis wasn't easy. In larger environments, it required the coordinated efforts of different groups such as the messaging team, which was responsible for managing Exchange Servers, and the Active Directory team, which managed domain controllers and access-related functions. One's lack of expertise in another's domain created difficulty even in communicating the requirements properly, thus introducing further delays in getting to the end result.

As Exchange scaled to higher user counts and ever more distributed environments, these limitations had to be addressed. A completely different approach to managing permissions and auditing access was required. This had to be accomplished while retaining Active Directory integration, which had its own benefits, such as the single repository of security principles and application configuration data. The seeds of RBAC were thus planted.

Exchange Server 2010 initially implemented RBAC, departing from the old ways of Active Directory ACEs/ACLs and implementing something completely new. We will delve into RBAC architecture a bit later in this chapter. However, one question immediately comes to mind: Is dependency on Active Directory for ACEs/ACLs completely gone? The answer to that question is no. For now, however, let's press on.

Understanding the Components of the RBAC Permissions Model

The RBAC permissions model in Exchange Server 2010 and Exchange Server 2013 consists of three major concepts: Who, What, and Where. Figure 6.1 will help you visualize the RBAC permissions model:

FIGURE 6.1
The core concepts of the RBAC permission model

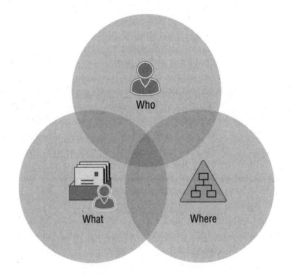

WHO

In technical terms, "Who" translates to the administrative users who are responsible for maintaining Exchange Server objects, such as server configuration, recipient objects, or end users who may be required to maintain their personal contact information. Compared with Exchange Server 2007 and earlier, while checking out the security permission on objects in Exchange Server 2010 or 2013, you may have noticed the inclusion of end-user permissions. While end-user permissions existed previously, there were no predefined roles in the delegation wizard. Neither was there a supported way for assigning permissions in Active Directory to allow users to carry out tasks such as editing their personal contact information. Solutions existed to implement such end-user permissions, but they weren't built into the product. It also wasn't easy to implement and maintain the product without investing in one or more third-party solutions. The Exchange RBAC model provides a simple method for assigning permissions and Exchange Server 2010/2013 tools, such as the Options section in Outlook Web App (OWA) (also known as Exchange Control Panel (ECP)), which allows users to perform pre-identified tasks that they are allowed to carry out easily. In RBAC terms, members of a role group, or role assignees (if permissions are directly assigned to a user instead of a group), represent the "Who" concept.

WHAT

The "What" concept translates to the objects or configuration steps that administrative users, or end users as identified in the previous section, should be able to manage, for example, an administrative user (who) is responsible for maintaining a mailbox database configuration (what). In RBAC terms, the collection of Exchange Management Shell cmdlets and parameters known as *management role entries* form predefined or custom *management roles*. These management roles define what the assignee is allowed to do. For administrators, they define which cmdlets and parameters will be available in the Exchange Management Shell or which tasks they will be able to carry out in the Exchange Administration Center. For end users, defined cmdlets and parameters are evident in the Exchange Control Panel in the form of fields that they can edit or tasks that they can perform, such as managing members of the distribution groups they own.

WHERE

The "Where" concept represents the scope of permissions that are assigned to an administrator or an end user. For example, a help desk administrator may be allowed to manage mailboxes of users located in the North America organizational unit (OU). The North America OU represents the location in this case. In RBAC terms, the scope of access where operations can be performed by administrators and end users is called the *management scope* or *management role scope*. There are two types of scopes: absolute and relative. An example of an *absolute scope* could be an OU or a set of users defined by a common attribute value such as Department = HR. A *relative scope* would be one where end users are only able to manage their own recipient object properties. Thus, the relative scope assigned to end-user permissions in RBAC is usually Self.

One additional RBAC component that isn't portrayed in the diagram is *management role assignments*. This component essentially ties the other three components together to make defined permissions effective. Until permissions and scopes are assigned to assignees (group or user), the permissions aren't effective.

As we progress throughout this chapter, you will have an opportunity to learn a bit more about each component of the RBAC model.

Planning Your Management Strategy

Wouldn't it be great if Exchange Server 2013 provided management roles and role groups that closely met the requirements of different administrative functions performed in your organization, such as administration, the help desk, or the legal department? While it is impossible for Microsoft to anticipate every possible scenario and to provide related management roles and other RBAC components out of the box, with Exchange Server 2013, Microsoft has done a great job in designing and creating 84 built-in management roles and 12 role groups that are available for immediate assignment.

Built-in management roles and role groups provide a starting point for an administrative strategy. The roles can be implemented as is or customized further to create roles and role groups that more closely map to your organization's requirements for secure access. After we briefly examine some of the built-in management roles and role groups, we will discuss how you can create new roles or customize existing roles to meet your requirements.

As made clear Chapter 1, "Business, Functional, and Technical Requirements," the most important thing that you must do before diving into the world of customizing the built-in management roles or creating new ones is to define your requirements. Failure to do so in most environments means using the default settings, which either provide more access than is required for a given administrative role or less access than is needed, hindering the ability of an administrator to accomplish the required task effectively.

One question that consistently arises is how to define the type of permission model required. In particular, how would an architect go about defining the required roles and permissions? Obviously, no single model fits all circumstances. To begin with, you need to look at the current roles and the responsibilities of those roles. Is your administrative model centralized? Do you have a group of administrators performing the same functions who back each other up? Do you have a decentralized IT model where each department admin is responsible for their location or region? Do you have a layered administration model where specialists manage a region and support local administrators while referring more serious issues to corporate IT personnel who might be in charge of the overall architecture and implementation?

Let's take the example of an office that has several hundred employees with three administrators responsible for managing the entire Exchange infrastructure. This might sound like a straightforward permissions model, with all three administrators being assigned the permissions that the Organization Management role group grants. This may appear on the surface to work well enough, but as you look beyond the administrators, you will realize that there may be support staff who don't necessarily perform Exchange management functions but who may need to verify recipient object status and other details before referring an issue to the Exchange administrators. In order to do so, they will need permissions. You may then find that the built-in Help Desk role provides more permissions than they need to perform their duties. At this point, even though it is a theoretically simple organization with minimal staff, you will begin to require a customized role for the support staff.

Taking things a step further, although this company has only a few hundred people, they are nevertheless producing intellectual property that requires the frequent involvement of legal advisors who also require access to mailbox search to ensure compliance. While again this might be a good case for using the built-in roles and role groups, you still need to investigate to see exactly what they need to do so that you don't risk granting them more access than they actually need. Ideally, this would be done in the planning phase before Exchange Server 2013 is deployed. If planning isn't done before deployment, the customization of role groups and role assignment may present challenges, such as communications to clarify changes and training to educate each group of employees who manage the Exchange environment. Changes made at a later stage in the deployment and operation phases can also present the danger of interruption to business.

Let's take another example of a large organization with worldwide offices and a layered IT administration model, where each group is responsible for tasks such as provisioning new users, managing backups, ensuring the health of the environment, and securing access. Each group may have separate duties that they perform while maintaining a common path of escalation for tackling complicated issues that they are unable to address on their own. While built-in roles and role groups may closely meet the requirements of a group, they might not have enough permissions, so a combination of roles may be required. The scope of the administrator's duties might be restricted to a particular area, which the built-in roles do not address, thereby providing more access than needed.

In summary, every environment is unique, so all need some form of requirements assessment regardless of their size. Without it, the environment may end up being implemented with a permissions model that does not meet the requirements and impedes administrators from performing their duties. Perhaps even worse, it may provide too much access, which could present a security risk.

Understanding Built-in Management Roles, Role Groups, and Role Association

Among the 12 built-in role groups, one of the most important is the Organization Management role group. It is not difficult to guess the amount of access a member of this role group is granted. As the name states, the members of this group are responsible for managing the entire Exchange organization and are granted access to almost but not all cmdlets and parameters that Exchange Server has to offer. There are certain management roles that are not granted even to the Organization Management role group members. The reasons for this include the need to secure data by blocking mailbox exports and discovery searches and blocking the ability to create unscoped top-level roles that can lead to administrators having too many permissions. Unscoped top-level roles are a complex area, and you need to understand the structure of RBAC better before we explain them. Therefore, we will discuss this topic fully later in this chapter.

In order to understand better exactly what Exchange and the Exchange Organization Management role group members in particular can do out of the box, it is useful to retrieve all of the existing roles and compare them to the roles assigned to the Organization Management role group. This is a pretty straightforward task in PowerShell. When run in Exchange Management Shell, the following command will return a list of all existing management roles, as shown Listing 6.1:

```
(Get-ManagementRole).Name | Sort
```

LISTING 6.1:   All existing management roles

```
(Get-ManagementRole).Name | Sort

Active Directory Permissions
Address Lists
ApplicationImpersonation
ArchiveApplication
Audit Logs
Cmdlet Extension Agents
Custom Mail Recipients
Data Loss Prevention
Database Availability Groups
Database Copies
Databases
```

Disaster Recovery
Distribution Groups
Edge Subscriptions
E-Mail Address Policies
Exchange Connectors
Exchange Server Certificates
Exchange Servers
Exchange Virtual Directories
Federated Sharing
Helpdesk Provisioning Script
Information Rights Management
Journaling
Legal Hold
LegalHoldApplication
Mail Enabled Public Folders
Mail Recipient Creation
Mail Recipients
Mail Tips
Mailbox Import Export
Mailbox Search
MailboxSearchApplication
Message Tracking
Migration
Monitoring
Move Mailboxes
My Custom Apps
My Marketplace Apps
MyAddressInformation
MyBaseOptions
MyContactInformation
MyDiagnostics
MyDisplayName
MyDistributionGroupMembership
MyDistributionGroups
MyMobileInformation
MyName
MyPersonalInformation
MyProfileInformation
MyRetentionPolicies
MyTeamMailboxes
MyTextMessaging
MyVoiceMail
OfficeExtensionApplication
Org Custom Apps
Org Marketplace Apps
Organization Client Access
Organization Configuration
Organization Transport Settings

LISTING 6.1:   All existing management roles *(CONTINUED)*

```
POP3 And IMAP4 Protocols
Public Folders
Receive Connectors
Recipient Policies
Remote and Accepted Domains
Reset Password
Retention Management
Role Management
Security Group Creation and Membership
Send Connectors
Support Diagnostics
Team Mailboxes
TeamMailboxLifecycleApplication
Transport Agents
Transport Hygiene
Transport Queues
Transport Rules
UM Mailboxes
UM Prompts
Unified Messaging
UnScoped Role Management
User Options
UserApplication
View-Only Audit Logs
View-Only Configuration
View-Only Recipients
WorkloadManagement
```

Next, run the following command, which will return all roles assigned to the Organization Management role group, as shown in Listing 6.2:

```
(Get-RoleGroup "organization management").Roleassignments | Get-ManagementRoleAssignment |
Where RoleAssignmentDelegationType -match "Regular" | sort role | ft role
```

LISTING 6.2:   Management roles assigned to the Organization Management role group

```
Get-RoleGroup "organization management").Roleassignments | Get-ManagementRoleAssignment |
Where RoleAssignmentDelegationType -match "Regular" | sort role | ft role

Role
----
Active Directory Permissions
Address Lists
Audit Logs
```

Cmdlet Extension Agents
Data Loss Prevention
Database Availability Groups
Database Copies
Databases
Disaster Recovery
Distribution Groups
Edge Subscriptions
E-Mail Address Policies
Exchange Connectors
Exchange Server Certificates
Exchange Servers
Exchange Virtual Directories
Federated Sharing
Information Rights Management
Journaling
Legal Hold
Mail Enabled Public Folders
Mail Recipient Creation
Mail Recipients
Mail Tips
Message Tracking
Migration
Monitoring
Move Mailboxes
Org Custom Apps
Org Marketplace Apps
Organization Client Access
Organization Configuration
Organization Transport Settings
POP3 And IMAP4 Protocols
Public Folders
Receive Connectors
Recipient Policies
Remote and Accepted Domains
Retention Management
Role Management
Security Group Creation and Membership
Send Connectors
Team Mailboxes
Transport Agents
Transport Hygiene
Transport Queues
Transport Rules
UM Mailboxes
UM Prompts
Unified Messaging
UnScoped Role Management
User Options

LISTING 6.2:   Management roles assigned to the Organization Management role group *(CONTINUED)*

```
View-Only Audit Logs
View-Only Configuration
View-Only Recipients
WorkloadManagement
```

When you compare the output of these two commands, you can see the roles that aren't assigned to the Organization Management role group members for their use.

Role Assignments

One thing that you may have noticed in the second command is the filter, which returns only roles that have the role assignment delegation type of Regular. This takes us right into discussing role assignments. Remember the component we discussed previously that connected all components together and made permissions effective? That component is called *role assignments*. The assignments are of two types: Regular and DelegatingOrgWide. The Regular assignments allow the assignee to have access to the Organization Management role entries, which are part of the assigned management role for purpose of execution. As an example, if a management role entry Get-Mailbox is part of the Mail Recipients management role, and an administrator is assigned access to that role using the Regular assignment, the administrator will be able to execute the Get-Mailbox cmdlet successfully from Exchange Management Shell.

Now let's assume for a moment that the assignment was of type DelegatingOrgWide instead. The administrator would not be able to execute the cmdlets that are part of the assigned management role. They will be able to create new Regular role assignments, however, that can allow other administrators in the organization to execute assigned cmdlets. These would be used to allow one administrator to set up delegation without actually being able to carry out the tasks they were delegating.

In summary, note the following about management roles and role groups:

♦   Multiple built-in management roles are created during the installation of Exchange Server 2013.

♦   Multiple role groups logically organize the multiple management roles into groups, which are also created during the installation of Exchange Server 2013.

♦   Members of each role group will be able to carry out the tasks allowed by assigned roles.

♦   Not all built-in roles are assigned to the Organization Management role group members using the Regular role assignment delegation type. There are several reasons for this, including prevention of accidental or intentional unauthorized access to mailbox data.

♦   While Organization Management role group members may not have access to all management roles to execute cmdlets, they can delegate them to others (including themselves) in the organization, enabling the tasks to be carried out by authorized administrators.

While you have seen all of the role groups in Listing 6.2, we will end this section by listing the default role groups. These include Compliance Management, Delegated Setup, Discovery Management, Help Desk, Hygiene Management, Organization Management, Public Folder Management, Recipient Management, Records Management, Server Management, UM Management, and View-Only Organization Management.

Under the Hood

Earlier we answered an important question about Active Directory dependency and ACEs/ACLs without going into any detail. Now that you understand the important components of RBAC, it is a good time to discuss how Exchange Server 2010 and Exchange Server 2013 achieve their granular permissions models without requiring Exchange or Active Directory administrators to delve into permissions on objects in Active Directory.

There are several ways this could be achieved. One possible solution might be that whenever an administrator customized any existing role or added new ones, Exchange made the necessary ACE/ACL changes in Active Directory. This would address the configuration aspect of the permissions problem, but auditing still requires a lot of work, since ACEs/ACLs are applied directly to the objects in Active Directory and thus need to be audited using Active Directory-related tools.

Another option is to create an Exchange System account in Active Directory and apply all of the necessary permissions that the Exchange System requires to this account. After the permissions are applied, Exchange can be coded to act as a gatekeeper and allow only authorized actions to be performed on Active Directory on behalf of the administrator. This option requires a tiered approach with at least two levels of permissions: one at Active Directory and the other at the Exchange layer. The benefit, however, is that the management of permissions can now be brought within the Exchange Server management boundary, making it possible for an Exchange administrator to assign granular permissions and allowing the auditing of Exchange Server-related actions performed by Exchange administrators.

As you might have guessed, the second approach has been implemented in Exchange Server 2010 and Exchange Server 2013. When Exchange setup is run, two important universal security groups are created in the Microsoft Exchange security group's OU. One is called *Exchange Trusted Subsystem* and the other is named *Exchange Windows Permissions*. All installed Exchange Server 2013 servers (and Exchange Server 2010 servers in mixed environments) are members of the Exchange Trusted Subsystem group. Exchange Trusted Subsystem is a member of the Exchange Windows Permissions group. Finally, the Exchange Windows Permissions group is assigned the required permissions on Active Directory objects so that Exchange Servers can make necessary changes such as adding new users, creating mailboxes for existing users, and so on. You might ask, "Why not just assign permissions directly to an Exchange Trusted Subsystem instead?" We don't apply permissions directly to an Exchange Trusted Subsystem, so that we have flexibility in splitting out permissions from Active Directory in order to allow Active Directory administrators to manage users and Exchange administrators to manage Exchange. We will return to this concept later in the chapter.

Now that you know how permissions are assigned in Active Directory, let's examine how they are applied on the Exchange side. Every time an administrator launches EAC or EMS, Exchange Server enumerates the role groups of which that administrator is a member. Next, it looks at all management role entries that are part of the assigned roles, and then it imports the permitted cmdlets and parameters into the shell session or enables the tasks in EAC. Since only permitted cmdlets are imported into the shell, the administrator cannot run cmdlets that are not assigned. They will only produce an error indicating that the cmdlet is not recognized. However, when an administrator issues permitted cmdlets, one more important check has to take place. While Exchange knows that the cmdlets are permitted based on role group membership, the object that the administrator is trying to create or modify may be out of the assigned scope. The check for management role scopes occurs before the changes are applied. If the administrative action passed all checks, the changes are then performed on behalf of the administrator by the Exchange Server account.

Active Directory permissions assigned to the Exchange Trusted Subsystem and checks performed by Exchange Server before implementing an administrative task make up the RBAC layers that prevent unauthorized actions while providing granular permissions assignments and auditing from within the Exchange Server management toolset.

Creating New Roles

As you learned earlier, Exchange Server 2013 provides multiple built-in management roles that serve as a starting point and that may also meet your requirements for administrative functions. However, if they don't meet your existing requirements, you can always create roles that do meet them.

When creating new roles, you must consider the following:

◆ *RBAC role assignments are cumulative.* If you assign multiple roles to an administrator, effective permissions are those that are most permissive of any of the assigned roles, not the most restrictive as some might assume.

◆ *With the exception of unscoped top-level roles, any new role created must use an existing role as a starting point.* This organizes two roles into a parent-child relationship. It is also possible to create a role based on a child role. In other words, the parent role doesn't have to be a built-in role. It can be another existing custom role. This could result in a grandparent-parent-child role relationship.

◆ *When a new role is created, it automatically inherits cmdlets and parameters from its parent role.* The customization can remove existing cmdlets or parameters, but it cannot add any cmdlets or parameters that did not exist in the parent role.

◆ *You can't edit built-in roles or roles that are parent roles to other custom roles.* There are no means to go in and amend any of the built-in roles or those that are parents to other custom roles. Instead, you need to use the built-in role as a template for a new custom role.

Armed with this information, you are now ready to create your first custom role. Let's assume that you want to create a role that closely matches the Mail Recipients management role. However, you do not want the administrator to be able to run disable-* cmdlets that are part of the built-in role. Since we know that built-in roles can't be changed, let's create a new role called Custom Mail Recipients. This is done using the following command:

```
New-ManagementRole -Name "Custom Mail Recipients" -Parent "Mail Recipients"
```

Now that we have a copy of the parent role, let's remove the cmdlets that we do not want administrators to be able to access using the following command:

```
Get-ManagementRoleEntry "Custom Mail Recipients\disable-*" | Remove-ManagementRoleEntry
```

At this point, we now have a customized role that, when assigned, will not allow administrators to run disable-* cmdlets.

Let's assume that, over time, the scope of the administrative function that manages mail recipients changes, and that it should now be able to disable mailboxes. We will need to add back in the corresponding cmdlet. Since the Disable-Mailbox cmdlet existed on role creation, it can then be added back in. Here's how to do this:

```
Add-ManagementRoleEntry "Custom Mail Recipients\Disable-Mailbox"
```

Here now is the level of granularity that you can achieve using the Exchange RBAC permissions model. Let's assume that, for your customized role, you want to allow all cmdlets that it includes, but you do not want to allow the –Arbitration parameter, which is part of the Disable-Mailbox cmdlet, to be used by administrators who are assigned the Custom Mail Recipients role. You can remove this particular parameter from the role as follows:

```
Set-ManagementRoleEntry "Custom Mail Recipients\Disable-Mailbox" -Parameters Arbitration -
RemoveParameter
```

Let's assume that you have multiple groups of administrators responsible for the same function that will be achieved by the role we just created. However, they are responsible for users in different locations; that is, West administrators should only be able to manage mail recipients in an OU called West. In this instance, you do not need to create multiple custom roles. The same custom role can be assigned to different role groups using different scopes limiting administrators to their boundaries.

Creating New Management Scopes

Let's continue building on what we have achieved so far. Now that we have our custom role, we need to create a scope to limit its use to users in the West OU. The administrators who will be assigned the Custom Mail Recipients role we created previously are responsible for mail recipient objects that are located in an OU called West. They should not be able to manage objects outside of the given OU. To achieve this goal, we will need to create a scope using the following command:

```
New-ManagementScope -Name "West Recipient Administrators" -RecipientRoot "exchange-d3.com/
West" -RecipientRestrictionFilter {RecipientType -eq "*"}
```

Using this command, we created a scope called West RecipientAdministrators, which restricts assigned administrators to the West OU in the exchange-d3.com domain, while no restriction is applied to recipient types.

There are other ways that you can create management scopes. Valid options include the following:

ServerRestrictionFilter   The scope applies only to the servers that match the specified filter.

ServerList   The scope applies only to the servers specified in the list. (Note: Server name isn't checked for errors.)

DatabaseRestrictionFilter   The scope applies only to the databases that match the specified filter.

DatabaseList   The scope applies only to the databases specified in the list.

Exclusive   As the name implies, only administrators who are explicitly assigned exclusive scopes can manage the objects protected by exclusive scopes. After exclusive scopes are created and before administrators are explicitly assigned the exclusive scopes, the objects protected by exclusive scopes cannot be managed by any administrator, including Organization Management role group members.

If you want to find out more about these scopes, then take a look at this URL, which is a handy reference for understanding and setting up the scopes we just discussed:

```
http://technet.microsoft.com/en-us/library/dd335146.aspx
```

Creating and Managing Role Groups

A *role group* essentially represents a group of users who are responsible for performing similar functions in managing your Exchange configuration. They could, for example, be help desk administrators, legal discovery officers, a delegated server setup person, or recipient management experts. As you learned earlier, Exchange setup creates 12 role groups. An Exchange administrator can always add more as needed. Role groups are created in Active Directory as Universal Security groups, and they are located in the Microsoft Exchange Security Groups OU.

The function of creating and managing role groups can be compared to managing security groups in Active Directory. Using Exchange cmdlets or management tools, you perform this function from the familiar EMS or EAC interface, eliminating the need to depend on Active Directory management tools and, at the same time, gaining the ability to audit administrative actions that are related to Exchange Server. If you were to manage those security groups directly from Active Directory management tools, Exchange would not be notified and administrative actions would not be logged, thereby requiring a reliance on the Active Directory logging infrastructure and tools to satisfy audit requirements and reporting.

So how do you go about creating a role group? Previously, we created a scope called West Recipient Administrators. Continuing to build on that scenario, we now need to create a group that represents recipient administrators who will be assigned the custom role we created for their respective scope. Let's call the role group West Recipient Admins. Creating the role group is a simple step:

```
New-RoleGroup "West Recipient Admins"
```

Observe the output, and you will notice that there are no roles assigned by default. The role group certainly doesn't have any members yet either. Also notice the managed by attribute, which is populated automatically and assigns the Organization Management group as manager of the new role group. This allows for future management of group membership by all organizational administrators.

Let's assume that we have a user called User1 who will be responsible for managing recipient objects in the West OU using the new role we created. Let's add User1 to the role group we just created:

```
Add-RoleGroupMember "West Recipient Admins" -Member User1
```

To remove a member from the role group, simply execute the Remove-RoleGroupMember cmdlet with appropriate parameters.

Creating New Role Assignments

The function of *role assignments* is to create a bond between a management role, a role group or a user, and a management scope. When these elements are combined, the permissions are made effective for assignees, whether it is a single user for direct assignment or a group of users who are members of a role group.

Earlier, we created a role named Custom Mail Recipients and a scope called West Recipients. We also created a role group for administrators responsible for managing West Recipients called West Recipient Admins. To close the loop and make the permissions effective, let's create the necessary role assignment using the following command:

```
New-ManagementRoleAssignment -Name "West Recipients-West Recipient Admins" -Role "Custom
Mail Recipients" -CustomRecipientWriteScope "West Recipients" -SecurityGroup "West
Recipient Admins"
```

By executing the preceding command, we have made the permissions effective. User1, who is a member of the role group, will now be able to execute cmdlets that are part of the custom role we created, within the specified scope.

There are several things to note before completing our discussion of role assignments:

- There are two types of write scopes: Recipient and Config.

    - *Recipient write scopes* are used when you want to manage objects stored in the Active Directory domain partition, and they usually represent security principles, such as a user or a group.

    - *Config write scopes* apply to configuration objects, such as database configuration or organization settings for transport. These are the objects stored in the configuration partition of Active Directory.

- The `RecipientOrganizationalUnitWriteScope` parameter allows us to define a scope that applies to a particular OU. In our current example, we have chosen not to use it so that we can demonstrate how scopes can be created, but we could have used this option instead. An example of this would look similar to the following command where `exchange-d3.com` is the domain where the OU named West is located, and it contains recipients that are in the intended scope:

    ```
    New-ManagementRoleAssignment -Name "West Recipients-West Recipient Admins" -Role "Custom
    Mail Recipients" -RecipientOrganizationalUnitScope " exchange-d3.com/West"
    -SecurityGroup "West Recipient Admins"
    ```

- Notice that there is no read scope parameter for this cmdlet. You can create scopes for restricting how Exchange objects can be manipulated, but currently there is no way to restrict read scope. It is always allowed for the entire organization, and it can be controlled using the `Set-ADServerSettings` cmdlet if the environment consists of multiple domains in a forest.

- When creating role assignments, if no scope is specified, the scope is inherited from the role being assigned. For built-in roles, the recipient write scope is always Organization and the configuration write scope is always OrganizationConfig. This information becomes very handy when troubleshooting RBAC-related issues.

- While you can assign scopes to role assignments, you cannot assign scopes to new management roles. Thus, any new management roles you create also have implicit write scopes of Organization and OrganizationConfig for recipient and configuration objects, respectively.

- If you are assigning an exclusive scope, you must specify the `–exclusiverecipientwritescope` or `–exclusiveconfigwritescope` parameter.

- If you are assigning an unscoped top-level role, you must use the `–UnScopedTopLevel` parameter.

- You can create multiple role assignments using the same role group. As discussed earlier, RBAC permissions are cumulative; so multiple role assignments will allow assignees to perform different functions as defined by the different roles that are assigned.

- While similar in concept, role assignment policies differ from role assignments in the way that they are used for assigning permissions to users, while scoping is relative, for example, Self. Role assignment policies can be assigned on a per-mailbox basis.

If you create a new role group and use the `-Roles` parameter, it will automatically create the required role assignments for you. This step is transparent, so bear in mind that you don't need to create role assignments manually afterward.

Understanding Role Assignment Policies

RBAC is designed to allow the delegation of frequently performed tasks to administrators or end users as required. Previously we discussed how to assign administrator permissions using roles, scopes, and assignments. But how do you assign permissions to users? How do you allow users to perform tasks such as changing their phone numbers? How do you delegate to them the ability to manage their distribution groups?

Delegation of permissions to the end user is managed by role assignment policies. The *Default Role Assignment Policy* is created during the installation of Exchange Server 2013. If you were operating in a coexistence environment using Exchange Server 2010, the policy is likely to have been in place since its installation.

The goal of the Default Role Assignment Policy is to give the end user the ability to perform basic self-service functions right out of the box. Following are some of the roles that are assigned to the Default Role Assignment Policy:

MyContactInformation   This role enables individual users to modify their contact information, including their street address and phone numbers.

MyDistributionGroupMembership   This role enables individual users to view and modify their membership in distribution groups in an organization.

MyBaseOptions   This role enables individual users to view and modify the basic configuration of their own mailbox and associated settings, such as Inbox rules.

Figure 6.2 depicts the relationships of the role assignment policy components:

FIGURE 6.2
Relationships of
role assignment
policy components

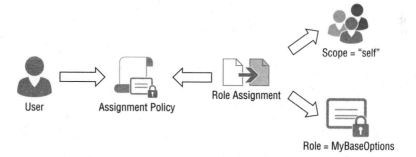

The roles just mentioned, as well as the other roles that allow administrators to delegate self-service tasks to users, are assigned in an assignment policy using the relative write scope of Self. The user mailboxes are then assigned to an assignment policy using the `set-mailbox` cmdlet. When a mailbox is created, it is automatically assigned the default policy. If you create a new policy and want it to be the default going forward, you need to specify the parameter `-IsDefault` when using the `New-RoleAssignmentPolicy` cmdlet. If you want the new policy to be assigned to existing mailboxes, you need to use the `Set-Mailbox` cmdlet and specify the `-RoleAssignmentPolicy` parameter.

Let's assume that the built-in Default Role Assignment Policy is assigned to all mailboxes in the organization, and you have just created new role assignment policy using the following cmdlet:

```
New-RoleAssignmentPolicy "Custom Role Assignment Policy" -Roles MyBaseOptions,MyDistributio
nGroups -IsDefault
```

This example uses only two roles; however, more roles can be added as required during creation. Since you used the -IsDefault parameter, the policy will be applied to all new mailboxes that are generated after the creation of the policy. However, it will not be applied to mailboxes that were made before the new policy was created and set as default. To apply the newly created policy to existing mailboxes, you must run the Set-Mailbox cmdlet, as shown here:

```
Set-Mailbox administrator -RoleAssignmentPolicy "Custom Role Assignment Policy"
```

This example applies the newly created policy only to a specified mailbox. If the same policy needs to be applied to all existing mailboxes, it can be achieved by running the following cmdlet:

```
Get-Mailbox | Set-Mailbox -RoleAssignmentPolicy "Custom Role Assignment Policy"
```

Care must be taken when running this cmdlet because this affects all mailboxes in the organization, and it can have disastrous effects if a wrong policy is assigned.

Role assignment policies can also be managed and created from EAC. Figure 6.3 shows the User Roles section of EAC and the Default Role Assignment Policy.

FIGURE 6.3
The Default Role Assignment Policy in EAC

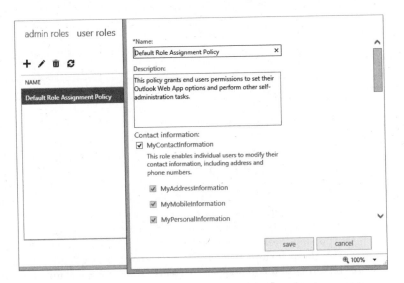

While you are in EAC, note the similarities between the Admin Roles and User Roles sections, which allow you to create, edit, and delete role groups (in the Admin Roles tab) or role assignment policies (in the User Roles tab).

In summary, role assignments are used to assign roles to role groups that allow administrative users to manage recipient or configuration objects, whereas role assignment policies are used to assign self-service abilities to end users.

Figure 6.4 helps you visualize all of the components of RBAC discussed so far, and it helps you to understand how each component relates to one another:

FIGURE 6.4
RBAC component interaction

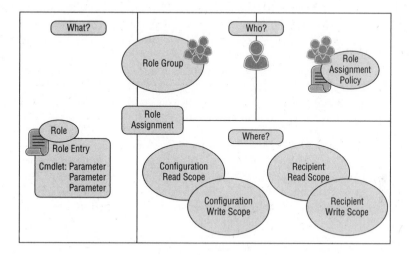

Applying Business Logic Using Unscoped Top-Level Roles

Next, we need to address unscoped top-level roles in depth. What's so special about them?

Let's look at the scenario where you need to grant access to non-Exchange cmdlets such as storage provider cmdlets provided by a PowerShell module from a vendor or a custom script that addresses business workflows related to your messaging environment.

Earlier we discussed creating custom roles. They had one important requirement: They must use a built-in role as a parent, hence inheriting cmdlets that are part of the parent role. Built-in roles are created for managing an Exchange environment, and therefore you wouldn't expect them to provide cmdlets for anything else. Given the understanding that business requirements or custom workflows may necessitate the ability to execute non-Exchange cmdlets from within EMS, what can you do? This is where unscoped top-level roles come in.

Think of unscoped top-level roles as empty containers. These containers can contain cmdlets from any PowerShell modules except for Exchange cmdlets. They can also contain custom PowerShell scripts. You can write scripts that contain Exchange cmdlets and assign them to unscoped top-level roles, but you cannot assign those cmdlets directly.

Since these are top-level roles, they cannot be scoped. If you interrogate an unscoped top-level role, you will notice that RoleType is UnScoped, and all read and write scopes are set to a value of NotApplicable.

Unscoped top-level roles are considered very powerful, and they can be detrimental to your environment if not implemented carefully. For this reason, even Organization Management group members do not have the ability to create unscoped top-level roles out of the box.

So how can you create unscoped top-level roles? The first step is to assign the required permissions to create them. Assigning the Unscoped Role Management role to a new role group or an existing role group does this. Let's assume that we want Organization Management group members to be able to create unscoped top-level roles. The following cmdlet syntax will help us get there:

```
New-ManagementRoleAssignment "Unscoped Role Management-Organization Management" -Role
"Unscoped Role Management" -SecurityGroup "Organization Management"
```

For the changes to be effective, you must open a new Exchange Management Shell session. After you do, you will be able to create new unscoped top-level roles.

Now let's walk through a scenario of a simple business requirement—that any new mailbox created in the environment must be created on a predefined provisioning database, and it must be assigned certain parameter values based on business-defined criteria. Let's assume that you have created a script and named it `Create-CustomMailbox.ps1`.

At this point, you have a couple of options. You could distribute this script to everyone who is responsible for creating new mailboxes in the environment. You would then need to assign all of the cmdlets you have used in the script to the administrators who will run the script. The administrators could then use the script itself, or instead they could decide to take matters into their own hands and attempt to perform manually any of the steps that script is supposed to accomplish using the cmdlets that you have assigned to them. As you can see, the situation has the potential to spiral out of control quickly.

Instead, the preferred solution is to create an unscoped top-level role and assign the role to administrators. This has several benefits:

◆ The script is never distributed. Instead, it must be copied to all Exchange Servers in the organization to which administrators can connect. The script must be copied to the `C:\Program Files\Microsoft\Exchange Server\V15\RemoteScripts` folder (substitute your installation path). The location is not shared and, since it is never distributed, administrators who are granted access to it cannot see its contents unless they also have access to the Exchange Servers and the script location.

◆ Another benefit of assigning the script to an unscoped top-level role is that you don't need to assign the Exchange cmdlets that are used within the script to administrators. Administrators can execute the script, but they can't execute the cmdlets directly. If you ever need to update the script, you know exactly how many copies you need to update and where they are located, unlike in the previous scenario where the distributed scripts could be located on any number of administrators' laptops, file shares, or other places beyond your knowledge or control.

Knowing all of the benefits of unscoped top-level roles, we're ready to create one for our imaginary script mentioned previously. The commands may seem familiar, but there are small differences about which you need to be aware. Start with the following command:

```
New-ManagementRole "Custom Mailbox Provisioning Script" -UnScopedTopLevel
```

What we have just done is to create an empty container. At this point, no role entry has been created, and that's exactly what we will do next:

```
Add-ManagementRoleEntry "Custom Mailbox Provisioning Script\Create-CustomMailbox.ps1"
-Parameters Name -UnScopedTopLevel
```

Notice the use of parameters. You can create a script that uses many more parameters. You must define all parameters here. In this example, there is only one parameter that we are allowing administrators to use with the script called Name. All that is left to do at this point is to assign the new role to a new role group or an existing role group. Here's how you can assign it to a new role group called Mailbox Provisioning:

```
New-RoleGroup -Name "Mailbox Provisioning" -Roles "Custom Mailbox Provisioning Script"
```

As we mentioned earlier, unscoped top-level roles provide flexibility and open up powerful possibilities. At the same time, they can open the door to disastrous results if, for example, your script contains harmful errors. Remember the scope? There is none. If the script isn't enforcing the required scoping and you set the script parameters to allow administrators flexibility, the results can be unforeseen and sometimes adverse. Once again, careful planning is a requirement and must be emphasized before recommending the use of unscoped top-level roles in any environment.

Reporting Effective Permissions and Cmdlet Usage

We have worked our way through the many ways of assigning permissions to users and administrators. Now we need to figure out how to report effectively who has which permissions, what objects they can manipulate, and, ideally, how to report historical usage for auditing or forensic purposes.

The starting point for this topic is the Get-ManagementAssignment cmdlet, which provides a very powerful parameter: –GetEffectiveUsers. When it's combined with another parameter, –WriteableRecipient, you can easily report who has access to a particular writeable object. Let's examine an example: You need to report on who has the ability to manipulate a mailbox named NDA Information. In this context, *manipulate* means the ability to move a mailbox, change quota, enable or disable a mailbox, and other such tasks that can be performed using Exchange cmdlets. The mailbox NDA Information is our writeable recipient. The command to report effective access looks like the following:

```
Get-ManagementRoleAssignment -WriteableRecipient "NDA Information" -GetEffectiveUsers
```

Let's take a look at another example. This time, we want to examine who has the ability to run the Remove-Mailbox cmdlet. This will be a multistep discovery process. First, you'll need to find all of the roles that contain the role entry Remove-Mailbox. Then you need to find all role assignments created for those given roles that negate delegating assignments, which don't grant execute access to assignees. The next step is to extract the effective users or role groups who are granted access.

With a little creativity and use of the PowerShell pipeline, you can easily combine multiple get-* cmdlets to report affected users quickly:

```
Get-ManagementRoleEntry "*\Remove-Mailbox" | foreach {Get-ManagementRoleAssignment -Role
$_.role -GetEffectiveUsers -Delegating:$false} | select effectiveusername -Unique
```

The issue that needs to be addressed is discovery after something has happened. An example might be, "Who deleted mailbox *x*?" Or "What was the last change made by administrator *y*?"

Exchange Server 2013 has implemented an auditing framework that addresses this effectively. The feature is called *admin audit logging*. It is turned on in Exchange Server 2013 by default. The logs are stored in a hidden system mailbox for 90 days. To understand the use of admin audit logging, we must look at the different types of cmdlets. There are cmdlets that only read information, for example, Get-*. Then there are cmdlets that actually manipulate objects, such as Set-* cmdlets. Another category is Test-* cmdlets. Not all of these cmdlets are important for logging. If you were to log Test-* cmdlets that are often used for monitoring the environment's health, it would clutter the audit log. Being configurable, the Admin Audit Log allows administrators to specify which cmdlets to log. The default settings log all cmdlets except Test-*and Get-*, thus tracking when someone makes a change. Using the Set-AdminAuditLogConfig cmdlet, an administrator can change the defaults and define specific cmdlets or parameters that need to be audited. Changes to the audit log configuration are always logged even when admin audit logging is turned off, which makes it very hard for administrators to cover their tracks!

So how is this auditing process actually implemented? It is done using a form of cmdlet extension agent called the *Admin Audit Log agent*. Every time a cmdlet is run, this agent is also run and, depending on the cmdlet, a log entry is generated. This agent is a system agent, which will prevent it from being disabled using the Disable-CmdletExtensionAgent cmdlet. The agent runs at the highest priority of 255, thus preventing any other agents from running at a higher priority and manipulating the audit process.

Once we have all of this audited information, we need a way to read the logs. There are two distinct ways of searching Admin Audit Logs from EMS:

Search-AdminAuditLog   This cmdlet produces search results and returns output to the screen, allowing for immediate analysis of results.

New-AdminAuditLogSearch   This cmdlet runs the search and returns results of the Admin Audit Log search to a specified mailbox. This can be very useful for searches that span longer periods and may take a long time to run before returning results.

Of course, there is also a GUI to enable access to the Admin Audit Logs. The Auditing tab can be accessed from the Compliance Management section of EAC. Figure 6.5 shows an example that will export all audited admin actions for the month of October 2014, and it will send the audit report to the Administrator mailbox.

FIGURE 6.5
The Admin Audit
Log being accessed
through EAC

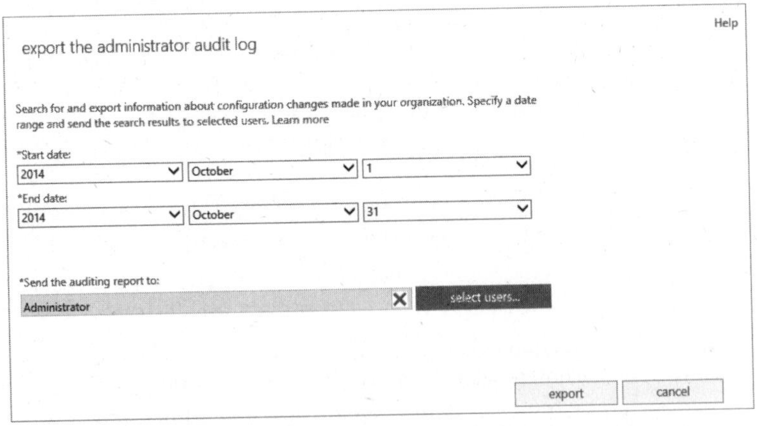

Help

export the administrator audit log

Search for and export information about configuration changes made in your organization. Specify a date range and send the search results to selected users. Learn more

*Start date:
| 2014 | October | 1 |

*End date:
| 2014 | October | 31 |

*Send the auditing report to:
| Administrator | X | select users... |

export   cancel

Understanding Split Permissions

There is one more aspect of permissions that we need to cover before moving onto the administrative tools of Exchange 2013. Out of the box, Exchange Server 2013 uses a *shared permissions model*. As an Exchange administrator, you are not only able to manage Exchange attributes of objects that reside in Active Directory, but you may also create security principles such as users and groups.

There are two built-in management roles that make this possible. One is called Mail Recipient Creation and the other is known as Security Group Creation and Membership. The Mail Recipient Creation role is assigned to the Organization Management role group as well as the Recipient Management role group. Members of these groups are able to create new users in order to create new mailboxes in an Exchange environment. The Security Group Creation and Membership role is only assigned to the Organization Management role group by default. This role allows Organization Management group members to create security groups and manage their membership by adding or removing members of the security groups. It is important to remember what we discussed earlier in the "Under the Hood" section. Each action taken using Exchange management tools is evaluated by RBAC and checked against permissions assigned to the user within the Exchange RBAC permissions model. If a user is an enterprise administrator in Active Directory but isn't assigned any permissions in RBAC, the user won't be able to create a user or security group using Exchange management tools, regardless of their permissions outside the scope of the Exchange Management framework.

The shared permissions model makes it very convenient for Exchange administrators to create and manage security principles in order to create new mailboxes and accomplish other Exchange-related tasks that depend on security principles. This also reduces dependency on Active Directory administrators when creation of security principles is required, and it allows for quick turnaround when necessary. Organizations that require a separation of duties to meet security requirements, often required to meet compliance standards to which the organization may be subjected, need a way to disallow shared permissions since they go against the requirement of separation of duties. In such organizations, splitting the permissions required to create security principles and those required to manage their Exchange-related attributes is a requirement that must be addressed.

Two Possible Models for Split Permissions

Exchange Server 2013 offers two possible means for creating this separation. The first is called *RBAC split permissions*. In this model, the separation of roles is achieved through the decoupling of the Mail Recipient Creation and Security Group Creation and Membership roles from the Organization Management role group and any other role groups that are not responsible for the creation of security principles in Active Directory. This is simply a matter of removing management role assignments from role groups. The roles are then assigned using new role assignments to the role groups that are responsible for managing the creation of security principles in Active Directory. Splitting permissions using this model allows for the use of Exchange management tools, such as EMS and EAC, to create users and security groups in Active Directory. While domain and enterprise administrators can always use Active Directory management tools to create and manage users and security groups, using this model offers flexibility and choice of tools.

Another possible way of achieving separation of duties is to implement the Active Directory split permissions model. In this model, the separation is achieved by decoupling permissions at the Active Directory level. The Exchange Trusted Subsystem group is not given any permissions to create users and security groups in Active Directory. Given that this is the group that underpins RBAC operations, it means that RBAC cannot be used to delegate permissions to create security principles in Active Directory. Creation of security principles is only possible using the Active Directory management tools, such as the Active Directory Users and Computers tool.

DECIDING BETWEEN THE TWO MODELS FOR SPLIT PERMISSIONS

There are many factors that must be considered in order to decide which split permissions model is appropriate for your organization. One of the considerations surrounds the specification of which management tools must be used to manage security principles.

- ◆ Are administrators allowed to use any tool at their disposal to create security principles? If the answer to this question is yes, the RBAC split permissions model works since it achieves the separation while offering the flexibility of tools that administrators can use.

- ◆ Are there any Exchange-related applications whose functionality relies on the creation of security principles? If yes, using the Active Directory split permissions model may break this functionality and could affect the performance and stability of such applications.

- ◆ Does your organization allow creation of security principles by services or applications? Some applications create security principles and depend on the RBAC permissions assigned to them.

- ◆ Do you want Exchange administrators to be able to manage the creation of role groups and management of membership of those groups? Split permissions don't allow such actions.

Answers to questions such as these, and whether your security requirements permit such actions, can help you choose the appropriate split permissions model.

If you decide to implement the Active Directory split permissions model, it becomes very important for you to understand that Exchange administrators will not only be prohibited from creating users and security groups, but they will also be barred from creating role groups, since they are security groups, and of course, they are blocked from managing the membership of role groups. This significantly increases the reliance on Active Directory administrators when creation and management of users and security groups are required. Flexibility is traded off in order to achieve separation.

Unlike the RBAC split permissions model, the Active Directory split permissions model achieves separation of duties by implementing permissions in the form of ACEs on Active Directory objects. Earlier, we discussed that during Exchange setup, the Exchange Windows Permissions group is granted the ability to create and manage users and security groups in Active Directory. The Exchange Trusted Subsystem group is created and added as a member of the Windows Permissions group. An important question that we didn't answer earlier was, "Why not just provide permissions to the Exchange Trusted Subsystem group directly?" As you can tell by now, it would make implementing Active Directory split permissions difficult if permissions were assigned directly. With the Exchange Windows Permissions group in place, implementing the Active Directory split permissions model becomes a simpler process.

IMPLEMENTING SPLIT PERMISSIONS

So how do you actually implement the Active Directory split permissions model? This can be done during Exchange setup using the Exchange Setup Wizard (which offers you an option to implement Active Directory split permissions) or using `setup.exe` from the command line with the parameters we'll specify shortly. If you did not implement Active Directory split permissions during Exchange setup, you can run `setup.exe` again with the `/PrepareAD` and `/ActiveDirectorySplitPermissions:true` parameters.

When setup is run with these parameters, changes are made in Active Directory. One of the changes is the creation of the Microsoft Exchange Protected Groups OU. It will become home to the Exchange Windows Permissions group when Active Directory split permissions are implemented. The Exchange Trusted Subsystem, which is usually a member of the Exchange Windows Permissions group, is removed from its membership.

Another important change takes place in RBAC role assignments. The regular role assignments that assigned the Mail Recipients and Security Group Creation and Membership roles are removed. Yet another important change that takes place is that the permissions assigned to the Exchange Windows Permissions group on the Active Directory domain object are removed. If the Active Directory forest contains multiple child domains, you must also prepare all of the domains either using the `/preparealldomains` or `/preparedomain` switches of Exchange setup. This is required to implement the necessary permissions changes across all domains.

While implementing Active Directory split permissions may seem like a relatively simple process, it requires careful consideration of your management model, third-party application dependencies, and flexibility in the use of management tools. It is also important to understand that, while split permissions can be achieved using Exchange 2013 setup, if you are in a coexistence environment with Exchange Server 2010 in place, the split also applies to Exchange Server 2010. Since RBAC wasn't implemented before Exchange Server 2010, Active Directory or RBAC split models aren't applicable to Exchange Server 2007.

Using EAC to Manage RBAC

Before we conclude the RBAC section of this chapter, we need to make sure that you understood that you are not limited to the use of EMS to manage RBAC. While EAC doesn't offer as much flexibility as EMS, it allows you to perform several RBAC tasks. Figure 6.6 shows the Permissions section of EAC. We have selected the Admin Roles tab, which shows the role groups that exist in the organization, including the built-in roles and any custom roles you may have created.

The Admin Roles section allows you to create new role groups, edit existing role groups, and remove role groups that are no longer in use. Creating a new role group is as easy as clicking the plus sign. Figure 6.7 shows the interface used when creating a new role group.

As you may have noticed, the interface is simple and straightforward. It allows you to select default and custom scopes, organizational unit scope, built-in or custom roles, and ultimately the members who will be part of this role group. The action is akin to using the `New-RoleGroup` cmdlet with appropriate parameters.

The interface to edit existing role groups is the same as shown in Figure 6.7. Modification of a role group may include changing the write scope, adding or removing management roles, and adding or removing group members.

Unfortunately, the EAC interface does not allow for the creation of management roles, the creation of management role scopes, or the customization of roles at this time. For those tasks, you must head back to EMS, as described throughout this chapter.

FIGURE 6.6
EAC Permissions
—Admin Roles

FIGURE 6.7
EAC Admin Roles—
New Role Group

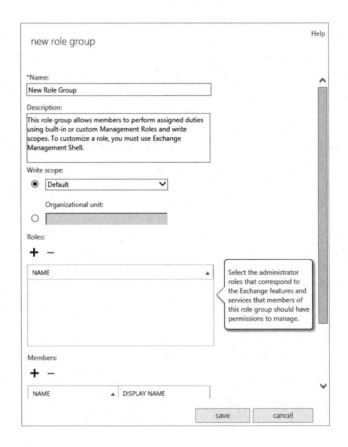

Administration

Earlier we discussed trends in management platforms and how advancements in technology and the introduction of cloud-based offerings affect what an administrator has come to expect from administrative tools today. The tools not only need to be more advanced to keep pace with today's technology, but they also have to have the ability to offer flexibility in tomorrow's environments. For example, tools need to provide only the functionality required by each administrator, making common tasks easy to carry out, while not hiding less frequently used components. Finally, with the growth of cloud-based systems, we expect a unification of management tools that enable both on-premises and online systems to be managed as one. With this goal in mind, we will now examine the Exchange administrative tools to see how they live up to these expectations.

 Real World Scenario

A View from the Product Group: Designing an Exchange Admin Center for On-Premises, Online, and Hybrid Environments

Over the last 15 years, Microsoft Exchange Server has undergone extraordinary growth from a small departmental mail system to the global mail server, calendaring, and contact management standard it is now. This growth was fuelled as email became a business-critical application. It is therefore not surprising that the Exchange management surface (the access and space where we manage Exchange) has developed massively over the same time period as it strives to meet customer demand for increased visibility of systems and granularity of control.

Of course, this rapid growth and development have not always resulted in a perfect administrative experience. Prior to Exchange 2010, the management experience was relatively simple—IT generalists who preferred a GUI-based experience relied on the single Exchange graphical management interface, while IT specialists who were more scripting savvy and who required tools to automate management or make bulk updates made use of the Exchange Management Shell. The choice was obvious.

With the release of Exchange 2010 and the introduction of the Exchange Online Service, Microsoft shipped another GUI-based management console called the *Exchange Control Panel* (ECP). The Exchange Control Panel was intended for tenant administrators to manage their organization and as an administrative method for users on the Exchange Online Service for Exchange 2010 running in hosted mode. (Hosted mode functionality is now deprecated.) Note that a *tenant* is the subdivision of the Microsoft public cloud within which an organization sits. It was designed from the ground up for the Web. For those early adopters of the Exchange Online Service, management was greatly simplified. Tenant administrators no longer had to worry about keeping servers up and running or maintaining database health, which meant that the management surface exposed in ECP focused primarily on managing online users.

Interestingly, some of the newer features introduced in Exchange 2010 on-premises, such as Auditing, eDiscovery, RBAC management, Group Naming Policy, and ActiveSync Quarantined Device management, could only be managed in ECP. This meant that in Exchange 2010, administrators had three ways to manage Exchange: the Exchange Management Console (EMC), the Exchange Control Panel (ECP), and the Exchange Management Shell (EMS).

continues

(continued)

As the Exchange Online Service has gained momentum and credibility, moving from versions based first on Exchange 2007, then on Exchange 2010, and now on Exchange 2013, more and more customers have started to use Microsoft Exchange Online, as witnessed by the launch of Office 365. This increase in usage and corresponding product group focus led to the discovery that there are many management scenarios that are applicable to both on-premises deployment and the online service.

Unfortunately, on-premises Exchange administrators who predominantly used EMC discovered that going online meant learning a whole new management tool. Worse yet, while seeing the business benefit of moving a part of the organization to the cloud, many organizations continued to require a part of the system to be on-premises. Those administrators were forced to learn multiple tools and to juggle between them. It was therefore critical that Exchange 2013 provided one management tool that provided a seamless, integrated way to manage all of Exchange, be it on-premises, online, or hybrid environments.

THE UNIFIED CONSOLE IS WEB BASED

EMC was based on MMC technology and remote PowerShell. These multiple dependency stacks were required before EMC could be fully functional. Large amounts of support data indicated that there was significant IT overhead with respect to the installation and updating of a client-based solution, and this led to increased costs and prolonged problem resolution. This consideration greatly influenced the decision of the product group to go with a web-based console. Additionally, with a standards-based web protocol, EAC can be accessed from anywhere a desktop computer is available. It even runs reasonably well, though not optimized for touch, on a tablet device.

The design of EAC adopts some of the key tenets of the Windows 8 style with a clean and simplified look and intuitive information organization. While the look and feel is refreshed, EAC's underlining technology stack, virtual directory, and protocol remain the same as for ECP. We opted to retain the name of the virtual directory/protocol as /ecp to avoid unnecessary changes to any customer's automation scripts that manage the virtual directory.

The design of the UI organization of EAC is based on large amounts of user research. Making the information intuitive and easy to find is the primary design goal. Based on their natural affinity, related features are organized into feature groups. For example, we prominently placed Resource Mailbox into its own feature tab called Resources, and we also created a Shared Mailbox management GUI for the first time under the Recipients feature group.

In every list view, a details pane is added to the right-hand side of the main list view. It displays the most frequently used attributes of the object selected, and it contains links to perform the most appropriate actions on that object. The attributes and actions are carefully chosen based on the type of the object being displayed. This UI design minimizes the user's need to click further on the object's property page to view a particular attribute. Users don't need to navigate off the view to perform a task directly applicable to the object, which might cause them to lose the original context. The design focuses on supporting administrators to allow them to get more done with less effort and time. In order to optimize performance, the details pane is loaded asynchronously.

As a matter of fact, performance was a big design consideration throughout EAC development. Underneath the EAC/ECP stack is local PowerShell rather than remote PowerShell. This directly contributes to significant performance improvement in overall UI responsiveness. For large organizations, rendering a list view with thousands of objects could take minutes or more, especially when the value of an attribute must be queried from individual Exchange Servers that may be located in distant remote sites. In such cases, the EAC UI loads the column displaying the attribute asynchronously. This is evident in the database master list view displaying the Mount/Dismount status. Of course, as with any design decision there are trade-offs, and the side effect of this change is that this particular column is no longer sortable.

One final enhancement to the new EAC design worth noting is the addition of the notification UI. This UI is added to provide administrators a consistent, all-in-one view of the long-running operations. When administrators issue a batch migration request for hundreds or thousands of mailboxes, or a PST import task on a large mailbox, the operations are naturally not instantaneous. In the past, the administrator was left in the dark until the operation completed or resulted in an error message. The new notification UI allows administrators to be informed of the progress of the long-running operation. Each supported asynchronous operation writes its progress periodically into a system mailbox. The UI then periodically checks for changes to this mailbox, and it notifies administrators via the EAC UI.

ONE CONSOLE TO RULE THEM ALL

The ultimate design goal of EAC is to achieve a single console to manage on-premises, online, and hybrid deployments of Exchange.

For on-premises deployments, EAC can be accessed via `http://<local host>/ecp`. For Office 365, the URL is `http://www.outlook.com/<tenant domain>/ecp`. The way features and feature groups are organized is largely identical for the on-premises and online EAC views. Attributes and actions that are not applicable to each view are removed via RBAC. This creates a familiar management experience for administrators. For organizations that choose to adopt a hybrid deployment, the same console can be used to connect to both the on-premises environment and the online tenant. It's a simple click to switch views. Access to each environment is independently authenticated. For ease of use, if ADFS is set up, single sign-on can be enabled such that the console can transparently use the online credential to sign onto the on-premises environment such that switching to the online system and vice versa becomes truly seamless. What's more, features like notification are designed such that even if administrators stay in the online view, they will still receive the notifications for long-running transactions happening in the on-premises environment.

DEFAULT PROXY ROUTING LOGIC

One thing that is not often considered is what happens behind the UI. In EAC, as it was for ECP and EMC in Exchange 2010, each task is supported by one or more cmdlets. The architecture of Exchange 2013 is simplified down to two roles: the Client Access server that primarily provides lightweight processing of proxy logic for each protocol access and the Mailbox server that provides data storage and handles the more heavy business logic. When a user accesses their email, the Mailbox server hosting the user's mailbox will respond to the access request. For EAC design, we needed to determine how the Client Access server will proxy the protocol and pick an appropriate Mailbox server to run the cmdlet.

The considerations were as follows:

◆ The ability to manage both current and legacy mailboxes in an interoperability environment

◆ To avoid creating hotspots and single points of failure

◆ To minimize any constraints placed on an Exchange deployment

continues

(continued)

What we came up with was a design that primarily anchors the cmdlet execution to the Mailbox server that hosts the administrator's mailbox. This provides an easy way to distribute administration load by creating multiple administrator accounts on different mailbox servers. The design logic will alternatively pick an appropriate mailbox server if the administrator does not have an actual mailbox. If we are talking about a user accessing their OWA options, then the cmdlet runs on the mailbox server hosting the user's own mailbox. This further helps eliminate the hotspot.

EXCHCLIENTVER AND SERVER PARAM OVERRIDE

As most of you are aware, Exchange is rarely deployed in greenfield scenarios where an Exchange environment doesn't already exist. Thus, there will likely be an earlier version of Exchange with which to interoperate. In such environments, EAC provides two handy parameters to override the default routing logic.

PARAM - EXCHCLIENTVER

In an interoperability environment, if an organization implements a single namespace, the version of EAC is decided by the version of Mailbox server that hosts the logged-on administrator's mailbox. This means that administrators with Exchange 2010 mailboxes will be redirected to Exchange 2010 ECP, and administrators with Exchange 2013 mailboxes will reach the Exchange 2013 EAC. While this works out well in many cases, some organizations don't necessarily upgrade their administrator's mailbox before upgrading user mailboxes. We needed to solve this design challenge to allow administrators with Exchange 2010 mailboxes to access Exchange 2013 EAC to manage any user mailboxes that had already been migrated to Exchange 2013.

Adding the ExchClientVer extension to the EAC URL solved this challenge. For Exchange 2010 admin users, when the extension (key/value pair) of ExchClientVer=15 is appended to their request to manage their organization, they will be proxied to the Exchange 2013 EAC instead of the Exchange 2010 ECP, for example:

```
https://.../ecp/default.aspx?realm=exchange-d3.com&exchclientver=15
```

For Exchange 2013 admin users, when the key/value pair of ExchClientVer=14 is appended to their request to manage their organization, they will be proxied to the Exchange 2010 ECP instead, for example:

```
https://.../ecp/default.aspx?realm=exchange-d3.com&exchclientver=14
```

The admin would need to log back on if they wanted to quit the override EAC session. Re-logon will take the user back to the default EAC or ECP experience.

Note that the parameter is only applicable for Exchange 2010 and 2013 coexistence deployments.

SEPARATING OWA OPTION FROM EAC

One final design challenge was that, given that ECP and OWA options were essentially one and the same in Exchange 2010, how could we achieve some clarity of separation now that EAC has become the main management interface for Exchange? We believe that the two concepts are fundamentally different, and by creating such separation, it allows the following:

UI Simplification and Ease of Use   When the administrator logs into EAC, they're managing their organization. When a user (even if that user is an admin) accesses the OWA option, they're changing their own email preferences.

The Ability to Configure Access Differently for OWA Options and EAC   This supports organizations with higher security needs for accessing OWA and OWA options from the Internet, while restricting the administrators managing the organization using EAC to the organization's internal network.

To access EAC, administrators would use the URL `https://exchange-d3.com/ECP`. For the same administrator accessing their own OWA option, the URL would be `https://exchange-d3.com/ECP/?rfr=owa`. When a user navigates from their OWA to OWA options, the URL is automatically appended to the query string key/value pair of `rfr=owa`.

The Exchange Management Tools

Exchange Server 2010 offered the Exchange Management Console and the Exchange Management Shell, and it introduced the Exchange Control Panel. Each tool used underlying PowerShell cmdlets and the RBAC framework to accomplish any given task. Both remote PowerShell and ECP offered the flexibility of using any Windows machine with PowerShell 2.0 and Windows Remote Management (WinRM) 2.0 installed to manage your Exchange Server 2010 environment remotely without the need to install the Exchange Server 2010 management tools. This was a departure from management methods in earlier versions of Exchange that required code to be installed on a management machine. While the concept of web-based administration tools wasn't new, the introduction of ECP promised ease of use and freedom, both to administrators and users, through the simple design of web management tools and the ability to use ECP anywhere you have a web browser. This was the beginning of self-service management in Exchange. Importantly, ECP even removed the requirement for PowerShell to be available on the local machine since it was entirely web based—operating on the remote server directly. Of course, given that it was the first iteration of a web-based management tool for Exchange 2010, ECP didn't provide feature parity with Exchange Management Shell or Exchange Management Console, but it nevertheless offered to perform many common administrative tasks simply and efficiently.

However, there were still issues with this mixed-toolset approach. Imagine an Exchange Server 2010 environment in a large multinational company where multiple groups of administrators support the environment from different locations around the globe. Now visualize each administrator needing to use EMC for administration. Can you spot the potential problem? As the servers are upgraded to newer service packs and update rollups, EMC installations quickly become outdated and, if not updated to match the server versions, the results could be unpredictable and sometimes undesirable. EMS mitigated this problem to an extent. While it offered flexibility, it required PowerShell 2.0 and WinRM 2.0 installation on client computers that were running Windows client versions older than Windows 7. If an administrator's workstation was running Windows 7, the required components were built in.

With the introduction of the EAC in Exchange Server 2013, Microsoft has taken the next logical step in unifying the management toolset. What some see as the demise of ECP, having a lifespan of only one version, in reality ECP has formed the basis for the new, improved web-based management toolset that not only promises to provide a fully featured management toolset that replaces EMC but also integrates management of your Office 365 tenant if you have a hybrid deployment. What this means is that we have moved away from the need to install code on management workstations, and we now have a common management toolset that can be accessed on almost any machine with a web browser. It also ties together the online and on-premises management toolsets.

Looking at the set of tools, EAC and EMS, you will see that EAC delivers an easy-to-use management interface that makes it simple to achieve the most common administrative actions and tasks, while advanced administrators have the ability to accomplish more demanding and complex tasks from the Exchange Management Shell. All the while, security is underpinned by the use of the RBAC framework.

Of course, as with any change to management tools, people will have to learn new things. Since Exchange 2007, there has always been a trade-off in Microsoft products between what could be carried out in PowerShell and what could be carried out in the GUI. In Exchange 2013, EAC does a good job, but people may want more. Looking back on Microsoft's history of advancing management tools, it would be safe to assume that EAC will continue offering more functionality over time.

What's New in EAC?

In the early development stages of Exchange Server 2013, some customers who deployed the beta software were disappointed to learn about the demise of EMC. They were also deeply concerned about how much of the functionality of EMC the EAC would replace and what functionality would only be achievable via the use of EMS or remote PowerShell.

Looking back at that not-so-distant past, earlier statements of Microsoft's willingness to listen to customer feedback as well as continually delivering enhancements to management toolsets are evident with general availability of Exchange Server 2013. Between the early beta versions and now, EAC has become a fully functional administration tool that is very capable. EAC promises to deliver a feature-rich administration experience while building on the sound pillars of a great toolset, including performance, simplicity, accessibility, and compatibility.

Benefiting from advancements in PowerShell 3.0, EAC is noticeably faster than the previous EMC. Even though web-based, it still feels snappier than using EMC on an Exchange 2010 server. Bulk edit functionality allows administrators to select multiple items for batch processing such as updating department information for multiple users at once, as shown in Figure 6.8. Notice the bulk edit options available in the right-hand pane when multiple recipients are selected. This type of capability blurs the line between yesterday's thick client and today's web-based administrative tool. Of course, things are not yet perfect. For example, we can't bulk mailbox-enable users in the EAC just yet.

FIGURE 6.8
EAC Bulk edit
functionality

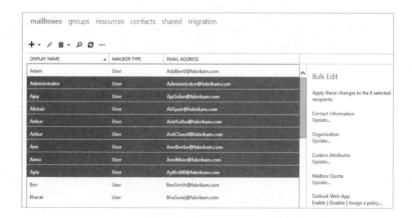

User interface improvements now also allow for support of long-running tasks such as exporting a mailbox to a PST file without blocking the user interface. This is accomplished through the implementation of synchronous execution of commands. Notifications of completion of long-running tasks and other conditions, such as certificate expiration, keep administrators informed without being intrusive, as shown in Figure 6.9.

FIGURE 6.9
EAC notifications

Simplicity is evident in the overall design of the EAC. The simple and lightweight user interface organizes tasks in categories that provide quicker access to actions that an administrator wants to perform. The mapping of tasks and categories is logical, which makes finding given actions a snap. The ability to customize the interface, such as column selection shown in

Figure 6.10, column width, and items per page, combined with persistence of personalized settings across sessions, makes you forget that Microsoft has traded a thick client for a web-based administration interface.

FIGURE 6.10
Adding and removing columns in EAC

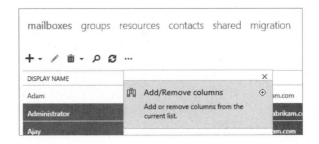

The user interface is also designed with accessibility in mind. The entire EAC is now fully accessible with the keyboard and provides enhanced screen reader support. It is also designed to perform well in high-contrast mode to cater to the needs of administrators with visual impairments.

Finally, support of 60 languages at launch and broader OS and browser support provide greater compatibility, which allows administrators to use the OS and browser of their choice while providing the full experience that EAC has to offer.

Securing Access to EAC

Although this chapter is not focused on security, it is worth touching on this issue here before covering it in more depth in Chapter 8, "Securing Exchange." While web-based administration tools deliver freedom of administration from any web browser, they also bring with them concern regarding secure access to those very same tools. There may be legitimate reasons to disallow access to EAC from outside the organization, for example. Thankfully, Exchange Server 2013 allows for such a provision.

Securing access to EAC can be accomplished in one of two ways:

Creation of a Second Website on the Client Access Server Role   Creating a second site allows separation of the internal site from the external site. Each site can be accessed using its respective internal or external URL for the EAC. This is the preferred option, because it requires the least amount of additional resources and administrative effort.

Separation of Internet-Facing Client Access Servers from Internal Client Access Servers   This method allows for separation of internal and external traffic to separate sets of client access servers, addressing the security requirements of external access to EAC while also potentially reducing the impact of external workloads on internal client access servers and vice versa. This approach comes with a higher implementation cost and higher administrative effort, thus making it less desirable.

After selecting one of the aforementioned options, the next step is to turn off access to EAC on the website that is configured for external access. Turning off access involves the simple step of issuing the following command in Exchange Management Shell:

```
Set-ECPVirtualDirectory -Identity "CAS01\ecp (default web site)" -AdminEnabled $false
```

Of course, you must identify the relevant ECP virtual directory for your environment. Performing this step will allow administrators to continue using the EAC internally while blocking access from outside their organization.

Hybrid Deployments and EAC

Earlier, we briefly discussed the EAC and its integrated management experience with an Exchange Online organization as part of an Office 365 tenant. Compared to the EMC provided in Exchange Server 2010, the EAC provides a handful of useful enhancements:

Hybrid Configuration Wizard   The first area of improvement is the Hybrid Configuration Wizard. The new wizard is sophisticated. The gaps that existed in EMC have been addressed. The experience of setting up a hybrid environment using the wizard has been greatly improved. What used to require two or more steps is now reduced to the single step of running the wizard.

Single Sign-On for Office 365 Users   If ADFS is deployed, single sign-on becomes available for users provisioned with Office 365. EAC is also able to leverage SSO for management.

Single Management Tool for Both On-Premises and Office 365 Users   Once your environment is configured for hybrid setup, EAC becomes the single management tool for both on-premises and Office 365 users. A single user interface can be used to move user mailboxes between on-premise servers and Office 365. Cloud on-boarding and off-boarding processes become easier as the requirement for multiple management tools is removed and the experience of managing the entire hybrid organization is unified through a single administration and management tool.

More details of hybrid deployments will be covered in Chapter 7, "Hybrid Configuration."

PowerShell and Exchange Management Shell

The PowerShell-based Exchange Management Shell provides the underpinnings upon which the EMC in Exchange Server 2010 and the EAC in Exchange Server 2013 are built. While EAC allows us to perform a good balance of tasks, EMS provides a shell-based management environment that can perform any task possible with Exchange. It also provides a robust scripting environment that paves the way to full automation of complex Exchange management tasks.

Unlike Exchange Server 2007, Exchange Server 2010 and Exchange Server 2013 rely on PowerShell remoting features. While Exchange Server 2010 requires PowerShell and WinRM 2.0, Exchange Server 2013 utilizes new and improved capabilities such as simplified syntax, workflows for long-running tasks, robust session reconnects, and more—all offered by Windows Management Framework 3.0, which includes PowerShell 3.0. Of course, just like EAC, PowerShell is also governed by RBAC.

When Exchange Management Shell is launched, it opens PowerShell and, using a script included with Exchange setup, connects to the closest Exchange 2013 server. When a remote session is created while connected, user permissions are evaluated using the RBAC framework, and the user is presented with a Shell session in which only commands for which the user is authorized are imported. The benefit of PowerShell remoting is that an installation of Exchange Management Tools is not required to manage an Exchange Server 2013 environment. Any machine with Windows Management Framework 3.0 installed can connect remotely to Exchange Server 2013 and manage the environment based on assigned permissions.

PowerShell Execution Policy

While PowerShell isn't the focus of this book, since we are on this topic, it is important to understand scripting security. If you create or use PowerShell scripts, you need to be aware of the four possible execution modes of PowerShell scripting:

Restricted Mode   This is the default execution mode. In this mode, the user is not allowed to run any scripts, including the ones that are digitally signed by a trusted certificate authority.

AllSigned Mode   This mode requires that a script be digitally signed by a trusted certificate authority before the script can execute.

RemoteSigned Mode   This mode allows scripts to run if they are created locally. Scripts that you may have downloaded from the Internet and other remote locations cannot execute and will fail.

Unrestricted Mode   This mode allows any script to run regardless of how it was acquired or its digital signing status. This mode is not recommended for obvious security reasons.

Use the following command from a PowerShell window with Local Administrator permissions to change these modes:

```
Set-ExecutionPolicy -ExecutionPolicy AllSigned
```

In this case, we are setting the policy to use AllSigned mode, but of course you can swap out that setting for any of the others listed here.

Once you have set the execution policy, you can then run scripts of your choice.

Scripts and Exchange

In its simplest form, a PowerShell script is merely a collection of cmdlets that allows for automating repetitive tasks. Of course, scripts can be somewhat more complex and can be expanded into complex workflows that can survive server reboots utilizing the new functionality offered in PowerShell 3.0.

Exchange Server 2013 provides you with a collection of scripts that can be used for various tasks, such as putting a host in Maintenance mode during maintenance. The scripts provided by Exchange setup are located in the `Scripts` folder within the Exchange Server 2013 installation path, and they can be accessed from the Exchange Management Shell by switching to the `$scripts` directory.

Summary

We have taken a journey through the changing world of management tools. Exchange 2013 is very much in keeping with these trends by moving to a predominantly abstracted model of management, whether through a web browser or from the Management Shell using remote PowerShell. The same tools allow this degree of management, whether the mailbox is in the cloud with Office 365 or on-premises with Exchange Server 2013. In either scenario, the flexibility to set specific permissions for your administrative teams is provided by the RBAC model, which, while potentially complex, allows great control.

Chapter 7

Exchange 2013 Hybrid Coexistence with Office 365

Exchange hybrid is the term used when an Exchange organization running in a customer or partner datacenter is connected to Microsoft Office 365. This configuration provides an extremely rich coexistence feature set that allows mailboxes to be hosted on-premises or in Office 365 while the end-user experience remains virtually the same.

This chapter discusses why you may want to evaluate Exchange hybrid, design considerations of this configuration, and tips from real-world deployments to help ensure that your Exchange hybrid project is a success.

What Is Exchange Hybrid?

Before we discuss Exchange hybrid, we should briefly touch on Office 365. *Office 365* provides cloud-based versions of some of Microsoft's major products, including Microsoft Office, SharePoint, Exchange, and Lync. In this context, the term *cloud* essentially indicates services that are hosted by someone else (Microsoft in this case) and that you can access over the Internet.

The services hosted by Office 365 are fundamentally the same as those that you can run in your own datacenter, with some slight differences. Microsoft adds the word *Online* to the names of these services so that Exchange becomes Exchange Online and SharePoint becomes SharePoint Online. These services are also generally abbreviated. Exchange Online is abbreviated as EXO, SharePoint Online is abbreviated as SPO, and so forth.

One of the main benefits of an online service is that you can take advantage of its continuous improvements as the feature set is enhanced. To simplify matters, each service has a fairly well-defined description.

Service descriptions for each service can be found at the following URL:

```
http://technet.microsoft.com/en-us/library/jj819284.aspx
```

High-Level Infrastructure Overview

Figure 7.1 shows a typical Exchange hybrid infrastructure. The services required for Exchange hybrid will be discussed in more detail later in this chapter.

FIGURE 7.1
Exchange Online
hybrid high-level
infrastructure
overview

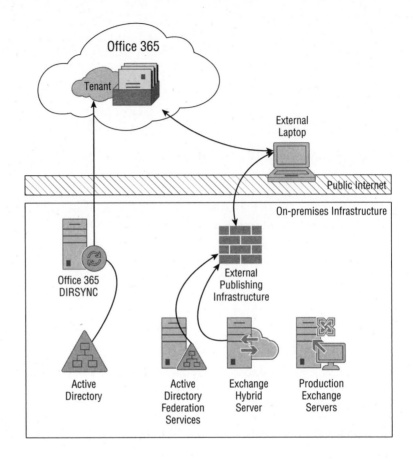

TENANT

Exchange Online is a *multi-tenant messaging* system. This means that customers have their own area within the Exchange Online service. Nonetheless, the servers that provide the services are shared with other customers. This is part of the reason why Microsoft can offer the service at such a low cost. From a customer and end-user perspective, however, the tenant that you are provided looks and feels like a totally isolated Exchange organization. That is, although the platform is shared, each tenant is a discrete and isolated instance of Exchange Server. Before you can begin to work with Exchange hybrid, you must have an Exchange Online tenant.

NOTE   Microsoft also provides a service known as Office 365 Dedicated. This service runs in Microsoft-owned datacenters, but the servers provided are dedicated to each customer. The service engagement model is much more demanding than it is for Office 365, however, and it requires a level of commitment and minimum scale to use this service. Additionally, it is much more expensive than Office 365.

More information about Office 365 Dedicated can be found here:

`http://technet.microsoft.com/en-us/library/jj879309.aspx`

Office 365 Directory Sync

Directory Sync (DirSync) is the process responsible for reading the local Active Directory and creating matching accounts in your Office 365 tenant. DirSync also copies attributes required to maintain a common global address list, across the entire organization. This process is discussed in Chapter 14, "Migrating to Exchange 2013." DirSync is also responsible for ensuring that the accounts created in your Office 365 tenant will be able to authenticate via your on-premises Active Directory Federation Services server.

DirSync Is Required for Single Sign-on

Single sign-on has dependencies on both DirSync and *Active Directory Federation Services (AD FS)*. AD FS requires that the identity object (user account) within Office 365 have attributes that allow it to be identified within the Microsoft Federation Gateway (MFG). The MFG is an identity trust broker that tells Office 365 where the authoritative authentication server is for each federated user account. In this instance, the MFG will store the URL for your AD FS server and require that each federated user be authenticated via the correct AD FS server before access to the service is granted.

Active Directory Federation Services

AD FS provides *single sign-on (SSO)* to Office 365. This means that a user needs to remember only a single account name and password that is stored in the local Active Directory; this is known as *identity federation*. When a user tries to log on to a mailbox hosted in their Exchange Online organization, they must first authenticate to the on-premises AD FS infrastructure. From an end-user perspective, the same account name and password are used to access local resources and resources hosted in Office 365.

Exchange Hybrid Server

A *hybrid server* is a standard, on-premises Exchange server that is being used to pass coexistence data between the on-premises Exchange servers and the Exchange Online service. This data might include email messages or availability data, such as when someone is free or when they are in a meeting. The hybrid server is also used to migrate mailboxes from on-premises to Exchange Online and vice versa in a hybrid configuration. The best way to think about the hybrid server is as the glue between your on-premises infrastructure and your Exchange Online infrastructure.

External Publishing Infrastructure

The *External Publishing Infrastructure* icon in Figure 7.1 refers to any infrastructure used to publish your internal servers to the Internet or provide Internet access for your end users. For Exchange hybrid to work, Exchange Web Services (EWS) and Autodiscover should be published to the Internet via some form of publishing infrastructure, such as a reverse proxy server, or directly via a load balancer. Additionally, client machines that are using Exchange Online will need to be able to connect to the service via the Internet quickly. For enterprise and small customers, this area often requires significant change to accommodate Exchange hybrid. We will discuss some of the design and deployment challenges later in this chapter.

Why Consider Exchange Hybrid?

One of the problems with Exchange hybrid is the hype that surrounds any cloud-based product or service. If you believe the hype, Exchange Online will cost virtually nothing, never fail, protect your data in the event of a disaster, dazzle your end users with added functionality and ease of use, upgrade itself automatically, and generally provide your organization with email nirvana. You can hear such sales claims at many Office 365 marketing events extolling the virtues of Exchange Online.

The reality, of course, is that, like most technologies, there are benefits to using Exchange Online as well as trade-offs; that is, you may gain some benefits by moving to Exchange Online, but you may also lose some flexibility and/or features. If you can handle such trade-offs, then you may stand to be in a better situation. However, as is true with all design decisions, in order to choose wisely you must know your requirements and define how you are going to meet them. In this instance, the most common approach is to work through your requirements and then search through the Office 365 service description documents to find evidence that they will be met effectively.

Benefits of Exchange Online

Exchange Online provides many benefits. Some of the main ones are stability, cost effectiveness, evergreen service contracts, and near-universal connectivity.

STABILITY

One benefit of Exchange Online is that the service is designed and operated by the Microsoft Exchange Product Group. This is the same team that writes the code for Exchange and operates and runs the Exchange Online service. Because of this, the developers who are responsible for specific features get to deal with problems in their own code firsthand, and they can then fix issues with better context in future product updates.

COST EFFECTIVENESS

Because of the scale of Exchange Online and shrewd operations processes, it is relatively inexpensive to run Exchange Online. This reduction in cost is passed on to customers. For example, the E1 plan, which provides SharePoint 2013 Online, Lync 2013 Online, and Exchange 2013 Online, includes a 25 GB Exchange mailbox that costs $8 per user per month. For a 500-user organization, this works out to $48,000 annually. This cost is predictable, and it includes continuous upgrades.

Another common benefit occurs when an organization needs to expand for a specific time period, such as for a big event. An on-premises customer would need to grow their infrastructure, which is very costly. An Exchange Online customer would just need to add more mailboxes, pay the per-month price per mailbox, and then close the accounts when the event is over, paying only for the resources they require.

EVERGREEN CONTRACTS

With an *evergreen service contract*, Microsoft automatically upgrades your Exchange service, free of charge, as soon as updates or new versions are available. For example, Microsoft upgrades Office 365 and all of the services it provides on a quarterly basis. An evergreen contract also includes major software version upgrades such as Exchange Server 2013. Customers are notified of the upgrade and any potential changes that they must make to prepare for the move. During the upgrade, the customer's data is moved over to the newer service platform. This is very appealing when compared to an on-premises migration.

WIDESPREAD CONNECTIVITY

Exchange Online is Internet based, and it supports all major client protocols. This means that you can connect to the service from virtually any operating system and use virtually any mail client. The provision of an always-on, always-accessible collaboration platform is great news for many customers who face the demands of a diverse and dispersed workforce, all wanting to use their own devices to access their data.

Trade-offs of Exchange Online

Adopting Exchange Online also has its downsides. We will now address the drawbacks of the same issues we just discussed.

STABILITY

Office 365 has had its fair share of service outages since its initial launch, though not all of these outages have impacted Exchange Online. These outages tend to be relatively short, that is, hours and not days. They usually impact only a subset of tenants. Nevertheless, if you are affected, you may be frustrated by the fact that there is nothing you can do about it because you are held accountable for a service outage over which you have no control. Microsoft is generally transparent about issues within Exchange Online and how to remediate them. They will also waive service charges when the service fails to meet its agreed-upon service levels. For most businesses, however, this is of little consolation because they would prefer to have a working service.

The trade-off in this area is not necessarily about total service availability—it's about control or the illusion of control. Many IT teams sense a need to retain control over the level of service that they provide. The reality is that few organizations can match or beat the service availability provided by Exchange Online. For many customers, however, the act of handing over control to a vendor is a tough pill to swallow. For others, the difficulty comes from a lack of direct involvement with the resolution process. For example, senior management may feel the need to help IT teams directly resolve problems.

Such positions are often unsubstantiated and based mainly on emotion. If a customer is presenting you with these types of objections to Exchange Online without quantitative evidence of service availability, then they just may not be ready for a cloud-based service. In our experience, these customers may benefit from a proof of concept or small production pilot to become accustomed to the differences via a hands-on process. Often, the initial pushback on cloud-based services is simply a fear of the unknown.

COST EFFECTIVENESS

Cost is without doubt the most common benefit that is touted for Exchange Online and Office 365 as a suite. However, it is not a given that it will always be cheaper. Large organizations often get discounts on hardware, and if their Exchange solution is based on cheap storage and commodity servers, then it is possible to provide a cost-effective Exchange solution on-premises. The real differentiator centers on operations costs and dependencies. Taking advantage of this cost saving, however, often requires a reduction in head count. Although possible, this is rarely achieved in practice. The most common scenario is that staff who previously were engaged in supporting the Exchange infrastructure are instead moved to support the Exchange Online dependency infrastructure, such as AD FS, DirSync, and Information Rights Management (IRM) solutions.

The upshot of this is that it is sometimes difficult to make a compelling business case for Exchange Online based purely on cost, especially if the business case does not include Lync Online and SharePoint Online, since the cost benefit of Office 365 is much harder to obtain without using the entire suite of products you are paying for.

EVERGREEN CONTRACTS

An evergreen service contract sounds like a great thing. Microsoft will automatically upgrade your Exchange service at no cost as soon as updates or new versions are available. There is a catch here, however—client supportability. As Exchange is upgraded, the supported client versions are often changed. Sometimes this may require a service pack upgrade, as it does for Outlook 2007 support with the version of Exchange Online released in 2013. Client support, however, is sometimes dropped, as it was in 2010 for Outlook 2003 in the upgrade from the Business Productivity Online Suite to Office 365.

An updated list of software requirements for Office 365 can be found at the following URL:

```
http://office.microsoft.com/en-gb/office365-suite-help/software-requirements-for-
office-365-for-business-HA102817357.aspx
```

The impact of using an evergreen service will vary from customer to customer. However, as a general rule, it means that all clients that use Exchange Online must have automatic updates enabled, and, more importantly, the organization must have a desktop upgrade program in place that is in lock step with Office 365.

Desktop upgrades can be disruptive and time consuming. Therefore, moving to Exchange Online requires strategic planning of the desktop. This topic is often not discussed during deployments, and it can come as a shock to customers when they receive their tenant upgrade notification and discover that they need to upgrade their operating systems and Office software within 12 months, which was neither planned nor budgeted.

Google is often criticized for making sweeping changes across their free and paid-for services, because such changes result in widespread user confusion. Microsoft takes a more enterprise-friendly approach to service upgrades. They usually introduce subtle feature changes and stability improvements on a quarterly basis and reserve more significant changes for major service upgrades, typically annually.

WIDESPREAD CONNECTIVITY

Exchange Online offers broad connectivity; that is, you can connect to it from anywhere in the world where you have an Internet connection. This has to be a good thing, right? Again, this depends on requirements. Some organizations encourage sharing of their data and let their employees connect their preferred devices to perform tasks, while others are much more restrictive about sharing their data and how it is accessed. For example, financial, insurance, security, government, and pharmaceutical companies are often conflicted about whether to allow their employees to use their own devices globally. Moreover, they are extremely concerned that someone outside of the organization might improperly gain access to their data.

The result of this conflict of requirements is that projects try to provide open access to services but also to restrict access to data. Historically, customers achieved this by deploying multifactor authentication systems and generally making remote access of their services exceptionally difficult. Moreover, once the Exchange service is moved out to Exchange Online, it becomes even more difficult to control access.

The following URL lists some steps that can provide some level of control:

```
http://technet.microsoft.com/en-us/library/hh526961(v=ws.10).aspx
```

The reality is that controlling data leakage by restricting access is complicated, expensive, and simply does not align well with an Internet service such as Exchange Online. Instead, use an Information Rights Management product, such as Active Directory Rights Management Service (AD RMS), to provide a more scalable and dependable solution. If neither of these solutions is appropriate, then perhaps Exchange Online is just not the right solution for this customer.

Design Considerations

In the early days of Office 365, the perception was that there was no need to design for it; that is, as the customer, you just need to click a few buttons, enter your credit card details, and you're all set.

Obviously, this is not correct, and even though Microsoft has provided a large portion of the Exchange service design, you still need to think about some of these design considerations when Exchange Online is part of the solution.

Many consulting firms will perform a *solution alignment workshop* for Office 365 deliveries. This process compares identified customer requirements to the corresponding Office 365 service descriptions in order to check that all requirements can be met. Additionally, the Office 365 dependencies, such as minimum client software versions, Active Directory, and network connectivity requirements, are discussed. Only when all of these discussions have taken place will the actual design and delivery work begin.

Solution Requirements

As we discussed in Chapter 1, "Business, Functional, and Technical Requirements," requirements form the fundamental building block of all design projects. If you do not know what the solution is required to do, then how do you know if the result is a success or failure? Moreover, how do you ensure that a design is fit for a given purpose if that purpose is not defined?

Requirements elicitation is no less important just because Exchange Online is part of your design. In fact, having precise requirements becomes even more important. Exchange Online has a service description that defines what it will and will not provide. If you discover a requirement in the middle of a project that Exchange Online cannot provide, then you have some difficult decisions to make. For example, do you abort the project and revert to an on-premises solution or simply fail to meet that requirement? This issue is at the heart of most customer dissatisfaction complaints with Exchange Online. Customers simply assumed that it would do what they needed it to do, and they only found out too late—after they had migrated—that it didn't meet their objectives.

Thus, whenever Exchange Online or any other aspect of Office 365 is in your solution design, be precise with your requirements definition. The requirements that you identify can then be compared against the Office 365 service descriptions, and any gaps are thus highlighted early on in the design process. Gaps can then be discussed and evaluated against the priority of the underlying requirement. For instance, is the requirement mandatory, or do you have any flexibility to change or drop it?

Be prepared to think creatively at this stage because many organizations have a predetermined operational and design philosophy that will need to be overcome before they are able to consume Exchange Online.

Solution Design

Once you have a clearly defined and agreed-upon set of requirements, you can begin the *solution design process*. Contrary to popular belief, this can often be more complex for an Exchange Online hybrid solution than for an Exchange on-premises solution. This is due to the huge wealth of experience that exists for designing and deploying Exchange on-premises solutions compared with the relative inexperience, even among the best consulting firms, with large-scale Exchange Online designs. There are also areas within an Exchange hybrid design that will be unfamiliar to many Exchange design teams, such as dealing with a large-scale Internet proxy bypass or the intricacies of network link topology and the variation of connectivity costs around the world.

The design also needs to focus on calculating service levels of combined services. For example, if Exchange Online provides 99.9 percent availability, your Internet service provider provides 99.9 percent link availability, and your firewalls are also 99.9 percent available, what is the maximum service level that you can provide to your end users? See Table 7.1 for a quick overview of how to approach this question. The percentages of availability of dependent services are multiplied together to show the combined service availability; that is, $99.9 \times 99.9 \times 99.9 = 99.7$. In this case, combining three services that are each a fundamental part of providing service to the end users results in an overall maximum service availability level of 99.7 percent.

TABLE 7.1: Combining service availability

SERVICE	AVAILABILITY	DOWNTIME (HOURS PER YEAR)
Exchange Online	99.9%	8.76
Internet service provider	99.9%	8.76
Firewall service	99.9%	8.76
Total	**99.7%**	**26.28**

The bottom line is that the solution design process for Exchange hybrid is exactly the same as for an Exchange on-premises solution. The design team must ensure that the solution can meet all of the requirements and that it will be operable and deployable within the customer's infrastructure and timescales. In reality, the focus of design attention switches from Exchange high-availability, storage, and performance to network link performance, latency, security, firewalls, and service availability. There is no less design work to be done. Rather, it involves different areas of technology than for an on-premises design. The most important thing to remember is that the design process remains the same—the solution design is created to meet the requirements.

Proof of Concept

A *proof of concept (POC)* is often used to showcase a potential design to the customer so that they can see exactly what will be delivered. One important thing to keep in mind when planning a POC is to know what you are trying to achieve. Many POC demonstrations deliver a perfect example of something that the customer is simply unable to achieve. For example, the POC is based on Windows 8 and Office 2013, whereas the customer is tied to Windows Vista and Office 2007 for another few years.

Try to define the success criteria for the POC after consultation with the customer. Find out what they want from the environment, and agree how best to present it effectively. Also remember that reality is often different than what the documentation suggests. Physically building and deploying a POC environment is a great way to expose problems and construct solutions early on in the design process.

For an Exchange Online hybrid POC, concentrate on the things that are special about a hybrid solution. The POC does not have to be feature complete—it could be used solely to demonstrate certain key features of the solution. Often, this might include the on-premises users sharing calendar availability data with users in Exchange Online or demonstrating data leakage prevention in action.

Do not confuse a POC with a pilot. A *pilot* is usually a feature-complete deployment, normally in or connected to the customer's production infrastructure. Real business users are moved over to the pilot with the goal of getting feedback on the use of the solution to share with the rest of the organization. Frequently, Office 365 documentation will refer to a *production POC*, which is actually better described as a pilot rather than a POC.

Deployment Planning and Preparation

As with any solution deployment, planning and preparation are required to ensure a smooth deployment. By far the most detailed walkthrough of configuring an Exchange Online hybrid deployment is from Henrik Walther. It is available at this address:

```
http://www.msexchange.org/articles-tutorials/office-365/exchange-online/
configuring-exchange-2013-hybrid-deployment-migrating-office-365-exchange-online-
part1.html
```

Additionally, Microsoft provides OnRamp for Office 365, which is an automated assistance tool that helps you gather configuration requirements and perform deployment readiness checks on your on-premises environment; see the following address:

```
http://technet.microsoft.com/en-us/library/jj993929.aspx
```

The following sections discuss high-level tasks that you should consider for your deployment of Exchange hybrid.

PLAN: IDENTIFY AND REMEDIATE CLIENTS

You should perform a client inventory as part of your Exchange deployment planning. This is equally as important for Exchange Online as it is for Exchange on-premises. You need to understand what clients are in use and then evaluate their suitability for Exchange Online. Clients may potentially need remediation or to be upgraded to ensure success.

PREPARE: REMEDIATE ACTIVE DIRECTORY OBJECTS WITH IDFIX

Exchange Online Directory Sync (DirSync) synchronizes Active Directory objects with the cloud. However, there are differences between allowable field values in your Active Directory and the directory service used within Office 365. Because of this, you should identify any Active Directory objects that have invalid entries and remediate them prior to beginning DirSync. Otherwise, you will need to remediate these errors post-DirSync installation, which is both time-consuming and tedious. Thankfully, Microsoft provides a tool called IdFix that identifies and remediates objects in the directory before installing DirSync.

IdFix is available for download at this address:

```
http://www.microsoft.com/en-us/download/details.aspx?id=36832
```

DEPLOY: REGISTER AN OFFICE 365 ENTERPRISE TENANT

Microsoft provides Office 365 tenants free of charge for POC and pilot use. Anyone can request a free 30-day trial tenant. Microsoft will also extend these tenants in the event that the POC or pilot duration goes beyond 30 days. The tenant can then be converted to a fully paid service if the customer chooses to purchase Office 365.

The address for the free Office 365 Enterprise E3 trial is as follows:

```
http://office.microsoft.com/en-us/business/office-365-enterprise-plan-e1-
FX103887102.aspx
```

> **KNOW YOUR PLAN**
>
> Office 365 offers a variety of different plans. You must choose your plan at sign-up. Because it can be difficult to change your plan later on, spend ample time up front deciding which plan type is best for you. A complete list of plans is found at the following URL. Note that not all offer a free trial.
>
> ```
> http://office.microsoft.com/en-us/business/compare-office-365-for-business-plans-
> FX102918419.aspx
> ```

DEPLOY: REGISTER DNS DOMAIN NAMES FOR THE TENANT AND ENABLE DIRECTORY SYNC

To use your new Office 365 tenant effectively, you will need to register your DNS domains. The process is relatively straightforward, and it requires that you perform some action within the DNS zone to identify yourself as the owner of that domain. This can take a few days to get right, however, especially if you have to pass the DNS change request on to a third party.

As a general rule, do not use your production domains in your trial tenants since it can be difficult to remove them later, and this can lead to delays when deploying into production. Instead, it is preferable to use a totally separate domain for POC testing against a trial tenant and then switch over to the production domains on the paid tenant once it is available.

Once the tenant is ready and DNS domains are registered, you should enable Active Directory synchronization. Do this as soon as possible, since it can take a day or so to switch on after enabling it in your tenant.

CONFIGURE INTERNET ACCESS INFRASTRUCTURE

Internet access can be one of the biggest changes between an Exchange on-premises design and a hybrid or full Exchange Online design. Once the mailbox has been moved to Exchange Online, the clients no longer access the Exchange server via the local network infrastructure alone and instead must traverse the Internet. In the early days of Exchange Online, proper attention was not paid to the design that was required, and this led to Outlook client traffic being processed by the same Internet proxy servers that handled all other Internet traffic, such as Facebook and Google.

Network latency is a critical part of the end-user experience. High network latency can cause significant delays in client responsiveness. The Internet proxy server is now adding to the network response time between Outlook and Exchange Online. To make this even more complex, the usage pattern for Internet proxy infrastructure generally has several spikes throughout the workday; that is, it rises dramatically first thing in the morning, during breaks, and at lunch time.

We strongly recommend spending some time to design a proxy bypass solution that directs traffic to Exchange Online as directly as possible via the best possible route, bypassing the Internet proxy server infrastructure. This both improves Outlook client responsiveness and reduces unnecessary load on the Internet proxy servers.

A current list of URLs and IP addresses in use for Office 365 is found here:

```
http://onlinehelp.microsoft.com/en-us/office365-enterprises/hh373144.aspx
```

In addition to client Internet access, a hybrid design also requires that Exchange Web Services and Active Directory Federation Services are correctly published and that the Directory Synchronization server has Internet access. There are many ways to publish web-based applications to the Internet securely, such as via Microsoft's Unified Access Gateway (UAG) or F5's BIG-IP appliance.

For UAG publishing information, refer to the following article:

```
http://blogs.technet.com/b/exchange/archive/2010/07/16/3410408.aspx
```

For F5 BIG-IP publishing guidance, refer to the following article:

```
http://www.f5.com/pdf/deployment-guides/f5-exchange-2010-dg.pdf
```

DEPLOY OFFICE 365 DIRECTORY SYNC

Deploying Office 365 Directory Sync is a fairly straightforward process for most organizations. Microsoft has automated the installation and simplified the configuration process for Forefront Identity Manager (FIM) to work with a single Active Directory forest and Office 365 tenant. The process is typically as simple as installing DirSync and then providing it with the credentials to access the local Active Directory and your Office 365 tenant. DirSync will then begin the synchronization process.

A few common problem areas with DirSync are presented in Table 7.2.

TABLE 7.2:   DirSync deployment common problems

ISSUE	NOTES
Access requirements	To install DirSync, you must provide the installation process with an enterprise admin account. This is a highly privileged account in the local Active Directory, and many customers are a little uneasy about doing this.
	It often helps to explain to customers that this account is not stored in the DirSync server, and it is only used during setup to create the MSOL_AD_Sync account in the forest root.
	Further information can be found at the following address: http://community.office365.com/en-us/wikis/sso/565.aspx
Tenant account expiry	During setup, the installation process will ask for an administrator account in your Office 365 tenant. This is used to create account objects. However, the default password expiration timeframe in Office 365 is 90 days. This of course means that DirSync will stop working every 90 days, and it will require that you reset the password.
	There are two ways to deal with this: either remember to change your password and reconfigure the DirSync account every 90 days, or use a specific account for DirSync that is set never to expire. The instructions for setting up a DirSync service account that never expires can be found here: http://blogs.technet.com/b/neiljohn/archive/2011/09/05/office-365-service-accounts-how-do-i-stop-dirsync-from-breaking-every-90-days.aspx
Proxy server configuration	DirSync requires an Internet connection so that it can communicate with your Office 365 tenant. However, many organizations still enforce authenticated proxy servers. The following article discusses some ways to check the proxy configuration: http://support.microsoft.com/kb/2517393
DirSync object limit	By default, all Active Directory objects are considered for synchronization to Office 365. For larger customers, this may not be desirable. To understand how to filter objects in DirSync, see the following article: http://technet.microsoft.com/en-us/library/jj710171.aspx
	If you need to synchronize more than 50,000 user objects, you will need to contact Office 365 support and request an increased DirSync limit. Also, you will need to use a full version of SQL Server 2008 rather than SQL Express for your DirSync database.
Domain controller unavailable	During the setup of DirSync, it will try to communicate with all domain controllers in all domains within the Active Directory forest. Make sure that the server on which you are installing DirSync has connectivity throughout the organization and that all domain controllers are online.

DEPLOY ACTIVE DIRECTORY FEDERATION SERVICES

As we have discussed, single sign-on requires that both DirSync and AD FS be installed in order to work. AD FS is usually split into two server roles: the AD FS server and the AD FS proxy server. The AD FS server is installed into Active Directory and configured as a farm. This allows multiple AD FS servers to be configured to provide fault tolerance. The AD FS proxy server is installed into the perimeter network and handles the secure publishing of the AD FS server farm to external clients or resources.

The most common problem during AD FS server installation and configuration is not having the correct certificates installed during the process. Make sure that you have requested your AD FS server certificates, that they have the correct names on them, and that they are correctly installed. Fixing problems caused by incorrect certificates and names is tricky, so spend a little extra time to get it right the first time.

The best source of information for AD FS deployment can be found at the following URL:

```
http://technet.microsoft.com/en-us/library/jj151794.aspx#bk_deployfsfarm
```

CONFIGURE EXCHANGE HYBRID

Back when Exchange hybrid was first launched with Exchange Server 2010, there was a checklist of more than 80 configuration steps that were required to get Exchange hybrid to work. Fortunately, Microsoft recognized that this was too complicated a process so they committed to the creation of a Hybrid Configuration Wizard. This wizard was first introduced in Exchange Server 2010 SP2. It is for this reason that we strongly recommend using a minimum of Exchange Server 2010 SP2 for your hybrid server.

If you are using a new Office 365 tenant that includes Exchange Server 2013, then you must use Exchange Server 2010 SP3 or Exchange Server 2013 CU1 as your hybrid server.

The Exchange Server 2013 CU1 version of the Hybrid Configuration Wizard has the following improvements over the Exchange 2010 version:

- Reduction of configuration tools

- Streamlined wizard

- Enhanced secure mail

- Improved centralized mail transport

- Integrated Edge Transport server

- Improved support for Exchange Online

- Detailed status in the configuration

- Improved Hybrid Configuration log

More information about these upgrades can be found at the following URL:

```
http://technet.microsoft.com/en-us/library/jj200790(v=exchg.150).aspx
```

Although the Hybrid Configuration Wizard simplifies the configuration process, it performs many actions "under the covers." Our advice is to read and reread the wizard prerequisites and make absolutely sure that you have met all of its dependencies before running it for the first time.

The TechNet guidance for the Hybrid Configuration Wizard can be found here:

`http://technet.microsoft.com/en-us/library/hh529921.aspx`

The following summarizes the prerequisites that must be completed before running the Hybrid Configuration Wizard:

◆ Office 365 Enterprise tenant obtained

◆ Custom domains registered in the tenant

◆ DirSync deployed and configured

◆ Active Directory Federation Services installed and configured

◆ Autodiscover DNS records created

◆ Office 365 tenant added into Exchange Admin Center (EAC)

◆ Public certificates installed for EWS and Autodiscover

◆ EdgeSync configured if using edge servers and hybrid secure mail is required

Common Deployment Hurdles

There are some common customer requirements that can mean that moving to Exchange Online is not viable. We will now discuss some of the more common problem areas and some potential solutions:

MULTIPLE ACTIVE DIRECTORY FORESTS

The standard version of Office 365 DirSync will only work with a single Active Directory forest. This can be a problem for many organizations, and it is something that many enterprise customers will need to solve before they can deploy Exchange hybrid. The primary method for solving this problem is simply to merge all of your Active Directory forests. Obviously, this is a non-trivial task and it is typically a project in its own right.

> **REMEMBER SUPPORTABILITY**
>
> Over the years, many design teams have tried to come up with creative solutions to the issue of Office 365 DirSync and multiple Active Directory forests. Some have even succeeded in developing homegrown solutions. However, the Office 365 team has not tested any of these solutions, and so they all remain unsupported. One of the main benefits of moving workload to the cloud is to make life simpler. If you find yourself in a position where you need to deploy an unsupported identity solution, consider deploying an on-premises Exchange infrastructure instead.

Nevertheless, there is a supported solution for Office 365 and multiple Active Directory forests with DirSync. The solution is to engage with Microsoft Consulting Services (MCS), which can help you deploy a custom version of Forefront Identity Manager (FIM) with the Microsoft Online management agent. Although this is a paid engagement, you do get a custom deployment of FIM, which might come in handy.

USER PRINCIPAL NAME

If your solution requires single sign-on, then you will need to deploy Active Directory Federation Services and DirSync. DirSync is required to synchronize your Active Directory objects to the Office 365 service, and AD FS is required to authenticate users and provide access to the Office 365 resources, as covered previously in this chapter.

One thing not addressed previously is that when you log onto Office 365, you need to use the *User Principal Name (UPN)* for your account. Typically, this is made up of your Active Directory forest name and your logon name. For example, my logon name might be `neilj` and my forest might be `company.local`, so my UPN would be `neilj@company.local`. The problem here is that Office 365 requires that you register your domain in public DNS so that you can verify ownership. Obviously, you cannot verify `company.local` since `.local` is not a valid public DNS domain. To make life slightly more difficult, Microsoft has recommended using `.local` or `.ad` for a little over 10 years, so the likelihood of coming across this situation is quite high.

The solution here is to rename the UPN to something that is a valid DNS domain (that you own). Therefore, my `neilj@company.local` account might become `neilj@exchanged3.com` instead. Changing UPNs in bulk can be done easily via ADModify, which is available at the following URL:

```
http://admodify.codeplex.com/
```

It is not always quite as simple as just changing the UPN, however. The UPN is often used to match certificates to user accounts via an Active Directory Certificate Authority. If end-user certificates are being issued via User Principal Name mapping, then when the UPN is changed, the certificates must be reissued at the same time. This will require some additional planning, and additional time should be included in your deployment if you need to change UPNs and reissue user certificates.

TRY TO MATCH UPN AND PRIMARY EMAIL ADDRESS

Since the formats of UPN and SMTP email addresses are the same, it can confuse users if they do not match. Consider the scenario where a user logon name for Office 365 is `neilj@exchanged3.com`, but their email address is `neil.johnson@exchanged3.com`. It is our experience that this mismatch of SMTP address and UPN results in confusion. If you are going to go to the trouble of changing UPNs, then consider making each user's UPN the same as their primary SMTP address. If you do this via ADModify, use the Account tab and set the UPN to be `%'mailNickname'%@yourdomain.com`.

DATA SOVEREIGNTY

Data sovereignty is the concept that data stored in a specific location is governed by the laws and taxation of the country in which it resides. Fundamentally, this idea is used to protect data and reduce tax bills. This concept is most commonly applied in finance, insurance, and pharmaceutical organizations that will typically have datacenters in countries such as Luxembourg, Switzerland, Bahamas, Cayman Islands, and Monaco where either the tax rates are lower or the law provides a level of banking privacy that makes storing money or data in that location beneficial.

There have been many discussions about the actual benefits of data sovereignty. The reality is that, given a serious enough offense, even a Swiss bank will hand over financial data if a "lifting order" is granted by a judge. Likewise, many governments have the right to seize data from companies that operate within their jurisdiction, which is often cited as a reason to store data offshore to prevent information from being seized. However, the reality is that most countries have rights to seize data from wherever it may be if there is supporting evidence to suggest that it is in the interest of national security (or is being located there to evade payment of taxes).

Despite this, almost every financial, insurance, or pharmaceutical company still insists on this method of data security. These types of organizations are extremely protective of their data, and getting their IT risk departments to approve a change of sensitive data location is an uphill struggle.

This is a problem for Office 365 since each tenant can only exist physically in one geographic region, that is, North America *or* Europe *or* Asia. You cannot have a tenant that spans these regions—you have to pick one at the time of tenant creation. (Office 365 actually uses the address that you type in to determine the best location for the tenant.)

Luckily, this is where Exchange hybrid comes in. Typically, only a fraction of the users in any organization that requires data sovereignty will in reality be affected by that requirement. This means that if, for example, 20 percent of the users have to keep their data in a specific location, then 80 percent of the users could be moved to Office 365. This model allows for a reduction in on-premises infrastructure while still meeting the organizational data sovereignty rules.

DATA LEAKAGE

Data leakage refers to the unapproved distribution of data. This may occur within the organization or externally. The news is often littered with companies that have lost sensitive data. Such examples include the British Ministry of Defense, which reported that 340 laptops had been lost or stolen between June 2008 and June 2010, and the loss of details about 1.2 million federal employee bank accounts by Bank of America in 2005.

Microsoft Office 365 is compliant with world-class industry standards, including ISO-27001, EU Model clauses, HIPAA-BAA, and FISMA, and it is verified by third-party auditors. However, when customers are presented with the paradigm shift of storing their data somewhere other than in their own datacenters, they are often a little uneasy about this prospect and want to understand how they can better protect their data. Often, the discussion of controlling data leakage is something that should probably have occurred many years earlier, and Office 365 is simply the catalyst that encourages a decision to be made.

The solution to data leakage is complex since it involves many factors. Imagine the differences between a lost laptop and an employee maliciously sending company confidential information to a competitor or to the press. Both constitute data leakage; however, one is accidental while the other is malicious.

The most common way to prevent data leakage with Office 365 is to integrate your tenant with an on-premises implementation of Active Directory Rights Management Services (AD RMS). This both encrypts sensitive data and controls who may access it, both inside and outside the organization. Bear in mind, however, that if someone really wants to share information with a competitor or the press, it is next to impossible to prevent it. Nevertheless, the likelihood of information getting into the wrong hands when storing your data in Office 365 is no worse than it is for an on-premises solution. If anything, you could argue that the Microsoft Office 365 datacenters are equally or maybe even more secure than most customer datacenters.

More information on using AD RMS for IRM with Exchange Server 2013 in hybrid deployments can be found here:

```
http://technet.microsoft.com/en-us/library/jj659052(v=exchg.150).aspx
```

UNSUPPORTED CLIENTS

As discussed previously in this chapter, Office 365 has a defined list of clients that are supported, especially versions of Microsoft Office. You should perform a client inventory to determine which clients you need to support. This also applies to Internet browsers if web-based services are being used, such as the Outlook Web App (OWA).

It can be quite difficult to deliver this news to customers who want to move to Exchange Online quickly, since it almost certainly means a fairly lengthy delay to their Exchange deployment project. However, it is also another area where Exchange hybrid can help. Hybrid allows some users to be moved to Exchange Online while others remain on the on-premises version. It also means that users can be migrated to Exchange Online as their client software is upgraded.

Of course, there is still the downside that the client or browser software needs to be upgraded at all. The reality is that customers eventually need to move forward to ensure security and a good user experience. Exchange Online is often just the catalyst that brings updates of client software versions into the discussion. Of course, some customers simply do not, or cannot, perform these types of desktop upgrades, and so this model may mean that they have to be very cautious about moving to Office 365.

Table 7.3 shows supported browsers and operating systems in Office 365. This table calls out that both Windows Vista and Windows XP will not be supported in Office 365 starting January 1, 2014.

TABLE 7.3:   Client and software support in Office 365

OPERATING SYSTEMS	WEB BROWSERS
Windows 8	Internet Explorer 10
	Latest version of Firefox
	Latest version of Chrome
Windows 7	Windows Internet Explorer 10 recommended
	Windows Internet Explorer 9
	Internet Explorer 8
	Latest version of Firefox
	Latest version of Chrome
Windows Vista with Service Pack 2	Internet Explorer 9 recommended
(Support ends January 1, 2014)	Internet Explorer 8
	Latest version of Firefox
	Latest version of Chrome

TABLE 7.3: Client and software support in Office 365 *(CONTINUED)*

OPERATING SYSTEMS	WEB BROWSERS
Windows XP with Service Pack 2 or 3 (Support ends January 1, 2014)	Internet Explorer 8 Latest version of Firefox Latest version of Chrome
Mac OS X 10.5, Mac OS X 10.6, or Mac OS X 10.7	Latest version of Firefox Safari 5 and later

http://office.microsoft.com/en-gb/office365-suite-help/software-requirements-for-office-365-for-business-HA102817357.aspx

Table 7.4 shows which Office versions are supported by Office 365 and what updates each requires.

TABLE 7.4: Office version support in Office 365

VERSION	NOTES
Microsoft Office 2010 with Service Pack 1	Customers who sign up for Office 365 after February 27, 2013 must apply all automatic public updates that were released before December 2012. Customers who signed up for Office 365 before February 27, 2013 must complete the following: By July 1, 2013, apply KB2553248. By April 8, 2014, apply all automatic public updates for Office 2010 that were released before December 2012.
Microsoft Office 2007 with Service Pack 3	Customers who sign up for Office 365 after February 27, 2013 must apply all automatic public updates that were released before December 2012. Customers who signed up for Office 365 before February 27, 2013 must complete the following: By October 1, 2013, apply KB2583910. By April 8, 2014, apply all automatic public updates for Office 2010 that were released prior to December 2012.
Microsoft Office 2003 All versions	POP3 and IMAP4 only. For more information, see the following URL: `http://go.microsoft.com/fwlink/p/?LinkID=254207`
Microsoft Office for Mac 2011 with Service Pack 3	Mac OS X 10.6 operating system or later required.
Microsoft Office 2008 for Mac version 12.2.9	Support ends April 9, 2013.

http://office.microsoft.com/en-gb/office365-suite-help/software-requirements-for-office-365-for-business-HA102817357.aspx

SINGLE SIGN-ON

This is one of the most misunderstood aspects of Exchange Online. For most people, the term *single sign-on* means not having to enter multiple passwords at logon. However, this is not strictly how it is applied in Exchange Online. Single sign-on in Exchange Online means that you have a single account and password, but it does not mean that you will not have to enter your password when you try to connect to Exchange Online. This is complicated further when we look at the authentication behavior for different client types. Typically, users accessing their mailbox via a web browser will experience true single sign-on in that they will not need to enter their password. Outlook, however, will prompt the user for a password. The user can chose to save their password, which will get rid of the password prompt until the user next changes their password.

This behavior is actually not a problem for most organizations, and although they would prefer that users not be prompted for passwords, the reality is that as long as the Exchange Online login name is sensible (their SMTP address, for example), they can usually manage to enter their password and click the Save Password check box without any concern. The problem arises when customer expectations are not set correctly at the outset and because the term "single sign-on" was taken literally and that customer expectation was never corrected.

Our advice here is to make sure that customers are aware of the potential change in user experience early on in the design process to give them time to get used to it. A POC can also help here. Demonstrating the actual logon experience to Exchange Online often alleviates any concerns. The bottom line, however, is that if a customer requires a seamless Outlook logon experience with no password prompts, then Exchange Online may not be the right solution for them.

VIRTUAL DESKTOP INFRASTRUCTURE

Desktop virtualization has experienced a recent rise in popularity. At its most basic, *Virtual Desktop Infrastructure (VDI)* is the replacement of powerful desktop computers with lower-power consoles that provide a virtual desktop running on large-scale virtual server farms. This works nicely for most applications, and it allows an end user to move freely from place to place. Moreover, when the end user connects to their virtual desktop, it is exactly as they left it, which is a nice user experience.

There are some problems, however, with Outlook on VDI. When Outlook is connected to Exchange Online, it is strongly recommended that you use cached mode. Cached mode helps Outlook perform well even if the network link is slow or of poor quality. When connecting Outlook to Exchange Online, the traffic must pass through several layers of network infrastructure and the Internet. Thus, it is likely that periods of poor performance will be experienced. This recommendation for using Outlook in cached mode when connected to Exchange Online is in direct conflict with Outlook on VDI. With Outlook on VDI, it is strongly recommended that you use online mode to avoid the need to store all of that Outlook cached data on the VDI infrastructure, which would be extremely costly.

The options here are limited. VDI and Exchange Online are simply not a great mix of technology. The best solution is our old friend the Outlook Web App. This works nicely since OWA is relatively tolerant to network performance and does not have the same storage capacity requirements as Outlook in cached mode. However, this does assume that OWA will meet end-user requirements, which is often not the case. Alternatively, you could configure Outlook to use online mode. Our experience here, however, is that Outlook in online mode is very sensitive to network performance, and the client may appear to hang for several seconds during periods of poor network performance.

Real World Scenario

AVOIDING AN EXCHANGE ONLINE PROJECT FAILURE

Some of the worst Exchange Online project failures could have been avoided by following the publicly available planning guidance and by defining requirements more diligently from the outset. For example, one project came to a standstill after the customer had been sold Exchange Online as part of Office 365. The project team went through what they thought was a detailed requirements-gathering process. This included discussing use cases, client versions, and so on. When asked about the client version, the customer replied, "Outlook 2010." What they failed to mention was that it was provided via a virtual desktop platform, and that they would not be able to switch on Outlook cached mode. A pilot was performed, and the end-user experience was unsatisfactory with Outlook in online mode. The business then advised the project team that OWA did not support all of the features required by their end users. This left the team with a customer that had purchased licenses for Office 365 that they could not currently use. In this instance, the customer chose to move their Exchange service back on-premises. This was a prolonged and painful process, which involved complex licensing changes and delayed their project by over six months.

Summary

Exchange Online in a hybrid configuration offers many customer benefits, but it is a standardized service offering with fixed support and feature boundaries. The trick to ensuring a successful Exchange Online deployment is to define the requirements more precisely than usual and to make sure that the customer is aware of any changes in the user experience that will result.

Be realistic when considering design service levels. Try to calculate the maximum service levels that you can meet by considering all of the links in the chain. In most cases, the Exchange Online SLA of 99.9 percent availability is not achievable in reality when you include the service levels of your firewalls, network, and Internet connections.

Try to avoid being caught up in the excitement and marketing hyperboles for cloud-based services. They are not the answer to every problem in the IT world. The old adage "If it sounds too good to be true, it probably is" should be considered at every stage. There are many benefits to Exchange Online; however, there are many dependencies and constraints to address before you can use the service. Understanding what you are getting for your money, and what it is going to cost you in terms of dependency remediation, is vital to making the right choices for Exchange Online.

Once the design process has begun, it is important to remember that, although Microsoft has designed and deployed Exchange in Office 365, you still need to design and deploy the hybrid infrastructure and connectivity. Plan for your network bandwidth requirements, upgrade links, and firewalls as appropriate. Remember that you are materially changing the quantity and direction of network data traffic for your messaging service.

Perform a proof of concept and production pilot in complex environments to catch environmental issues with customer infrastructure and to demonstrate the actual end-user experience. This can help to alleviate the fear of change.

Before deployment, remember to run through the validation tools mentioned in the chapter to check that the environment is ready for Exchange Online hybrid:

◆ Microsoft Office 365 Deployment Readiness Tool

    `http://community.office365.com/en-us/forums/183/p/2285/8155.aspx`

◆ Microsoft Connectivity Analyzer Tool

    `https://testconnectivity.microsoft.com/?tabid=client`

◆ Microsoft OnRamp Tool

    `https://onramp.office365.com/onramp/`

◆ IdFix DirSync Error Remediation Tool

    `http://www.microsoft.com/en-us/download/details.aspx?id=36832`

Also, remember to use the Exchange Server Deployment Assistant, which will create a customized deployment and preparation plan for you.

    `http://technet.microsoft.com/en-gb/exdeploy2010/default(EXCHG.150).aspx#Index`

Chapter 8

Designing a Secure Exchange Solution

As a messaging consultant, you know that some of the most complex areas in designing a Microsoft Exchange solution are those relating to security. There are a number of reasons for this. Primarily, security and the technology used to address security considerations are a minefield and a discipline in their own right. This makes understanding security concepts and the ability to talk in the same language as your security officer a challenge from the outset. When and if you manage to overcome this hurdle, further frustration is likely to develop from a lack of requirements and the disparity between the vision and the reality of your design. You will then need to reason with and facilitate key stakeholders to identify and agree on a way to move forward.

More than any other area of the design of a Microsoft Exchange solution, determining how the solution is to be secured requires an array of skills. The goal of this chapter is to help you understand and develop those skills, from comprehending the concepts and vocabulary needed, to appreciating the functionality within Microsoft Exchange Server 2013 that can be deployed to meet the project's requirements. Deploying a secure Microsoft Exchange solution often relies on dependent infrastructures, so we'll discuss the wider infrastructure components in order to provide you with a thorough understanding of how a project's requirements can be met in full.

In addition, this chapter will provide you with useful insights to prepare you for the awkward questions from your security officer and enable you to elicit the security requirements in a concise manor, thus avoiding the lengthy and soul-destroying security workshops and the spectrum of confusion that will arise from that disparity between the vision and the reality!

Should you wish to skip this chapter, we urge you, at the very least, to read and understand the section "How Real Is the Threat Today?" This section alone should encourage you to read on.

Why and What to Secure?

Before plunging into the "how," it is vital that you understand the "what" and "why." That is, what is security and why is it important? How real are the security threats and risks to a messaging infrastructure today?

What Does Security Mean?

Because of a number of security incidents that have occurred since the first release of Microsoft Exchange Server, and with the onset of *ubiquitous computing* (the embedding of microprocessors in everyday objects), the meaning and significance of security have changed. Consequently, the technology used to avoid security risks and threats has also matured. As you will learn later in this section, message security is now integral to Exchange Server thanks to Microsoft's Trustworthy Computing (TwC) initiatives and Secure by Default principles.

Email is no longer accessed only from the workplace, using one device and one access endpoint. User demand, driven by ubiquitous computing, has created a need for flexible access and, of greater concern from a security perspective, a desire for uncontrolled access. Securing a messaging infrastructure implies securing email on a wide spectrum of devices and classifying and protecting data in motion.

When we speak about security, we are talking about risk acceptance and probability. It is the job of the security officer to assess the risk and probability of security threats and then to determine what must be done to avoid or mitigate those threats and risk. Consequently, securing a messaging infrastructure means different things to different organizations. As consultants, it is our job to understand the meaning of security for a particular organization and then decide how best to address it during design.

How Real Is the Threat Today?

The financial impact of viruses spread during the early versions of Microsoft Exchange Server (and messaging systems in general) is estimated to be approximately $16.7 billion in labor costs, tool expense, productivity loss, and lost income. Since mid-2000, the impact of such mass-mailing viruses has been reduced. To eradicate mass-mailing viruses, such as "Anna Kournikova," "I Love You," and "MyDoom," Microsoft addressed vulnerabilities within Outlook. More recently, the use of cloud-based message hygiene services has grown, providing a dynamic level of intelligence. As a consequence, antivirus software vendors have increased their capabilities in terms of identifying and reacting to viruses more quickly. In addition, many organizations have deployed edge antivirus protection. Although the impact of such viruses has been greatly reduced, other more insidious threats still remain.

Those of you who experienced the epidemic mass emailing of viruses may believe that the threat of email-related viruses has been eradicated. Delving into the statistics produced by antivirus software vendors shows that, on the contrary, the threat is still significant. The December 2012 issue of the Symantec Intelligence Report states that 1 in 277.8 emails contains *malware* (malicious software), 1 in 377.4 emails contains *phishing* attacks (the act of attempting to acquire information such as usernames, passwords, and credit card details by masquerading as a trustworthy entity), and 70.6 percent of all email was reported as spam. By example, in an organization with 50,000 users, each of whom receives, on average, 10 email messages per day through the Internet, 500,000 messages in total inbound will be received from the Internet; of these, on a daily basis,

- ◆ 800 emails will contain malware.
- ◆ 1,325 emails will contain a phishing attack.
- ◆ 353,000 out of 500,000 messages will be spam.

The probability of an attack depends on multiple factors including current level and depth of protection, the industry in which the organization operates, and the geographies in which the organization does business. Organizations based in the United States are more likely at risk than those in any other country. India and the United Kingdom also have a high probability of receiving emails containing phishing attacks because of the large installed base of technology found in those countries.

Aside from malware, spam, and phishing attacks, unauthorized access to network and email data is extremely prevalent today. In the majority of cases, hackers will use one of the following methods to gain unauthorized access to users' email accounts:

◆ Observe the user type in the password, and subsequently attempt to match the typing pattern to gain access.

◆ Profile the user in social media websites and collect user intelligence to allow the hacker to guess the user's password.

◆ Obtain password as a result of a successful malware or phishing attack.

Over the last two years, fewer mass-mailing attacks have been launched as hackers focused on high-value cybercrime, such as *spear phishing*, that is, targeted attacks, directed at specific individuals or companies. In such cases, attackers gather personal information about their target to increase their probability of success. Since 2009, hackers have launched damaging cyber raids on multinational organizations such as Coca-Cola, BG Group, ArcelorMittal, and Chesapeake.

Coca-Cola's email system was infiltrated by an email sent to the deputy president of Coca-Cola's Pacific Group, appearing to come from the CEO. The email contained a malicious link, which when clicked, transparently began downloading malware including a *keylogger*, which records and logs the keys struck on a keyboard. The reported aim of the attack was to ex-filtrate files relating to Coca-Cola's ultimately unsuccessful $2.4 billion acquisition of China's Huiyuan Juice Group. It is clear that, although the impact of such threats is not as obvious as it was during the mass-mailing virus attacks, the threat is still very real, and a good security officer will be aware of current threats and methodologies, tools, and techniques used to penetrate corporate email systems.

What Is Necessary to Secure?

As a messaging consultant, you must understand the likely security concerns of an organization so that you are adequately prepared to determine, communicate, and challenge (if necessary) the proposed security requirements.

During research conducted in April 2012, Mimecast, a company that developed a platform that uses cloud computing to deliver email management, held 500 interviews with IT decision makers across a range of company sizes, industry sectors, and regions. The June 2012 "Shape of E-mail" report concluded that while the level of concern regarding mobile and remote access to email is very real (39 percent and 41 percent of organizations, respectively, agreed), organizations are more concerned about email-based viruses (55 percent) and email security breaches in general (55 percent).

In August 2006, Microsoft classified the four major threats to a messaging and collaboration infrastructure as follows:

Malware   Many viruses and worms are designed to infect millions of computer systems rapidly across the world using the Internet, email, and instant messaging.

Spam   Businesses are being overwhelmed with unsolicited email that is sapping network resources and flooding email inboxes. Spam is not only a threat to corporate productivity; it has become a common carrier for malicious code. As a result, the messaging infrastructure is a critical focal point for businesses in the fight against malicious software.

Unauthorized Network Access   Security procedures and policies that are adequate to protect LAN data can be ineffective when the network is opened to outsiders for messaging and collaboration. In addition, hackers are now using more sophisticated application-layer attacks.

Unauthorized Data Access   Businesses are increasingly concerned with sensitive information leaking outside the business through the messaging and collaboration infrastructure.

Although the threats have matured and are now more sophisticated than in 2006, this threat classification still applies.

Later on, we will take a look at the Microsoft Exchange functionality that can be used to secure the platform against such threats. For malware and spam, we will consider the new built-in functionality designed to provide protection alongside a cloud-based service. To address unauthorized network access, we'll look at how to secure external access, how to secure remote client access, and the options available to *harden* Microsoft Exchange Server 2013 servers. In the concluding section, we will consider data encryption (at rest, in motion, and long-term storage). Finally, should the integrity of the system be compromised, we'll consider the built-in auditing capabilities of Exchange Server 2013.

Handling Security Conversations

Conversations relating to security are almost always unpredictable. Despite this, it is essential that you win the trust of the security officer. If you understand the threats to the organization and have a firm grasp of the technology, you are halfway there. The aim of this section is to provide you with some useful insights so that you can become that trusted advisor.

It is vital that during the early design stages of an Exchange 2013 solution, you involve the security team, not just in collecting the security requirements but also by keeping them informed of your progress and ensuring that you gain an understanding of the organization's current security strategies. Keeping the security officer on board with the design can be the difference between the success or failure of the project. The security officer has the power to veto the project if they do not buy into the solution. It is not uncommon to see entire strategies fail, whether the strategy is Bring Your Own Device (BYOD), Exchange Online, or creating a dynamic/flexible work style, if the messaging consultant doesn't gain support from the security team from the start.

The Challenges

Over the last 10 years, the authors have held, facilitated, and learned from many meetings with security teams. Let's take a look at the challenges that you may face when interacting with them:

Challenge #1: Complexity Comes with a Cost   It is inevitable that the security team will want the most secure solution technically possible—after all that is their job! However, this level of security will sacrifice both simplicity and the overall user experience, and, as a consequence, not all organizations will choose the most secure solution. Each security requirement must be weighed against the threat, assessed against both the impact, should the integrity of the system be compromised, and the technical complexity that will result from the requirement. In addition, the resulting design must be assessed against the ability to manage and maintain it throughout the projected life cycle of the platform.

Challenge #2: Management Vision Is Disconnected from the Corporate Security Policy   "I want a flexible workforce." "We must move toward a BYOD strategy." "We have a long-term strategy to move to Exchange Online." We have heard such statements time and time again from senior key stakeholders and IT decision makers. Then, several hours later, after meeting with the security officer, we have learned: "We don't publish any Exchange services directly to the Internet today; our only means of external access, by policy, is via a virtual private network." Having foresight to recognize this disconnect, between the reality and the vision, will save you hours of negotiation later in trying to resolve this problem instead of letting the strategist solve it.

Challenge #3: Dependent Infrastructure Is Not Available   A requirement has been defined to provide secure external access to email services. In addition, a requirement to be able to prevent users from printing, forwarding, and copying email has also been defined. You have collected the security requirements from the security officer, and you now need much more infrastructure than just Microsoft Exchange. Although reverse proxy platforms and Active Directory Rights Management Service (AD RMS) clusters, which can be used to protect data through the application of user rights, are typically utilized as "shared infrastructure," the security officer will likely inform you that your project is the first to require the infrastructure. Suddenly, wider infrastructure costs become a stark reality. Make sure that you call out any infrastructure dependencies and associated costs as soon as the requirement is defined and validated.

Challenge #4: Lack of Understanding of Regulatory Policies and Data Jurisdiction Laws   If you work for a multinational corporation and are planning the consolidation of mail services into just one country, or you are considering a move to Exchange Online as part of the Office 365 offering, your security officer is likely to present you with data jurisdiction laws as to where data may and may not reside. We have yet to find a security officer who can articulate clearly data jurisdiction laws. We have come to believe that it is a little like explaining the offside rule in soccer! Data jurisdiction laws are complex, and you may have to adhere to several different data protection acts depending on the location of the business, the cloud provider, and the provider's datacenters. Make sure that the guidance and requirements that you are given are crystal clear and not open to interpretation.

Challenge #5: The Obstructive, Prudent Security Officer   Quite often, you may encounter a security officer who bombards you with questions rather than a set of defined requirements. For example, they may ask, "Why is Microsoft Exchange Server so secure?" The sections that follow will assist you in answering some of these tricky questions. Always remember that a security officer has the duty to protect the organization from threats, and it is their responsibility should the security of the system be compromised. Empathize, make sure you understand their real concerns, and don't be too eager to dismiss their cautiousness.

Challenge #6: Dealing with Unreasonable Demands   Many security teams, especially those teams that are part of larger IT outsource providers, may need to adhere to an industry security standard, for example, ISO 27001. Sometimes, an inaccurate interpretation of that standard is behind demands that you implement the impossible. For example, we were once faced with the statement "Secure Sockets Layer allows client-initiated renegotiation. This must be disabled." If you are challenged with what you believe is impossible functionality to implement, you may need to understand the default behavior of the system to know why you have been given such a task in the first place. It is almost always possible to conform to a required standard by other means.

The sections that follow will help you articulate how Microsoft Exchange Server is secure, either intrinsically due to the software engineering approach, by the components that are secure by default, or by design.

Trustworthy Computing

In 2002, Microsoft implemented the *Trustworthy Computing (TwC)* initiative. Bill Gates defined Trustworthy Computing as "computing that is as available, reliable, and secure as electricity, water services, and telephony." Microsoft has invested in and matured their Trustworthy Computing initiative over the last 11 years. Today Microsoft delivers Trustworthy Computing in the following ways:

The Security Development Lifecycle This is the framework that is used when Microsoft develops software. The *Security Development Lifecycle (SDL)* framework involves approach, processes, and people, and it is not solely concentrated on the traditional software engineering life cycle. Microsoft employees are taught the SDL—what should be done and what must not be done. Other companies have now officially adopted the SDL, and it has become an open framework.

Microsoft Security Response Center The Microsoft Security Response Center (MSRC) is a group of people within Microsoft who track the vulnerabilities within Microsoft software.

Microsoft Malware Protection Center The Microsoft Malware Protection Center (MMPC) provides analysis of malware threats and how to handle them.

Product Certifications The Product Certifications team concentrates on gaining certifications for Microsoft software against local industry security standards.

Security Industry Alliances The Security Industry Alliances team manages alliances with security-focused organizations.

Microsoft Exchange Server is no exception to this process, and versions as early as Microsoft Exchange Server 2003 were developed in accordance with the Trustworthy Computing initiative. Let's take a look at the impact this initiative has made on Microsoft Exchange Server 2013 by examining what is "Secure by Default."

SECURE BY DEFAULT

The ability to articulate to your security officer how Microsoft Exchange is secure is vital. As messaging consultants, we are often asked by a security officer to explain how Microsoft Exchange Server is made secure. Let's discuss how this question is best answered using the right security language.

It is always best to begin by explaining how Exchange Server is *Secure by Default*, that is, right out of the box. Table 8.1 provides you with some of the information you will need to explain this to your security officer. Most of these capabilities were introduced during the SDL of Microsoft Exchange and thus were present in early versions of Exchange. For this reason, we focus both on these capabilities and those that were newly introduced in Exchange 2013.

TABLE 8.1:   Security capabilities in Microsoft Exchange 2013

CAPABILITY	DESCRIPTION	NEW IN EXCHANGE 2013
Secure client to server communications	HTTPS to secure communications between clients and servers (Autodiscover, OA, OWA, EWS, OAB, ActiveSync, POP3, and IMAP4).	No
POP3 and IMAP4	Disabled by default. POP3 and IMAP services on the Client Access role and the Mailbox server role are disabled by default.	No
Transport security	SMTP uses certificates to encrypt and authenticate the SMTP protocol between Mailbox servers and Edge servers and partner organizations. By default, Exchange 2013 servers will always attempt to communicate via TLS but will automatically fail over to unsecure SMTP if the destination server does not support TLS.	No
Secure Edge synchronization	Edge synchronization process: Encryption of LDAP traffic between Edge servers and Exchange 2013 Mailbox servers.	No
Native antimalware functionality	By default, malware filtering is enabled in Microsoft Exchange Server 2013. The default antimalware policy controls your company-wide malware filtering settings.	Yes
Role-based setup	Ensures that only the intended roles and services are installed on the target server by performing a server hardening by default. Limits communication to the ports required for the installed services and processes running on each server role.	Yes
Administrator access to users' mailboxes	Since Microsoft Exchange Version 5.5, administrators with Full Exchange privileges do not, by default, have access to every mailbox within the organization. An administrator who has Full Exchange privileges can grant herself rights to a specific mailbox.	No
Exchange services—local authority	Exchange services no longer run under a single server account to which administrators (and others) used to know the password. Exchange services run under the local system or the network service security context.	No
RBAC	Introduction of RBAC in Microsoft Exchange 2010 provided the ability for a more granular-level assignment of permissions to users and groups. It is now possible to adhere to a least-privilege principle.	No
Always up-to-date setup	When the setup utility is run, the user is given the option to download and use the latest rollups and security hot fixes. The setup executable itself is updated.	Yes

(CONTINUES)

TABLE 8.1: Security capabilities in Microsoft Exchange 2013 *(CONTINUED)*

CAPABILITY	DESCRIPTION	NEW IN EXCHANGE 2013
Auditing reports	From within the EAC, you can run reports or export entries from the mailbox audit log and the administrator audit log. The mailbox audit log records whenever someone other than the person who owns the mailbox accesses a mailbox. This can help you determine who has accessed a mailbox and what they have done. The following reports are now available within the EAC: ◆ Non-owner mailbox access report ◆ Administrator role group report—Reports changes that are made to role groups ◆ In-place discovery and hold report—Reports changes that have been made to in-place discovery and hold ◆ Per-mailbox litigation hold report—Reports users who have been placed on litigation hold ◆ Export mailbox audit logs—Searches for and exports information about non-owner access ◆ Export the administrator audit log—Searches for and exports information about configuration changes made in the organization	Yes
Transport rules	Enhancements have been made to transport rules. New predicates, such as `AttachmentHasExecutableContent`, `MessageContainsDataClassifications`, `SenderIPRanges`, `GenerateIncidentReport`, `ReportSeverityLevel`, and `RouteMessageOutboundRequireTLS`, provide the administrator with more flexibility and control when implementing data loss prevention rules.	Yes
Information Rights Management (IRM)	IRM provides the ability to control what a user can do with a message. IRM is now compatible with Cryptographic Mode 2, an Active Directory Rights Management Services (AD RMS) cryptography mode that supports stronger encryption by allowing you to use 2048-bit keys for RSA and 256-bit keys for SHA-1. Additionally, Mode 2 enables you to use the SHA-2 hashing algorithm.	Yes
Message throttling	The ability of the administrator to set a group of limits on the number of messages and connections that can be processed by the Exchange 2013 server. These limits can prevent unintentional exhaustion of system resources. For example, they could be used to prevent a mass-mailing worm.	No

SECURE BY DESIGN

In software engineering terms, *Secure by Design* means that the software has been designed from the ground up to be secure. You are now able to articulate the process that Microsoft uses and the capabilities that are provided to ensure that Microsoft Exchange Server is secure by default. In infrastructure design terms, when the term Secure by Design is applied, it refers to how the environment has been made secure throughout the design phase.

How secure you make the environment depends on the security requirements that you gather from the security officer, and those requirements should accurately reflect and address the probability of threat, the impact should the system be compromised, and the overall risk to the organization.

As messaging consultants, you have an extremely important task to accomplish in helping to define the security requirements of the Microsoft Exchange Server estate. Quite often, it is your role to understand the generic security requirements (for example, all Exchange data, databases, and logs must be encrypted). You must then translate these into the components that must be implemented and configured (for example, all Exchange servers must be encrypted using Microsoft BitLocker). When the security requirements are well defined, the translation process is relatively straightforward, but as you will learn in the next section, these requirements can often be quite ambiguous.

REQUIREMENT ELICITATION

How do you build a security policy for your business, and what is a sensible starting point? Start by simply asking your security officer this question: "What are the existing corporate security policies, and how are they implemented today?" The response to this question largely depends on the type of customer. Some customers know they should have security but don't know a lot more. A customer who still believes in all of the old best practices when securing Exchange is likely to take the belt-and-braces approach, that is, to secure everything possible, because it is too complicated to try to understand the business requirements and the functionality to meet those requirements. Finally, those clients who have strict security policies in place for a good reason, such as organizations that handle classified information, may respond, "Where should we start?"

One of the most important approaches within infrastructure architecture is not to assume but to reason. While it is important to understand how security is implemented within the current system, do not assume that it is a true reflection of the real requirement; for the majority of customers, this will not be the case. Frequently, the required security policies are not implemented because of a lack of functionality or capability within the product, a lack of investment, or simply that the functionality is too complex both to implement and support.

Real World Scenario

PROBABILITY OF A THREAT

Recently we were with a client, gathering the security requirements. One of the defined requirements was that "all methods of external access must be secured by a second factor of authentication." We later discovered that this client had implemented Microsoft Exchange ActiveSync within their current Exchange platform but that access had not been secured by a second factor. When we challenged the client, we learned that the security officer would be comfortable signing off on a solution that implemented sufficient security controls (for example, ActiveSync device policies) should it prove difficult to implement a second form of authentication.

continues

(continued)

So why the change of heart? One of the main causes of this is the probability of threat. Because a less-secure solution was in place, and the organization was confident in it since no attack or compromise had been evident, the security officer was willing to sign off on a security solution that did not utilize a second factor of authentication. This decision, however, did not truly consider the impact of an attack. For this reason, security requirements must be defined and classified using a *must/should/could* approach, that is, what the system *must* do, what it *should* do, and what it *could* do.

Frequently, the difference between a *must* and a *should* requirement is a tradeoff between the risk, the investment required to implement, and the complexity and maintainability of the solution within the production environment. For that reason, it is vital that when requirements are being defined, you can articulate the cost, complexity, and supportability of the functionality required to meet the requirement.

One challenge remains when defining the security requirements for the solution; that is, how do you deal with customers who know they should have security but don't know a lot beyond that? These are customers and security officers who are not able to provide you with their requirements; consequently, your job is then to tease the requirements out of them. For those customers, we find that a list of questions is helpful. Table 8.2 provides a good starting point.

TABLE 8.2: Questions for defining security requirements

QUESTION	CONSIDERATION AND SOLUTION
Do you have any requirements for the encryption of data at rest?	Protect against unauthorized data access.
	Exchange 2013 alone cannot encrypt Exchange data. However, Windows BitLocker can be used to encrypt Exchange data stored on the Exchange servers.
Do you have any requirements for the encryption of data in transit?	Protect against unauthorized data access.
	Client to server traffic is secure by default. Are there any requirements to secure SMTP traffic (i.e., to use TLS)? Is there a requirement for end-to-end encryption of message data (i.e., the use of S/MIME and/or cloud based to encrypt messages)?
Do you have any requirements for the encryption of data in long-term storage?	Protect against unauthorized data access.
	How are tape backups to be secured? (Does the backup solution encrypt the data on tape?). Who has access? Are backup tapes kept off-site?
Do you have any requirement that users apply digital signatures to emails so that the recipient can verify the validity of the sender?	Protect against unauthorized data access.
	AD RMS required.

(Continues)

TABLE 8.2:   Questions for defining security requirements   *(CONTINUED)*

QUESTION	CONSIDERATION AND SOLUTION
Do you have requirements for enabling users to protect email content with Information Rights Management controls? **Is there a requirement to prevent users from copying/forwarding/printing emails?**	Protect against unauthorized data access. AD RMS required.
Are there any firewalls in between sites and servers or clients of which this solution should be aware?	Protect against unauthorized network access. May affect supportability of Exchange 2013, depending on the implemented firewall rules.
Do you have the ability to use an internal PKI? Where external certificates are required, do you have a preferred third-party supplier?	Protect against unauthorized network access. Securing client to server traffic.
Do you have a requirement to classify data? Is there data in the environment that if leaked would cause a significant impact on the organization?	Protect against unauthorized data access. Common in government agencies. Often these types of organizations have a requirement to classify data on levels of impact. Hub transport rules can be implemented to recognize and classify data.
Is there a requirement to implement address book segmentation so that some users do not have permission to view other users within the address book?	Protect against unauthorized data access. Address book policies required.
Is there a requirement to provide two-factor authentication for external access methods?	Protect against unauthorized network access. Applicable to Exchange ActiveSync, Outlook Web App, and Outlook Anywhere. Client certificates, IPSec, VPN, DirectAccess, soft/hard security tokens.
Can wildcard certificates be used?	Protect against unauthorized network access. Wildcard certificates can make configuration simpler, but have some constraints in usage. In addition, by security policy, some organisations will not allow the use of wildcard certificates.
Is there a requirement to implement a least-privilege, granular-permissions model for system administrators?	Protect against unauthorized network access. The Active Directory administrative model should follow the least-privilege model to ensure that only the required privileges for a specific job role are granted.

(CONTINUES)

TABLE 8.2:   Questions for defining security requirements *(CONTINUED)*

QUESTION	CONSIDERATION AND SOLUTION
Is there a requirement for system administrators to have separate user accounts and administrator-level accounts?	Protect against unauthorized network access. These accounts should always be separate and not be shared by a group of users.
Must the solution include the ability to log authorized and unauthorized access to users' mailboxes?	Protect against unauthorized data access. Enable Mailbox Auditing
Must the email system provide the capability to scan internal emails (that is, messages sent and received between internal users) for spam and malware?	Protect against malware and spam. Enable antimalware and antispam agents on Mailbox servers.

Now that you have a defined set of requirements, adequately categorized in the appropriate manner, let's take a look at how to meet these requirements using native operating system or Microsoft Exchange 2013 functionality, through the use of third-party software, or through a combination of all three.

Designing a Secure Exchange Solution

Given that the security officer is likely to articulate requirements against the perceived threats, this section of the chapter is designed to provide you with an understanding of the capabilities that can be implemented to secure the solution and mitigate those specific threats. For example, how to protect the environment from spear-phishing attacks (discussed previously in this chapter) is covered in the section "Protecting against Malware and Spam" that follows. Implementing functionality to protect against unauthorized network access, for example, securely publishing Exchange using reverse proxy solutions, is covered in the "Protecting against Unauthorized Network Access" section, and so on.

Protecting against Malware and Spam

Typically, an organization will require protection against malware and spam using a multi-layer defense barrier. Within the industry, this is commonly referred to as *defense in depth*. In addition to this security principle, organizations may wish to ensure that the different layers cover a broad spectrum of products, vendors, and suppliers. For example, an organization that subscribes to Symantec Cloud Services to provide malware and spam protection will then not implement Symantec Mail Security for Microsoft Exchange 2013, Symantec Endpoint Protection for Windows 2012, and Symantec Endpoint Protection for their client base.

Following is a brief overview of different layers of message protection and offerings:

Cloud   *Cloud-based message hygiene services* provide essential protection while virtually eliminating the need to manage hardware and software on-premises. Typically, a cloud-based message hygiene service will accept emails on behalf of the organization. (A configuration change is required to point the organization's MX records to the cloud-based service provider.) As spammers continuously become more clever, protection needs to be dynamic so that the environment can be protected fully as threats change. If you plan to protect the organization from threats using on-premise products exclusively, this can consume a lot of effort and resources, and thus the virus update process is more likely to be protracted, leading to an increased risk of threat. Recently, Microsoft has invested heavily in their Exchange Online Protection (EOP) cloud-based service, because they determined that this was the best and most efficient way of providing that dynamic service to their customers. With EOP, Microsoft can see what is happening across multiple organizations from a broader perspective and proactively target threats a lot faster (made possible through spam-aggregation techniques, for example). Other cloud-based message hygiene services include Symantec Cloud, Postini (Google), Comodo AntiSpam Gateway, and Total Defense Email Security Service, among others.

In April 2011, Gartner reported: "SaaS secure Web and e-mail gateways frequently provide efficiency and cost advantages, and a growing number of offerings are delivering an improved level of security that exceeds what most organizations can achieve with on-premises software or appliances."[1]

Perimeter *Perimeter protection* provides a vital layer of security between the Internet and a corporate messaging environment. Without perimeter protection, SMTP connections can be made and emails sent directly to servers on the internal network from either a cloud-based message hygiene provider or directly from the Internet. When an SMTP server is deployed in the organization's perimeter network, messages are routed through the SMTP message hygiene server, thus providing additional virus filtering and connection security. Currently, as organizations adopt cloud-based message hygiene services, and as confidence grows in these solutions, some organizations are opting to remove the virus-filtering capability from the on-premise perimeter network to reduce the administrative burden. For perimeter protection, Microsoft provides the Exchange Edge Transport server role. Other solutions include but are not limited to Clearswift SECURE Email Gateway, McAfee Email Gateway, Cisco IronPort, and Websense Email Security Gateway.

Platform There are two considerations when providing *platform-level protection* on Microsoft Exchange servers: protecting the message transport layer and protecting the server file level. As of September 2012, Microsoft announced that they were retiring their Forefront Protection for Microsoft Exchange, which was additional software that could be installed to provide malware and spam filtering. In Microsoft Exchange Server 2013, the ability to filter malware and spam has been built into the product, as you learned in the previous section. Exchange 2013 uses transport-level agents to scan email for spam and malware. While the antispam agents typically run on the Edge Transport role, these too can be enabled and run on the Mailbox server along with malware scanning. It is also possible to disable the malware filter if you wish to use another product to provide this functionality. Such products include Trend Micro ScanMail Suite for Microsoft Exchange, Symantec Mail Security for Microsoft Exchange, and McAfee Security for Email Servers. All of these vendors have updated their software to run with Microsoft Exchange Server 2013.

In addition to application-level protection, it is advisable that the operating system and the files on a Microsoft Exchange server be protected from malicious code. This is commonly known as *file-level protection*. However, it is vital to make sure that the appropriate Exchange file and directory-level exclusions are in place to avoid issues with Exchange Server 2013. Refer to the following TechNet article for additional information:

```
http://technet.microsoft.com/en-us/library/bb332342.aspx
```

---

[1]*"Moving E-Mail and Web Security to the Cloud" (Gartner, 2011).*

Let's take a closer look at the Microsoft offerings and the built-in functionality now included within Exchange 2013 for each of the layers defined here.

CLOUD: EXCHANGE ONLINE PROTECTION

Exchange Online Protection (EOP) is the replacement for the recently retired Forefront Online Protection for Exchange (FOPE), Microsoft's hosted email gateway. EOP provides comprehensive email protection (through multiengine antivirus) and continuously evolving antispam protection. It also boasts enterprise-class reliability, flexible policy rules, and a streamlined administration console with detailed reporting.

Some major improvements have been made to this latest version of EOP, including the use of an integrated console, common policy rules (built on the same stack as the Exchange transport rules), and some spam-handling improvements. EOP performs both inbound and outbound filtering.

Microsoft's recommended guidance for Exchange Server 2013 security is to use EOP alongside the Exchange Server 2013 built-in antimalware and antispam features, removing the management and administration overhead of the Edge Transport server role.

Deploying EOP involves the following four, high level activities:

1. Adding and verifying domain ownership and setting up the MX record(s). This step involves manual configuration of your mail Exchange (MX) record within your corporate DNS external provider to point to the EOP servers.

2. Configuring EOP antimalware and antispam settings.

3. Creating rules to meet the business needs.

4. Running the Hybrid Wizard. The Hybrid Wizard will set up the appropriate connectors for secure mail flow between your on-premises Exchange 2013 server and EOP.

If you wish to set up rules based on users/groups or user attributes within Active Directory, or if you want to synchronize safe/blocked senders lists, you will also need to set up and run Directory Synchronization, which takes advantage of the Office 365 DirSync process.

EOP uses several methods to block spam. *Connection filtering* is the first line of defense that blocks spam at a TCP layer. EOP uses the *Spamhaus* and internal databases to block connections from known spammers. (Spamhaus is an international organization that tracks email spammers and spam-related activity.) Eighty percent of spam is captured at this layer. EOP will automatically add those sending over 90 percent spam to the internal block list. However, you cannot rely on this method alone, because spammers now send only five to nine messages from one IP address.

The second layer is *sender-recipient filtering*, which is reported to block up to 15 percent of all spam based on internal lists and sender reputation. When the EOP servers receive the HELO (or EHLO) command, the sending host/service name is checked against a list of banned hosts.

The third layer is *content filtering*, which blocks the final 5 percent of all spam based on the internal lists and heuristics. Included within the content filter is the capability of blocking certain URLs within emails. This protects against phishing attacks and, more significantly, the spear-phishing attacks discussed earlier in the chapter. A geographically distributed Microsoft team exists entirely to watch mail streams, keep all of these lists and rules in check, and work out new content rules.

EOP also offers good protection against *spoofing*, which is an email message with a sending address modified to appear as if it originates from a sender other than the actual sender of the message. To accomplish this, EOP utilizes *sender policy framework (SPF)* and sender ID filtering. SPF records, once implemented on external DNS zones, identify authorized outbound email servers. Unlike FOPE, EOP provides granular options for the detection and management of spam, including the ability to block bulk mail and block email based on a language and/or geography.

Multiple engines facilitate antimalware capabilities within EOP. Other enhancements over FOPE include the introduction of a new action to remove unsafe attachments but still deliver the message content. Once detected, EOP can send a notification message to the sender of the undelivered message and to a system administrator. This capability can be enabled/disabled for internal/external users separately.

EOP also provides the ability to configure customized mail rules. This capability is built upon the Exchange transport rules engine. Rules are *comprised* of conditions used to identify specific criteria such as sender, receiver, and keywords within a message, *actions* that are applied to email messages that match the conditions, and *exceptions* that identify messages to which a transport rule action should not be applied. In addition to the functionality provided in Exchange Server 2010, both EOP and the on-premises version of Exchange 2013 allow rules to be run between certain dates and to run in a test mode, with or without notifications. Having the ability to run transport rules in a test mode with notifications is ideal when configuring rules within EOP to block messages, because it allows you to test rules before inadvertently blocking critical messages.

Most importantly, to help the security officer assess the probability of a threat, EOP provides built-in granular reporting options that present a clear view on spam filtering and malware attacks. One constraint to bear in mind, however, is that only 60 days of summary data and 7 days of detailed data are provided.

Finally, EOP provides a streamlined management console, as shown in Figure 8.1, for control over the settings for antispam and antimalware, RBAC, domain management, message tracing, and quarantine management. If you have an Exchange Enterprise Client Access License (ECAL) with services or you are an Office 365 customer, you will also have the ability to connect to EOP through PowerShell.

EDGE TRANSPORT SERVER

To act as an ingress and egress point for Internet email, the *Edge Transport server* must be deployed into the organization's perimeter network. Given that the Edge Transport server is not installed on the internal network, for most organizations this means that the server is not joined to a domain. However, larger enterprises sometimes have domain(s) dedicated to the perimeter and, in that scenario, Microsoft will support the Edge Transport server being joined to a domain. When the Edge Transport server is not domain-joined, configuration and recipient information that the Edge Transport server requires is stored in Active Directory Lightweight Directory Services (AD LDS). Internal Active Directory information can be synchronized (commonly known as *EdgeSync*) to the Edge Transport server by subscribing the Edge Transport server to an Active Directory site. This associates the Edge Transport server with the Exchange organization. Once established, the EdgeSync process enhances antispam features by providing the capability to perform recipient lookups and *safelist aggregation*, which refers to the ability to collect data from the user's safe/blocked senders list in Outlook. Once the data is collected, the Edge Transport server can use it to reduce the number of false positives. The EdgeSync process also provides the ability to secure SMTP communications with partner domains using mutual transport layer security.

FIGURE 8.1
EOP streamlined management console

The Exchange 2013 version of the Edge Transport role was not shipped when Exchange 2013 reached general availability in early December 2012. Therefore, it is possible to coexist (and even deploy) Exchange 2010 Edge Transport servers with Exchange 2013 servers. Additional information about the Edge Transport server role is available at the following TechNet address:

```
http://technet.microsoft.com/en-us/library/bb124701(v=exchg.141).aspx
```

It is important to be aware of some essential considerations if you plan to use Exchange 2010 Edge Transport server to protect your Exchange 2013 infrastructure. These considerations are as follows:

◆ Exchange 2010, Service Pack 3 is required on all Exchange 2010 Edge Transport servers that are to coexist within the same environment as the Exchange 2013 infrastructure.

◆ Exchange 2007 or Exchange 2010 Edge Transport servers may be used.

◆ When subscribing the Edge Transport server to an Active Directory site, the server can be subscribed to a standalone Exchange 2013 server or a combined Mailbox server and Client Access server. You are unable to subscribe the Edge Transport server to a standalone Exchange 2013 Client Access server. This is because the Transport service now exists on the Mailbox server and not on the Client Access server role.

◆ The edge synchronization (EdgeSync) process cannot be set up and configured from within the Exchange Administration Center. This will not be possible until an Exchange 2013 version of the Edge Transport server is released. Currently, the edge synchronization process can only be set up using PowerShell.

INTERNAL ANTIMALWARE AND ANTISPAM PROTECTION

Microsoft Exchange Server 2013 is the first release of this product to provide basic, built-in antimalware protection. In previous versions, if you required Exchange-level protection for Exchange, you either deployed Forefront Protection for Exchange (FPE) or a third-party product such as Trend Micro's ScanMail. Historically, Exchange administrators have experienced many instability issues with third-party products using the Virus Scanning API (VSAPI) to provide antimalware and antispam functionality. Microsoft has elected to build in protection for their products as native functionality, rather than having an extra, third-party layer on top. This doesn't mean, however, that a third-party product cannot be used instead of the built-in functionality.

By default, malware filtering is enabled and the antispam agents are disabled on the Exchange 2013 Mailbox server role. It is recommended that you enable the antispam agents on the Mailbox server role if your organization has not deployed an Edge Transport server role in the perimeter network. The Exchange 2013 antispam agents that run on the Exchange 2013 Mailbox server role are installed and enabled by default on the Edge Transport server.

The following list defines the antispam agents and, should they be enabled, the order in which they are applied to the message in transit on the Exchange 2013 Mailbox server:

Sender Filter Agent   Assesses incoming messages against a blocked sender list.

Recipient Filter Agent   Assesses incoming messages against a blocked recipient list.

Sender ID Agent   Checks sender IP address to determine if the sender is spoofed or not.

Content Filter Agent   Assigns a *Spam Confidence Level (SCL) rating* from 0 to 9 to each scanned message: the higher the rating, the more likely the message is spam. The administrator can configure the content filter to delete, reject, or quarantine the messages according to the allocated SCL level.

Protocol Analysis Agent   Assesses the sending server reputation against multiple criteria.

The following agents, available on the Edge Transport server, are not available on the Exchange 2013 Mailbox server role. Should there be a requirement for you to deploy either of these two antispam agents, you will need to deploy an Edge Transport server.

Connection Filtering Agent   Uses a variety of IP block lists and IP allow lists to determine if the remote server is allowed to establish a TCP connection.

Attachment Filter Agent   Allows the administrator to configure which attachments are filtered based on filename, extension type, or MIME content type.

Although they are disabled by default, the antispam agents maybe enabled on the Exchange 2013 Mailbox role with the following command:

```
& $env:ExchangeInstallPath\Scripts\Install-AntiSpamAgents.ps1
```

Once this command is run, you must restart the Microsoft Exchange Transport service on the Mailbox server.

Because malware scanning is enabled by default on all Mailbox servers, messages are scanned for malware when sent to, or received from, a Mailbox server. EAC can be used to configure your default, organization-wide malware filter policy. To be able to configure any of the antispam and antimalware functionality within Exchange Server 2013, you must be a member of either the Organization Management or Hygiene Management RBAC role group.

EAC provides simple management of the default malware policy, which can be found under the Protection menu item. EAC provides the ability to choose how you wish email to be treated should malicious code be detected. Options are provided to delete the entire message or to delete all attachments and replace with either default or custom text. The administrator also has the option to send customizable notifications to both the sender and the system administrator. You can also differentiate between internal and external senders.

EAC blocks the ability to create new malware filters, but the following shell command is available to do this:

```
New-MalwareFilterPolicy -Name <Name>
```

Although you may be able to create new malware filter policies from PowerShell, you will be unable to scope the policy (which renders making new policies useless). Within EAC, the default policy is shown as being Scoped To: All Domains. From this, you can take some comfort in knowing that Microsoft does have plans to enable the scoping of malware filter policies in future releases.

By default, Exchange 2013 will check for new malware engines every hour. Doing so requires an Internet connection. Engine updates can also be invoked manually from an Exchange server that has Internet connectivity by running the following script:

```
& $env:ExchangeInstallPath\Scripts\Update-MalwareFilteringServer.ps1 -Identity <FQDN of
server>
```

Currently there is no published guidance on how to download an engine update from a non-Exchange server. This procedure is required if your Exchange 2013 servers are not configured to connect to the Internet, but it is anticipated that the procedure will be the same as it was for updating the scan engines in Microsoft Forefront Protection for Exchange (except for a code change to download only one engine). This procedure is defined in following support article:

```
http://support.microsoft.com/kb/2292741
```

There are two options available to stop messages from being scanned by the antimalware filter on a Mailbox server. The first action is to disable the filter. Malware scanning should be disabled if you opt to run a third-party product (for example, Trend ScanMail) as a replacement for the native functionality. If you disable the malware scanning, the agent will stop and no further engine updates will be performed. The following script can be run to disable the malware filter:

```
& $env:ExchangeInstallPath\Scripts\Disable-Antimalwarescanning.ps1
```

Once this script has been run, you will be prompted to restart the Exchange Transport service. Should you wish to re-enable the agent, it will perform an engine update when the following script to enable it is run:

```
& $env:ExchangeInstallPath\Scripts\Enable-Antimalwarescanning.ps1
```

To unhook the antimalware agent temporarily for troubleshooting purposes, it is recommended that you implement a *bypass*. Although the agent is then bypassed, the engine is kept up to date. You can bypass the antimalware agent with the following command:

```
Set-MalwareFilteringServer -BypassFiltering $true
```

You can re-enable it using the $False parameter. Note that this command does not require you to restart the Exchange Transport service, causing no disruption to mail flow.

To ensure that you understand whether the built-in antispam and antimalware capabilities will meet your requirements, here is a summary of the constraints present within the initial release of Microsoft Exchange Server 2013:

◆ Malware policies cannot be scoped to specific users/groups/domains.

◆ Antimalware functionality does not provide the ability to quarantine messages. Microsoft decided that given these messages contain active malicious code, no one (including administrators) should have access; therefore, the messages are deleted.

◆ The malware agent runs only one engine—the Microsoft engine. This is the same engine that is used in System Center Endpoint Protection.

◆ There are no reporting capabilities. As you learned earlier, this functionality has been added to EOP.

◆ Messages are scanned only at the transport layer. Microsoft has removed the VSAPI from the store. This removes the ability to scan messages at rest. This may increase risk, especially if you are planning a migration from a different email system, such as Lotus Notes.

◆ Antispam agents can only be enabled and configured on an Exchange 2013 Mailbox server using PowerShell.

◆ Antispam and antimalware configuration cannot be defined and managed centrally; that is, there is no process by which the configurations can be replicated to each server (although a PowerShell script can be used to configure each server with the same settings).

◆ If you enabled the antispam agents on the Mailbox server role, you are unable to perform both connection and attachment filtering. If you require this functionality, you will need to deploy an Edge Transport server.

◆ When configuring sender and administrator malware notifications, it is not possible to use message elements to compile the custom message, for example, using the [Time] element to embed what time the malware was detected within the customized message notification.

Protecting against Unauthorized Network Access

It will soon be common for email users to access their corporate email solution mainly from a device that is not connected to their corporate network. With the majority of users accessing an email infrastructure externally, securing that access and the infrastructure that is used to permit that access becomes critical. In this section, we examine the options to make Exchange services securely available externally and how to secure communications between devices and the Exchange environment.

SECURELY PUBLISHING EXCHANGE 2013 SERVICES

It has been possible to provide external browser-based access to Microsoft Exchange since version 5.5, although most organizations were not faced with strong demand until Exchange 2003 was released. At that point, the demand for providing external connectivity to Outlook Web Access grew. Since then, organizations have become savvier with their externalization strategy, investing heavily in network perimeter zones to ensure that network access to all enterprise infrastructure is secured by an additional network layer between the untrusted Internet and the organization's local area network. When working with a wide range of clients, we always find it refreshing to learn of new names for perimeter networks, from Secure the Perimeter (STP) to the Purple Zone. While perimeter zones provide a single location whereby external access can be simply managed, secured, and monitored, in so doing, organizations ultimately provide a single point of attack for potential hackers. For this reason, many large organizations, with Microsoft being no exception, are currently reconsidering their strategies for providing external access.

Historically, Microsoft promoted the use of an Internet Security and Acceleration (ISA) server to publish Microsoft Exchange services securely to the Internet using a variety of designs. Some of these designs included Exchange front-end servers to be placed in the perimeter zones along with the publishing server. Since Exchange 2007, installation of a Client Access server in a perimeter network zone has not been supported, relying heavily on the publishing server, and more recently Forefront Threat Management Gateway (TMG) 2010, to secure communications to the internal Microsoft Exchange infrastructure.

In September 2012, Microsoft announced that no further development will take place on Forefront TMG and that the product will no longer be available for purchase as of December 2012. Mainstream support will end for Forefront TMG on April 14, 2015, and extended support will end on April 14, 2020. Once mainstream support has ended, Microsoft will not provide any non-security hotfix support (unless an extended hotfix agreement has been purchased), offer any design changes, or honor any feature requests, and they will not provide any no-charge incident support or service any warranty claims.

Should you wish to use a Microsoft product to secure external access to Microsoft Exchange 2013 by performing pre-authentication, what are your options? Forefront Unified Access Gateway (UAG) 2010 will be the only publishing option available to purchase from Microsoft going forward, although Forefront TMG server will continue to work with Exchange 2013 and be supported until April 2015. For the initial release of Exchange Server 2013, Microsoft did not recommend using UAG to publish Exchange 2013 services. This is due to the incompatibility of the Outlook Web App and the deep URL inspection that UAG performs. However, this was recently resolved in the Service Pack 3 release for UAG 2010.

If you plan to use Forefront TMG 2010 to publish Exchange 2013 services securely to the Internet, it is important that you follow the publishing guidance provided for Exchange 2010. There are some important amendments to this guidance, however, that need to be addressed to make this work:

- Don't be alarmed that there is no Exchange Server 2013 Publishing Wizard available within Forefront TMG when you attempt to set up the publishing rules. The Exchange 2010 Publishing Wizard can be used.

- Kerberos Constrained Delegation (KCD) preauthentication is currently not supported. If you require Forefront TMG to perform pre-authentication to Active Directory, only Basic or NTLM authentication is currently supported. Microsoft intends to address this in the first cumulative update of Exchange Server 2013.

- Once you have set up the rule to publish OWA 2013, and if you have configured TMG to provide OWA forms-based authentication in front of Exchange, on the OWA publishing rule Application Settings tab, you will need to change the Published server logoff URL from `?cmd=logoff` to `/owa/logoff.owa`. This is to stop TMG from sending you to the OWA FBA form that is disabled.

◆ There is a requirement to add a supplementary publishing rule to ensure that OWA 2013 apps continue to work if TMG is providing forms-based authentication.

More information about publishing Exchange Server 2013 using TMG can be found here:

```
http://blogs.technet.com/b/exchange/archive/2012/11/21/publishing-exchange-server-
2013-using-tmg.aspx
```

If your organization has already bought the required TMG licenses, you are able to continue to deploy and use TMG 2010 to publish Exchange 2013 services. It is vital to ensure that your company has a roadmap to move away from TMG within the next three to five years. Be mindful that licenses can no longer be purchased, so before you steam ahead and deploy into production, check to be sure that you have all the licenses that you will need. If your organization is new to publishing Exchange services and wishes to publish Exchange 2013 services to the Internet, and if you have not yet purchased Forefront TMG licenses, your best option is to purchase and deploy Forefront UAG 2010.

It is likely that more publishing options will become available from other vendors as Microsoft Exchange Server 2013 matures. If your organization has a strong Defense in Depth security strategy, it is likely that you will have a requirement that prohibits you from using Microsoft's Forefront TMG or UAG products within the perimeter network.

It is important that the requirements drive the adoption and deployment of a reverse proxy solution, and that it isn't simply assumed that one is required. Many enterprises, including some of the largest, publish Client Access servers directly to the Internet; that is, they do not use TMG, UAG, or a third-party product. If preauthentication is not required, then a hardware load balancer can be deployed at the network edge (the device must support this deployment scenario) to accept HTTPS traffic and to forward that traffic directly to the Client Access server.

SECURING REMOTE CLIENT ACCESS

By default, all communications between the client (be it Outlook Anywhere, Outlook Web App (OWA), or ActiveSync) and Exchange 2013 are secured by using Secure Sockets Layer (SSL). Exchange 2013 requires the use of digital certificates installed on the servers themselves to create the SSL-encrypted channel that is used for client communications. So even though you have the ability to encrypt data communications between the client and the server, your security officer will remind you that it doesn't help if your identity has been stolen and someone has logged onto OWA with your password. As you learned at the beginning of this chapter, about 40 percent of those surveyed were concerned about the threat posed by remote and mobile working. Thus it is quite possible that your security officer will require the ability for remote access not only to be encrypted but also to be secured by a second factor.

Two-factor authentication is an authentication principle that requires the presentation of two or more factors: a knowledge factor (something the user knows) and a possession factor (something the user has). In principle, two-factor authentication decreases the probability that the requester is presenting false evidence of its identity. The ability of a solution to provide a second form of authentication is increasingly becoming a requirement because of the ease at which passwords can be compromised, mainly through nontechnical methods such as coercion, *user profiling* (which involves hackers guessing passwords based on information disclosed on social network sites), bribery, and users simply writing them down. Finally, it is possible for a savvy hacker to make a mental note of a user's password by watching the user type in their password on a keyboard in a public location.

What are your options with Exchange 2013 when faced with a requirement to secure external access with two-factor authentication? Client certificates can be used to prove the identity of the connecting user, and the "something the user has" criterion for two-factor authentication is then met with the client certificate. If your security officer accepts this as a valid second factor, then the security of that client certificate must also be addressed as part of the solution, for example, by certifying how the certificate is securely stored on the device.

If you use Forefront TMG to publish Exchange, support for certificate-based authentication was built into Cumulative Update (CU) 1 for Microsoft Exchange 2013. The initial release of Exchange 2013 could not use certificate-based authentication because of a lack of support for Kerberos Constrained Delegation. There are two important considerations for certificate-based authentication: First, it is the only supported method (without using additional software and/or services, such as PhoneFactor) to provide two-factor authentication for ActiveSync and mobile devices. Second, Outlook Anywhere does not support the use of certificate-based authentication (using any Outlook version). Certificate-based authentication can also be used with OWA, when the Forefront UAG server publishes OWA. More information on how to configure Forefront TMG with certificate-based authentication for OWA and EAS and Forefront UAG for OWA can be found in the following white paper:

http://www.microsoft.com/en-us/download/details.aspx?id=302

Configuring IPSec on the endpoint that is used to publish Exchange to the Internet has previously been recommended for use with Exchange 2010. IPSec does not require any significant investment in infrastructure, and it can be provisioned easily. In addition, both Forefront TMG and Forefront UAG work well with an IPSec-based security solution. More appropriately, it can also be used to secure authentication for Exchange 2013. (The reality is that Exchange neither knows nor cares about it.)

Given that any connection attempt made to the endpoint must first succeed at the IPSec negotiation layer (rather than just the username/password layer), configuring IPSec is a way to provide the second factor and thus reduce the possibility of a *denial-of-service (DoS)* attack. When IPSec is enabled on either the Forefront UAG server or the TMG server, only clients with the proper credentials can establish a connection, and both computers need to agree to communicate with each other before application access is permitted. IPSec can be used to secure OWA, OA, EWS, and Autodiscover. It is generally not used for EAS, since it is not natively supported on mobile devices. A quick overview of the requirements and configuration process for IPSec follows:

Client Certificates   Both the client and server must have certificates installed. Only clients with a valid machine certificate issued by a CA that is trusted by the Forefront TMG/UAG server can connect and authenticate.

IPSec Filters and Policies   These must be configured on the client (for outbound communications) and the Forefront UAG/TMG server (for inbound and outbound communications). The filters and policies stipulate that communications (to a specific IP address) must be secured with IPSec. They also define the authentication method, the encryption policy, and the security settings used.

Firewall Access Rules   Configured on the Forefront TMG or UAG server, firewall rules allow the IPSec traffic (UDP 500 or UDP 4500) through the access point, allowing the client and server to negotiate an IPSec connection.

Although IPSec is a cost-effective way of providing two-factor authentication, it is sometimes perceived as a difficult solution to manage and maintain. This is largely due to two limitations: First, the configured IPSec policies on the clients contain IP addresses and not the DNS addresses of the connection endpoint(s). Therefore, should an IP address change, the IPSec polices must be updated. (This is the reason why IPSec policies must be configured as part of a GPO, so that it is possible to update them centrally and distribute them automatically to all client machines.) Second, the use of IPSec is known to place a processing overhead on network cards (although this is understood to be less than that required for SSL). However, the advantages of using IPSec with Exchange 2013, in that both Outlook Anywhere and OWA support it as a two-factor authentication solution, and that it does not require the use of third-party software, outweigh its limitations.

Unquestionably, establishing a VPN connection before using Outlook Anywhere or OWA facilitates the use of two-factor authentication. However, this authentication process is not transparent to the user, and with the growth of working remotely, the process of having to establish a VPN connection is perceived by users as unnecessary overhead. Similar to VPN, *DirectAccess* (Microsoft's solution for providing users seamless access to their corporate infrastructure from virtually any Internet connection) also facilitates two-factor authentication with the advantage that the connection and authentication process is transparent to the user. However, the limitations to and solution requirements for DirectAccess are not trivial: They are Windows 7 Ultimate/Enterprise or Windows 8 (if DirectAccess with Windows Server 2012 is used) domain-joined clients and Forefront UAG as the preferred edge solution.

Thus far, all of the two-factor authentication access methods considered require that software, policies, and/or certificates be specifically installed or configured on the client. What are your options if you have a requirement to provide two-factor authentication for OWA when being used in a kiosk scenario? In this case, when the asset is not owned by the organization, and the organization is not in control of the client machine (for example, a computer in an airport), you do not have the luxury of being able to install any additional software and/or updates. Third-party products have been available for Exchange 2010 to secure and provide two-factor authentication for OWA by integrating with IIS and requiring the use of either a hardware or software token (for example, a one-time secret code or one-time password). Through its recent acquisition of PhoneFactor, Microsoft now owns a native solution with the ability to secure OWA via the two-step verification process. Other third parties such as Swivel (Office 365 solutions), ArrayShield, and Duo Security are all examples of companies that provide two-factor authentication solutions for OWA. At the time of this writing, however, none have updated their products to work with OWA 2013.

PhoneFactor leverages the user's mobile device as the "something you have" trust factor. A PhoneFactor agent runs within the corporate network, intercepts the OWA SSL requests, and sends them to the cloud-based PhoneFactor service. A phone call, text message, or a notification is then sent from the PhoneFactor cloud-based service to the user's mobile device. Once the user approves or denies the access request from their mobile device, it returns the access result to OWA. In contrast, Messageware provides the functionality to filter OWA logons by IP address or location, an OWA CATCHA challenge, and other functionality (such as secure email attachment viewing, navigation, and session protection) to secure OWA 2013 logons and sessions.

Two-factor authentication for OA using smart cards (as discussed in the following TechNet article) is not supported in the current release of Microsoft Exchange Server 2013, although it is expected to be supported in future releases:

http://technet.microsoft.com/en-us/library/hh227263(EXCHG.141).aspx

For those of you who may be wondering about claims-based authentication (AD FS) support in Exchange 2013, or perhaps even managed to make it work, Microsoft does not support OWA or OA using claims-based authentication. Thus it is not something that you should recommend as a two-factor solution to the security officer.

Table 8.3 summarizes the available methods for two-factor authentication with Microsoft Exchange Server 2013.

TABLE 8.3: Two-factor authentication methods for Microsoft Exchange Server 2013

AUTHENTICATION METHOD	REVERSE PROXY SOLUTION	CLIENT ACCESS METHOD SUPPORTED	PROS AND CONS
Certificate (client)	TMG	OWA and EAS	*Pro*
			TMG configuration well documented.
			Con
			Need to make sure that certificates on devices can be managed.
			Will not function until release of Microsoft Exchange 2013 CU1 to address issues with KCD.
Certificate (client)	UAG	OWA	*Pro*
			TMG configuration well documented.
			Con
			Need to make sure that certificates on devices can be managed.
			Will not function until release of Microsoft Exchange 2013 CU1 to address issues with KCD.
IPSec	TMG or UAG	OWA and OA	*Pro*
			Does not require any additional infrastructure.
			Con
			Can be difficult to set up and manage (IP filter list).
			External client requires a machine certificate.
			EAS is also supported, although the capability is not built into the native mobile email clients.

(CONTINUES)

TABLE 8.3:   Two-factor authentication methods for Microsoft Exchange Server 2013   *(CONTINUED)*

AUTHENTICATION METHOD	REVERSE PROXY SOLUTION	CLIENT ACCESS METHOD SUPPORTED	PROS AND CONS
VPN	N/A	OWA and OA	*Pro* Widely accepted method for facilitating two-factor authentication. *Con* Not transparent to user. Poor user experience.
DirectAccess	UAG	OWA and OA	*Pro* Transparent to user. *Con* Heavy on infrastructure (UAG server required).
Software or hardware tokens (for example, PhoneFactor, RSA, or smart cards)	N/A	OWA	*Pro* Can be used in kiosk scenarios. *Con* Requires third-party infrastructure and software. Some are not yet available for Microsoft Exchange Server 2013. Hardware tokens are difficult to manage.

Protecting against Unauthorized Data Access

In this section, we examine some of the common concerns that may require attention to ensure that corporate messaging data is secured in such a way as to protect against unauthorized data access. To understand fully the range of concerns within this area, it is paramount to appreciate the potential threat.

This section is divided into three parts:

◆ The security of data in transit—This section addresses the vulnerability of messages being read and accessed by unintended parties while in transit.

◆ The security of data at rest—This section focuses on the vulnerability of data in intermediary storage, for example, data stored within the Exchange databases.

◆ The security of data in long-term storage—This section tackles the vulnerability of data stored in long-term storage and often "off-site."

Security of Data in Transit

Ensuring that messages are securely transferred to their destination is a fundamental require-ment and thus the functionality that facilitates this is expected. Microsoft Exchange Server 2013 provides a variety of options to facilitate the secure exchange of messages. Nonetheless, it is important to understand the default behavior and whether this meets the defined requirement(s).

For messages that are transferred within the Exchange organization, all mail flow between Exchange 2013 servers is secured by Transport Layer Security (TLS). By default upon install, all Exchange 2013 servers are configured with a self-signed certificate that facilitates this TLS encryption of SMTP traffic. TLS encryption is mandatory for all SMTP communications between Mailbox servers.

NOTE   It is possible to disable TLS encryption. One situation for doing so might be if you are utilizing WAN optimization devices.

In addition, messages that are accepted for delivery by the Front End Transport service into the Exchange 2013 organization are streamed (because there is no SMTP queuing functional-ity on the Front End Transport service) to the relevant delivery group via TLS. Furthermore, all traffic between Edge Transport servers and Exchange 2013 Mailbox servers is both authenticated and encrypted.

For messages that are being sent externally from within the Exchange organization, whether these are routed through the Client Access server or straight to an Edge server, Exchange 2013 will always attempt delivery to the remote SMTP server via opportunistic TLS. By default, Exchange Server 2013 will always try to negotiate TLS by issuing the `StartTLS` command dur-ing the initial SMTP conversation exchanges. Interestingly, even if the self-signed certificate has expired, opportunistic TLS will still work as long as the target server accepts the `StartTLS` command. To that end, it is important to understand that, by default, a significant proportion of outgoing mail will be encrypted via opportunistic TLS without the need for any further configuration.

Is opportunistic TLS sufficient to meet your requirements? There are two distinct factors that will help you determine this based on the requirements that have been defined. It is vital to understand that opportunistic TLS will only encrypt the communication session, and that it will do so only if both the sending and receiving server can negotiate a TLS session. If there is a requirement to ensure that encryption is enforced to a particular domain/partner, *or* that the SMTP traffic must be both encrypted *and* authenticated (that is, that the sending and receiv-ing server validate their authenticity), then mutual TLS must be configured. From experience, the requirement to enable *Domain Security*, which describes the functional components (that is, the certificates, connector configuration, and Outlook functionality that enables mutual TLS), is most commonly driven by the requirement of organizations to communicate securely with a third-party vendor, service provider, or outsource agency. A simple example is a retail company with the requirement to send all email via an encrypted and authenticated session to their bank, such as retailbankprovider.com.

Should you be faced with the requirement to enable Domain Security, the following steps provide a high-level overview on how this must be performed:

1. On Mailbox or Edge server (if you have deployed the latter), make sure that the following parameters are set on the Send connector, `Set-SendConnector`:

   `DomainSecureEnabled` is set to `$true`.

If you created the Send connector via EAC and chosen the Partner connector type upon creation, this value will already be set to `$true`.

`DNSRoutingEnabled` is set to `$true`.

`IgnoreSTARTTLS` is set to `$false`.

2. On the Mailbox or Edge server (if you have deployed the latter), make sure that the following parameters are set on the Receive connector, `Set-ReceiveConnector`:

`DomainSecureEnabled` is set to `$true`.

`AuthMechanism` is set to TLS.

3. On the Mailbox server (these changes will be replicated to the Edge server), run the `Set-TransportConfig` cmdlet to specify the domain with which you want to send domain-secured email, for example:

`Set-TransportConfig -TLSSendDomainSecureList "retailbankprovider.com"`

4. On the Mailbox server (these changes will be replicated to the Edge server), run the `Set-TransportConfig` cmdlet to specify the domain with which you want to receive domain-secured email, for example:

`Set-TransportConfig -TLSReceiveDomainSecureList " retailbankprovider.com "`

5. Make sure that the FQDN on the Send connector matches the `DomainName` parameter within the server(s) certificate.

If you are planning to implement Domain Security, there is one final consideration: Domain Security isn't supported when outbound email is routed through an Exchange 2013 Client Access server. The `FrontendProxyEnabled` parameter on the `Set-SendConnector` cmdlet is used to configure whether outbound email is routed through the Client Access server. By default, outbound mail is not routed through the Exchange 2013 Client Access server.

New to Exchange Server 2013 is the ability to set a transport rule to enforce TLS encryption. This is achieved by the new transport rule action, `RouteMessageOutboundRequireTLS`. This new action enforces the use of TLS encryption when routing messages externally. If TLS encryption isn't supported, the message is rejected and not delivered. Figure 8.2 shows a sample transport rule being created to meet a requirement that when all members of the Retail group's Senior Executive Team (SET) send emails to retailbankprovider.com, TLS encryption is applied. Should TLS encryption not be possible, the message will then be rejected. In this example, Domain Security is not configured for the stipulated recipient domain. Thus, TLS encryption will not be enforced for users who are not members of the RetailSETMembers group.

One final concern may remain in the security of data in transit, and that is the security of database availability group (DAG) replication traffic. Given that DAG replication is now supported over wide area networks, it is possible that DAG data may be replicated over unsecured WAN links. By default, network encryption is only used on DAG networks when replicating across different subnets. Network encryption utilizes Kerberos security to provide authentication between Exchange servers. Should there be a requirement for a more stringent level of encryption on the DAG network, the `Set-DatabaseAvailabilityGroup` cmdlet can be used to configure the encryption settings. Possible encryption settings for DAG network communications are listed in Table 8.4.

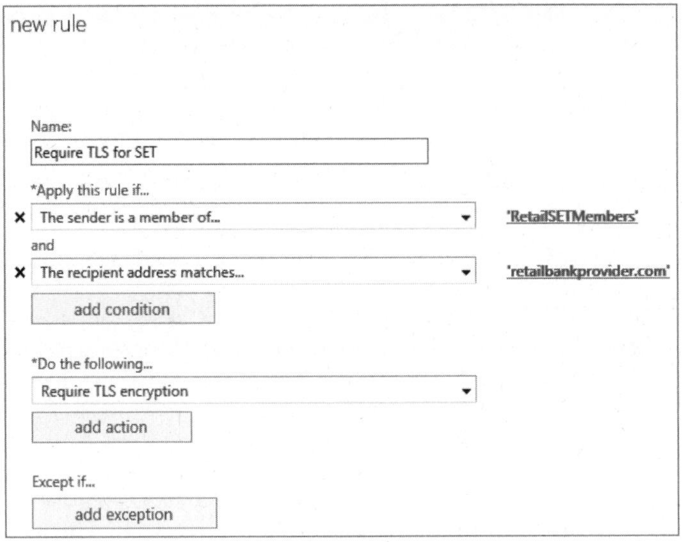

FIGURE 8.2
Configuring transport rules to set up TLS

```
new rule



Name:
┌─────────────────────────────────────────────────┐
│ Require TLS for SET                               │
└─────────────────────────────────────────────────┘
*Apply this rule if...
✕ ┌───────────────────────────────────────┬───▼─┐   'RetailSETMembers'
  │ The sender is a member of...           │     │
  └───────────────────────────────────────┴─────┘
  and
✕ ┌───────────────────────────────────────┬───▼─┐   'retailbankprovider.com'
  │ The recipient address matches...       │     │
  └───────────────────────────────────────┴─────┘
     ┌─────────────────────┐
     │    add condition    │
     └─────────────────────┘

*Do the following...
  ┌───────────────────────────────────────┬───▼─┐
  │ Require TLS encryption                 │     │
  └───────────────────────────────────────┴─────┘
     ┌─────────────────────┐
     │     add action      │
     └─────────────────────┘

  Except if...
     ┌─────────────────────┐
     │   add exception     │
     └─────────────────────┘
```

TABLE 8.4:   Possible encryption settings for DAG network communications

SETTING	DESCRIPTION
Disabled	No network encryption is used.
Enabled	Network encryption is used on all DAG networks for replicating and seeding.
InterSubnetOnly	Default setting. Network encryption is used on DAG networks when replicating across different subnets.
SeedOnly	Network encryption is used on all DAG networks for seeding only.

Security of Data at Rest

To prevent data at rest from being accessed, stolen, or altered by unauthorized persons, some organizations will consider the application of encryption or Information Rights Management on messaging data. Whether data is at rest on Exchange servers, workstations, laptops, or mobile devices, the risk of unauthorized data access will vary, generally depending on the portability of the device. However, the impact on the organization of unauthorized data access could be considerable and could cost millions.

PROTECTING DATA AT REST ON SERVERS AND CLIENTS

Let's initially consider the risk of unauthorized data access to the messaging data stored on a Microsoft Exchange server. Historically, prior to the centralization of messaging services,

Exchange servers may have resided in remote and unsecured areas. However, by today's standards and because of the trend toward centralization, it is common for Exchange servers to be secured within corporate datacenters. Therefore, the risk of unauthorized physical access is reduced. That being said, the risk is still there.

What happens when an engineer walks off-site with a disk (especially a disk that has been part of a JBOD configuration), which may store a complete copy of an Exchange database? Should that data be unsecured, a corporation will be at the peril of an untrustworthy (and perhaps external) engineer. In addition, once the data is removed from the site, how can you guarantee its security? Even if the disk has a flaw, this alone will not render the data inaccessible. There are native tools and many third-party utilities that can access data within an Exchange database .edb file, removing the requirement for having to perform a complete restore. Given such concerns, you may be faced with a requirement to encrypt data that is at rest (that is, the Exchange databases) on the Exchange servers. If so, what are your options?

By default, data that is at rest on an Exchange 2013 server is not encrypted. Unlike Lotus Notes, Exchange does not provide any native, application-layer functionality to encrypt the mailbox databases. However, *BitLocker*, a full disk-encryption feature that is included in Windows Server 2008 and Windows Server 2012, is supported for use with Exchange Server 2013 and specifically on volumes that hold Exchange data. At present, it is the only disk-encryption software that is supported for use with Exchange Server 2013. If you plan to use BitLocker to encrypt the data stored on the Exchange server, you should be aware of the following considerations and recommendations:

◆ If you wish to leverage the pre-startup system integrity verification, which ensures that data is accessible only if the computer's boot components appear unaltered and the encrypted disk is located in the original computer, when procuring the hardware that will be used for your Exchange 2013 servers, you must ensure that Trusted Platform Module (TPM) version 1.2 or version 2.0 is installed. In addition, a server with TPM must also have a trusted computer group-compliant BIOS or UEFI firmware. Disk encryption alone does not require a TPM.

◆ Windows 2012 was the first version of Windows to build in support for disk encryption on both iSCSI and Fibre Channel-connected disks. Therefore, if you are planning to present your storage to the server over Fibre Channel or iSCSI, you must deploy Exchange Server 2013 on Windows Server 2012 and not Windows Server 2008.

◆ Network file systems, software-based RAID systems, bootable and non-bootable virtual hard disks, and dynamic volumes are all *not* supported for use with BitLocker.

◆ The operating system must be formatted with NTFS.

◆ You must make sure that when Jetstress is run against the storage subsystem prior to deployment, BitLocker is enabled against the volumes where the Exchange data resides.

To enable BitLocker on Windows Server 2012, the feature must be installed from Server Manager. Once installation is complete, a reboot will be required. It is recommended that BitLocker be installed before the node is joined to a DAG. Once the data is encrypted, BitLocker is known to have a slight performance impact on the server—a 1–3 percent CPU overhead. The IOPS performance impact on an Exchange server with BitLocker enabled is reported to be insignificant.

The risk of unauthorized access of data stored on portable devices is today a significant concern to organizations, largely due to the growth of mobile devices and the increased security risk they bring. Organizations are not only concerned with sensitive corporate data being leaked from emails, but they are worried about data such as user personally identifiable information, address book data (stored in the Outlook offline address book), and the ability of an unauthorized user to view locally stored company IM conversations, which may be stored within an offline copy of the user's mailbox.

To secure data at rest on laptop computers, most organizations have a device encryption policy that often requires the use of disk encryption software such as BitLocker. On client machines, Microsoft BitLocker can be used alongside Windows 7 and Windows 8. Once BitLocker is enabled on a laptop computer, encrypting the entire Windows operating system volume on the hard disk, including the Outlook data files such as the Offline store (`*.ost`), personal address book (`.pab`), and offline address book (`*.oab`), will prevent unauthorized access should the laptop be stolen. In addition, BitLocker will encrypt additional data volumes on the device and protect against access to the data on the disk should it be removed from the laptop.

PROTECTING CONTENT USING INFORMATION RIGHTS MANAGEMENT

Enabling BitLocker on portable Windows devices is the best and most comprehensive solution to prevent against unauthorized data access. In addition to BitLocker, Exchange Information Rights Management may also be used to prevent data leakage from within the Exchange organization. Exchange IRM uses Active Directory Rights Management Service (AD RMS) to apply both encryption and permissions to emails to prevent recipients from taking an action on the email (such as printing, copying, forwarding, and replying). Exchange 2010 SP3 and Exchange Server 2013 now support AD RMS cryptographic mode 2, which supports RSA 2048 for signature and encryption and SHA-256 for signature. This provides the ability to deliver a stronger level of encryption. It is important to understand that although, like S/MIME, AD RMS encrypts email, it also provides the ability to apply Information Rights Management to the email. Once an S/MIME email has been decrypted, there is no control over what the recipient can do with the information contained within the email.

To enable the use of IRM to protect Exchange data, an AD RMS server must be deployed within the Active Directory forest. AD RMS functionality can be added to a Windows 2008 or Windows 2012 server by adding the Active Directory Rights Management Services role. Rights policy templates must then be defined. The *rights policy template* outlines the rules and conditions applied to the content protected by using the template. AD RMS clients (Windows 7 and Windows 8 are AD RMS clients by default) are then able to request the rights policy templates stored on the AD RMS server/cluster and download and store them locally on the client computer. Figure 8.3 illustrates a sample set of rights policy templates, defined on an AD RMS server, which can be used with Exchange Server 2013 and Microsoft Outlook.

Predominately, AD RMS is used to encrypt a subset of data that is at rest, for example, one that is based on a user requirement and the user manually applies a template or a template is applied programmatically to a subset of users. AD RMS is not commonly used to encrypt all data at rest, as BitLocker can, because of the administration and performance overhead.

There are three ways to apply IRM (an AD RMS template) to a message:

◆ Users manually apply the rights policy template within Outlook or OWA during the composition of a message. Figure 8.4 illustrates the availability of the previously defined AD RMS templates once they're propagated to the Outlook client.

FIGURE 8.3
Rights policy
templates for use
with Outlook and
Exchange

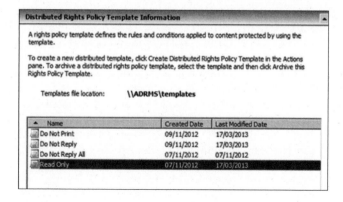

FIGURE 8.4
Selecting an RMS
template in Outlook

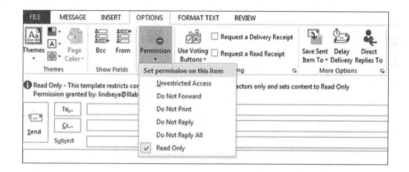

◆ Apply IRM to a message via the use of hub transport rules. Figure 8.5 shows the creation of a new hub transport rule in EAC, which applies Read Only rights to an email that is sent from the senior executive team (DL-RetailSET) to all retail store workers (DL-AllStoreWorkers). Messages that are sent by members of the senior executive team distribution group to all store workers will now be marked Read Only. Consequently, store workers will be unable to reply, forward, print, or copy the email. Only when the message enters the transport pipeline on an Exchange 2013 server will the encryption and rights management policies be applied.

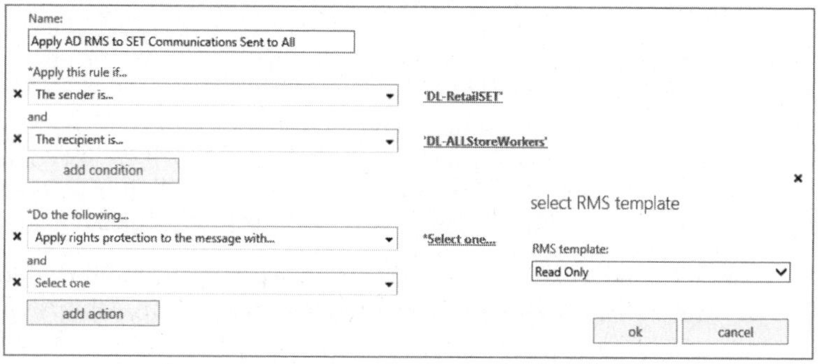

FIGURE 8.5
Creating a hub
transport rule in
EAC to apply an
RMS template

◆ Use Outlook protection rules to apply AD RMS rights policy templates. Outlook protection rules are similar to transport protection rules in that an AD RMS template is applied based on message conditions. However, unlike transport protection rules, Outlook protection rules are applied from within Outlook 2010 or Outlook 2013 before the message leaves the computer and enters the transport pipeline on the Exchange 2013 server. One clear advantage of this is that messages protected by an Outlook protection rule are also saved in an encrypted format in the Sent Items folder of the sender's mailbox. Outlook protection rules are automatically distributed to Outlook using Exchange Web Services. For Outlook to apply the rule, the AD RMS policy template that is specified within the rule must be available on the user's computer. Outlook protection rules are stored within the organization context with Exchange, and therefore the new-OutlookProtectionRule cmdlet only needs to be run on one Exchange 2013 server. The following command creates a new Outlook protection rule declaring that messages sent from users in the SET department (as defined within the AD Department field) should be Read Only:

```
New-OutlookProtectionRule -Name "Senior Executive Team" -FromDepartment "SET"
-ApplyRightsProtectionTemplate "Read Only"
```

Three predicates are available for use with Outlook protection rules:

FromDepartment This predicate looks up the sender's Department attribute in Active Directory and automatically IRM-protects the message if the sender's department matches the department specified in the rule.

SentTo This predicate deals with messages sent to specified recipients or distribution groups.

SentToScope This predicate automatically IRM-protects messages sent inside or outside the organization. You can use the SentToScope predicate with the FromDepartment predicate to IRM-protect messages sent by a particular department to internal users.

To ensure that users accessing their company's email from outside the external network can consume IRM-protected content, the AD RMS server (or cluster) must be published externally. Specifically, there are two URLs that must be published: the licensing URL, which specifies the rights that users have to the content, and the certification URL, which must also be configured on the AD RMS server (or cluster).

END-TO-END ENCRYPTION USING S/MIME

Whereas AD RMS provides the capability both to encrypt and rights-protect email content, *S/MIME* (Secure/Multipurpose Internet Mail Extensions) only provides encryption for email content. S/MIME is sometimes referred to as end-to-end encryption, or writer-to-reader encryption, because messages are encrypted from the initial source (sender or writer) to their target destination (recipient or reader), and the encryption is preserved throughout the message transfer. In addition to encryption, S/MIME also supports the digital signing of a message to provide authentication, non-repudiation, and data integrity. In contrast to AD RMS encryption, S/MIME is based on an industry-standard RFC, and therefore messages can be decrypted and read within a non-Microsoft email client. Both Outlook 2013 and Outlook for Mac 2011 support S/MIME encryption. However, the Exchange 2013 RTM version of OWA does not provide support for S/MIME encryption (although we expect that this support will be added in SP1).

Typically, S/MIME is not widely deployed because of the overhead of maintaining and exchanging user certificates. Both sender and recipient require a certificate (with the recipient requiring a copy of the sender's certificate), which is bound to the sender's validated email address. Old certificates must also be retained, so that historical emails can be decrypted and read. S/MIME certificates can be purchased from a supplier such as Symantec, and most suppliers have an option for a free trial. Once purchased, S/MIME certificates must be renewed, downloaded, and installed once a year. They must also be installed on every device on which the user wishes to send or receive S/MIME messages.

If a certificate is required to decrypt each sender's email, organizations are then unable to decrypt messages to enforce policy compliance or to scan messages for antimalware. For this reason, messages that are encrypted with S/MIME are able to bypass the newly built-in anti-spam and antimalware capabilities in Exchange Server 2013. In addition, S/MIME encrypted messages cannot be decrypted when performing an eDiscovery search/export, unlike with AD RMS protected content.

Cloud policy-based encryption services, such as Symantec Policy Based Encryption and Exchange Hosted Encryption (EHE), which is part of the Exchange Online Protection offering from Microsoft, can reduce the burden of maintaining individual user certificates across a multitude of devices. With such services, an administrator will stipulate a set of rules (policies) for which messages must be encrypted. Typically, these services will then distribute to the recipient a link to the encrypted mail, where it can be opened from within the cloud encryption service. Within EHE, administrators are able to define encryption policies based on recipient domains, email addresses, message body content (via regular expressions), recipients, IP addresses, and email attachments.

PROTECTING DATA ON MOBILE DEVICES

With the increase of *Bring Your Own Device (BYOD)* strategies, it is now common for users to access their company's email from multiple, and more often than not personal, devices. Even if users do not have this functionality today, the likelihood is that they will expect it, creating a demand that leaves organizations baffled as to how to provide such authorized access without increasing the risk of unauthorized data access. In this final section, we'll examine the options available to secure data at rest on mobile devices.

Windows Phone, Blackberry Enterprise Service, and Good for Enterprise all offer capabilities for the encryption of data stored on mobile devices. Device encryption in Windows Phone 8 utilizes BitLocker technology to encrypt all internal data on the phone with 128-bit Advanced Encryption Standard (AES). Encryption is enabled either by an Exchange ActiveSync (EAS) policy or a device management policy. Once enabled, BitLocker conversion automatically begins encrypting the internal storage. The encryption key is protected by the Trusted Platform Module that is bound to UEFI Trusted Boot, in order to ensure that the encryption key will only be released to Trusted Boot components. With both PIN lock and BitLocker enabled, the combination of data encryption and device lock would make it extremely difficult for an attacker to recover sensitive information from a device. Device security settings are managed by native Exchange 2013 ActiveSync policies, which in the main are largely unchanged from previous versions of Exchange Server.

Good for Enterprise provides containerization of the device to create distinct partitions—a personal partition and a corporate partition—on the device (iOS, Windows Phone, or Android) to ensure that data is segmented and, as such, can be managed differently (including the ability to wipe the corporate partition while leaving the personal partition intact). Good uses AES 192-bit encryption on the corporate partition to secure the data. In addition, all data in transit between the device and the enterprise firewall is also encrypted by the same method. The Blackberry Enterprise Service also provides the same containerization through the Blackberry Balance functionality, although it uses a stronger (AES 256-bit) method of encryption. Data transfer between the Blackberry device and the Blackberry Enterprise infrastructure is also encrypted either by AES 256-bit encryption or Triple Data Encryption Standard (Triple DES), depending on how the service is configured. Both the Good and Blackberry Enterprise Service software provide additional functionality for mobile device management, which delivers a more granular level of control than the Exchange Server 2013 native ActiveSync capability.

Since Exchange Server 2010, users have been able to create and view IRM-protected messages on the Windows Phone. Windows Phone is the only smartphone currently available that includes a built-in capability to handle rights-protected email and documents. Apple iOS does not support IRM natively. Devices that support Exchange ActiveSync protocol version 14.1 (Exchange 2010 SP1 and higher), including Windows Phones, can support IRM in Exchange ActiveSync. The device's mobile email application must support the `RightsManagementInformation` tag defined in Exchange ActiveSync version 14.1 for this to work. It is possible for users of other devices to consume IRM-protected email messages, but a third-party app is required to facilitate this.

iOS devices support S/MIME encryption through the native mail app, while Good for Enterprise can provide S/MIME encryption functionality to Windows and Android phones. (Neither Windows nor Android OS natively supports S/MIME encryption at present.) For Blackberry devices to support S/MIME, the S/MIME Support Package for BlackBerry smartphones is required, and it must be installed on the Blackberry device to enable users to create and view S/MIME-encrypted content. For all devices, use of S/MIME requires the transfer of the S/MIME private key to the device.

Table 8.5 summarizes the options available to secure data on mobile clients.

TABLE 8.5:   Options available to secure data on mobile clients

MOBILE CONNECTION METHOD	METHODS OF ENCRYPTION SUPPORTED	DEVICE CONTROL
Windows Phone	Data at rest encrypted by BitLocker. IRM. S/MIME: Requires third-party app (Good).	Security settings applied via Exchange ActiveSync Polices.
iOS Devices	S/MIME. IRM: Requires third-party app.	Security settings applied via Exchange ActiveSync Polices.
Good for Enterprise (iOS, Android, Windows Phone)	Data at rest and in transit is encrypted with strong AES 192-bit encryption. S/MIME. IRM: Requires third-party app.	Data containerization via Good Enterprise container. Security settings applied via Good Mobile Control Policies.

(CONTINUES)

TABLE 8.5:   Options available to secure data on mobile clients   *(CONTINUED)*

MOBILE CONNECTION METHOD	METHODS OF ENCRYPTION SUPPORTED	DEVICE CONTROL
Android	S/MIME: Requires third- party app.	Security settings applied via Exchange ActiveSync Polices.
	IRM: Requires third-party app.	
BlackBerry	Data at rest encrypted with strong AES 256- bit encryption.	Data containerization via BlackBerry Balance technology.
	Data in transit is encrypted with strong AES 256-bit encryption or Triple Data Encryption Standard (Triple DES).	Security settings applied via Exchange ActiveSync Polices.
	S/MIME.	Enterprise Mobility Management provides capability for granular security controls.
	IRM: Requires third-party app.	

Security of Data in Long-Term Storage

Many organizations are now using Exchange native resiliency to protect against failure. In so doing, they are negating the need to have a point-in-time, offline backup of Exchange data (either on disk or tape). Some organizations, however, will still have a requirement for a point-in-time backup. In the authors' experience, this is usually done to satisfy one of the following criteria:

◆ Protect against administration/automation errors

◆ Provide the ability to recover complete mailboxes after the deleted mailbox retention period has expired

◆ Provide the ability to recover to a completely separate and offline datacenter

Should the organization have a requirement to make frequent backups of Exchange data and there is also a strict requirement for data encryption, how the data is secured in long-term storage (on disk or tape) should also be considered. Given the movement of tape media and the likelihood that third parties are involved in that movement to off-site storage, encryption of data stored on disk or tape is imperative. There are two options for encryption of data on tape storage media: software or hardware encryption. Most enterprise-strength tape backup systems, such as IBM's Tivoli Storage Manager with Tivoli Data Protection for databases, use in-built software encryption to satisfy this requirement. Alternatively, there are third-party products that offer software encryption to backups as a bolt-on.

The availability of hardware encryption of tape media depends on the tape device used. In general, hardware encryption offers a lower performance overhead than software-based encryption.

Auditing and Reporting

Despite efforts to secure the Exchange environment, should unauthorized access be attempted and be successful, Exchange Server 2013 provides a new auditing interface within the

Compliance Management section of the Exchange Administrator Center (EAC) to track access, audit administrator changes, and report on compliance status. The interface is split into two distinct sections, with reporting functionality provided on the left and the functions to export mailbox and administrator audit logs on the right, as shown in Figure 8.6.

FIGURE 8.6
Auditing capabilities within Exchange Server 2013

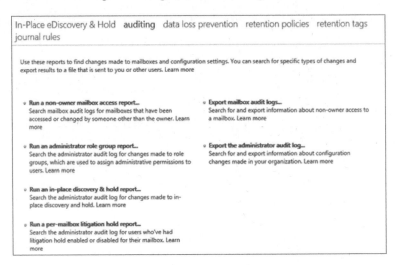

More information on auditing reports can be found in the following TechNet article:

```
http://technet.microsoft.com/en-us/library/jj150497(v=exchg.150).aspx
```

This section is provided as an overview for the reader and to illustrate the types of results gained from searches and the output of the reports.

AUDITING AND REPORTING USER MAILBOX ACTIVITY

By default, the auditing of user actions within a mailbox is disabled. When enabled, mailbox auditing will log administrator and/or delegate actions (such as hard and soft deletion, logging on/off, or SendAs) that are performed within a mailbox. Mailbox auditing does not log the actions of the mailbox owner. To enable mailbox auditing on a mailbox for the administrator and delegate, the following cmdlet can be used:

```
Set-Mailbox -Identity "LindseyA" -AuditEnabled &true
```

Mailbox auditing can be enabled for all mailboxes with the following cmdlets:

```
$UserMailboxes = Get-mailbox -Filter {(RecipientTypeDetails -eq 'UserMailbox')}
$UserMailboxes | ForEach {Set-Mailbox $_.Identity -AuditEnabled $true}
```

To verify that mailbox audit logging has been enabled for all users, run the following command:

```
Get-Mailbox | FL Name, AuditEnabled
```

There are multiple ways in which the audit log entries can be viewed. The quickest way is to perform a search against the audit log using PowerShell. This can be achieved using the

Search-MailboxAuditLog cmdlet. Alternatively, a non-owner mailbox access report can be run from the EAC via Compliance Management ➤ Auditing. Figure 8.7 shows a report detailing that delegate fullmsxadmin performed a soft delete of a mail item in Lindsey's mailbox.

FIGURE 8.7
Report showing actions taken by fullmsxadmin

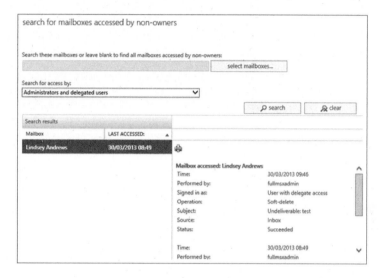

EAC can also be used to export a copy of the mailbox audit log between specific dates, for specific or all users, and it can send the export to a specified mailbox, as shown in Figure 8.8.

FIGURE 8.8
Sample export of the mailbox audit log

AUDITING AND REPORTING ADMINISTRATOR ACTIVITY

Within Exchange 2013 administrator audit logging is enabled by default. With administrator logging enabled, when an administrator makes a change within the Exchange organization, that change is tracked within the audit log. The Search-AdminAuditLog cmdlet can be used to search the administrator log, and granular searches are possible based on the cmdlet that the administrator has run. The PowerShell output shown in Figure 8.9 provides a sample search of the admin audit log. This PowerShell code searches the administrator log to find out when auditing was enabled on all mailboxes.

FIGURE 8.9
Sample search of the admin audit log

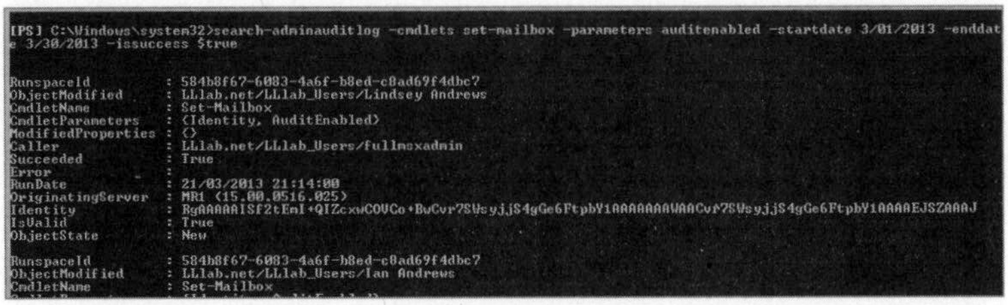

```
[PS] C:\Windows\system32>search-adminauditlog -cmdlets set-mailbox -parameters auditenabled -startdate 3/01/2013 -enddat
e 3/30/2013 -issuccess $true

RunspaceId         : 584b8f67-6083-4a6f-b8ed-c8ad69f4dbc7
ObjectModified     : LLlab.net/LLlab_Users/Lindsey Andrews
CmdletName         : Set-Mailbox
CmdletParameters   : {Identity, AuditEnabled}
ModifiedProperties : {}
Caller             : LLlab.net/LLlab_Users/fullmsxadmin
Succeeded          : True
Error              :
RunDate            : 21/03/2013 21:14:00
OriginatingServer  : MR1 (15.00.0516.025)
Identity           : RgAAAAAISf2tEmI+QIZcxwCOVCo+BwCvr7SWsyjjS4gGe6FtpbY1AAAAAAAWAACvr7SWsyjjS4gGe6FtpbY1AAAAEJSZAAAJ
IsValid            : True
ObjectState        : New

RunspaceId         : 584b8f67-6083-4a6f-b8ed-c8ad69f4dbc7
ObjectModified     : LLlab.net/LLlab_Users/Ian Andrews
CmdletName         : Set-Mailbox
```

Using EAC, the full administrator audit log can also be exported and sent to a specific mailbox. The log is sent in `.xml` format, as shown in Figure 8.10.

FIGURE 8.10
Example of full administrator audit log

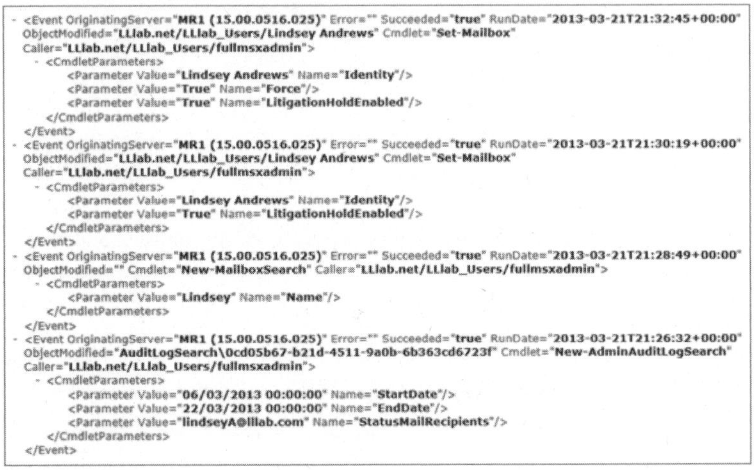

```
- <Event OriginatingServer="MR1 (15.00.0516.025)" Error="" Succeeded="true" RunDate="2013-03-21T21:32:45+00:00"
  ObjectModified="LLlab.net/LLlab_Users/Lindsey Andrews" Cmdlet="Set-Mailbox"
  Caller="LLlab.net/LLlab_Users/fullmsxadmin">
  - <CmdletParameters>
      <Parameter Value="Lindsey Andrews" Name="Identity"/>
      <Parameter Value="True" Name="Force"/>
      <Parameter Value="True" Name="LitigationHoldEnabled"/>
    </CmdletParameters>
  </Event>
- <Event OriginatingServer="MR1 (15.00.0516.025)" Error="" Succeeded="true" RunDate="2013-03-21T21:30:19+00:00"
  ObjectModified="LLlab.net/LLlab_Users/Lindsey Andrews" Cmdlet="Set-Mailbox"
  Caller="LLlab.net/LLlab_Users/fullmsxadmin">
  - <CmdletParameters>
      <Parameter Value="Lindsey Andrews" Name="Identity"/>
      <Parameter Value="True" Name="LitigationHoldEnabled"/>
    </CmdletParameters>
  </Event>
- <Event OriginatingServer="MR1 (15.00.0516.025)" Error="" Succeeded="true" RunDate="2013-03-21T21:28:49+00:00"
  ObjectModified="" Cmdlet="New-MailboxSearch" Caller="LLlab.net/LLlab_Users/fullmsxadmin">
  - <CmdletParameters>
      <Parameter Value="Lindsey" Name="Name"/>
    </CmdletParameters>
  </Event>
- <Event OriginatingServer="MR1 (15.00.0516.025)" Error="" Succeeded="true" RunDate="2013-03-21T21:26:32+00:00"
  ObjectModified="AuditLogSearch\0cd05b67-b21d-4511-9a0b-6b363cd6723f" Cmdlet="New-AdminAuditLogSearch"
  Caller="LLlab.net/LLlab_Users/fullmsxadmin">
  - <CmdletParameters>
      <Parameter Value="06/03/2013 00:00:00" Name="StartDate"/>
      <Parameter Value="22/03/2013 00:00:00" Name="EndDate"/>
      <Parameter Value="lindseyA@lllab.com" Name="StatusMailRecipients"/>
    </CmdletParameters>
  </Event>
```

ROLE GROUP, IN-PLACE DISCOVERY, AND LITIGATION REPORTS

The administrator is able to use EAC to understand what changes have been made within RBAC and, more specifically, to management role groups. Use the Run An Administrator Role Group Report section of auditing to search for changes made to management role groups. Figure 8.11 shows an administrator role group report listing the recent changes made to the UM Management, Records Management, and Hygiene Management role groups. The search interface also allows the administrator to execute searches within a specific data range and/or to search for changes made only to specific management role groups.

If you have enabled a user for litigation hold using either EAC or PowerShell, the Run A Per-Mailbox Litigation Hold report is useful for determining which users are placed on litigation hold. Note that this does not include users who have been enabled for in-place hold via the eDiscovery center. Figure 8.12 illustrates the results of this type of report.

FIGURE 8.11
Recent RBAC role
changes showing
up in the role group
report

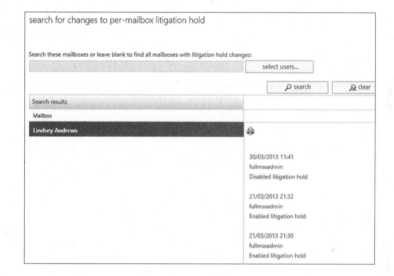

FIGURE 8.11
Recent RBAC role
changes showing
up in the role group
report

FIGURE 8.12
The results of a
Litigation Hold
report

For users who have been enabled for 'In-Place' hold either through EAC or the eDiscovery Centre, the 'Run an In-Place eDiscovery & Hold report' feature can be used to search the administrator audit log to determine the In-Place hold changes made. Note that this report also includes users which have been enabled for Litigation Hold, using the legacy method (EAC, "recipients," "mailbox features," "Litigation hold").

Summary

The goal of this chapter was to provide you with a pragmatic approach to security by understanding the security threats posed to an organization's email data in today's environment. We endeavored to help you understand the real concerns of security officers and IT departments and how the security features in Exchange Server 2013 can be used to address and mitigate those concerns. This chapter attempted to arm you with the knowledge of how Exchange Server 2013 is secure by default and what your options are for securing the infrastructure by design.

The chapter was structured in such a way as to guide you through the crucial conversations you must have with the security officer during the design phase and in addressing the security of data in transit, data at rest, and data in long-term storage. You learned what native functionality Exchange Server 2013 provides to audit and report on security breaches if all security precautions fail. In addition, this chapter provided you with an overview of periphery technologies, such as reverse proxy solutions and mobile device security technology, to afford you a comprehensive view of the client access landscape and how to secure that access into the messaging infrastructure.

This chapter also delivered an overview of the security components that are new to Exchange Server 2013: the native antimalware and antispam capabilities, the ability to enforce TLS through transport rules, new auditing and reporting capabilities, the ability for AD RMS to support more recent cryptographic modes and the enhancements which have been made to make the setup routine more secure.

In 2012, it was stated that the average security breach costs organizations $5.5 million each. Thus, if there is one thing that you *must* take away from this chapter, it has to be a firm belief in the importance of security issues and the dire consequences posed if you are unable to elicit security requirements effectively.

Chapter 9

Compliance

The amount of information the world generates is constantly growing. Much of it ends up as email, with people regularly having mailboxes that are gigabytes in size. Of course, because of the history of Exchange storage, it is also the case that people have moved mail out of their mailbox and into PST files. When you couple this with ever-increasing regulation of business that affects the flow of information, you are faced with a significant challenge that needs to be addressed.

This chapter will take you through a discussion of compliance. We will introduce you to the regulations that businesses face, cover the conversations that you need to be having with your organization's legal department, discuss the policies that need to be set, and examine what Exchange functionality is available to implement those polices.

Overview of Messaging Compliance

The first step to be taken in understanding compliance is to know what regulations apply to your organization. If you have been working for a particular industry for some time, you are likely to be aware of such regulations. If not, start your research now. Most likely, this will involve a discussion with the local management chain or legal team. We also provide some useful URLs later in the chapter.

The challenge of compliance is that it is often led by a general understanding of regulations rather than by hard fact. This means that one legal advisor may interpret the rules one way, while another takes a different approach. In this way, one organization in an industry may come up with a vastly different approach to policy than another in the same industry. No matter, you must be guided by *your* legal team's understanding of a regulation and then seek to create a policy that offsets the risk to *your* organization.

It is here that your job really begins. Once you have the policy in hand, you need to look at the situation from a technological point of view. Although you may be designing a new system from scratch, it is more likely that you will be coping with an existing mail system.

Email can exist in a multitude of places, not only mailboxes. For example, *PST (Personal Storage Table)* files, which were introduced in the earliest versions of Outlook dating back to 1997, have become a major issue for email administrators because they contain huge amounts of information that is not readily accessible to them. The files can also become corrupt and thus lose that information. Alongside the PST, which is very much a personal archive, is the organizational archive. This is often based on a third-party solution that exploits Exchange's journaling functionality. *Journaling* ensures that a copy of everything that passes through transport is captured and held in a specific mailbox. For small systems where mail flow is limited, that journaling mailbox may be all that is needed. For situations where that mailbox is immense, however, it is common to integrate with a third-party program, such as Zantaz EAS or Symantec Enterprise Vault.cloud. These products will monitor the journaling mailbox and extract mail out of it into their own database on a scheduled basis. In this way, they build up their own fully searchable repository of email. These systems can also be used to archive other information within the organization from repositories such as SharePoint. Nowadays, there are also online varieties like Mimecast, which can provide other solutions as well, such as resilience in the event of your system being down.

All this means is that information is being removed from Exchange; that is, it is no longer stored in the native format in which it arrived. It also implies buying, learning, and maintaining a third-party system. The thinking these days is that, given that Exchange can store 100 GB+ per mailbox, why not just keep the data in Exchange and make it safe, searchable, and secure there?

Whatever the situation, you need to come up with a response to the policy that ensures compliance on the part of your organization. We will return to this later in the chapter. For now, let's look at the types of regulation that your organization may face so that you will be comfortable with the elements that go into a compliance policy.

Regulations

Email is a central capability for almost all organizations and, over the last 15 years, it has become firmly accepted as a legal document of record that stands up to scrutiny in court. This means that organizations need to include email records when required to disclose information. It is therefore very important to understand which regulations apply specifically to email. We are not by any means lawyers, and by no means do we aim to provide legal advice. Nevertheless, what we intend to do here is to set out examples of the more common regulations and concerns that apply to email in various countries. It is then up to you to work with your organization's legal team to understand the specifics of how these regulations affect your situation.

U.K. Data Protection Act   The United Kingdom's Data Protection Act (DPA) specifies that "emails can be caught by the Act if they identify living individuals and are held, in automated form, in live, archive or back-up systems, or have been deleted from the live system but are still capable of recovery. They may also be caught if, despite having been deleted from the electronic system they are stored in paper form, in relevant filing systems." (To be clear, "caught by the Act" indicates that the item falls under the jurisdiction of the DPA.)

For more information, see the following page:

```
http://www.dft.gov.uk/vca/data-protection-act-guidance-on-compliance.asp
```

Assuming that your email information comes under the Act, some of the important specifics are as follows:

- ◆   Email is kept no longer than necessary.

- ◆   Email is kept secure from unlawful or unauthorized processing or accidental loss or erasure.

This means considering the ability to remove data once it is no longer relevant and ensuring that the data is securely held. Also significantly, this means keeping that data safe and secure so that it is not leaked or transferred to others. Finally, you must also be able to provide data to the owner upon request.

U.S. Patriot Act   This act gives the U.S. government various powers to safeguard national security. In particular, it allows the U.S. government to intercept all messages that are "relevant to an ongoing criminal investigation." In essence, the Act provides the ability to require access to data via closed subpoena.

Like the DPA, this legislation is mostly concerned with the search and provision of data. However, it does have the interesting aspect of a potential clash between legislative bodies when concerning cloud-based systems run by U.S. firms.

For example, for the majority of the companies that we deal with regularly that fall within the jurisdiction of the European Union, any request under the U.S. Patriot Act needs to be viewed in the context of the EU Data Protection Directive, which is an example of a safe harbor law. This prohibits EU firms from transferring data overseas other than to countries that have signed up to meet the EU standards. The issue arises where certain national laws, like the U.S. Patriot Act, potentially overrule the agreement with the EU. This is of particular interest when considering a cloud-based service such as Office 365.

More and more often, we see an acceptance of the risk of the U.S. government requiring data, not least of which is because the United States has signed up for the EU safe harbor standards, and also because the benefits outweigh the risks. Finally, it is very often the case that were governments to require certain information, this could, in any case, be routed via the local security agencies that, particularly in the U.K., have good relations with comparable bodies in the U.S.

Freedom of Information Act   Freedom of Information Act (FOIA) legislation is found in many countries including the U.S. and U.K. For example, the U.K. Freedom of Information Act 2000 provides access to data held by public bodies as follows: "Anyone can make a request for information, including members of the public, journalists, lawyers, businesses, charities and other organizations. An information request can also be made to any part of a public authority. You may have a designated information requests team to whom the public can make their requests. However, members of the public will often address their requests to staff they already have contact with, or who seem to know most about the subject of their request. When you receive a request you have a legal responsibility to identify that a request has been made and handle it accordingly. So staff who receive customer correspondence should be particularly alert to identifying potential requests. You normally have 20 working days to respond to a request." The basic point here is that this is a regulation set up to allow the public as a whole (be it from journalists or directly) to gain access to data that will allow them to hold public organizations to account.

More information can be found on the following site:

http://www.ico.gov.uk/for_organisations/freedom_of_information/guide.aspx.

This regulation is all about being able to search for and provide information that is requested, within a prescribed time frame.

Health Insurance Portability and Accountability Act   Health Insurance Portability and Accountability Act (HIPAA) is a U.S. law that applies to healthcare entities that governs the use, disclosure, and safeguarding of protected health information (PHI). This could be medical records or data relating to administrative or financial matters. It imposes requirements on covered entities to sign business associate agreements with their vendors that use and disclose PHI. In this case, the regulation is concerned with the protection and privacy of data, which in the case of email means ensuring suitable encryption of data both at rest and in transit. (Both of these topics are covered in Chapter 8, "Designing a Secure Exchange Solution.") It also means preventing leakage of data, which is a topic we will cover shortly in this chapter.

For a great introduction to HIPAA and how it affects email, see the following site:

`http://luxsci.com/blog/what-hipaa-says-about-email-security.html`

Sarbanes-Oxley Act   The Sarbanes-Oxley Act (SOX) is a U.S. law born out of the Enron scandal, and it is administered by the Securities and Exchange Commission (SEC). It has three guiding rules:

1. You must not destroy, falsify, or alter records.

2. An auditor must maintain all audit or review work papers for a period of five years from the end of the fiscal period in which the audit or review was concluded. (This has the potential to require both the auditor and, in practice, the auditee to maintain these records.)

3. The third rule defines the types of records that need to be stored, comprising all business records and communications, including electronic communications created, sent, or received in connection with an audit or review and which contain conclusions, opinions, analyses, or financial data relating to such an audit or review.

You can see how this regulation is concerned with data protection and immutability.

Payment Card Industry Data Security Standard   The Payment Card Industry Data Security Standard (PCI-DSS) is a proprietary information security standard for those involved in handling cardholder information. The aim is to ensure that a minimum level of security is in place for those who store, process, and transmit cardholder data to prevent identity theft and card fraud. All transmissions must be audited, encrypted, and regularly tested. Often this involves using secured networks and isolating the data to certain systems.

In terms of email systems, PCI-DSS requires that this type of data either be encrypted or prevented from being sent over email in the first place. If this type of data is sent out over email, encryption is a must and so is careful protection with firewalls and malware safeguards to prevent infiltration that allows access to data.

Companies (Trading Disclosures) Regulations 2008   This U.K. regulation is derived from a European law on how businesses identify themselves. If your business is a private or public limited company or a Limited Liability Partnership, this regulation amends the Companies Act of 2006, and it requires all of your business emails (plus your letterhead and order forms) to include the following details in legible characters:

◆   Your company's registered name (for example, XYZ Ltd.)

◆   Your company registration number

◆   Your place of registration (for example, Scotland, England, or Wales)

◆   Your registered office address

Further information can be found in the PDF file found at the following address:

`http://www.legislation.gov.uk/uksi/2008/495/pdfs/uksi_20080495_en.pdf`

In Exchange terms, this means adding a footer or disclaimer to emails.

Having covered many of the major regulations that affect the flow of information, and having noted that the majority of them concern data privacy, retention, and provision, we shall now move on to look at how this affects the required policies.

Designing Your Policies

Making sure that you have policies in place and then sticking to them is the single most important element of compliance. It is simply not acceptable to say that compliance issues haven't been considered when working with Exchange. Different policies will have fundamentally wide-ranging effects on the requirements for which you are designing Exchange. It is therefore imperative that you reach out to your legal team early on as part of your project.

Discussions with the Legal Department

When working with specialist professionals, it is essential to understand their language. Therefore, we strongly recommend that you get to know the "lay of the land" when it comes to regulation. Check out the following resources to start building an understanding of what might apply to your situation:

http://en.wikipedia.org/wiki/Compliance_(regulation)

http://www.metrocorpcounsel.com/articles/7216/email-screening-compliance-european-regulations

http://www.itgovernance.co.uk/compliance.aspx

http://searchsecurity.techtarget.co.uk/resources/Compliance-Regulation-and-Standard-Requirements

Regulations rarely spell out exactly what is required; that is, they are open to interpretation. This means that your organization needs to interpret the regulation appropriately and be able to show, in good faith, that it has made a reasonable effort to comply with the particular regulation. The fact that interpretation is involved opens up the potential for some rather extreme policies. It is at this point that an experienced consultant or architect needs to have the tough discussion that could very well save the organization money.

As an example, you may be able to bring up the fact that organization X in the same industry is doing things a little differently. It is very important that you challenge the status quo and present different possibilities. For example, keeping email forever, just because that is what has always been done, is going to cost your organization a significant amount of money. To this end, continue to push the legal team to make a decision. It is at this point where leveraging the senior sponsor of a project can make a difference. If you can convey accurately the complexity and cost implications of an open-ended, keep-everything-forever approach, you can often use the sponsor to guide the legal team into an appropriate response.

Typical Requirements

As you saw in the discussion of some of the most common regulations, they very often had the same effect on the operation of Exchange. These are not the only constraints on Exchange design, however. It is also necessary to manage the day-to-day operation of the platform. Therefore, you will likely have two major types of requirements in your compliance policy. The first set of requirements is driven by regulation and the second set is driven by day-to-day needs, such as the message size limit. It is important to understand that the legal team will drive one set of requirements and business sponsors will drive the other set of requirements.

What follows is an examination of the typical requirements you will need to consider when designing your compliance policy.

RETENTION OF DATA

You must weigh everything specified in the regulation and then consider your approach to whether it is better to retain data or not to retain data. Some organizations take the approach that all mail will be removed after one year no matter what. Other organizations delete all mail after thirty days unless it is specifically called out as a record and stored in a separate system. This is not an approach we would generally recommend, because it has a nasty habit of interfering with peoples' ability to do their jobs, becoming as irritating as the old need to manage mailboxes with small quotas. Other organizations must plan for very long data-retention cycles. Those building certain sensitive facilities with a long life may require access to those emails many decades into the future. In general, however, maintaining email for seven years for tax purposes is one of the more familiar requirements in the financial space.

Of course, you may require different retention periods for different types of users. For example, your standard policy might be to keep data for two years, but a specific regulated team might require a policy that provides for longer retention of data. You might also give users the ability to mark certain items specifically to allow them to be retained longer than the standard two years.

Once you have defined the retention periods and which groups are affected, you must be specific about the type of data required. Different archiving solutions can capture different levels of information. For example, are you required to capture all metadata related to messages, such as a point-in-time breakdown of members of distribution lists to whom the mail was sent? Or, is it a requirement to capture the BCC field of a mail? If so, then some form of envelope journaling is necessary. You may also be required to maintain visibility of Calendar and Notes entries in Exchange. Users have been known to attempt to get around ethical walls by leaving notes in shared calendars for the next shift to act upon.

Finally, you must define where data is to be held. For example, many organizations are desperately trying to reduce their reliance on PST files. You should consider making it part of your policy that all data should be held in Exchange because, for the lifetime of the product, there will always be a way to transfer data between versions. It also means that there are largely no blocking factors preventing upgrades that can occur when you have different third parties involved.

ABILITY TO RETRIEVE DATA

Having the data is one thing, but actually being able to get it back in a timely fashion is another. We've worked with customers who ended up with a mess when going back through ancient Exchange 5.5 database backup tapes to locate mail needed for a particular HR dispute. This underscores the importance of considering the length of time that you need to retain data. Once you have decided on a particular period, it makes a great deal of sense to maintain this data live and immutable if necessary. Given that Exchange can now make full use of up to 8 TB hard drives, keeping data live no longer means going back through ancient backup tapes, all stored in the wrong format.

INTEGRITY/IMMUTABILITY

Assuming that you can retrieve the data, you also often need to prove that it hasn't been tampered with. This is one area where companies often focus on a particular solution: write-once, read-many (WORM) media. In effect, regulations mostly state that it must be possible to prove the integrity of the data. Naturally, this can be done in several different ways through the use of both hardware and software. Exchange uses the software method by marking items as on hold. It then prevents updates to those items behind the scenes while letting users continue to work in the normal way. Any changes are captured, and a new version is created. Discovery teams then have full access to this history. Validation of data integrity can be provided through the provision of SHA-256 hashes for exported content, which can be checked using Electronic Discovery Reference Model (EDRM)-compatible software.

SECURITY OF DATA

Of course, by retaining all of this data, you must take care to protect it. It is all too common to hear about data leakage, which can be extremely costly financially while damaging the reputation of an organization at the same time. Security is covered in depth in Chapter 8, where we discuss auditing and rights management. However, we will also touch on a few security-related elements in this chapter, particularly concerning data loss protection.

IDENTIFICATION OF YOUR ORGANIZATION

Another aspect of regulation covers the need to identify your organization. Thus, it is a common requirement that all business communications, including email, show your company information such as name, address, and registration details. This is usually covered as an email footer or disclaimer.

GENERAL GOOD PRACTICE

As mentioned in the introduction to this section, policy requirements are not only driven by regulation. You must also cover some of the more mundane aspects of a mail system, such as whether or not personal email use is allowed and whether mail size limits exist. While these are not very exciting, they will form part of the consideration around your design.

Compliance Policy

Once you have decided on the elements that need to be contained within the compliance policy, you need to prepare the document that will then be communicated. In many situations, this document will need to be signed in some form by the staff. This may be a function of their terms of employment or as an additional procedure. The key point about this type of document is that it needs to be clear and concise so that users fully understand what they are signing.

The following elements should be included in the compliance document:

EXEC SUMMARY

Give a quick introduction to the policy and what it covers, that is, email security and compliance. Cover the goals of the policy.

ROLES AND RESPONSIBILITIES

Cover which groups are responsible for the policy and what they need to do to implement it.

COVERAGE

State to whom the policy applies. Be specific about different organizational units, systems, and employees. Explicitly call out any exceptions to the policy in this section.

ACTUAL POLICIES

This part of the document is where you must define the policies. This will be the largest section, and it will form the guidance for your design. Make sure to cover all aspects of email compliance, including not only the regulatory issues and your responses to them that you may face (encryption, data retention/deletion, and so on) but also more mundane matters, such as personal use of email and mail size limits.

PROCESSES

Cover the actual steps to be taken to put the policy into action in this section—how it will be enforced and how it will measure compliance. You may consider making this section an appendix in order to keep the user-readable material concise.

CONSEQUENCES FOR VIOLATION

As with any policy, you need to define a clear set of responses should it be violated. Here you should cover the consequences of the first, second, and third violations.

REVISION DATE

Define when the policy will be reevaluated and checked in order to determine if it is still meeting the relevant regulations.

APPENDICES

The following appendices are also part of a compliance policy:

Reference Material   Links to any regulations to which the policy intends to comply

Associated Documentation   Links to any related documents

Revision History   Coverage of updates

Compliance Solutions

Having looked at the regulations and the policy elements that drive the topic of compliance, we will now move on to considering how these elements come together and how they can be implemented. We will identify the various aspects of Exchange that can be brought to bear on the problem of compliance. We will cover retention policies, archiving, discovery, immutability, and leakage protection. We will do this while examining the choices we would make when working with a selection of companies.

Exchange Functionality

Before we introduce our scenario customers, we will cover the features and functions in Exchange 2013 and Office 365 that will help you meet compliance policy requirements.

JOURNALING

Journaling has been available in Exchange since the earliest versions. It enables administrators to capture a copy of every item that passes through transport. It will capture the entire message envelope, meaning that BCC fields and the breakout of the membership of distribution lists are captured. It can be used as part of a compliance solution, although items that don't pass through transport, such as calendar items or Lync instant messages, are not captured. Journaling is often used in conjunction with a third-party archiving system, either on-premises or online, because it generates large volumes of data in a small number of mailboxes.

We are starting to see organizations move away from journaling toward In-Place Hold, as described in a later section. One challenge of journaling, as with many compliance mechanisms, is the ability to provide a view into encrypted emails. Only IRM-protected items can be decrypted in journal reports, because IRM is integrated tightly with Exchange, as mentioned later. S/MIME emails cannot be viewed.

TRANSPORT RULES

Transport rules have been a core component of Exchange since Exchange 2007. They enable a great deal of control over mail flow. They provide a wide variety of conditions that can be used to select mail and an equally large number of actions that can be carried out. They also allow exceptions, which further enhance their usefulness. Some examples of their use include moderating a percentage of email, implementing mail blocking based on a keyword, encrypting/rights that protect a mail, and routing mail to a manager as required. In Exchange 2013, transport rules have been enhanced specifically to provide mail-filtering capabilities for Exchange Online Protection, which is covered in Chapter 8. For example, transport rules can now be set in motion for a particular time period and can also be set to operate in test mode only, which provides a mechanism to review policies before full operation commences.

DATA LOSS PREVENTION

All organizations have sensitive data that, if leaked, would damage their reputation at the very least if not cost them financially. *Data Loss Prevention (DLP)* is a new feature of Exchange 2013 that builds on the existing transport rules capabilities by providing sensitive data classifications and policy templates to help meet common requirements in a variety of different locations around the world. For example, classifications exist to detect common personally identifiable information, such as social security numbers and passport numbers. Similarly, there is a classification for credit card data, which is useful in PCI-DSS scenarios. Exchange 2013 includes 40 policy templates out of the box and 47 sensitive data types.

DLP in Exchange 2013 can scan deep into attachments to locate specific email items, and it can then select from the multitude of actions afforded to it by transport rules. In addition, integration with Outlook 2013 enables the user to be involved in the process through Policy Tips. These tips enable users to be educated about policies and even be enabled to override a policy, while being required to give specific business reasons for doing so. All of this can be audited to provide suitable mechanisms of oversight.

INFORMATION RIGHTS MANAGEMENT

Information Rights Management (IRM) is another technology to which Exchange provides access, both at the transport layer and in Outlook, as covered in Chapter 8. Setting an IRM template on a mail item is one of the transport rule actions. Using IRM for encryption and lockdown means that because Exchange can be deeply integrated with IRM, the mail can be decrypted as it flows through the system to allow other scanning, such as AntiVirus/AntiSpam, and other transport rules to operate before being re-encrypted and passed on. This is different from encryption systems like S/MIME, where no further scanning is possible, because Exchange cannot decrypt the mail item. Outlook users can also apply IRM templates to mail items directly through the client. In the new version of Office 365, IRM is available in Exchange Online.

MESSAGE RECORDS MANAGEMENT

Message Records Management (MRM) capabilities have been included in Exchange for some time using Recipient Update Service policies. Exchange 2013 is somewhat more developed in this area. Exchange 2013 provides a system of tags to be built into retention policies and applied to different groups of users. Tags can be used either for deleting a mail or for moving a mail to an Archive mailbox. Tags can operate on the mailbox as a whole or on individual folders within the mailbox. It is also possible for administrators to make the tags mandatory or to give the user Personal tags, which gives the user a choice about what settings to put on their mail items. In this way, there can be a balance between enforcing policy while still giving the user a degree of control over the way they deal with their mailbox. A user can have only one policy applied to their mailbox. These policies are then implemented by the Managed Folder Assistant, which processes all mailboxes over a specified time period to enact the policy on each email. Tasks, calendars, and mail items can all be covered by the policy.

IN-PLACE ARCHIVING

In-place archiving provides a user with a secondary mailbox. This mailbox can either be held on the same database as the primary mailbox or be held somewhere else including, through a hybrid deployment, in the cloud with Office 365. The in-place archive has a different quota from the primary mailbox. Users can populate information manually by dragging in PST files, or the files can be automatically imported through PowerShell by administrators or by using the Microsoft PST Capture tool or a similar third-party tool. Once old archives have been migrated in, new information is moved to the archive from the primary mailbox by Move tags, as previously mentioned. Note that the in-place archive is only accessible online; it is not cached to an Outlook Offline Storage Table (OST) file like the primary mailbox.

IN-PLACE HOLD

Added as a feature in Exchange 2010, the ability to place a mailbox on *litigation hold* signifies that the data within that mailbox is immutable. No changes are possible to the original items. Edits are captured and saved to versions. The end user is not affected, but discovery officers have full access to the entire history. In Exchange 2013, this feature has been further enhanced to include not only full mailboxes but also specific data located through a discovery query. Also, time-based holds have been made possible so that data does not need to be kept indefinitely. Instead, it can be held for a defined period of time.

eDISCOVERY

With the ability to hold large amounts of data comes the need to search that data. In Exchange 2010 and Exchange 2013, search capabilities are provided to those with the correct discovery

RBAC role. This provides access to a web portal where the discovery officer can search and pre-view data before exporting it. Exchange 2013 and SharePoint 2013 are further enhanced through the provision of a new Case Management portal. This portal allows legal teams to carry out complex searches across data from SharePoint, Lync, and Exchange. This data can be put on hold and exported in an industry-standard way through the use of an EDRMS manifest file.

Administrator Audit Logging

As discussed in Chapter 8, Exchange 2013 provides the ability to track all actions carried out by administrators, thus enabling change control processes to be monitored and policies to be enforced.

Mailbox Audit Logging

Given that the mailbox is where data is held, monitoring access makes a lot of sense. Exchange 2013 allows you to monitor end-user access, delegate access (whether administrative or end-user enabled), and administrator access to mail items. It even goes as far as showing who sent a par-ticular item.

Having introduced the features available, we will now move on to consider the different scenarios in which they might be used.

Exchange 2013 Compliance Scenarios

We will now use scenarios that represent real-world examples to illustrate the choices and deci-sions that different companies need to make with regard to compliance. Naturally, we do not intend these scenarios to be followed exactly. Rather, they are to provide examples of the type of thinking that occurs and the processes that might be implemented in certain situations. Given your particular circumstances and attitude toward risk, you will likely make different decisions.

 Real World Scenario

Company A

Company A is a small business in an unregulated industry with 250 employees that needs to protect itself from occasional HR issues. The company has had HR disputes in the past and, when moving to Exchange Server 2013, it wants to take the appropriate steps to avoid such troubles going forward.

The thought process for such a company could go in several different directions. First, it could move its current mail system to the cloud with Office 365. This, of course, would be the subject of all the usual cloud decision framework elements, covered in the Microsoft Technical Fit Assessment, available at the following location:

    http://www.microsoft.com/en-us/download/details.aspx?id=21538

Because it does not operate in a regulated industry, the major challenge for a small organization like Company A is bandwidth availability. Assuming that the cloud is a suitable solution, then Company A would migrate its messaging system to Office 365. From a compliance perspective, this makes matters very simple. As a starting point, it now has a much larger mailbox, which means that use of PST files can be prevented and that all data can be brought into Exchange Online.

continues

(continued)

For more information on planning for Office 2013 GPOs, see the following article:

`http://technet.microsoft.com/en-us/library/cc179077.aspx`

Given the size of the company, it is likely that the Microsoft Exchange PST Capture tool can be utilized to move the data. For more information about the details of the PST Capture tool, see the following article:

`http://technet.microsoft.com/en-us/library/hh781036(v=exchg.141).aspx`

Once the data is moved, Company A needs to consider data retention. Users tend to keep everything, so it makes sense to implement some basic retention policies. By default, Office 365 has a selection of policies in place, as can be seen in the following article:

`http://technet.microsoft.com/en-US/library/dd297955(v=exchg.150).aspx`

This article provides a very useful rundown of the technology behind retention policies and how to implement them. What is important is that the majority of tags are of the personal type. There are two retention policy tags and one default policy tag. Only the two retention policy tags are set to delete data automatically. These remove objects from the deleted items and junk mail folders after 30 days. Nonetheless, they do allow those objects to be recovered through the deleted items recovery area. Therefore, if you wanted to implement a default two-year retention policy that will delete all mail over two years in age, you would need to create a new retention tag, as shown in the following graphic, and then assign it to the policy. The following page lists procedures for setup and management of tags and policies:

`http://technet.microsoft.com/en-US/library/jj150558(v=exchg.150).aspx`

new tag applied automatically to entire mailbox (default)   Help

*Name:
Default Retention - Remove 2 Years

Retention action:
○ Delete and Allow Recovery
● Permanently Delete
○ Move to Archive

Retention period:
○ Never
● When the item reaches the following age (in days):
730

Comment:
This is Company A default retention policy - Remove all items older than 2 years.

save   cancel

Having set up the system to allow mail to be retained, it is important to know how this mail can be located when the need arises. There are three possibilities for searching Exchange data. First, you can search via the SharePoint eDiscovery portal. This is not available, however, if you have not either installed SharePoint or you do not have a SharePoint subscription if using Office 365. The second option is through the use of PowerShell. While PowerShell is extremely flexible, it is also rather complex. This leaves the third and standard option of searching through the Exchange Admin Center. To allow a discovery officer to search Exchange data, you must make sure that they have the relevant RBAC role. In this case, membership in the Discovery Management role group is required. For a full breakdown of the discovery search capabilities of Exchange, see the article found at the following URL:

```
http://technet.microsoft.com/en-us/library/dd298021(v=exchg.150).aspx
```

For procedures regarding the management of eDiscovery capabilities, the following page is useful:

```
http://technet.microsoft.com/en-us/library/dd298014(v=exchg.150).aspx
```

Finally, as all companies must, you will have to identify yourself in email. To do so, you can use a simple transport rule. Exchange 2013 has a new interface for configuring transport rules, and it has an out-of-the-box option for adding a disclaimer. Open EAC and navigate to the Mail Flow/Rules sections. Select the plus icon and, on the drop-down menu shown in the following graphic, select Apply Disclaimers.

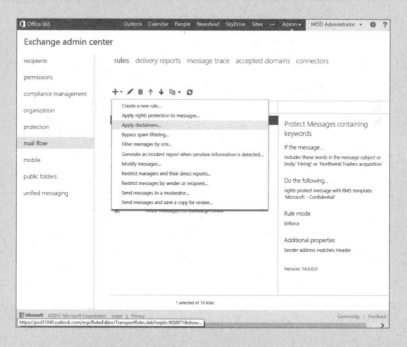

continues

(continued)

You are next presented with a group of options. First, give the disclaimer a name. You may create several names for different parts of the organization if you wish. You must be specific about when you want the disclaimer to apply, which in this case is when the mail is sent to a recipient outside the organization. Finally, specify the disclaimer text and a fallback option if, for some reason, the disclaimer can't be applied. As you can see in the following graphic, there are many other possibilities. These are covered in depth in the articles associated with these sites:

```
http://technet.microsoft.com/en-us/library/dd351127.aspx

http://technet.microsoft.com/en-us/library/aa998315.aspx

http://technet.microsoft.com/en-us/library/bb124352(v=exchg.141).aspx
```

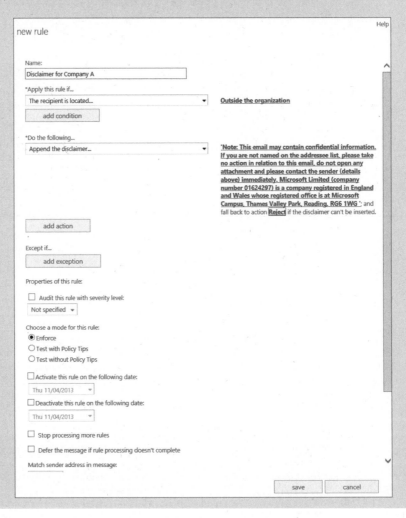

Should Company A decide to stay with an on-premises solution, then deployment of Exchange 2013 would allow it to use large, cost-effective hard drives deployed directly in the servers. It could provide high availability by replicating the data and then implementing the same type of policies, as it would have for Office 365. Of course, the company would have to consider backups, but for a small number of users—even if these users have 25+ GB mailboxes—this should not be a major issue for a basic backup-to-disk system.

 Real World Scenario

ORGANIZATION B

Organization B is a governmental body that is required to provide data to the public via the Freedom of Information Act. Public-sector organizations generally work with sensitive data, which is classified at certain levels. More information about these levels in the U.K. can be found at the following URL which requires downloading. Similar examples exist for all major jurisdictions:

```
http://www.cesg.gov.uk/publications/Documents/business_impact_tables.pdf
```

Organization B is particularly determined to ensure that data is not leaked from the organization. Over the years, a large collection of PSTs has grown, because PSTs provided the only way possible to keep mailboxes small.

As with Company A, when considering the design of an Exchange compliance policy for Organization B, you have options regarding on-premises and cloud-based deployments.

With the recent announcement that Office 365 has received IL2 accreditation in the U.K., it is now open for use in many public-sector and government organizations, as discussed in the following article:

```
http://blogs.msdn.com/b/msbluelight/archive/2013/02/06/microsoft-office-365-
receives-g-cloud-il2-accreditation-from-cabinet-office-for-use-across-the-uk-
public-sector.aspx
```

Given that Organization B works with data that requires higher levels of security, it has decided to stay with an on-premises deployment of Exchange 2013. Also, for a different reason—that is, HR disputes versus Freedom of Information Act requests—the key requirement of being able to search and provide data to relevant parties is the same as for Company A. Thus, it is worth noting here that you should give thought to the interface chosen to perform searches.

As mentioned previously, the two GUI-based tools for searching are the EAC and the eDiscovery portal in SharePoint. While the EAC tool provides access to search, previews results, and then exports them to a discovery mailbox, the SharePoint portal is far more advanced. It provides a full case-management system, allowing different cases to be separated and permissions to be applied as needed to different discovery officers. It also provides real-time updates in search statistics and an improved export mechanism. Therefore, Organization B should weigh the frequency and complexity of it search requirements in order to choose the correct search mechanism.

continues

(continued)

Organization B also faces another very common issue: dealing with the accumulation of PST files. Many government organizations have outsourced mail platform delivery. To this end, they are often stuck behind the times in terms of design and delivery of messaging best practices, simply because of the sheer increase in contractual charges. This means that, up to this point, Organization B has had small mailbox quotas of 100 MB for a standard user and up to 750 MB for senior leadership. These size limits caused the growth of PSTs as users fought to remain within quota while retaining the data needed to do their jobs.

At this stage, Organization B is renegotiating its outsourcing agreements, which puts it in a position to dictate new terms. It has opted for a new storage platform, which is scaled to provide large 10 GB mailboxes for all users. This will enable Organization B to bring all of the data from the PST files back into Exchange. The major benefits of this approach are that users will no longer have to manage their quota constantly, data will not be exported out of Exchange, and backup challenges will be removed. Of course, it also means that all of the old data is now searchable and manageable through the use of Message Records Management policies.

Before beginning the process of importing all of the old data, Organization B will need to consider the age of the data and its importance to the organization. It may well be that some people have very old data. It is often the case that an organization will decide to put a reasonable limit on the data imported—five years, for example. This is what Organization B has decided. As discussed further at the end of this scenario, communication is key when making this change to avoid a user backlash. Decisions surrounding the amount of old mail to be imported will also need to be tied into the sizing discussion for the platform as a whole.

Once you have determined which PST data will be brought into the Exchange mailboxes, you have to decide how to get the data migrated. This can be harder than it sounds. You may be dealing with a huge amount of email that has the potential to overload both the network and Exchange if handled incorrectly. Generally, the first step is to migrate the user to their new mailbox. This makes a large mailbox available to them. Then it makes sense to turn off the ability to write new data to existing PST files and to prevent the creation of new ones. This turns the existing PSTs into an archive of old data with no possibility for modification by the user. This change is made using Group Policy in Active Directory. As a starting point, review the following article to understand Office 2013 Group Policies:

```
http://technet.microsoft.com/en-us/library/cc179176.aspx
```

Group Policies are widely used in almost all organizations, so make sure that you discuss this with your Active Directory specialists. When you've decided on the best approach for application, download the Group Policy Administrative Template files from the following website:

```
http://www.microsoft.com/en-us/download/details.aspx?id=35554
```

Once you download and install the template files, you will find a spreadsheet called `office-2013grouppolicyandoctsettings.xlsx`. In this spreadsheet, you will see details of all of the policies that can be applied. The particular policies in which you are interested are found in the `outlk15.admx` template. These policies are described here:

◆   Prevent users from adding PSTs to Outlook profiles and/or prevent using Sharing-Exclusive PSTs.

By default, users can add PSTs to their Outlook profiles and can use Sharing-Exclusive PSTs for storing SharePoint lists and Internet calendars. You can use this setting to limit a user's ability to store mail in a decentralized fashion. You can also block the use of PSTs completely, but be aware that blocking all PST files disables Outlook features such as SharePoint lists and Internet calendars. If instead you allow only Sharing-Exclusive PSTs to be added to user profiles, PST use is still limited but the Outlook features that rely on special PSTs are not disabled. The setting that allows Sharing-Exclusive PSTs to be added blocks users from creating new folders in the Sharing-Exclusive PST, copying existing mail folders from their default store to the PST, and copying individual mail items to the root of the PST.

◆ Prevent users from adding new content to existing PST files.

This setting prevents users from adding any new content to PST files linked to their profiles.

Having prevented the creation of new PSTs and the addition of data to old ones, you can now consider the migration of old data into the Exchange mailboxes. Following are several approaches for accomplishing this:

Ask the users to use Outlook to import PST data into their new mailbox. We have seen this work occasionally or perhaps as a supplemental method. However, it is mostly an option in smaller organizations where there are relatively savvy users and where those users have bought into the change. Challenges occur because this can tie up Outlook clients for lengthy periods of time and because, as an administrator, you have no control over the bandwidth used or the logs created on the Exchange server. There may be a massive spike of imports that could overload the system, so this needs to be managed carefully with a communication plan.

Ask users to disconnect PSTs from Outlook and copy them to a central location. Then use PowerShell to import. The first issue here is again trusting end users to do as they are requested. Next, it is important to implement a suitable naming convention. Otherwise, identification and automation of the process of getting the PSTs imported will be a challenge. This method does give you more control over the import process, which means proper scheduling can be applied to prevent overload of Exchange. PSTs are all copied over the network at a time selected by individual users. For more information about the process required, review the following article:

http://technet.microsoft.com/en-us/library/ee633455.aspx

Use a specialist tool designed specifically to migrate PSTs into Exchange. As with many administrative tasks, various specialist tools can ease the migration process as compared to the use of built-in or PowerShell-based automation. The task of PST migration is no different. Microsoft provides the Microsoft Exchange PST Capture tool, which is designed to search out and copy PST data from across the network into Exchange on-premises or online. Additional information about this tool can be found in the following articles:

http://www.msexchange.org/articles-tutorials/exchange-server-2010/management-administration/microsoft-pst-capture-tool-part1.html

http://technet.microsoft.com/en-us/library/hh781036(v=exchg.141).aspx

The Microsoft Exchange PST Capture tool offers various features, including an agent that needs to be installed on client PCs to allow non-specifically defined PSTs to be located.

continues

(continued)

The agent will allow the local PC and any attached drives to be searched for PSTs. It will also allow PSTs to be imported directly to the primary mailbox or to an archive mailbox. Of course, there are some limitations with a free tool. The Microsoft Exchange PST Capture tool only looks at the file owner to determine the ownership of the PST. It doesn't open up the PST and discovery sender and recipient information to better analyze the true owner. Therefore, you would need to assign PSTs manually to their true owner if they are not detected correctly. Another issue is that it can't use the Volume Shadow Copy Service (VSS) to capture PSTs open in Outlook. Perhaps the most important issue here is that the PST Capture tool does not allow data meeting a certain date range to be imported. This highlights the attention to detail required when evaluating whether a tool meets your requirements. The PST Capture tool will import all data from the PSTs chosen for import. In our scenario, where you want to import only data that is less than five years old, this is a showstopper.

You must therefore look elsewhere for a specialist tool. In the past, we have used a couple of products from TransVault. This company specializes in data migrations from various archive storage systems. *TransVault Insight* provides an enterprise-ready PST capture-and-migration solution that can overcome the issues described for the free Microsoft tool.

In this instance, you would weigh the cost of the tools versus the need to meet the requirements. It may be possible to automate some date range options using PowerShell, so if that was the only issue causing the move to a third-party tool, you may decide to use the free Microsoft tool for the bulk of the newer PSTs and then use PowerShell to automate the migration of the older ones.

As with any migration of large quantities of data, always carry out suitable benchmarking to ensure that you understand both the demands on the system (network, storage, and performance) and also the likely time that the migration will take so that you can appropriately inform users when their data will be available.

The final major requirement in this scenario is the need to protect Organization B from potential data leakage. Exchange 2013 is the first version of Exchange to include a Data Loss Prevention (DLP) system in the box. For an overview of the system, read the following article:

```
http://technet.microsoft.com/en-us/library/jj150527%28v=exchg.150%29.aspx
```

There have been a variety of third-party tools designed to carry out this task. However, since this demand has previously only been met in Organization B using the limited capabilities of older Exchange versions, we will investigate the integrated solution so as to hold to the principle of simplicity of management, integration, and design. DLP is an Enterprise Client Access License feature of Exchange, so you'll need to consider the cost of the solution in your recommendation.

Obviously, the most important element of the DLP solution is to decide what constitutes information that you need to protect. Most public-sector organizations use some form of protective marking scheme, such as the one detailed here:

```
http://protectivemarking.co.uk/images/downloads/gpms.pdf
```

Thus, you have ready-made categories that users are familiar with to assign to documents and emails. When dealing with email, categorizations are used to represent the different levels of restriction. Outlook provides the ability to apply categories manually. However, if this process needs to be mandatory for each mail sent, as it is in many of the more security-conscious firms, then a third-party add-in, such as those provided by Boldon James, needs to be implemented. Categorizations have existed for quite some time, but some of the actions that can now be taken in Exchange when sensitive data is detected are vastly improved.

Some of the requirements in this area may be as follows:

◆ Route a mail to a manager or compliance officer for validation/moderation.

◆ Route mail of a specific classification that is destined for a specific location over a special connector, which will then apply Transport Layer Security.

◆ Apply a special amendment to the header of the message that will then trigger a separate encryption system farther down the chain.

◆ Block a mail from being sent externally.

◆ Block a mail from being sent at all.

There may also be special situations where you want to ensure that users are not using the wrong categorization. In such cases, the major improvement in Exchange 2013 is that there are various built-in ways to detect sensitive data types. As mentioned in the "Exchange Functionality" section, there are 47 data classifications built into Exchange. You can use these classifications and extend them further to operate as a means of double-checking that suitable classifications have been applied to mail. They can also be used to capture any special cases, such as mail about a specific project. The following graphic shows the interface where you can configure rules based on sensitive data types. As you can see, it is just another transport rule.

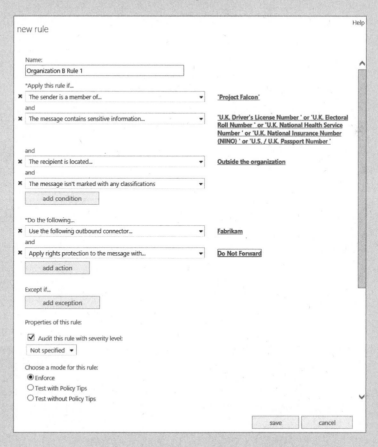

continues

(continued)

Naturally, a big part of the DLP solution is what happens when an incident is detected. Exchange provides auditing capabilities that enable notification of both the end user and the compliance team. In Outlook 2013, Exchange can provide warnings called *Policy Tips* to users, as shown in the following graphic, where detection of credit card information has been made.

You can elect to have users manually click to override a Policy Tip, either with a single click or by forcing them to enter a business justification. All of these elements are captured, and they become part of the audit report that can be sent to a compliance team. A sample report is shown in the following graphic.

These audit mails are structured in a regular fashion, as shown in the following article:

```
http://technet.microsoft.com/en-us/library/jj150534(v=exchg.150).aspx
```

It is possible to extend the capability of the solution further than just sending a mail to a mailbox for manual processing. For example, based on the coverage of EWS in Chapter 11, " Extending Exchange," it is possible to set up a reporting app that takes further action on various audit logs.

The DLP system in Exchange 2013 is the initial version. As such, it has areas that can be improved. For example, it is not possible to tie into external databases, perhaps to validate certain IDs.

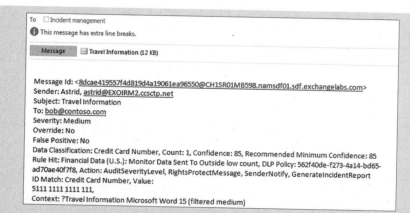

Equally, it is currently not possible to implement *fingerprinting* of documents, a process whereby a checksum is run on sensitive documents and then fed into the DLP system. Any document matching the checksum can then be matched as a sensitive data type. That being said, this solution will fit many scenarios, and it is a huge step forward from the basic capabilities Organization B had implemented in previous versions of Exchange, based on simple transport rules.

One final note is that DLP in Exchange is also extensible, so you can build additional templates and classifications to fit your needs better. More information on the required processes can be found in the following article:

```
http://technet.microsoft.com/en-us/library/jj674310(v=exchg.150).aspx
```

 Real World Scenario

COMPANY C

Company C is a global banking organization that has offices in Hong Kong, London, and New York as well as numerous retail branches worldwide. It has to address strict regulatory compliance issues, and it already has a third-party archiving system in place.

A major financial firm is likely to be using a broad range of systems, so let's assume that SharePoint and Lync are already deployed. We will also assume that there is a storage strategy in place, which predominantly makes use of managed SAN storage.

It is clear that many of the conversations already covered in the previous scenarios will also be applicable here. For example, the use of retention tags and policies to provide a mechanism for keeping data for a certain time period also applies to Company C. A DLP mechanism provided by a third party is also in place. In situations where a major component is already deployed, a review of the requirements, as described by the design document, is often a useful prompt to reevaluate whether new functionality in the Exchange platform will meet those requirements.

continues

(continued)

Obviously, change for the sake of change is not necessarily sensible, so you should undertake these reviews systematically and with an open mind. In Company C's case, it makes sense to stick with the existing solution, because it is deeply embedded in its processes and it offers certain niche functionality, particularly around built-in workflow as opposed to needing to develop this functionality anew for Exchange 2013. Finally, as with Company A, a suitable disclaimer will be added to mail using transport rules in each jurisdiction.

As with all of the other organizations, there is the discussion about whether or not to use cloud-based services. While financial organizations have been reluctant to place their data in a public cloud infrastructure, that mentality is evolving. For example, the Dutch financial services firm Robeco recently moved its infrastructure to Office 365 after an agreement with the Dutch National Bank on regulation, as detailed in the case study at the following URL:

```
http://www.microsoft.com/casestudies/Microsoft-Office-365/Robeco/Financial-
services-provider-Robeco-leaps-from-the-stone-age-to-the-21st-century-with-cloud-
solution/710000002301
```

In the case of Company C, it elected to deploy a hybrid cloud-based solution. For the first time, all branch users will be given email and portal access based on Office 365. Highly regulated traders will be retained on the on-premises servers for the time being.

The key requirements in this scenario include the following:

◆ Consideration of the archiving system in light of the new functionality in Exchange, SharePoint, and Lync

◆ Dealing with the storage of data for a subset of users in an immutable fashion as required by regulators

◆ Searching for data and providing it to counsel on a large scale

We will start by considering the archiving situation, because it has a direct impact on the other requirements. The third-party archiving system that is in place currently would need to be upgraded to work with Exchange 2013. As covered in the introduction to this case study, this means that it is an ideal time to explore whether things could be simplified through the use of new native Exchange features. As in Exchange 2010, Exchange 2013 continues to provide an archive mailbox, which is a secondary mailbox for users. Data can be moved by policy or be moved manually to the archive, and it can be accessed only when the client is connected to the server; that is, when it is online.

The existing archiving platform has been used both as a platform for discovery of data in Exchange and SharePoint and as long-term immutable storage via integration with specialist WORM storage. It can also be used as a method for keeping the size of a mailbox relatively small, given the reliance on expensive SAN storage. Recalling the discussion in Chapter 5, "Designing a Successful Exchange Storage Solution," the Exchange team won the argument about using the SAN storage and was granted an exception to use much cheaper direct attached storage. This has the added benefit of providing much more space for mailboxes. Thus, there is a reduction in the need to archive solely to keep mailboxes small. Exchange 2013 provides support for mailboxes of up to 100 GB in size, so even the heaviest email users are likely to be able to maintain data for seven years and not hit their quota. Also, given the improvements in keeping the data in Exchange, from Exchange 2007 to Exchange 2010 and Exchange 2013, it makes sense given that future versions are likely to improve this capability even further and hard disk drives will continue to grow in size while becoming less costly to purchase.

The company will also be moving to Outlook 2013, which means that it will have control over the amount of mail synchronized down to each client machine OST file, as shown in the following graphic.

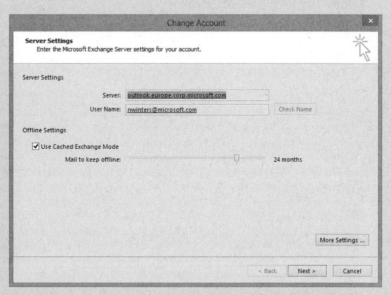

From a client perspective, a benefit of moving to a single, large mailbox approach is that the ability to search for data from any client—mobile, desktop, or browser—is simplified to using native tools. This means that there is no longer a need to integrate with add-ons for OWA or Outlook.

The client archive is the simplest area to move into Exchange, because its primary goal was to keep the mailbox small, which is no longer an issue with Exchange 2013. The next major consideration is the journal. This is used to ensure that copies of all items that pass through transport are held in a secure, immutable location. Journal objects are placed in one or more mailboxes that are specially secured on separate servers because of the sensitive nature of the content and the workload that this approach generates. The third-party system monitors these mailboxes and regularly pulls data out into its own system. One of the challenges of this approach is that items that do not pass through transport, like Notes or Calendar entries, are not captured. This leaves a potential loophole to be exploited. Another challenge is the level of resources dedicated to special mailbox servers. While journaling still exists in Exchange 2013, there are other ways to maintain records for the long term without special servers and without removing data from Exchange.

The new method for retaining data immutably for various periods of time is called *In-Place Hold*. There are various options available, which allow significant flexibility:

◆ *Indefinite hold* is similar to the Litigation hold feature you may be familiar with from Exchange 2010. This ensures that all items from mailboxes are held indefinitely.

◆ *Query-based hold* again holds all items indefinitely. However, the items to be held are based on a query that you specify.

◆ Finally *Time-based hold* is used to capture all of the data for a specific time. In a financial setting, we store data for all of our mailboxes for seven years.

continues

(continued)

For more information on In-Place Hold, including the method through which it achieves immutability, check out the following article:

```
http://technet.microsoft.com/en-us/library/ff637980(v=exchg.150).aspx#scenarios
```

It is likely that automation of Hold applications will be carried out through PowerShell as part of the mailbox provisioning process. For more information on configuration see the article at the following address. Pay particular attention to the `ItemHoldPeriod` parameter:

```
http://technet.microsoft.com/en-us/library/dd298064(v=exchg.150).aspx
```

There are a couple of downsides to not using journaling, because the In-Place Hold feature does not capture the Distribution List membership at the point of receipt as the journal would. It also doesn't capture the BCC field. However, inbound mail arrives in mailboxes and thus can be located. The use of the BCC field will show up in the Sent Items field of a mailbox. While not a perfect match for existing functionality, the move to this retention method means that the third-party archiving system can be retired, thus allowing significant savings. Another benefit, which helps tip the balance, is that with the 2013 releases of SharePoint, Lync, and Exchange, the process of data retention can be extended across the platform. SharePoint can integrate with Exchange to provide the search portal, which we will discuss shortly, and Lync can make use of the immutable storage area in the Exchange mailbox to store its own communication records, thus providing a unified approach. For more information about Lync archiving integration to Exchange, see the following blog post, or read Chapter 17 of *Mastering Microsoft Lync Server 2013* (Wiley, 2013):

```
http://blogs.technet.com/b/nexthop/archive/2012/07/23/integrating-exchange-2013-
preview-and-lync-server-2013-preview.aspx
```

As with any other business decision, there is a tradeoff between risk and reward. In this case, the proposed solution is deemed suitable.

Removing the third-party archive naturally leads to the discussion of getting data from A to B. There are currently no native Microsoft tools available to carry out this type of migration, other than resorting to PSTs. It may be possible for the archive solution to repopulate items into individual mailboxes. However, this usually causes a problem due to storage on the existing mail platform not being sized appropriately. Also, given that the archive system is the system of record, it is very important that a complete audit trail be maintained. To this end, we have observed several companies working with another of the TransVault products, *TransVault Migrator*, to get data into Exchange or Office 365 with a complete audit trail.

Before completing the discussion of data retention, we must cover the one outstanding major element that the third-party system was providing, that is, search. Given the complexity of searches carried out and the sheer number of difference cases, we will opt for the Case Management system provided by the SharePoint eDiscovery portal.

We covered the majority of steps required to get SharePoint and Exchange talking to each other in Chapter 10, "Collaborating with Exchange." Following is a group of links that provide good information about the processes required for setup of discovery search. The first URL is to the SharePoint TechNet site, and it contains a listing of the relevant information in the correct order and links to all other relevant locations. The next URL provides a suitable overview of features that can be found in the SharePoint eDiscovery Center.

```
http://technet.microsoft.com/en-us/library/fp161514(office.15).aspx
http://technet.microsoft.com/en-us/library/fp161513(v=office.15).aspx
```

The eDiscovery Center in SharePoint shown in the graphic here allows members of the Discovery Management RBAC role to search for and retrieve data from Exchange, just as they would by using the EAC, as discussed with Company A. The added capabilities for returning data from SharePoint mean that this offers a one-stop shop for data discovery and retention, because queried data can also be put on hold. Interestingly, Time-based hold is not configurable from the SharePoint eDiscovery Center. This must be configured from PowerShell or through EAC.

When you enter the eDiscovery Center, as shown in the following graphic, you will likely create a new case. This essentially creates a new SharePoint site under the main eDiscovery Center.

Permissions can be applied and basic details about the case can be provided, as shown in the following graphic.

Once the case is created, you'll see the simple dashboard shown in the following graphic, which provides a quick and easy view of the sources (eDiscovery Sets) and the queries. You also get basic statistics on the case.

We begin by creating an eDiscovery Set, as shown in the following graphic. This combination of sources can be SharePoint sites or Exchange mailboxes and basic queries that will get us to a starting point of data to refine further.

Throughout this process, you are presented with statistics. It is easy to set up the basic filters around date, sender/author, and domain. At this point, you can also choose to put this data on hold. Finally, you can also preview the data in order to be sure that you are retrieving what is needed.

continues

(continued)

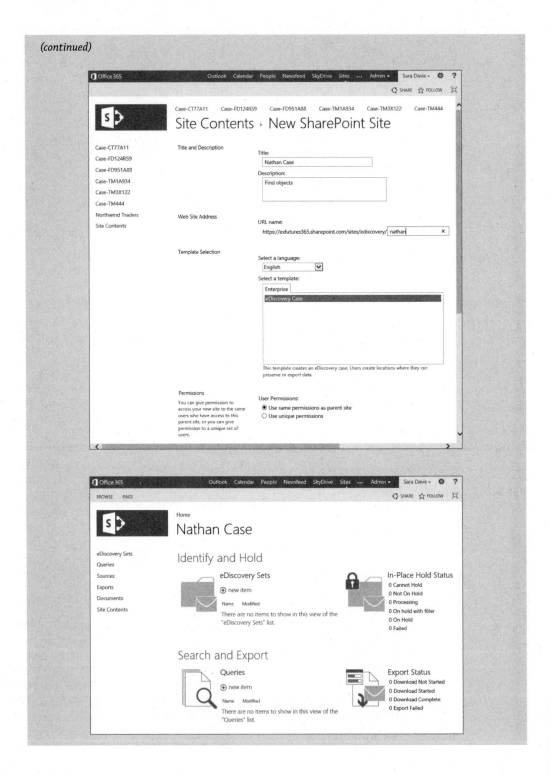

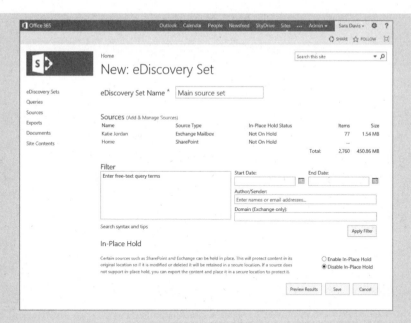

The key thing to remember throughout the discovery process is that you will likely start with a huge data set, but what you really need is the minimal amount of data relevant to the case in order to hand it over to counsel. It is not uncommon to have to search hundreds of mailboxes. This will return gigabytes of data, which if handed over to counsel would increase costs astronomically. Therefore, you go through a process of filtering the data using the new *Keyword Query Language (KQL)*. For more information about KQL, see the following article:

```
http://msdn.microsoft.com/en-us/library/ee558911.aspx
```

Once you have the basic sources you need, you then go on to create complex and detailed search queries using KQL, starting from the case summary page shown in the following graphic. When creating the search query, you are constantly provided with statistics, real-time updates, and filters to further refine the data set, as shown in the graphic. You can see that there are tabs to show Exchange and SharePoint data in different views. In this case, you are looking at SharePoint data. Hovering over one of the items located at any time will give you a quick preview, and clicking the item opens it either in a browser (for a site or email) or in one of the Office Web Apps, if a document.

Once you have filtered the data down as much as required, you are ready to complete the process by exporting the data. An export is carried out based on a query set. When you go to create a new export, you will be prompted for a query to base it on. This will open the query, as shown in the graphic, and if you move to the bottom-right of the window, you will find the Export button. Once you click this button, you will be able to configure the export including naming it, selecting options for de-duplication of data, and including object versions and objects that are not searchable, such as those protected with S/MIME encryption, as shown in the following graphic.

continues

(continued)

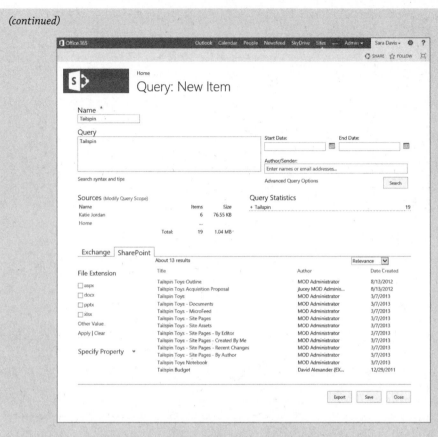

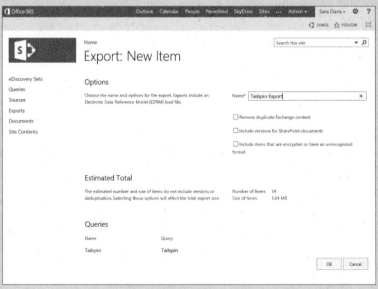

Finally, after clicking OK, you see a screen that allows you to either start the export of all of the results or simply generate a report of the results, as shown in the following graphic. Either choice launches the browser app shown in the next graphic, which prompts you for a location to save the results and then completes the export.

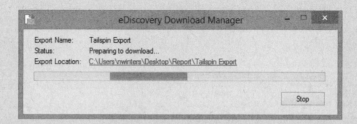

The top half of next graphic shows the results, which include the reports. If only the reports are downloaded, then you'll see the files in the bottom half of the graphic.

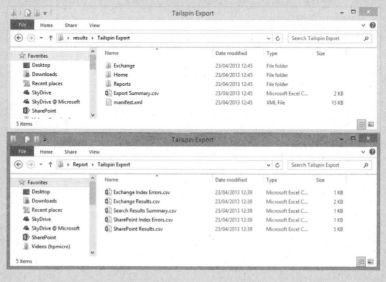

continues

(continued)

Upon drilling into the results, you can see that they are provided with a manifest file that conforms to EDRM standards. This manifest file, as shown in the following graphic, contains detailed information about all of the actions taken to accomplish the search. Significantly, it is provided in a standard format so that it can be imported into existing toolsets used by legal teams. Equally important is the fact that it contains an SHA-256 hash of each document, which suitable software (that many legal teams already use) can read and use to prove that the document has remained unchanged during the export process.

```
<?xml version="1.0" encoding="UTF-8"?>
- <Root xmlns:xsd="http://www.w3.org/2001/XMLSchema" xmlns:xsi="http://www.w3.org/2001/XMLSchema-instance"
  CaseId="95bb8422-dc7e-40d2-92a2-4afb71b8a446" DataInterchangeType="Update" Description="Tailspin Export" MinorVersion="1"
  MajorVersion="1">
  - <Batch>
    - <Documents>
      - <Document MimeType="application/vnd.ms-outlook" DocType="File" DocID="Tailspin Export-Katie Jordan-04.23.2013-
        1245PM">
        - <Files>
          - <File FileType="Native">
              <ExternalFile Hash="SHA256:cb1f7ba80339231b77f0e07c5f79bbb32f9c5c78a229e74b62741dab5f38d8b0"
              FileSize="271360" FileName="Tailspin Export-Katie Jordan-04.23.2013-1245PM.pst" FilePath="Exchange"/>
          </File>
        </Files>
      </Document>
      - <Document MimeType="application/vnd.ms-outlook" DocType="Message"
        DocID="AAMkADBhZWExNzljLTQxNTUtNGYxMi1hNmE3LTczYzBjMjdmNDAwOQBGAAAAAAAfnU7Ia390TZDgJiIeJo4CBwDbHGUcri
        - <Tags>
            <Tag TagValue="Tailspin Export-Katie Jordan-04.23.2013-1245PM.pst/AAAAAL5OLH1HW5xOtcyggoSRqdEkACAA"
            TagDataType="Text" TagName="TargetPath"/>
            <Tag TagValue="The "Tailspin Toys" site has a new mailbox" TagDataType="Text" TagName="#Subject"/>
            <Tag TagValue="2013-03-07T10:26:41" TagDataType="DateTime" TagName="#DateSent"/>
            <Tag TagValue="2013-03-07T10:26:46" TagDataType="DateTime" TagName="#DateReceived"/>
            <Tag TagValue="Tailspin Toys" TagDataType="Text" TagName="#From"/>
            <Tag TagValue="Alex Darrow; Allie Bellew; Anne Wallace; Aziz Hassouneh; Belinda Newman; Bonnie Kearney; David
            Longmuir; Denis Dehenne; Dorena Paschke; Fabrice Canel; Garret Vargas; Garth Fort; Janet Schorr; Julian Isla;
            Junmin Hao; Kari Furse; Katie Jordan; Molly Dempse" TagDataType="Text" TagName="#To"/>
            <Tag TagValue="False" TagDataType="Boolean" TagName="#HasAttachments"/>
            <Tag TagValue="Normal" TagDataType="Text" TagName="#ImportanceFlag"/>
            <Tag TagValue="False" TagDataType="Boolean" TagName="#ReadFlag"/>
        </Tags>
        - <Locations>
```

For more information about the EDRM standards, browse to the following address:

```
http://www.edrm.net/
```

The topic of oversight has not been covered in any of these case studies, because we already covered several aspects of Exchange that also contribute to maintaining compliance in Chapter 8, "Designing a Secure Exchange Solution." In particular, the ability to audit not only mailbox access but also administrative actions means that you constantly have a log of all that goes on within the system. Ensuring that you are making regular audits and checking programmatically that those people who should have access actually do have it to the broader roles, such as Discovery, is critical to avoiding accidental or deliberate compliance breaches.

Overall, the move to large, cheap storage and away from the third-party archive systems translates to a simpler experience for users and administrators and a general reduction in operating costs. It does require migration of data from the old archive system, which nevertheless has a cost attached to it. However, in the long term, it sets up an easy migration to future versions of Exchange or to Office 365 because the data is now in a standard format.

Communication

Throughout all the company case studies, we have not touched on the topic of communication. In any system rollout, it is absolutely critical to have constant communication with end users. An evangelization approach should be taken, to inform and educate the user base that the change is coming and why. Just telling users that something is about to happen often causes resentment. Therefore, making sure that you explain the need, giving examples, and then detailing what will happen and when makes the whole process flow much more smoothly. This is particularly important in those cases where a new policy will start to remove old mail or where a change in working practice surrounding PSTs will take place. If this is not communicated effectively, users will feel like they are losing flexibility as PSTs are removed and possibly losing access to mail as the policy kicks in. You must explain that the larger mailboxes help them retain such flexibility without the overhead and risk of PSTs, and that the policy helps keep the organization compliant with data-protection regulations.

Summary

In this chapter, you learned that there are simply no default answers when it comes to compliance. Make sure that you get good guidance from your legal team, and be sure that you understand the basics of the regulations yourself. Take advantage of the opportunity to push back on existing policies. Make sure that standard operating procedures require that you regularly review these policies to maintain compliance, and be certain that your design is fulfilling the intent of requirements effectively. If necessary, show the costs of different compliance options to give the business clear information that feeds into its policy decisions.

When it comes to implementation, Exchange provides a massive toolset. Think through each choice carefully, because there are many possibilities ranging from Microsoft to third-party tools. In the end, working to keep things simple is always a sensible approach. Therefore, looking to remove PSTs, keeping data in Exchange, and making use of built-in search and hold facilities is likely to provide a manageable and cost-effective solution for many organizations.

Chapter 10

Collaborating with Exchange

At its core, Exchange is often defined as a groupware product. From the outset, it was intended to be a collaborative software suite, and although it has evolved over time, the fundamental purpose of Exchange remains to help people work better together.

In this chapter, we're going to discuss exactly what makes Exchange a collaborative product—what is in the current version of Exchange that helps users collaborate right out of the box? Moreover, when you add in the full suite of Office Server products, how does this improve the end-user experience and allow them to get better value out of Exchange and its related products?

What Is Collaboration?

Before we dive into the discussion about *how*, let's again ask *why*?

Email is great, isn't it? Ask someone a question and get a response (hopefully). *Collaboration* is about working together as an organization, that is, the ad hoc day-to-day mixing and matching of opportunities, problems, and questions. First and foremost, by collaborating with each other, you can find the solution faster, distribute the effort, and provide peer review on important actions. Second, collaborating involves working together on larger projects, such as working together to build a messaging system. This requires the ability to collaborate on the creation of good quality documentation and to arrange meetings to keep people in the loop. Finally, groups of people need to collaborate to accomplish their job roles, such as a sales team dealing with many sales opportunities or an IT service desk receiving many customer queries.

Now let's think about what you can do with Exchange itself. There's nothing better than being able to deliver all of the functionality a customer wants without having to add in extra products, whether that's SharePoint, Lync, or third-party applications or utilities. Of course, that's not to say that such supplementary products aren't important. For some of these examples, for instance, products specifically tailored for collaborating on certain job roles may fit better than Exchange alone.

At the very core of Exchange is the email service, a function that is central to the way most organizations do business. Though Twitter, Yammer, and other social media products are often touted as email replacements, it remains key to the modern business. Email is the product people use every day to keep in touch, to keep colleagues up to date with news, to find opportunities, or to collaborate on new ideas. Yes, there are other great ways to talk to your colleagues, but at this point the end user is most likely to send and receive email as their primary form of communication.

The downside of email is its over-reach and the constant flow of information, duplication of content, and, of course, the Reply All storms that we've all experienced. To counter such issues, organizations must periodically reevaluate the way they use email.

The key to getting people to collaborate better with email is knowing how best to use it. With Exchange, this means implementing the right features and training users to work with email in an efficient way so that it becomes a focused tool rather than a constant distraction and productivity drain.

The kinds of features that help improve the core email experience for end users include such things as keeping a well-maintained address book so that they can find the right people quickly, mailing tips to help users understand the consequences of clicking Send, and putting the right client on their computers so that they can take advantage of the latest improvements. Then there is the hands-on training, such as teaching people how to manage their mailbox properly so that they can focus on the collaborative work they need to do instead of having to wade through a pile of emails before they can begin to work as a team.

Basic Collaboration with Email

Now let's delve a little deeper into the core topic of email and, in particular, how to enable people to wrest back control of their inbox so that when a new email message is received, it's a positive experience.

The Client Experience

First, let's examine the key differentiator between a good and a bad email experience. The email client on the user's desktop is far too often overlooked when upgrading Exchange, which is the wrong approach.

Setting the oldest client supported by Exchange as the baseline might be a quick win in terms of up-front time and investment, but such decisions always have repercussions farther down the road. Because email collaboration is all about helping people to be more productive working together, leaving them with a dated tool that can't access new features is a bad solution. Furthermore, older clients like Outlook 2007, though supported by Exchange 2010 and above, miss out on all of the great features that the newer versions of Exchange bring with them.

Conversation view is one of those features that may get a frosty reception when users first encounter it, but it's a key ingredient in bringing down that inbox overload. Think of it as a prerequisite for a better user experience. You might want to encourage users to leave the feature on for a week and see if they want to go back. Often, you'll find that users will stick with the smaller inbox once that list of 100 email messages is reduced to a handful of conversations.

Implementing the correct *Mail Tips* is key to making sure people don't over-collaborate. Could there be such a thing? In this case, we're referring to unnecessary messages or unknowingly sending messages to a very wide audience. If you think about a couple of very common scenarios, you'll begin to see the benefits. First up, take Mail Tips that show when someone is out of the office. We've all returned from vacation and dreaded opening our inbox, just waiting for the deluge of messages that we need to slog through, invariably finding out that half the people who emailed received the out-of-office message and had to look elsewhere for the information they needed. Automatic Replies, a built-in and enabled-by-default Mail Tip, ensures that people are notified up front, saving both them and you time. You just need Outlook 2010 or above to use it.

A second scenario is the practice of mechanically sending messages to a large number of people—the epidemic known as Reply All. We've all done it, and often a number of people will join in the Reply All frenzy by asking others not to click Reply All, thus making the situation worse. This is known as the *large audience threshold* in Exchange 2013. By default, a large audience is 25 people, but it can be configured to a suitable size for each organization.

You might want to change the large audience threshold to something more appropriate. Finding the right size isn't an exact science. There are two factors worth taking into account: organization size and group metrics. A large audience in a company of 30 people might be only 15 people. In a larger organization, this figure might well be 50 or more. So take into account the overall size of the organization and the groups who collaborate, such as departments or teams. The goal is to find a happy medium where users only see the large audience warning when they are sending an email to too many people. If they are working in a team of 25 people in an organization of 1,000 employees and often need to email everyone in the team, the warning will be soon ignored if the threshold is set too low.

The following TechNet article describes the procedure for configuring large audience size settings:

```
http://technet.microsoft.com/en-us/library/jj659068(v=exchg.150).aspx
```

Another feature that sits atop the large audience warning is *group metrics*. This background process, executed by default on the server that generates the Offline Address Book, updates each Distribution Group object in Active Directory with group metrics data. Often, you won't need to make any configuration adjustments to this feature, but if your design for Exchange excludes the Offline Address Book, then you'll need to configure group metrics manually. The configuration steps can be found in the TechNet article mentioned previously.

Helping Users Learn to Collaborate

It's all very well to provide end users with the collaboration features we've discussed, but without a clear plan to communicate how to take advantage of these features, those who may benefit most from these features will simply carry with what they've been doing up to this point—now possibly complaining about the new version of Outlook deployed to their desktop without any training.

It should come as no surprise that the key to getting it right is by first listening to users and understanding their needs. Email isn't something many users think they need training for, so you may find that your customer and its end users aren't overly enthusiastic about Outlook 2013 training. Thus the approach you take needs to sell the benefits of the upgrade to the user base and give them the information they need in a form they can digest and in way that makes sense to them.

Beyond user training, management buy-in is also essential. While it's common for the Exchange 2013 project you are working on to have executive-level project sponsorship, there must be a willingness on the part of management to effect change within the organization. Therefore, getting the right members of the management team onboard with collaborative features is critical. You might find this task daunting, as you are turning what some may have originally perceived to be a transparent infrastructure upgrade into an end-user-facing project. However, in so doing you or your customer will get the broadest return on investment in the form of more productive staff.

After listening to users and getting the project sponsors on board with the need for user education, what kinds of options are available to you? You're likely get some great suggestions from interested users who buy into the project at an early stage, so take this feedback to heart. Often, they'll be relaying what worked for them from an earlier project or previous employer. If no great ideas emerge, don't worry. There are several common approaches that work as an alternative to formal Microsoft training courses.

The first approach is to look at video guides that can provide quick snippets of information. If a user doesn't have to give up an afternoon to sit through a dull training session and instead can watch a series of videos tailored to the organization's approach at collaboration, it's going to be received very well. We've seen a mix of in-house videos, custom videos, and off-the-shelf packages from training providers that has done the job. We're not talking about setting up a film studio here; a good screen-casting package may be all that's necessary.

If you've deployed Lync, another great approach is to use it to run remote sessions. This combines the convenience of end users being able to attend without having to leave the office with face-to-face sessions with users who prefer a workshop style. After all, why not let the session on collaboration with Exchange be collaborative itself?

Finally, make the drive to educate users about new collaborative features of Outlook and how to use email effectively, a formal exercise. Keep a record of who has been trained so that you can ensure that everyone who needs to use the new features your implementation provides can take advantage of them.

The Address Book: a Place to Find and Get to Know People

If social media has taught us anything, it's that people are inquisitive by nature. It's human nature to want to find out more about the people with whom you interact. With people nowadays being happy to upload their profile pictures to Facebook, Twitter, LinkedIn, and so on, the initial barriers to uploading a contact picture have already been broken down.

Exchange 2010 introduced the ability to import contact photos into Active Directory, using the thumbnailPhoto attribute to store 96×96-pixel photos. This has been reimagined in Exchange 2013 in number of ways. Exchange 2013 now supports high-resolution photos with 648×648-pixel photos being stored in the user mailbox, alongside a smaller, lower-footprint 48×48-pixel photo in Active Directory. This enhancement affects Lync the most, but it isn't the only improvement of this type. An enhancement that will facilitate better collaboration is the ability of an end user to change their own photo from within Outlook Web App and view contact photos within OWA as well as Outlook. An example of the contact photo feature in OWA is shown in Figure 10.1.

FIGURE 10.1
Contact photo in
OWA

Now a user can easily log onto OWA, set their preferred contact photo, and experience a message thread that's far more social. On top of that, Outlook now provides features that allow contact pictures from LinkedIn and other social media sources to be integrated for better interaction with external users, as shown in Figure 10.2.

FIGURE 10.2
Photos and social
feeds in OWA or
Outlook

As you can see from Figure 10.2, the experience is significantly improved when you can "see" to whom you're sending or from whom you're receiving email. Instead of a purely text-based thread, you now have a much more social experience. In the thread in Figure 10.2, you can see that we're not just making use of internal contact photos; we're providing rich collaboration between external parties using contact photos from the business social network LinkedIn.

While we're on the subject of people, another major change in Exchange 2013 is the move from storing contacts to storing people. While this may seem like semantics, it highlights that, in most situations, we want to talk to a person rather than search for the relevant contact. Therefore, Exchange 2013 now helps us bring all of the information about a person together in one place, whether internal to the organization from a SharePoint feed and Active Directory account or external information from LinkedIn or Facebook. This allows us to achieve a better understanding of the people with whom we are communicating.

Shared Mailboxes

The other dimension to basic mailboxes is a *role-based mailbox*, and this is where we pick up the basics of real collaboration in Exchange. *Shared mailboxes,* even alongside a CRM or service desk system, are often a key part of the system that a team uses to provide a single point of contact for their customers. Many organizations still set up distribution groups today to fan out email to a sales team or helpdesk address, when shared mailboxes would allow them to view email as a team and allow them to collaborate more effectively in their day-to-day work.

While a shared mailbox might seem simple enough, it's one of those features that give teams the biggest advantages of public folders and mailboxes with few of the drawbacks. Because a mailbox is associated with a role, someone who moves into the team immediately benefits from the shared history and knowledge that the shared mailbox contains. If they move elsewhere in the organization, they don't have to carry the same baggage that they might have with their personal mailbox.

A shared mailbox is also less likely to be on a bunch of busy distribution groups and, in some cases, it might not even need to receive mail from outside the organization. Who doesn't like a spam-free mailbox?

Creating and Managing Shared Mailboxes

Shared mailbox management gets a makeover within the Exchange Admin Center. There is now a new dedicated tab for shared mailboxes, simply named *Shared*. Figure 10.3 illustrates how this makes finding and managing shared mailboxes a lot simpler.

FIGURE 10.3

The Shared mailbox tab in EAC

The improvements in shared mailboxes extend to the management of permissions, often something that confuses new administrators who are used to the permissions model in Exchange 2003. Within the settings for each shared mailbox, you no longer have to manage Full Access and Send As permissions separately from the mailbox itself. You can modify these properties alongside other Shared mailbox settings, as shown in Figure 10.4.

FIGURE 10.4

Managing Shared mailbox permissions

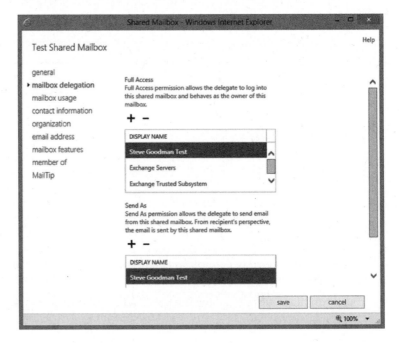

All in all, it's a simplified experience for whoever is tasked with the management of Exchange. However, if they're used to managing shared mailboxes using the same methods available in Exchange Server 2010, it's important that they understand how things have changed and how the new methods streamline day-to-day management.

Automatic Mailbox Mapping

One new feature introduced in Exchange 2010 Service Pack 1, and improved in Exchange 2010 Service Pack 2, is the ability to map the shared mailbox within Outlook automatically for users with permissions granted. It's common for administrators who don't deal with end-user desktops to question where this would be useful. For example, some Exchange administrators use the mailbox permissions to grant themselves rights to a user's mailbox for troubleshooting purposes, and they simply don't want the mailbox to show in their normal Outlook profile. Thus the benefits of this feature may pass them by.

Where this feature really excels is with end users and desktop support teams. No longer do users need to add shared mailboxes into Outlook manually—it all happens behind the scenes. This feature is controlled by the Active Directory multi-value attribute msExchDelegateListLink, which is stored on the base user account for the shared mailbox itself. The distinguished names of user mailboxes with permissions to access the shared mailbox are stored and used by Outlook to determine which shared mailboxes to attempt to map.

The good news is that this feature can be switched off where appropriate. However, the option to do so is not exposed through the Exchange Admin Center itself. You'll need to use the Add-MailboxPermission cmdlet with the -AutoMapping:$false parameter, as shown in the examples on the cmdlet's TechNet reference article:

```
http://technet.microsoft.com/en-gb/library/bb124097(v=exchg.150).aspx
```

Accessing Shared Mailboxes from Mobile Devices

One shortcoming of shared mailboxes is that protocols like EAS do not provide users with the ability to access shared mailboxes alongside their normal mailbox. When planning to deploy shared mailboxes, you need to bear this in mind. While this may not have been a major problem in the past, when a mobile device was often only a companion for occasional access to email, a world of users equipped with Apple iPads, Microsoft Surface RTs, and other tablet devices means that users expect to be able to accomplish a greater amount of their daily work away from the confines of a desktop PC.

If you need to provide this access, then you have a number of options to consider as part of your deployment:

- ◆ Instruct users to access the Outlook Web App for shared mailbox access.

- ◆ Create a password and enable the underlying Active Directory account associated with the shared mailbox.

- ◆ Implement certificate-based authentication for EAS to avoid distributing shared mailbox passwords to users.

These options are not without their issues. For example, managing the password on a shared mailbox can be troublesome. If password policies dictate regular password changes, then each shared mailbox user must update the password on their device. The same goes for certificate-based authentication in a scenario where a user has their access of a shared mailbox revoked. In this case, you may need to deploy updated certificates to devices to ensure that only those with valid access are able to access the shared mailbox.

Of course, this doesn't even touch on the challenges associated with implementing certificate-based authentication for the wider user population. These challenges can be overcome, however, with a mobile device management solution that allows administrators to manage individual mobile device profiles centrally.

The Outlook Web App therefore appears to be the easiest option, and thankfully the experience across a huge range of devices and different screen types is significantly improved in Exchange 2013. This addresses the main point of consideration, which is ensuring that the tablet experience is consistent for users rather than disjoined from their day-to-day experience. This will be a different experience from using the device's built-in ActiveSync access, and you may find that the lack of push notifications for new mail presents an issue. In that case, you will have to consider one of the previous options.

Resource Mailboxes

While easy to confuse with shared mailboxes, *resource mailboxes* perform a different function within Exchange and your organization. A shared mailbox represents a role or even a group of people, whereas a resource mailbox represents some sort of object.

When it comes to collaboration, this type of mailbox fills the gap between collaborating electronically and collaborating in the real world. Where do you collaborate face to face? There are two types of Resource mailboxes, Room and Equipment. They allow you to represent both your meeting rooms and other resources within Exchange. For example, as part of any collaboration, you may want to use an LCD projector to pull your ideas together on a large screen or to include a colleague in the meeting by booking some time in a videoconferencing-equipped room.

Implementing Resource Mailboxes

Let's examine how end users use resource mailboxes in Exchange with an example scenario. Let's say that you want to schedule a meeting and find a room in your building to host the meeting. You'll create the meeting request, in this case within Outlook Web App, and choose Add A Room, as shown in Figure 10.5.

FIGURE 10.5
Adding a meeting room into an OWA invite

After choosing your building, you'll then be shown a list of the available rooms within that building, as shown in Figure 10.6.

You then pick the room you want to use and send out the invite. That's how simple it is for end users to manage room mailboxes. If the meeting request requires approval, whoever is responsible for the room will be given the option to accept or decline the request.

FIGURE 10.6
Choosing a specific room

You'll need to not only create the room mailboxes themselves but also to create distribution groups to organize your rooms. That's where those buildings you saw listed in Figure 10.5 come from; they are simply distribution groups within Exchange that we've changed to room lists. You can see the process for changing distributions groups to room lists in the following code snippet:

```
Set-DistributionGroup -Identity "Building 1" -RoomList
Set-DistributionGroup -Identity "Building 2" -RoomList
Get-DistributionGroup
Name DisplayName GroupType PrimarySmtpAddress
---- ----------- --------- ------------------
Building 1 Building 1 Universal Building1@Exchange-D3.com
Building 2 Building 2 Universal Building2@Exchange-D3.com
```

Management of resource mailboxes is improved in Exchange 2013. Key attributes, including the following, can be managed from the Exchange Admin Center, as shown in Figure 10.7:

◆ Room capacity.

◆ Delegates for managing booking requests that allow all requests to be accepted automatically or for one or more individuals to be responsible for approving requests.

◆ Booking options including the ability to allow recurring meetings, to schedule meetings outside of working hours, to set meeting lead time and durations, and to configure custom reply messages when booking a room.

FIGURE 10.7
Managing rooms in Exchange Admin Center

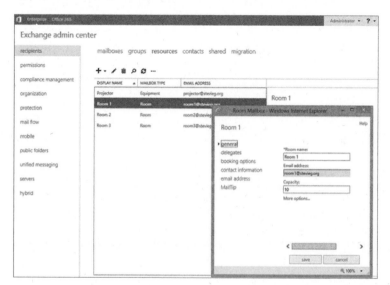

TIP When helping to plan resource mailboxes, do not overcomplicate the implementation. Management of advanced options can be tricky, as is helping users understand how to manage and book resources. Keep it simple and within the user interface. Otherwise, those managing resource mailboxes will simply give up on the feature and seek out something easier to use, like public folders.

Public Folders

One of the new features in Exchange 2013 is *public folders*. Before you say that public folders aren't a new Exchange feature, that they were supposed to be long dead, and that no one should be using them, let's clarify our first statement. We're not talking about the old public folders; instead, we're talking about modern public folders, that is, the prodigal child of the old public folders—the trendy new public folders that everyone is talking about. The best thing about them is that they're a bit like the old public folders but without all the problems.

Users often liked public folders, but IT administrators tasked with managing them often didn't like them at all. Problems like replication have given public folders a bad name, and from an architecture point of view, the fact that public folder databases replicated content via SMTP didn't fit well into the modern world of database availability groups (DAG) and block-mode replication. Beyond that, for smaller organizations using Exchange Standard Edition, a public folder database uses up one of five valuable databases that they can mount. Moreover, in previous versions of Exchange Online, part of the Office 365 offering, no support was available for public folders, except in the dedicated offering. Modern public folders fix all of these problems, but they also provide some different challenges.

Sometimes when you create a shared mailbox, an administrative task, versus one that end users can handle, is just too difficult to accommodate when people work together on a short-term project. Equally, although you might think a site mailbox would be a better, more modern approach, what happens if SharePoint is not available in your organization? Thus, in certain types of collaboration or deployment scenarios, what's needed is a simple location to store a team calendar or perhaps an archive of a distribution group. In these cases, using modern public folders makes sense. Another benefit is that they're something many users already know well. Of course, the challenge is knowing when and where to deploy modern public folders or when it's better to use a different Exchange feature or indeed SharePoint. This is something that you need to think through for your organization so as to provide the best solution possible.

As mentioned earlier, modern public folders in Exchange 2013 have removed many of the management challenges of the previous version. Nevertheless, this doesn't mean that an organization should continue to use public folders the same way they did previously. The push since Exchange 2007 to move away from developing applications that run atop public folders was certainly valid. There are now much better platforms for applications, and public folders should be seen as a place for simple collaboration that doesn't warrant the more complex approach of solutions such as shared mailboxes or site mailboxes. The architectural changes in Exchange 2013 mean that in addition to thinking about the role of public folders, you need to consider how to handle the removal of multi-master replication, since public folders formerly handled the replication of content to a distributed group of users rather well.

Structure of Modern Public Folders

Before we look at how public folders are distributed in Exchange 2013, let's take a moment to remember how public folders worked before. To keep things simple, let's examine a simple scenario. You have three users all on different mailbox databases, each with a different public folder database assigned. Each public folder is replicated to each public folder database, as shown in Figure 10.8.

FIGURE 10.8
Sample public folder setup

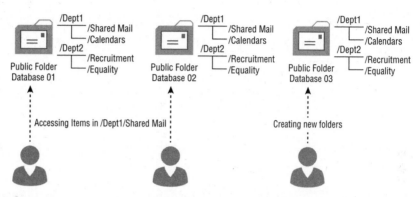

Replication issues aside, it's a fairly straightforward scenario. Changes to public folder content can be applied to the local copy of the data. Each user could feasibly be on a different continent with slow links in between and not see a delay in using the local public folder. Of course, if the different users make multiple changes, there will be a delay in replicating, but you have a simple structure that, while less than ideal, gives an easy-to-predict setup.

Move onto modern public folders, and you'll immediately see the changes highlighted by Figure 10.9. You're moving to a single-copy, single-master role. Public folders do not live in public folder databases, and they are instead located in public folder mailboxes that, like any other mailbox, live in a single mailbox database. This means that you have the immediate benefit of DAGs to make public folders highly available and can tap all of the database structure improvements that have occurred over the last few versions of Exchange. However, you've lost the multimaster model. Moreover, you've lost the ability to replicate content between different locations entirely (other than in a traditional DAG). The only aspect of public folders that is replicated is the hierarchy, or the public folder tree, where a single writeable copy exists. You can see how this works in Figure 10.9.

As you can see, you now have a tree-like structure where a single public folder mailbox, which can only be active in a single location in an international organization, holds the writable copy of the entire hierarchy.

You can also see that when users access a public folder, they will access the data within the sole public folder mailbox within which the public folder lives. For teams working in a single region or with low latency networks that provide fast access to the mailbox server hosting the public folder mailbox, there is unlikely to be a problem. However, for an organization with slow links between collaborating workers there may be a challenge to regularly access data with acceptable speed.

Therefore, when planning to enable and implement public folders within Exchange 2013, consider how they are used within the organization at present. If you're performing a new implementation, then consider how teams will work together when using this great feature.

FIGURE 10.9
An example
of the modern
public folder
infrastructure

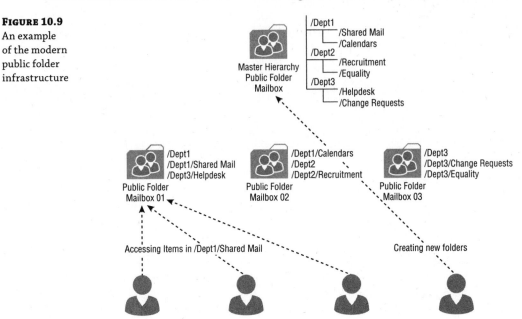

Distribution Groups

Distribution groups allow the sending of email to a large number of mailboxes, mail-enabled users, or contacts via a single email address. One-to-many and many-to-many communications through distribution groups are both important aspects of making email useful. They are a way of getting people to converse and can help harness an organization's knowledge. However, they can sometimes be a productivity killer and an inefficient way of managing that knowledge. You may have been a member of many distribution groups in a large organization and were so overwhelmed by emails that they were filed away in a folder with thousands of other unread messages. You got so far behind on the conversation that it was hardly a collaborative tool. At best, it was a makeshift knowledge base—one that was often only maintained in individual inboxes. You don't want your customer or end users to experience this situation, so let's see exactly how you can use the features available in Exchange to turn things around to provide a great collaborative experience.

The overall experience of creating and managing distribution groups hasn't changed greatly from Exchange 2010. The key features remain the same. The administrator can manage distribution groups centrally or delegate management to end users. Groups can be configured to allow only certain senders, such as members of the group, or they can be moderated so that the individuals responsible for the group must approve or deny messages before they are sent out to all of the members of the list.

You can read more about the specifics of managing distribution groups in the following TechNet article:

```
http://technet.microsoft.com/en-gb/library/bb124513(v=exchg.150).aspx
```

When it comes to planning for generic distribution groups, you must consider the impact on Active Directory and mailbox servers, because both of these will perform the bulk of the work. Because distribution groups are universal groups within Active Directory, they must be replicated to all Global Catalog servers within the Active Directory forest. If you are planning many distribution groups with a significant number of members, make sure that you consider the impact this will have on the domain controllers that support the Exchange infrastructure.

Additionally, from a mailbox server perspective, be sure to take into account the impact that implementing large numbers of new distribution groups will have on your design. If you've sized the Exchange infrastructure based on average message sizes and daily send/receive counts from the existing organization, then how will it impact your deployment if distribution groups become a popular resource?

If your aim is to build a bustling set of distribution groups where people share knowledge, you should ask questions and encourage members to discuss this with their colleagues because this is highly likely to impact the average send and receive figures that you used to design your mailbox server infrastructure. If the distribution groups are to be implemented as part of your Exchange project, then you'll also find it hard to judge the popularity of additional distribution groups. Therefore, some estimation is required unless you can use the current version of Exchange to conduct a limited pilot.

Another sizing option is to consider a two-tier approach to distribution groups. In this case, you set up a system where a minority of users subscribes directly to the list while the majority of users access distribution group archives through public folders. This has the additional benefit of making the knowledge more broadly available with all of the relevant historical information, rather than it being tied to individual inboxes. The lines do not need to be solid, but take care not to confuse the users with too many options!

Self-service management of distribution groups has been a key feature of Exchange to some degree for many versions. However, the ability of users to create new distribution groups based on a naming policy was only introduced in Exchange 2010. This feature is important because you really cannot leave it to end users to choose their own names for their distribution groups. If no naming convention is enforced, the team that keeps Active Directory in order will soon be displeased—battles will erupt on who should have a certain name, and no one will know the purpose of each group. Therefore, putting in place a naming policy that users can follow to create distribution groups keeps everyone happy.

Improvements in Exchange 2013 let you configure the Group Naming Policy via the Exchange Admin Center or the Exchange Management Shell. The Exchange administrator can design the naming policy and pick attributes to integrate into the naming policy, including custom strings, as shown in Figure 10.10.

FIGURE 10.10
Using Exchange Admin Center to manage the distribution Group Naming Policy

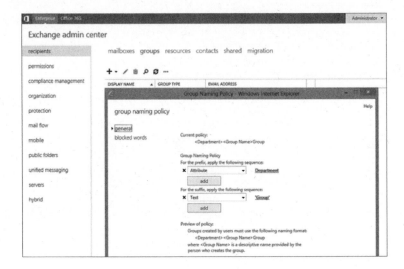

After setting these options, you may be more inclined to allow certain groups of users to create groups. This is done using RBAC policies, as depicted in Figure 10.11. The highlighted option lets you change the Default Role Assignment Policy to allow all mailbox users to create groups by granting MyDistributionGroups rights to everyone.

FIGURE 10.11
Granting rights to users to create distribution groups

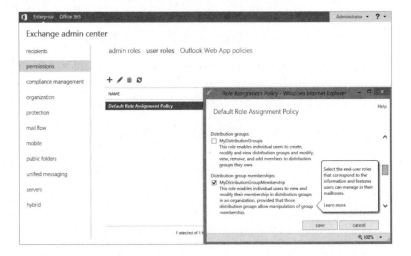

Of course, you may choose to restrict certain users to this ability. Doing so, however, is less dangerous once a policy is in place to enforce the naming convention. You'll see that when a user attempts to create a new distribution group via the Options page of the Outlook Web App, the new distribution group will be created according to the policy in place, as shown in Figure 10.12.

FIGURE 10.12
Notification that a new distribution group has been created following the specified naming policy

You can read more about group-naming policies, including the specific features and attributes available, in this TechNet article:

```
http://technet.microsoft.com/en-us/library/jj218693(v=exchg.150).aspx
```

Site Mailboxes

Finally, let's examine site mailboxes. If you haven't heard the term before, it might seem a bit foreign to you. But if you've used SharePoint, you will certainly be aware of the term *SharePoint site*. A *site mailbox* is a mailbox associated with a SharePoint site. A team of people working together on a project or common goal will most likely use a site mailbox. The same rules that apply to setting up a SharePoint site for a project, including shared documents and project communications, also apply to site mailboxes.

Before Exchange 2013, a group of users working together on a project might start with a SharePoint site and then create a subfolder in their email inbox to store all project-related content. Yes, they could use a shared mailbox, but that just adds another place where they could store content apart from SharePoint. A site mailbox pulls that project information from SharePoint and then combines it with Outlook. It's not uncommon for people working on a project to have a SharePoint site and to send people links to the updated documents in SharePoint or even to email a document from SharePoint to someone else who has access to the site. Site mailboxes provide a great view of the site's documents as a repository in Outlook alongside messages related to the project. The great thing with site mailboxes is that the user can maintain the same behavior. They can email documents straight out of the SharePoint site from Outlook and automatically minimize duplication. Site mailboxes accomplish this by allowing Outlook to work behind the scenes to replace the attachment with links to the message, thus maintaining the version history in SharePoint. Figure 10.13 shows site mailboxes in action, with the Documents folder in Outlook representing the Document Library in SharePoint.

FIGURE 10.13
The site mailbox in Outlook showing documents from SharePoint

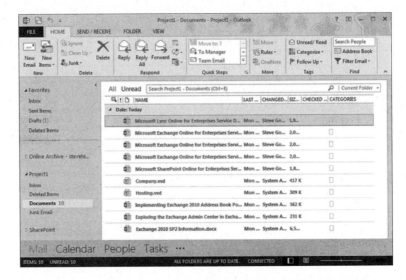

The user interaction doesn't end there. End users can manage a site mailbox themselves rather than relying on an administrator. The major difference from an Exchange administrator's perspective is that this is implemented through SharePoint. That's right—you won't find an option within the Exchange Admin Center to create a site mailbox.

Site mailboxes manifest themselves to the user as an app within SharePoint. A user responsible for their SharePoint site looks through the Apps You Can Add section and simply picks Site Mailbox, as shown in Figure 10.14.

FIGURE 10.14
Adding a site mailbox

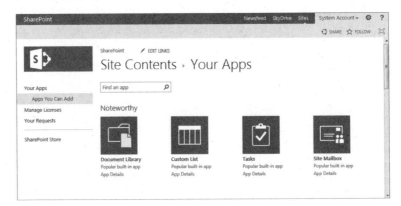

After choosing to create the site mailbox, the user needs to wait a while for synchronization to complete. After a short while, they'll find that they can access the site mailbox through SharePoint or via Outlook 2013.

A major concern of IT professionals with the distribution of control from administrators to users is over-proliferation of mailboxes and the potential for data regulation issues. Here one of the most exciting developments in site mailboxes plays an important role. As mentioned, site mailboxes are provisioned from SharePoint. Permissions are matched to the SharePoint site, and the site mailbox pops up in the user's Outlook client automatically, similar to a shared mailbox. What makes this special is that it allows SharePoint life cycle policies to apply, not only to the SharePoint site but also to the site mailbox. Therefore, an administrator can be secure in the knowledge that users can create SharePoint sites and site mailboxes for use on a project, but that they are restricted to the time limit that the administrator has set. At the end of the time period, the user may be prompted to ask for an extension, or the content could simply become archived. Then, at a later date, the content could be automatically deleted, both across SharePoint and across the site mailbox. In this way, control is maintained and the organization retains a clean, secure infrastructure.

Finally, it is important to note that to use site mailboxes, you must have compatible clients and servers. On the server side, users' mailboxes must be on Exchange Server 2013 and the SharePoint site must be on SharePoint Server 2013. On the client side, if you want users to be able to use the desktop version of Outlook, implementing Outlook 2013 is essential unless you plan for users to access site mailboxes through SharePoint and the Outlook Web App only.

Implementing Site Mailboxes

Not only are site mailboxes a cross-product offering, they are also fairly complicated to set up. Microsoft's TechNet document, while generally excellent, doesn't lead you step by step through the implementation of site mailboxes, and it assumes a fair amount of SharePoint knowledge. Therefore, to complete this chapter, we'll guide you through the implementation of site mailboxes in an Exchange 2013 environment, covering the core steps of the installation procedure and linking to TechNet for very specific items, like worthwhile scripts.

SharePoint 2013 Prerequisites

As with all software programs, there are guidelines that should be followed to ensure an ideal experience. We recommend reviewing and adhering to the SharePoint 2013 software and hardware requirements documented in the following article:

```
http://technet.microsoft.com/en-us/library/cc262485.aspx
```

USER PROFILE SYNCHRONIZATION SERVICE

While we will cover the configuration details later in the chapter, the *User Profile Synchronization Service (UPSS)* is one element you should be particularly aware of prior to installing to ensure that you don't have to redo your install. The UPSS synchronizes user information between Active Directory and SharePoint.

It is very important to select the correct version of SharePoint and the correct database option to install. The reason for this is that not all SharePoint versions allow the use of the User Profile Synchronization Service. This is important because you need a way of getting user information (such as email addresses) synchronized from the Active Directory into SharePoint. It is this process that allows the automatic provisioning and permissioning of sites to propagate to site mailboxes.

Of course, it is possible to perform this syncing of accounts manually. It is highly advisable that you install the UPSS with SharePoint to do this work. Otherwise, you will set yourself up for a manual operations nightmare. This requires a full version of SQL (not SQL Express), a 64-bit edition of SQL Server 2012, or a 64-bit edition of SQL Server 2008 R2 Service Pack.

SQL INSTALLATION

Having covered the key concept of UPSS and why a certain version of SQL is needed, now let's install it. We are not going to cover every possible step—we will only address the basics to get you up and running. The rest of the SQL install can be done with default settings.

To install the minimum required SQL configuration, install the components selected in Figure 10.15.

FIGURE 10.15
Installing the minimum SQL components

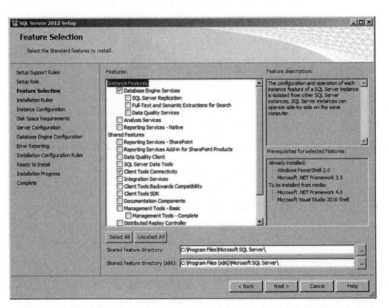

Configuring the SharePoint Server

Once SQL is installed, you need to get SharePoint up and running. Once again, we will not cover the complete installation. Essentially, you need to perform a full installation of SharePoint Server using the Complete installation type using a simple wizard. Next, you will run the SharePoint Server 2013 Configuration Wizard, again following the wizard's prompts to create a new server farm.

Once SharePoint is installed, a series of steps is required to get it up and running and talking to Exchange. These steps are covered in the next few sections.

CONFIGURING THE SHAREPOINT FARM

Once SharePoint 2013 is installed on the SQL server, you need to configure the farm. Do so by following these steps:

1. The Central Administration console should launch automatically, prompting the Farm Configuration Wizard. If the wizard does not launch automatically, open the SharePoint Central Administration console by choosing Start ➤ All Programs ➤ Microsoft SharePoint 2013 Products ➤ SharePoint 2013 Central Administration.

2. On the left-hand side, select Configuration Wizards.

3. Click Launch The Farm Configuration Wizard.

4. Click OK to accept the customer experience program.

5. Click Start The Wizard.

6. Select Use Existing Managed Account.

7. Accept the default settings for the remaining options and click Next.

8. Wait for the "Working on it" screen to close. This can take up to 20 minutes to complete.

9. Once the wizard is finished, it will ask you to create a site collection.

10. You don't want to create a site collection at this point, so click Skip, as shown in Figure 10.16.

FIGURE 10.16
Skip creating a site collection.

CREATING AN SSL WEB APPLICATION

By default, an HTTP (port 80) application is created automatically. However, for secure access to your site mailbox document store, you need to create an SSL site collection. But before doing that, you need to create an SSL web application. This is done using the following steps:

1. From the Central Administration console, click the Application Management link on the left.

2. Click Manage Web Applications near the top of the page, as shown in Figure 10.17.

FIGURE 10.17
Choose Manage
Web Applications.

3. Click the New button at the top left of the page.

4. Leave the option set to Create A New IIS Site.

5. Change the port to **443**.

6. Select Yes for Use Secure Sockets Layer (SSL).

7. Scroll down to the URL, and change it to the FQDN that will be accessible:
   `https://<SP_FQDN>`.

8. Scroll to the bottom of the page and click OK.

9. Wait for the Create New Web Application screen to disappear, which will bring you to an Application Created screen.

10. Click OK.

11. You should now see a SharePoint - 443 web application, as shown in Figure 10.18.

FIGURE 10.18
SharePoint - 443
web application
created

12. Check Internet Information Services Manager to verify that a corresponding site has been created. To do so, launch Internet Information Services Manager. Expand your SharePoint server name in the Connections pane, and click Sites. In the middle pane, you should see SharePoint – 443, and the site should be started. If it's not started, it may be that you did not select Use Secure Sockets Layer (SSL) in step 6, thus creating a binding conflict. If so, go back and remove the incorrect application, and create a new one with the correct settings.

CREATING A SITE COLLECTION ASSOCIATED WITH THE SSL WEB APPLICATION

Once you have created the SSL web application, you need to create the corresponding SSL site collection. Here's how:

1. Choose Application Management of the left-hand side of the Central Administration console.

2. Click Create Site Collections.

3. At the top, right-hand side, click the drop-down menu beside Web Application.

4. Select Change Web Application.

5. Select the SharePoint - 443 application.

6. Type in the title **Secure** (or a name of your choice).

7. Scroll down, and enter **Contoso\administrator** for the Primary Site Collection Administrator, as shown in Figure 10.19. (Use your own domain rather than Contoso.)

FIGURE 10.19

Enter the administrator for the site collection.

8. Click OK.

9. After a few moments, you will see a confirmation page.

CONFIGURING PROFILE SYNC WITH SHAREPOINT

The Profile Synchronization service synchronizes properties, such as your email address, from your account in Active Directory to your user profile in SharePoint. Although it is not mandatory to configure the service, it is very beneficial. For site mailboxes to function properly, each user must be populated into SharePoint with an email address. If you do not configure profile synchronization, these properties will need to be added manually through Application Management ➤ Manage Service Applications ➤ User Profile Service Application ➤ Manage User Profiles.

To set up profile sync, follow these steps:

1. Click System Settings on the left-hand side of the Central Administration console.

2. Select Manage Services On Server, as shown in Figure 10.20.

FIGURE 10.20

Choose to Manage services on server.

3. Scroll down and click Start beside the User Profile Synchronization Service.

4. Type and confirm the password for the Administrator account.

5. Click OK.

6. The service will enter a starting state. It will take some time for it to start.

7. Refresh the Services page, and make sure that the User Profile Synchronization Service is started, as shown in Figure 10.21.

FIGURE 10.21
Make sure the service is Started.

8. Choose Application Management on the left-hand side of the Central Administration console.

9. Select Manage Service Applications, as shown in Figure 10.22.

FIGURE 10.22
Choose Manage service applications.

10. Scroll down and select the User Profile Service application.

11. Select Configure Synchronization Connections, as shown in the Figure 10.23.

FIGURE 10.23
Then choose Configure Synchronization Connections.

12. Click Create New Connection.

13. Type in the name **AD Connection**.

14. Type in the forest name **Exchange-D3.com**. (Use your own forest FQDN here.)

15. Enter the username and password, for example:

Username: **Exchange-D3\Administrator**

Password: **Password1**

16. Click Populate Containers.

17. Click Select All.

18. Click OK.

19. Wait for the "Working on it" screen to complete.

20. You should now have a new synchronization connection to Active Directory, as shown in Figure 10.24.

FIGURE 10.24
Your new synchro-
nization connection

21. Choose Application Management again.

22. Click Manage Service Applications.

23. Scroll down and select the User Profile Service application.

24. Click Start Profile Synchronization.

25. Select Start Full Synchronization.

26. Click OK.

27. Refresh the page and, at the bottom right, you should see that it has started synchronization. Refreshing the page occasionally will notify you of the different synchronization stages. You will also see user profiles populated, as shown in Figure 10.25.

FIGURE 10.25
User Profiles

Profiles	
Number of User Profiles	36
Number of User Properties	93
Number of Organization Profiles	1
Number of Organization Properties	15
Audiences	
Number of Audiences	1
Uncompiled Audiences	0
Audience Compilation Status	Idle
Audience Compilation Schedule	Every Saturday at 01:00 AM
Last Compilation Time	Ended at 4/20/2013 1:00 AM
Profile Synchronization Settings	
Synchronization Schedule (Incremental)	Every day at 01:00 AM
Profile Synchronization Status	Idle

28. If you do not see new user profiles populated, check the Application log on the SharePoint server for errors. A common issue occurs when the credentials you added in step 15 do not have access to the SQL database.

INSTALLING EXCHANGE WEB SERVICES API ON SHAREPOINT SERVER

SharePoint communicates with Exchange much like other applications these days using web services. In order for SharePoint to communicate with Exchange, you need to install the relevant Web Services API on the SharePoint server. This is done using the following the steps:

1. Go to the Microsoft Download Center, and download EWSManagedAPI.msi to a folder on the SharePoint server.

2. Change the location in the command prompt to the directory where the file was downloaded.

3. Run the following command to begin the install:

```
msiexec /i EwsManagedApi.msi addlocal="ExchangeWebServicesApi_
Feature,ExchangeWebServicesApi_Gac"
```

4. Click through the install, making sure to select Everyone when prompted, as shown in Figure 10.26.

FIGURE 10.26
Allow Everyone to see the preview.

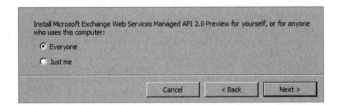

Install Microsoft Exchange Web Services Managed API 2.0 Preview for yourself, or for anyone who uses this computer:

- ⦿ Everyone
- ○ Just me

| Cancel | < Back | Next > |

5. Once EWS is installed, you will need to run IISReset from the command prompt.

CONFIGURING CERTIFICATES FOR SHAREPOINT

Given that you are using the SSL web application that you set up previously, you need to make sure that you have all of the relevant certificates. There are three options for installing an SSL certificate on a SharePoint SSL site:

◆ A self-signed certificate

◆ A certificate from a corporate certificate authority

◆ A certificate from a third-party trusted root certificate authority

If you use a self-signed certificate or a certificate from an internal certificate authority, you will need to make sure that certificate provider is in the trusted root authority of the client. When installing in a production environment, it is far better to use fully trusted certificates from either a public or private certificate authority.

When using a certificate from a certificate authority, you need to assign bindings to the site, as shown in Figure 10.27.

FIGURE 10.27
Setting the certifi-
cate for the website

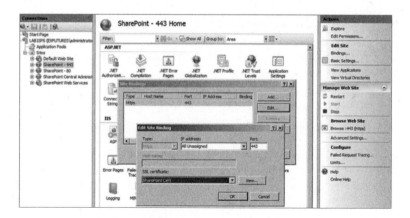

You've now finished preparing SharePoint, so we can move on to Exchange.

Preparing the Exchange 2013 Server

Just as with SharePoint, there are a few preparatory stages needed to make integration work in Exchange 2013. Specifically, this means getting Autodiscover and certificates set up correctly on Exchange 2013.

CONFIGURING AUTODISCOVER

Since all of this integration functionality relies on web services, you need to configure the Exchange 2013 Autodiscover service to be available on an FQDN. The FQDN can be left as the client access server name, but it is best practice to configure it as a load-balanced URL. The attribute you need to configure on Exchange 2013 is AutodiscoverServerInternalURI.

NOTE   Mail is the name space chosen in the example. Any name space is fine, however, as long as it can be resolved to the Exchange server or to the Virtual Internet Protocol or to the Virtual Internet Protocol (VIP) address of the load balancer.

1. From the Exchange 2013 Management Shell, run the following:

   ```
   Set-ClientAccessServer -AutoDiscoverServiceInternalUri https://mail.exchange-D3.com/
   autodiscover/autodiscover.xml
   ```

2. Configure a host record in DNS that points either to your Exchange server or to the VIP of your load balancer.

3. Make sure DNS is refreshed on the SharePoint server.

4. Also make sure that you have an Autodiscover A record in DNS.

NOTE   For all of this to work, you must also ensure that the usual name spaces are configured correctly and that certificates are set up on Exchange.

Creating and Configuring a Connection from SharePoint to Exchange

There are several steps required to get Exchange to communicate with SharePoint and to get to the stage where a site mailbox can be created. These steps are discussed in the following sections.

CONFIGURING OAUTH

Once Autodiscover is correctly configured and working, you need to create an OAuth connection from SharePoint to Exchange and assign service permissions on SharePoint. *OAuth* is an open standard for authorization. OAuth provides a method for clients to access server resources on behalf of a resource owner (such as a different client or an end user). It also provides a process for users to authorize third-party access to their server resources without sharing their credentials (typically, a username and password pair), using user-agent redirections. OAuth is the basis for the integration of the different Office 2013 servers.

In order to configure the OAuth connection, you first need to retrieve and install the metadata document from Exchange in SharePoint using the following steps:

1. Open the SharePoint 2013 Management Shell on CONSPS01, and run the following cmdlet:

   ```
   New-SPTrustedSecurityTokenIssuer -Name Exchange -MetadataEndPoint https://mail
   .exchange-D3.com/autodiscover/metadata/json/1
   ```

2. You should now see the output shown below:

   ```
   IsSelfIssuer                   : True
   NameId                         : 00000002-0000-0ff1-ce00-000000000000@Exchange-D3.com
   RegisteredIssuerName           : 00000002-0000-0ff1-ce00-000000000000@Exchange-D3.com
   IdentityClaimTypeInformation   : Microsoft.SharePoint.Administration.Claims
                                    .SPTrustedClaimTypeInformation
   Description                    :
   SigningCertificate             : [Subject]
                                      CN=Microsoft Exchange Server Auth Certificate
                                    [Issuer]
                                      CN=Microsoft Exchange Server Auth Certificate
                                    [Serial Number]
                                      15288EBE4000F7B04F982947B8B5413D
                                    [Not Before]
                                      10/28/2012 2:58:37 PM
                                    [Not After]
                                      10/2/2017 3:58:37 PM
                                    [Thumbprint]
                                      3A361E221741A3AD1E6D4F2A17A959F8F374804B
   AdditionalSigningCertificates  : {}
   MetadataEndPoint               : https://mail.exchange-d3.com/autodiscover/metadata
                                    /json/1
   IsAutomaticallyUpdated         : True
   ```

```
Name                        : Exchange
TypeName                    : Microsoft.SharePoint.Administration.Claims
                              .SPTrustedSecurityTokenService
DisplayName                 : Exchange
Id                          : 9072f81a-c3fb-488c-a197-95cc77255b96
Status                      : Online
Parent                      : SPSecurityTokenServiceManager Name=SecurityTokenService
                              Manager
Version                     : 1861210
Properties                  : {}
Farm                        : SPFarm Name=SharePoint_Config
UpgradedPersistedProperties : {}
```

For security purposes, it is strongly advised that OAuth authentication be maintained over an SSL connection.

3. To ensure that this is maintained, run the following cmdlets:

```
$sts = Get-SPSecurityTokenServiceConfig
$sts.HybridStsSelectionEnabled = $true
$sts.AllowMetadataOverHttp = $false
$sts.AllowOauthOverHttp = $false
$sts.Update()
```

GRANTING PERMISSIONS

You must now grant the Exchange service Principal Full Control permissions to the SharePoint site subscription. You can repeat this process for multiple sites if they have been previously provisioned. To make it simple, you can use some variables as follows:

1. Type the following variables in the SharePoint Management Shell, replacing the URLs with your own:

```
$webAppUrl1="https://sps"
$exchangeDomain="Exchange-D3.com"
```

2. Run the following cmdlets that make use of the variables to set the required permissions:

```
$exchange=Get-SPTrustedSecurityTokenIssuer | Where-Object -FilterScript {$_.DisplayName
-eq 'Exchange'}

$app=Get-SPAppPrincipal -Site $webAppUrl1 -NameIdentifier $exchange.NameId
$site=Get-SPSite $webAppUrl1

Set-SPAppPrincipalPermission -AppPrincipal $app -Site $site.RootWeb -Scope
sitesubscription -Right fullcontrol -EnableAppOnlyPolicy
```

3. Repeat these steps for each URL in step 2.

ENABLING SITE MAILBOXES, SETTING THE TARGET DOMAIN, AND CHECKING THE CONFIGURATION

Now that the SharePoint sites have been permissioned between SharePoint and Exchange, you need to enable site mailboxes and set the Exchange Server site mailbox target domain for the SharePoint farm:

1. Run the following cmdlet from the SharePoint Management Shell:

```
Enable-SPFeature CollaborationMailboxFarm
```

2. Type the following code snippet. Repeat for each SharePoint URL in the previous section:

```
$webApp=Get-SPWebApplication $webAppUrl1
$webApp.Properties["ExchangeTeamMailboxDomain"] = $exchangeDomain
$webApp.Update()
```

3. Run the `Check-SiteMailboxConfig.ps1` script available from the following TechNet article:

   http://technet.microsoft.com/en-us/library/jj552524.aspx/

   The output of the script is shown in below:

```
Step 1: Checking for Exchange Web Services
Found Exchange Web Services in Global Assembly Cache
Exchange Web Services Version: 15.00.0516.014

Step 2: Checking for https web application
Found Web Application at https://sps/ that uses HTTPS
WARNING: Web Application at http://sps/ does not use HTTPS. Site Mailboxes will not work
on this Web Application.

Step 3: Checking for trusted Exchange Servers
Found trusted Exchange Server at mail.exchange-d3.com
Exchange Server at mail.exchange-d3.com has Full Control permissions
Exchange Server at mail.exchange-d3.com has App Only Permissions

Step 4: Report current Site Mailbox Configuration

Web Application Site Mailbox Configuration: https://sps/
Exchange Site Mailbox Domain: exchange-d3.com

Web Application Site Mailbox Configuration: http://sps/
Exchange Site Mailbox Domain: exchange-d3.com

Trusted Exchange Services: mail.exchange-d3.com
Site Mailboxes are enabled for Farm
```

Configuring the Connection from Exchange to SharePoint

Having set up SharePoint to communicate with Exchange, you must now configure Exchange to talk to SharePoint.

To establish the OAuth trust from Exchange to SharePoint, you need to run the `Configure-EnterprisePartnerApplication.ps1` script from the `<Path>\scripts` directory on your Exchange server as follows, where `<SP_FQDN>` is the URL for the SharePoint SSL root site collection that you want to configure:

```
.\Configure-EnterprisePartnerApplication.ps1 -ApplicationType Sharepoint -AuthMetadataUrl
https://<SP_FQDN>/_layouts/15/metadata/json/1
```

Running the script does the following:

1. A partner application account is created in Active Directory called SharePointEnterprise-ApplicationAccount. (If this account already exists, -1 will be appended to the account name to make it unique.)

2. The following Exchange Role-Based Access Control roles are assigned to this account. The roles enable both site mailbox and EDiscovery functionality:

    a. User Application

    b. Legal Hold Application

    c. Mailbox Search

    d. Team Mailbox Lifecycle Application

    e. Legal Hold

3. Once the roles have been assigned, you establish the OAuth trust between SharePoint and Exchange by pulling the metadata from SharePoint (for instance, `https://sps/_layouts/15/metadata/json/1`) and create a partner application using the linked account SharePointEnterprise-ApplicationAccount.

At this point, you have completed all of the steps, and you should be able to log into a SharePoint site and add a site mailbox, as discussed earlier in the chapter.

Summary

In this chapter, we looked at some of the old and new features that make Exchange the best collaborative platform available. As you've seen, some involve retraining users to help them better understand how to make email an efficient product. In other cases, a bit more effort is required on the part of those who are planning and managing Exchange to determine the best way to implement it.

As with any adoption of technology, the implementation may seem straightforward, but if you don't spend time planning up front, you may wind up spending considerably more time, relatively speaking, correcting mistakes later on.

Finally, we explored the big new collaborative feature in Exchange 2013, site mailboxes, and we worked through the steps necessary to implement the feature. A single collaborative feature on its own is rarely sufficient to encourage users to collaborate effectively, and simply throwing a multitude of features at end users will result in widespread confusion. Therefore, remember to consider how each feature will be used when planning your Exchange 2013 organization so that you can communicate this effectively to the people who will reap the day-to-day benefits.

Chapter 11

Extending Exchange

As a messaging platform, Exchange has grown over the years into a highly competent and cohesive system with a vast range of functionality. Nevertheless, that doesn't preclude Microsoft from extending Exchange's functionality or leveraging it through other systems.

This chapter examines the use of Exchange as a messaging platform to build upon and touches on where it resides within the Microsoft catalog of products. We will begin by investigating the concepts and capabilities Exchange provides to developers for creating custom solutions, and we will then discuss the thought processes behind integrating Exchange with other Microsoft and non-Microsoft systems.

Accessing Exchange Programmatically

In this chapter, we will examine how you can use the development interfaces provided by Exchange 2013 to meet the business requirements that you may have for your email system that can't be solved with the standard out-of-the box features of the product. First, we will cover the interfaces that are available to create applications, scripts, and add-ins in Exchange 2013, and then we will cover how you can go about writing application code.

This chapter will focus on using Exchange Web Services (EWS), which is now the primary *application programming interface (API)* for developing code that accesses an Exchange mailbox. We will also look at a few of the new and exciting features in Exchange 2013, such as in-place eDiscovery and mail apps for Outlook, and we will discuss how these new features can be leveraged as solutions in your environment.

As with many other Microsoft products, Exchange 2013 comes with a rich array of development interfaces that allow you to extend and customize the functionality of the product. For IT professionals, it can be confusing trying to decide when you should consider using these development interfaces, and the very mention of writing code can send some scurrying for cover. However, if you really want to add value to your Exchange Server organization, even some simple PowerShell scripts can save you a lot of money on third-party software and give you a rapid return on investment.

A major reason why you may find yourself turning to the development interfaces occurs when you try to fulfill a request for functionality that cannot be provided using the standard features of the product. Also, those who are managing very large Exchange environments can benefit greatly from the ability to write custom reports for otherwise standard requests, such as mailbox usage, message tracking, or the ability to configure certain mailbox features and settings automatically. Automation of these types of tasks can greatly reduce the number of man-hours required to manage a complex environment while simultaneously making your end users more productive. Another instance when you may want to look at the development interfaces occurs when you have a great idea and need to create a new and innovative client application.

Where do you start and what can you do? As soon as you mention development, many IT professionals think of off-the-shelf product applications. While this is one part of the development ecosystem, the Exchange development space also involves other, more home-brew-type projects. Here are some examples:

◆ Creating a script to provision new users automatically and configure their mailbox defaults

◆ Making a script to move data during migrations, or pushing certain data to an archive

◆ Creating an application that enhances the Outlook and OWA client interfaces

◆ Creating a transport agent that performs custom routing of emails

◆ Creating an application to process inbound messages automatically

◆ Performing custom discoveries of information stored in mailboxes and public folders

Many of these tasks can be performed with a minimal amount of code and development skills, so they are not out of reach for most IT professionals willing to stretch themselves a bit. In the end, any code or script you create is just a list of instructions that you're asking the server to perform on your behalf. What takes time is working out the order and logic of those instructions and then reading the results. While this process can be time consuming, the reward of increased agility in problem solving and the rapid return on investment are well worth it.

Exchange 2013 builds on the existing development interfaces introduced in previous versions of Exchange to provide a richer development experience, particularly focused on using standard Internet protocols such as HTTPS. As already mentioned, EWS has been promoted to the primary API for developing applications that run against an Exchange mailbox in Exchange 2013. EWS uses SOAP (XML) to provide the standard message format for the exchange of information between the Exchange Server and your application client.

WHAT IS SOAP?

SOAP is a standardized messaging framework that clients use to communicate with Web Services. It's been used in Exchange since Exchange Server 2007 with the inception of EWS. A SOAP request and response are made up of three parts: an envelope, a header, and a body. The SOAP request is transmitted to and from the server over HTTPS.

While the Outlook client still primarily uses MAPI to access the Exchange store (albeit tunneled through RPC over HTTPS), new Exchange 2013 features, such as in-place eDiscovery and mail apps, use EWS as the endpoint for accessing Exchange.

Where Do I Start?

If you have made the decision to write some Exchange code but you're not a developer, just where to begin can be a little confusing. The first question to ask if you want to do something simple is, "Can I write a PowerShell script that uses EWS to accomplish the tasks I want to perform?" PowerShell scripts require a minimum of investment, and they can be written in a text editor like Notepad or a visual IDE, such as the PowerShell IDE or PowerGUI. Such visual scripting IDEs simplify the process of creating scripts, and they also allow the use of code snippets, which can save you a lot of time. *Code snippets* are partial or fully formed code blocks that you can copy and paste into your own application code or script. These can greatly reduce the amount of time it takes to prototype an application or script. The next step up from writing a simple script is creating a .NET application. For this, you will need Visual Studio. If you are a first-time developer, Microsoft provides a free version of Visual Studio called *Visual Studio Express* that you can use to build .NET applications.

Taking EWS for a Test Drive without Writing Any Code

If you are still not sure about EWS and what you can access using it, there is a great tool produced by Matt Stehle, a Microsoft senior application development manager. The tool is called the *EWSEditor*, and you can download it at `http://ewseditor.codeplex.com/`. With this simple GUI application, you can execute most of the EWS operations without needing to write any code, as well as view the syntax used in the requests and responses that may be important if you are building code that uses raw SOAP.

How Do You Connect Your Code to Exchange?

All EWS operations are executed through a Client Access Server (CAS) in your Exchange organization. On each CAS, there is a virtual directory in IIS that points to the underlying EWS files, such as `exchange.asmx` and `service.wsdl`, which we will discuss later. To allow any piece of EWS code to post requests to Exchange, you need to specify the URL path to the EWS `exchange.asmx` file. The URL that you would use within your code to connect to Exchange is usually determined using Autodiscover, which was covered in Chapter 3, "Exchange Architectural Concepts." The URLs that Autodiscover returns are those that are configured via the `Set-WebServicesVirtualDirectory` EMS cmdlet. If you need to know the URL to use for EWS and you can't obtain it via Autodiscover, you can find it using the `Get-WebServicesVirtualDirectory -Identity` EMS cmdlet. For example, review the following code snippet:

```
Get-WebServicesVirtualDirectory -Identity EWS(Default Web Site)
```

Where Do You Run Your Code?

One of the big advantages of using EWS is that it's designed to be used over HTTPS. Thus, all the code and scripts you write to use it can be run remotely (where port 443 is available). As a general rule, you should avoid running any code directly on your Exchange Servers—there is little advantage to doing this, and errors in your code or scripts may cause your server to become unreliable. Generally, the default EWS throttling setting within Exchange will offer some protection against errant pieces of code causing problems for your Client Access Servers or Mailbox role servers. If you are planning on doing a lot of development work, it is a good idea to build a virtualized development environment in order to avoid testing your beta code and scripts within your production environment.

Considerations for the Cloud

Exchange organizations can now be configured in a number of different ways that may affect which APIs you can use to access an Exchange mailbox. For example, in any one organization, mailboxes can be located on-premises, in the cloud, or in a mixture of the two. This leads us to consider the following:

Latency   If your application transfers a lot of data to and from Exchange, then you need to consider the impact of a change from a LAN-based to a cloud-based environment. The time it will take to transfer data and the latency of certain operations will increase for a cloud-based system, thus affecting the responsiveness and viability of some applications.

Throttling   Since Exchange 2010, *throttling*, or the ability to regulate workload based on server resources available, has been enabled by default to enhance server reliability by ensuring that one user or one application doesn't consume an excessive amount of server resources. In an on-premises environment, the ability to configure and control throttling policies to suit your application is available. In a hosted environment, the ability to configure throttling policies isn't generally provided. The default throttling policies are biased toward the actions of one user; however, the usage profile of a given application may make it possible that it will consume sufficient server resources to cause the throttling budget to be exhausted. To cope with throttling, applications should be written to deal with exceptions that are caused by it and use *EWS impersonation*. Using EWS impersonation means that your EWS requests are executed in the security context of the owner of the mailbox. From a throttling perspective, this means that the throttling budget of the mailbox owner rather than the calling service account is charged.

Choosing the Right API for Exchange Development in Exchange 2013

If you are embarking on a new development project, or you are evaluating or writing a scope of works for an application that you're going to ask another company to develop, there are many different aspects to consider. Some of the Exchange APIs, such as the Mailbox APIs MAPI and EWS, have overlapping functionality, while some server-management tasks; for example, require the use of the Exchange Management Shell cmdlets, which are the only method you can use to provision mailboxes.

Choosing the correct API to use for development requires that you map out the requirements of the application that you wish to develop first. Then you can match those requirements against the functionality that each API provides. To demonstrate this, let's look at a few real-world scenarios and the development choices available.

 Real World Scenario

SCENARIO 1: LINE OF BUSINESS AUTOMATION APPLICATION THAT PROCESSES INCOMING MAIL

Customer A has a mailbox called Sales Orders. Distributers send sales orders for their product to Customer A's mailbox in the form of email attachments. Customer A requires an application that will monitor this mailbox for new messages and then process them on arrival. If a message has an attachment that is a sales order, it will download the sales order, process the contents, and upload the order into the company's enterprise resource planning (ERP) system using a third-party API. After processing, the mail then needs to be moved to a separate folder in the mailbox called Processed Sales Orders. If the message isn't a sales order, the application should forward the message to another mailbox for the sales staff to process.

In this scenario, all that is required is an API that can access a mailbox. For this type of application, Exchange Web Services is the best API to use in Exchange 2013. EWS can be used to poll the mailboxes on a timed interval. EWS streaming notifications can also be used if real-time response to new emails is required. EWS allows full access to the attachments, and it also contains operations to move and forward messages. All of the code that is written can run in a completely automated manner, without the need for any user input.

We will demonstrate code for performing these actions in the EWS samples section of this chapter.

 Real World Scenario

SCENARIO 2: CLIENT-SIDE, USER-PRODUCTIVE ENHANCEMENT

Company B's sales department receives a lot of inquires via email. To help them process these customer requests more efficiently, they would like to have information from their customer relationship management (CRM) system displayed in-line in any message received. Users need this information for email that is accessed inside shared mailboxes. Company B has users that use both Outlook Web Access (OWA) and Outlook, and they require that the workflow be the same across each client.

In this scenario, the application must interact with the client that an end user is using, and it will also need access to the shared mailbox. The primary functionality in this scenario can be fulfilled by a mail app for Outlook and the Outlook web app that uses the Office JavaScript API to access the mailbox and extend the user interface in Outlook and OWA. Mail apps for Outlook must be hosted on an IIS server.

This application is for internal company use only. This means that it can be hosted on an internal system and then published to selected users remotely as required. The company could also choose to host their web apps using Azure if they are using a cloud-based email system like Office 365.

We will show how to create a suitable example application in the "Mail Apps for Outlook and the Outlook Web App" section of this chapter.

 Real World Scenario

SCENARIO 3: CUSTOM ROUTING APPLICATION IN THE OUTLOOK CLIENT

Company C has a requirement that all email sent to a subset of email addresses in one particular domain be routed via a particular SMTP smart host. They also require that the sender address be rewritten to a single sender address when messages are marked in a particular way.

In this scenario, the application must interact with the messages when they are in the transport pipeline. Building a transport agent using the Transport Agent SDK and the transport pipeline's events and public objects fulfills this requirement. A routing agent and the OnResolved Message event can be used to set a routing override on a message so that it will be routed via a specific SMTP smart host. The address rewriting can also be performed within the transport agent events.

Transport agents provide the ability to extend the functionality of the transport pipeline by allowing you to build custom applications that execute at different points in the transport pipeline. The transport pipeline is the processing that happens on a message as part of the message-transfer process. This starts at the beginning of the SMTP conversation at the TCP connection and runs to the delivery of the message to the Exchange store. Note that transport agents can't be extended to the Mailbox store, so they can't be used to access messages in a mailbox or route messages to particular mailbox folders (other than the Junk Email folder). Some uses for transport agents are gateways to external non-SMTP servers, such as fax or SMS gateways, domain catchalls, enhanced mail routing, or antispam handling.

There are three different types of transport agents:

SMTP Receive Agents *SMTP receive agents* are designed to respond to messages coming into and going out of an organization. They can be used to respond to an event that happened during an SMTP conversation or to perform Catch-All-type functionality for incoming email.

Routing Agents *Routing agents* are designed to allow you to catch a message just after submission or at a different point in the transport pipeline. Some uses for routing agents are to modify the message contents or perform custom routing functions for a particular recipient.

Delivery Agents *Delivery agents* allow you to deliver messages from your SMTP Exchange Server environment to a system that doesn't use the SMTP protocol. They are used for providing delivery messages to the foreign system and providing acknowledgement for each successful message delivery.

The transport architecture has been changed in Exchange 2013, and this affects the location and placement of transport agents. The Transport service is now split into three different services. Table 11.1 lists the new services that make up the transport architecture and the transport agents supported by each service.

TABLE 11.1: Exchange 2013 Transport service and transport agent support

SERVICE	AGENTS SUPPORTED	SERVER ROLE
Front End Transport service	SMTP receive agents	Client Access Server
Transport service	SMTP receive agents, routing agents, and delivery agents	Mailbox Role Server
Mailbox Transport service	No third-party agents supported	Mailbox Role Server

For more information on developing transport agents, you should download and read the Exchange 2013 Transport Agent SDK from MSDN.

Real World Scenario

SCENARIO 4: AUTOMATION OF MAILBOX PROVISIONING

Company D's HR department needs to be able to provision mailboxes and contacts in the company's Exchange organization when new employees are hired. After the mailbox is created, a specific configuration should be applied to the mailbox and a welcome email, personalized for the user, should be sent.

In this scenario, Exchange Management Shell (EMS) commands need to be used to provision the mailboxes. The commands can be run from managed code using remote PowerShell and the automation class libraries. The personalized welcome message could also be sent from the EMS, but EWS would be a better choice since it provides greater formatting options.

While not strictly an API, the EMS cmdlets are the primary mechanism for the automation of administrative tasks on Exchange. These may include the provisioning of mailboxes, adding/removing/changing email addresses on objects, and the configuration of the default setting for mailboxes. Also, EMS cmdlets are the primary mechanism used to access reporting information on mailboxes, such as retrieving the size of mailboxes, the details of quota usage, or message-tracking information.

Real World Scenario

SCENARIO 5: MIGRATION OF AN EXISTING APPLICATION THAT USES MAPI DURING A MIGRATION TO EXCHANGE 2013

Company E has been running Exchange since version 5.5. They are now seeking to migrate to Exchange 2013. Over the years, they have purchased or developed a number of applications and scripts that use MAPI over RPC to connect to Exchange. Some of these applications are critical to the business and can't be offline for any significant period of time.

In Exchange 2013, all MAPI connections need to be encapsulated using RPC over HTTPS. This means that any existing applications that use a direct RPC/TCP MAPI connection will need to be rewritten to use RPC over HTTPS. For applications that use the Collaboration Data Objects (CDO) version 1.2.1 library, which uses RPC/TCP, Company E will need to get an updated version of this DLL that supports RPC over HTTPS and make changes to their application to create RPC over HTTPS profiles. Microsoft has deemphasized MAPI in 2013, and it is recommending that all new development be done using Exchange Web Services.

For Company E, any scripts that use CDO 1.2 can easily be rewritten to use EWS and tested against their current Exchange 2010 Servers before migration. For the applications that they have developed themselves in the past, changing the source code to use the new version of CDO 1.2 before the migration would be most prudent. In the long term, however, moving these applications to EWS should be planned. For any third-party applications, they will need to contact the original vender to obtain a new version of the application that is supported in Exchange 2013 before the migration can take place.

We will take a sample VBS script written in CDO 1.2 and rewrite it in PowerShell and the EWS Managed API later in this chapter.

Other Exchange APIs

For the sake of completeness, you should be aware of one other development interface—the Exchange ActiveSync protocol. The *Exchange ActiveSync protocol* is designed to allow mobile devices to synchronize email, calendar, contacts, and tasks with Exchange Server. The XML structures used within the Exchange ActiveSync protocol are *tokenized*, meaning that they are more compact, which reduces the size of the data transferred between the server and the client.

Other features included in Exchange ActiveSync are policy mechanisms used to enforce standard configuration settings on mobile devices. ActiveSync is the best protocol to use when building a mobile device email client because of the policy and tokenization features. Nevertheless, custom mobile applications that need to access just one type of mailbox data may make better use of EWS, which will reduce the overall development effort needed to build and maintain an application.

NOTE   You need a specific license from Microsoft to develop Exchange ActiveSync clients.

Exchange Web Services in Exchange 2013

In this section, we will go into detail about what EWS is and how you can use it. While this may have a slight developer slant to it, the information covered is important to understand when using EWS.

EWS is now the preferred API to use when building applications in Exchange 2013. It was introduced in Exchange 2007, and it allows access to Exchange mailbox data and allows you to perform mailbox client functionality such as Out of Office (OOF), free/busy lookups, and so on. EWS uses SOAP (XML) to provide the standard message format for the exchange of information between the Exchange Server and the client. There is nothing you need to do to enable EWS in your Exchange environment, because it's enabled by default and used in many of the core areas in Exchange. For example, since Outlook 2007 and Exchange 2007, EWS has been used to provide access to OOF and free/busy information. In Exchange 2013, the new eDiscovery functionality is built on top of EWS. EWS is backward compatible with Exchange Server dating back to version 2007. However, newer features and operations are only available in certain versions of Exchange, so it is important that you take this into consideration if you are supporting multiple version of Exchange.

A major advantage of EWS compared to other mailbox access APIs is that all communication between the client and server is performed over HTTPS. This allows you to take full advantage of the flexibility and functionality of web services technology in your client applications. It also means that any client that supports these standard Internet protocols, regardless of operating system, can run applications that can interact with an Exchange mailbox via EWS. This allows you to support both Windows and non-Windows platforms, such as Linux, Apple's iOS, and Android.

In Exchange 2013, EWS has been enhanced to provide support for new server functionality as well as improved accessibility to existing mailbox data. New features in EWS in Exchange 2013 include the following:

◆ eDiscovery: The ability to search all folders in a mailbox using Keyword Query Language (KQL) searches

◆ Archiving: The ability to copy from primary mailbox to archive

- ◆ Personas and unified contact store access
- ◆ Operations to manage retention policies
- ◆ The ability to access the GAL photo of a user
- ◆ Mail apps for Office 2013
- ◆ Support for authentication using identity tokens

When you're thinking about writing code for EWS, there are three methods that can be used: the EWS Managed API, Web Services Description Language proxy objects, and raw SOAP. The actual method you use will depend on the platform in use and the language in which you wish to write the code. For most development scenarios involving .NET applications, the EWS Managed API is the best method of the three because it greatly reduces the amount and complexity of the code you need to write.

Following is a description of the three different available methods.

EWS Managed API

If you're developing applications that will run on a Windows platform in .NET, the ESW Managed API offers the best and easiest method for building Exchange applications. The EWS Managed API is a Microsoft-developed and supported client-side library that offers an intuitive object model, which reduces the complexity of the code you need to write. This both reduces the time it takes to develop an application and makes for less-error-prone code. Another advantage of the EWS Managed API is the detailed documentation and number of examples available from Microsoft and third-party websites. All of the samples shown in this chapter make use of the EWS Managed API.

Web Services Description Language Proxy Objects

Most development applications, such as Visual Studio, support the ability to scan for the operations provided by a particular web service. To do this, they use the *Web Services Description Language (WSDL)* file for the web service and generate strongly typed objects based on this definition. These objects allow you to write code more easily using a standardized object model, without needing to worry about the serialization and deserialization of the web service's SOAP requests and responses. The difference between this and the EWS Managed API is that the latter's objects are designed to be more developer friendly and intuitive, which reduces the amount of code you need to write, thus decreasing complexity and debugging time. Nonetheless, proxy code is still useful in that some EWS operations aren't included in the EWS Managed API.

Raw SOAP

For some applications where you can't use the EWS Managed API or proxy code, using raw SOAP is the only option. An application that uses raw SOAP requests must build the XML EWS SOAP request manually and parse the XML SOAP responses that are returned from the server. An example of an application that makes use of raw SOAP requests and responses is the makeEWSRequestAsync method of the Office JavaScript API that is utilized in the mail app for Outlook, a new feature in Office 2013 and Exchange 2013.

Connection and Authentication

The first thing that any EWS application requires is that you discover and authenticate to the CAS through which the EWS requests will be communicated. Autodiscover is the best method for discovering the EWS URL for a Client Access Server in most organizations. With the EWS Managed API, SOAP-based Autodiscover is used, which is the most efficient method. However, if you aren't using the EWS Managed API, you may want to look at using POX-based Autodiscover.

POX-BASED AUTODISCOVER

Plain Old XML (POX) Autodiscover allows you to send a plain XML Autodiscover request and retrieve the configuration information from a mailbox that will include the EWS URL of the CAS to which to send EWS requests. The POX request/response is what you see when you perform an Outlook test autoconfiguration. Listing 11.1 shows POX-based Autodiscover in action.

LISTING 11.1:   How to perform a POX-based Autodiscover against Exchange Online using C#

```
//SMTP Address of Mailbox
String MbMailbox = "user@exchange-d3.onmicrosoft.com";
//UserName and Password of account to use for authentication
String UserName = "upn@exchange-d3.onmicrosoft.com";
String Password = "password123";
//Autodiscover End Point for Office365
String AutoDiscoURL = "https://autodiscover-s.outlook.com/autodiscover/autodiscover.xml";
NetworkCredential ncCred = new NetworkCredential(UserName,Password);
String EWSURL = null;
String auDisXML = "<Autodiscover xmlns=\"http://schemas.microsoft.com/exchange/autodiscover/
outlook/requestschema/2006\"><Request>" +
        "<EMailAddress>" + MbMailbox + "</EMailAddress>" +
        "<AcceptableResponseSchema>http://schemas.microsoft.com/exchange/autodiscover/
outlook/responseschema/2006a</AcceptableResponseSchema>" +
        "</Request>" +
        "</Autodiscover>";
System.Net.HttpWebRequest adAutoDiscoRequest = (System.Net.HttpWebRequest)System.Net.
HttpWebRequest.Create(AutoDiscoURL);
byte[] bytes = Encoding.UTF8.GetBytes(auDisXML);
adAutoDiscoRequest.ContentLength = bytes.Length;
adAutoDiscoRequest.ContentType = "text/xml";
adAutoDiscoRequest.Headers.Add("Translate", "F");
adAutoDiscoRequest.Method = "POST";
adAutoDiscoRequest.Credentials = ncCred;

Stream rsRequestStream = adAutoDiscoRequest.GetRequestStream();
rsRequestStream.Write(bytes, 0, bytes.Length);
rsRequestStream.Close();
adAutoDiscoRequest.AllowAutoRedirect = false;
```

```
WebResponse adResponse = adAutoDiscoRequest.GetResponse();
String Redirect = adResponse.Headers.Get("Location");
if (Redirect != null)
{
    adAutoDiscoRequest = (System.Net.HttpWebRequest)System.Net.HttpWebRequest.
Create(Redirect);
    adAutoDiscoRequest.ContentLength = bytes.Length;
    adAutoDiscoRequest.ContentType = "text/xml";
    adAutoDiscoRequest.Headers.Add("Translate", "F");
    adAutoDiscoRequest.Method = "POST";
    adAutoDiscoRequest.Credentials = ncCred;
    rsRequestStream = adAutoDiscoRequest.GetRequestStream();
}
rsRequestStream.Write(bytes, 0, bytes.Length);
rsRequestStream.Close();
adResponse = adAutoDiscoRequest.GetResponse();
Stream rsResponseStream = adResponse.GetResponseStream();
XmlDocument reResponseDoc = new XmlDocument();
reResponseDoc.Load(rsResponseStream);
XmlNodeList pfProtocolNodes = reResponseDoc.GetElementsByTagName("Protocol");
foreach (XmlNode xnNode in pfProtocolNodes)
{
    XmlNodeList adChildNodes = xnNode.ChildNodes;
    foreach (XmlNode xnSubChild in adChildNodes)
    {
        switch (xnSubChild.Name)
        {
            case "EwsUrl": EWSURL = xnSubChild.InnerText;
                break;
        }
    }
}
```

SOAP-BASED AUTODISCOVER

POX-based Autodiscover was deemphasized in Exchange 2010 in favor of SOAP-based Autodiscover. The latter has the advantage of supporting batch requests when you need to perform discovery for multiple users in one operation. SOAP-based Autodiscover also provides the ability to request only those settings that you need, and this reduces the size of the Autodiscover response.

Listing 11.2 shows how to perform a SOAP-based Autodiscover. The process is as follows: When using the EWS Managed API to perform an Autodiscover, the client-side library will first try to discover the EWS endpoint using the Active Directory SCP records. If this lookup fails, DNS Autodiscover is then tried. In some Exchange organizations, disabling the first SCP check would provide a more optimized discovery. To do this, the EnableScpLookup property can be used.

LISTING 11.2: How to perform a SOAP-based Autodiscover using the EWS Managed API to get the EWS URL and version of Exchange

```
String MbMailbox = "user@exchange-d3.onmicrosoft.com";
String UserName = "upn@exchange-d3.onmicrosoft.com";
String Password = "password123";
NetworkCredential ncCred = new NetworkCredential(UserName, Password);
String EWSURL = null;
String EWSVersion = null;
//Create Autodiscover Object
AutodiscoverService asAutodiscoverService = new AutodiscoverService();
//Set Credentials
asAutodiscoverService.Credentials = ncCred;
asAutodiscoverService.EnableScpLookup = false;
asAutodiscoverService.RedirectionUrlValidationCallback = RedirectionUrlValidationCallback;
//Define array for setting to retreive
UserSettingName[] unUserSettings =  new UserSettingName[2] { UserSettingName.
ExternalEwsUrl,UserSettingName.ExternalEwsVersion };
GetUserSettingsResponse adResponse = asAutodiscoverService.GetUserSettings(MbMailbox,
unUserSettings);
//Retrieve the Results from the Autodiscover response
EWSURL = (String)adResponse.Settings[UserSettingName.ExternalEwsUrl];
EWSVersion = (String)adResponse.Settings[UserSettingName.ExternalEwsVersion];
```

AUTHENTICATION

Authentication is an important consideration when creating an application or script that uses EWS. By default, users in Exchange can access only their own mailbox and nothing beyond basic free/busy information for other users. This means that if your application is going to access mailboxes other than that belonging to the current user (the user running the application), you will need to configure permissions on the mailboxes you wish to access.

EWS supports several authentication methods. As you would expect, NTLM and Basic authentication are available, plus Exchange 2013 adds the new token authentication using *server-to-server authentication (OAuth)*. This allows you set up partner applications whereby you can authenticate and create a token in one application and then use that token to authenticate to Exchange or another third-party web service without specifying the credentials for that user. The two partner applications that Exchange 2013 supports at release to manufacturing (RTM) are Lync 2013 and SharePoint 2013, both of which support OAuth and server-to-server (STS) authentication. Once EWS is configured, you can generate a token on SharePoint 2013 or Lync 2013 and then use this token to authenticate with Exchange.

Another use of token authentication is to help support single sign-on in mail apps for Office. The EWS Managed API now includes a partner DLL library named `Microsoft .Exchange.WebServices.Auth.dll`, which is used to validate user-identity tokens sent from an Exchange Server so that your third-party web service can implement authentication for these claims.

How Token Authentication Works

Token authentication facilities in Exchange 2013 provide the power to build applications that support *single sign-on (SSO) authentication*. Exchange 2013 uses the JSON web token (JWT) format for identity tokens. The token is signed but not encrypted, using a public key that is held and replicated to all Exchange Servers in your Exchange organization.

An example where token authentication can be used is in mail apps for Office. Within the mail app, you can generate a token that can then be used to make a request to another web service within your organization that requires user authentication. The other (non-Exchange) server that you want to authenticate against must have the ability to validate the token and then associate the unique identifier from the token with a set of credentials for which you're requesting access. To validate a token, a server application can use the validation library from the `Microsoft.Exchange.WebServices.Auth.dll` partner library included with the EWS Managed API.

The other way of using token authentication is by setting up a partner application in Exchange 2013. This is done using the `Configure-EnterpriseApplication.ps1` script that is included with Exchange. For example, with this script you can set up Lync 2013 or SharePoint 2013 to be a supported partner application. This means that you can generate tokens within your SharePoint or Lync applications and then use these tokens to authenticate against a user's mailbox to retrieve mailbox data. This can allow you to extend your SharePoint and Lync applications into the Exchange data store without the need to prompt the user for credentials.

More information and guidelines for using token authentication are found in the Exchange SDK `http://msdn.microsoft.com/library/exchange/`.

AUTHENTICATING AND ACCESSING DIFFERENT USER MAILBOXES

EWS has two authentication access modes that can be used when accessing a mailbox other than the primary mailbox or the archive associated with the account being used to authenticate to Exchange. *EWS impersonation* can be used when you have an application or service account that needs to access many accounts. When impersonation is used, the application or service user account that has been granted impersonation rights will have the same rights as the user whom they are impersonating. This allows you to have an application act on a mailbox's data as the owner and provides the security implications that go along with this. There is no way to constrain impersonation in Exchange, that is, to constrain it to just the Calendar folder. Thus, once access is granted, the impersonator will always have full rights or owner access to a mailbox. Another constraint of impersonation is that you can't impersonate a disabled account. For example, when the Meeting Room and Resource mailboxes are disabled by default, these accounts cannot be impersonated by default. Listing 11.3 demonstrates how to use impersonation in the EWS Managed API to impersonate another user and access that user's inbox.

LISTING 11.3:   How to use impersonation in the EWS Managed API to impersonate another user and access that user's inbox

```
String UserName = "ApplicationUserName";
String Password = "ApplicationPassword";
String Domain = "exchange-d3";
String EmailAddress = "user@exchange-d3.com";
```

```
var Version = ExchangeVersion.Exchange2013;

ExchangeService service = new ExchangeService(Version);
service.Credentials = new NetworkCredential(UserName, Password, Domain);
service.AutodiscoverUrl(EmailAddress);

//Set Impersonation to the Target Mailbox you want to impersonate
service.ImpersonatedUserId = new ImpersonatedUserId(ConnectingIdType.SmtpAddress,
UserPrimarySMTPAddress);
//Bind to the Inbox folder of the Impersonated Mailbox
Folder InboxFolder = Folder.Bind(service, WellKnownFolderName.Inbox);
```

The other access mode available is *EWS delegation*. This is the conventional method to use when a user account needs to access a mailbox other than its own. Delegation means that discretionary access control lists (DACLs) on the mailbox and mailbox folders are used to determine whether the requesting user can access a mailbox or particular mailbox folder. The advantage delegation may have over impersonation is the ability to constrain the access to resources. For example, if the application you are creating needs to access only the Contacts folder of the other user's mailbox, then rights need to be granted only to this particular folder. Full rights can also be granted explicitly to the mailbox via the Add-MailboxPermissions cmdlet. Listing 11.4 demonstrates how to use delegation in the EWS Managed API to access another user's inbox.

LISTING 11.4:   How to use delegation in the EWS Managed API to access another user's inbox

```
ExchangeService service = new ExchangeService(ExchangeVersion.Exchange2013);
service.Credentials = new NetworkCredential(ApplicationUserName,
ApplicationPassword, Domain);
service.AutodiscoverUrl(ApplicationEmailAddress);
//Specifiy the SMTP Address of the destination Mailbox in the FolderId
FolderId InboxFolderId = new FolderId(WellKnownFolderName.Inbox,
"User@exchange-d3.com");
//Bind the delegate's Inbox
Folder InboxFolder = Folder.Bind(service, InboxFolderId);
```

Accessing Mailbox Data

In terms of data, when you break down what constitutes a mailbox, it's pretty simple: A *mailbox* is a container that holds folders, each containing items and other folders. A folder itself has three collections: one for normal items, one for *folder associated items (FAI)*, and a third for *soft deleted items*, which was used in previous versions of Exchange and more commonly known as the *dumpster* of a folder.

The dumpster's operation changed in Exchange 2010 with the introduction of *single item recovery (SIR)*, so you no longer need to be concerned with it. With SIR enabled, when you Shift-Delete an item from a folder or when it is purged from deleted items, it is copied into the Recoverable Items folder under the NON_IPM_Subtree of a mailbox (for the duration of the retention period).

EWS Identifiers

To access a folder or item using EWS, you must know the EWS identifier associated with that item or folder. This EWSID is a Base64 encoded identifier that Exchange will use to determine what object you want to access. These IDs change on items and folders. For example, if an item is moved between folders, deleted, or copied, a new ItemID is created for the copied item. The fact that these ItemIDs can change means that you should be careful when using them as permanent, non-changing identifiers that you can reference in your application. While the ID won't change if the item doesn't change location in the mailbox, once an ItemID has changed, there is no way to search for the item based on the old identifier. This means your application likely won't function. This is where storing other identifiers, such as pidtagSearchKey, can be useful. This ID doesn't change, and it can be used to search for an item that has been deleted, for instance, and may now be in the Recoverable Items folder mentioned earlier.

To determine what the EWSID is for a particular item or folder, Exchange provides two search operations. The first is called *FindFolders*, and it allows you to search for folders in a mailbox. The second is called *FindItems*, and, as the name suggests, it allows you to search for items within a particular folder. These search operations can be used with search constraints, called *restrictions* in EWS, or *SearchFilters* in the EWS Managed API.

Folder and Item Properties

The heart of the Exchange Server product is the Information Store service, which acts as a special type of database and property store. In Exchange, instead of a single email being stored as one object or a large binary blob, it is stored as a collection of properties in the Exchange store. The manner in which these properties are stored in the Exchange database has changed and evolved as the information store developed. IT professionals who are familiar with information store development over the years are aware of the storage enhancements that have continued into Exchange 2013. However, the way in which these properties are enumerated, primarily via MAPI since the early versions of Exchange, has remained unchanged. The one thing to keep in mind that can impact the performance of any programmatic operation you do is that some properties are real, while others are calculated; some may also be indexed, while others are not.

A basic example of a property of an object is the subject of a message. In EWS, there are strongly typed objects for the common object types you use in Exchange, such as email messages, contacts, and appointments. These strongly typed objects provide access to the first-class object properties like the subject, body, sender, recipients, and so forth. These strongly typed objects and properties, however, don't cover all of the properties of a message. Exchange also allows for the provision of custom properties by users and application developers to support the needs of custom workflows and applications.

Any property in EWS can be accessed and set via the *extended property definition*, which contains information about the data type of the property and a property identifier that uniquely identifies the property. In reality, however, you only need to use extended properties when no strongly typed property definition exists. To demonstrate this concept, following is an example of setting the subject on an email message using the Managed API via the strongly typed email message object's subject property:

```
EmailMessage message = new EmailMessage(service);
message.Subject = "Email Subject";
```

This is an example of setting the subject using its extended property definition:

```
// Example of setting the Extended property for the subject on a message
EmailMessage message = new EmailMessage(service);
ExtendedPropertyDefinition pidTagSubject = new ExtendedPropertyDefinition(0x0037,
MapiPropertyType.String);
message.SetExtendedProperty(pidTagSubject, "Email Subject");
```

The idea of these examples is that when you're writing a program or script, you may see a property in Outlook that you can't find as a property in the Managed API or WSDL object classes. In such cases, you will need to use the extended property definition to set, change, or remove these properties. To help you determine what the property tags and property data types should be for an extended property definition, you should use a MAPI editor like OutlookSpy or MFCMapi. These MAPI editors allow you to view all of the extended properties of a particular Exchange object, which is an invaluable tool when doing any Exchange development. Figure 11.1 shows the Subject property highlighted in MFCMapi. Under the Tag column, you will see `0x0037001E` listed. In this example, the `0x0037` is the property tag and `001E` is the data type.

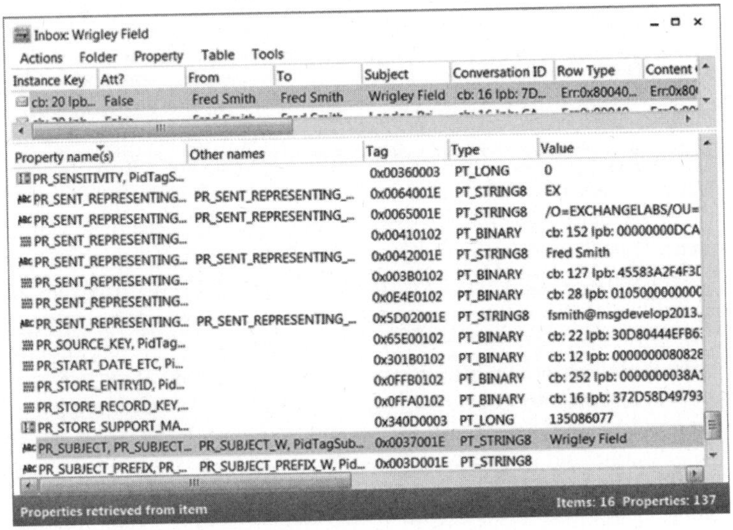

FIGURE 11.1
Using MFCMapi to show the extended property ID of the Subject field of a message

ACCESSING FOLDERS

If you are writing an application that requires access to one of the well-known folders in a mailbox, such as the Inbox, Contacts, Calendar, Journal, or Sent Items, EWS provides a direct method for accessing these folders through the distinguished `folderIdTypes`. This allows you to refer to a folder using a more user-friendly name and have Exchange still understand what you mean. It also allows you to deal with issues surrounding localization, when you have mailboxes that use different languages. In the case where your mailbox has a localized Inbox, Calendar, or Contacts folder display name, the same distinguished name is still used. With the EWS Managed API, this is provided via the `WellKnownFolderName` enumeration. The `WellKnownFolderName` enumeration maps to the distinguished `folderIdType`, and it is the easiest way of obtaining access to many important folders within a mailbox. For example, to access a user's Calendar folder, you can use the following code:

```
CalendarFolder CalFld = Folder.Bind(service,WellKnownFolderName.Calendar);
```

If you wanted to access a user's Recoverable Items folder (the Dumpster, v2) instead, you could use the following code:

```
Folder RecoverableItemsDeletions = Folder.Bind(service,WellKnownFolderName.
RecoverableItemsDeletions)
```

Once more, if you want to access the user's Archive mailbox, you can use the following code:

```
Folder AFld =Folder.Bind(service,WellKnownFolderName.ArchiveMsgFolderRoot);
```

As you can see, these are all relatively straightforward. If instead of accessing one of the well-known folder types you need to access a user-created folder, such as one that is a subfolder of the Inbox, then you need to use the FindFolders operation to search for a folder based on a search parameter. For example, Listing 11.5 illustrates how to address a subfolder of the Inbox by searching for it based on the folder's display name.

LISTING 11.5: How to address a subfolder of the Inbox by searching for it based on the folder's display name

```
Folder InboxFolder = Folder.Bind(service, WellKnownFolderName.Inbox);
SearchFilter FolderSearchFilter = new SearchFilter.IsEqualTo(FolderSchema.DisplayName,
FolderName);
FolderView FolderView = new FolderView(1);
FindFoldersResults ffResults = InboxFolder.FindFolders(FolderSearchFilter, FolderView);
if (ffResults.TotalCount == 1)
{
    Folder SubFolder = ffResults.Folders[0];
}
```

ACCESSING ITEMS

Just like accessing folders, to access an item using EWS, you need to know its EWSID. Unlike folders, however, there are no `WellKnownItemIDs`, so unless you have stored the EWSID externally, perhaps in a SQL database, to access any mailbox item you will first be required to use the FindItems operation. The FindItems operation in EWS allows you to enumerate the items within a mailbox folder, with or without a search clause. For example, Listing 11.6 demonstrates how you can enumerate all of the items within a particular mailbox's Inbox folder and output the subject. This example shows you how to use *paging*, which means telling the server in the request to return large result sets in smaller increments. This is an important method to use when working with Exchange 2010 and above because of the implementation of throttling. In order not to overload the server and run afoul of throttling, we have asked the server to return only 1,000 items at a time per request. Refer to the following site for more information about throttling:

`http://technet.microsoft.com/en-us/library/dd297964%28v=exchg.141%29.aspx`

LISTING 11.6: How you can enumerate all of the items within a particular mailbox's Inbox folder and output the subject

```
Folder InboxFolder = Folder.Bind(service, WellKnownFolderName.Inbox);
ItemView itItemView = new ItemView(1000);
FindItemsResults<Item> fiResults = null;
do
{
    fiResults = InboxFolder.FindItems(itItemView);
    foreach (Item itItem in fiResults.Items) {
    Console.WriteLine(itItem.Subject);
    }
    itItemView.Offset += fiResults.Items.Count;
} while (fiResults.MoreAvailable == true);
```

Searching for Items

While enumerating items may be okay for some scenarios, in most instances where you need to access items, you will need to use a search restriction. A *search restriction* is analogous to a *where* clause in a SQL query, and it limits the items that a FindItems operation will return. In Exchange 2013, as well as the Exchange store search and the Exchange Search service (content indexing), EWS supports searching all folders within a mailbox in a single operation using the new eDiscovery operations.

EXCHANGE SEARCH SERVICE (CONTENT INDEXING)

The *Exchange Search service* allows you to query Exchange's content indexes. This gives you the ability to query text within messages and indexed properties more easily, without the need for an expensive item-filter operation. In this context, we consider *expensive* to mean something that has a significant impact on the performance of a server and/or the amount of time it takes to return the results to the requesting user. The Exchange Search service runs on the Mailbox server, and it is responsible for building and maintaining the content indexes. New messages are indexed as soon as they arrive in a mailbox folder, which ensures these indexes are always up to date. Exchange Search also allows you to search for content inside attachments (that is, for attachment types for which an IFilter is available on the server). The attachment content search feature is an exclusive one that is not available by means of an Exchange store search. (See the "Exchange Store Search" section that follows.)

Exchange Search uses search-optimized indexes to provide a reliable and consistent method for querying mailbox items. However, because the number of properties that are included in these indexes is limited, it is not always possible to make use of a content index search, depending on the particular properties that you might need to query. Listing 11.7 shows how you can use an *Advanced Query Syntax (AQS)* filter to search for a message.

LISTING 11.7: Using an AQS string to search for messages

```
String AQSString = "Subject:\"Good Coffee\"";
ItemView itemview = new ItemView(1000);
FindItemsResults<Item> fiitems = FindItems(WellKnownFolderName.Inbox, AQSString, itemview);
```

EXCHANGE STORE SEARCH

Exchange store search is the conventional search method that has been used since Exchange 2007. It represents an evolution of previous search services used by the Exchange Mailbox store. If you used filtering in CDO 1.1 or exMAPI, then you have used the Exchange store search. Exchange store search creates a dynamic restriction on the folder you are querying that is similar to how a Search folder works. Exchange store search performs a sequential scan of all messages in the target search scope on the Exchange Server. Because no indexes are used, there are no restrictions on the properties that can be queried. Nevertheless, on folders with a large number of items, these types of queries may not perform optimally and may also impact overall server performance. Sample code needed to perform an Exchange store search is shown in Listing 11.8.

LISTING 11.8: Using a search filter to perform an Exchange store search

```
[Updated GS]
String SrchValue = "Good Coffee";
var SrchProp = EmailMessageSchema.Subject;
ItemView iv = new ItemView(1000);
SearchFilter sf = new SearchFilter.ContainsSubstring(SrchProp, SrchValue);
FindItemsResults<Item> fiResults = null;
fiResults = service.FindItems(WellKnownFolderName.Inbox, sf, iv);
```

In-Place eDiscovery in Exchange 2013

In-place eDiscovery is a new feature introduced in Exchange 2013 that allows you to use EWS to search all folders in a mailbox with a single operation. It also contains a variety of new features and actions that can be used either via the eDiscovery console, which is available to IT professionals and administrators, or programmatically within an application or script. Table 11.2 lists the new operations that have been added to EWS to support eDiscovery.

TABLE 11.2:   New operations added to EWS to support eDiscovery

OPERATION NAME	DESCRIPTION
GetHoldOnMailboxes	Gets the status of a query-based hold, which is set using the SetHoldOnMailboxes operation
GetSearchableMailboxes	Gets a list of mailboxes on which the client has permission to search or perform eDiscovery
SearchMailboxes	Searches for items in specific mailboxes that match query keywords
SetHoldOnMailboxes	Sets a query-based hold on items

In-place eDiscovery is really more than a series of new search operations—it's the new strategy for dealing with "big data" stored within mailboxes and archives. With mailbox capacities expected to average 100 GB in the near future, this feature will become increasingly important in enabling you to handle the data stored in these large mailboxes in the future. The eDiscovery operations that are now part of EWS allow you more easily to query data, place a hold on items to prevent their removal, and de-duplicate the items found to help with the processing of the discovered data. *De-duplication* means that if an individual item is the same as other search results, it will be shown only once in the results. The log will show all of the locations of that file. While many of these features are designed to be used in a legal context, they are extensible for use in many other application scenarios.

PERMISSION REQUIREMENTS FOR EDISCOVERY

Note that before you can perform any eDiscovery operations, you need to have been granted rights to do so via the Discovery Management RBAC role.

EDISCOVERY AND KQL

Keyword Query Language (KQL) has been introduced in Exchange Server 2013 for use in building search criteria for any eDiscovery operations you wish to perform. A KQL query consists of one or more free-text keywords or phrases and/or property restrictions. In addition, you can combine KQL query elements with one or more of the available operators to build more complex queries. In this context, operators are things like the Boolean AND and NOT or equate operations like = or <, >. KQL queries are case-insensitive and limited to 2,048 characters. An example of making a free-text KQL query for the phrase "Microsoft Exchange 2013" would be as follows:

```
MailboxQuery mbq = new MailboxQuery("\"Microsoft Exchange 2013\"", msbScope);
```

An example of using a property restriction where you wanted to search for messages where the subject was "Microsoft Exchange 2013" would be as follows:

```
MailboxQuery mbq = new MailboxQuery("Subject:\"Microsoft Exchange \"", msbScope);
```

Wildcards are also supported in KQL queries. For example, you might want to write a query like the one in Listing 11.9 to find the number of hits obtained for a query for Exchange 20x compared to one for Exchange 2003.

LISTING 11.9:   Using wildcards with the `MailboxQuery` class

```
MailboxQuery mbq = new MailboxQuery("Exchange NEAR(1) 20*", msbScope);
MailboxQuery mbq2 = new MailboxQuery("Exchange NEAR(1) 2003", msbScope);
MailboxQuery[] mbqa = new MailboxQuery[2] { mbq,mbq2 };
```

PROCESSING THE RESULTS OF AN eDISCOVERY OPERATION

When you perform an eDiscovery operation, you have the option of either getting only statistics or retrieving results in preview items format. Getting the statistics means that you will get an estimate of the number of messages the search will return for each of the keywords or search predicates you use. This can be useful if you're looking to find the most efficient query to make or the correct operator to use. For example, if you have a folder used to store a mailing list where people talked about problems with their Exchange Server, then you could use the sample code in Listing 11.10 to determine the number of items where the different versions of Exchange were discussed.

LISTING 11.10:   Using the NEAR operator with the `MailboxQuery` class

```
MailboxQuery mbq2 = new MailboxQuery("Exchange NEAR(1) 2003", msbScope);
MailboxQuery mbq3 = new MailboxQuery("Exchange NEAR(1) 2007", msbScope);
MailboxQuery mbq4 = new MailboxQuery("Exchange NEAR(1) 2010", msbScope);
MailboxQuery[] mbqa = new MailboxQuery[4] { mbq1,mbq2,mbq3,mbq4 };
```

The results you would receive for a statistics-only query would look like those shown in Listing 11.11.

LISTING 11.11:   eDiscovery search results in statistics format

```
<t:KeywordStats>
  <t:KeywordStat>
    <t:Keyword>Exchange NEAR(1) 20*</t:Keyword>
    <t:ItemHits>2506</t:ItemHits>
    <t:Size>477698732</t:Size>
  </t:KeywordStat>
  <t:KeywordStat>
    <t:Keyword>Exchange NEAR(1) 2003</t:Keyword>
    <t:ItemHits>1248</t:ItemHits>
    <t:Size>375585600</t:Size>
```

```
    </t:KeywordStat>
    <t:KeywordStat>
      <t:Keyword>Exchange NEAR(1) 2007</t:Keyword>
      <t:ItemHits>1197</t:ItemHits>
      <t:Size>129445974</t:Size>
    </t:KeywordStat>
    <t:KeywordStat>
      <t:Keyword>Exchange NEAR(1) 2010</t:Keyword>
      <t:ItemHits>91</t:ItemHits>
      <t:Size>4536168</t:Size>
    </t:KeywordStat>
  </t:KeywordStats>
```

When you use the preview-only `SearchResultType`, instead of getting the keyword statistics, you will receive a preview item for each of the keyword item hits. These preview items can be de-duplicated to ensure that the same item isn't shown multiple times. For preview items that are returned, a subset of the most common properties on the items is shown so that you can perform more client-side filtering if required. The preview items can then also be processed separately, and actions like Copy, Move, Delete, or Hold can be performed on each of the search hits.

PUTTING EDISCOVERY INTO ACTION

There are many potential uses for eDiscovery, but it will be used primarily for legal discoveries. These legal discoveries will allow your legal team to search across a selection, or even across all mailboxes, to locate specific data that is perhaps relevant to litigation.

There are several things you need to determine when you want to perform a discovery:

◆ The keywords you wish to query

◆ Whether you want to query for a particular item property

◆ What operators you want to use

◆ How you are going to process the result

In the next example, Listing 11.12, we are going to do a free-text keyword query using the search term "share trade." We are going to use the `ONEAR` operator, which allows us to search for two different keywords that have a variable proximity. In this example, it will search for the word "share" that has the word "trade" within a two-word proximity. This is just one example of the more complex searches that can be performed using KQL and eDiscovery compared to the AQS searches that we had in Exchange 2010.

LISTING 11.12:   Using eDiscovery to do a proximity search

```
//Get the Mailboxes to Search using the GetSearchableMailboxes Operation
GetSearchableMailboxesResponse gsMBResponse = service.GetSearchableMailboxes("user@
exchange-d3.com", false); MailboxSearchScope[] msbScope = new
MailboxSearchScope[gsMBResponse.SearchableMailboxes.Length];
Int32 mbCount = 0;
foreach (SearchableMailbox sbMailbox in gsMBResponse.SearchableMailboxes)
```

```
{
    //Get the referenceId for the use in the eDiscovery operation
    msbScope[mbCount] = new MailboxSearchScope(sbMailbox.ReferenceId, MailboxSearchLocation.
All);
    mbCount++;
}


SearchMailboxesParameters smSearchMailbox = new SearchMailboxesParameters();
MailboxQuery mbq = new MailboxQuery("\"share\" ONEAR(n=2) \"trade\"", msbScope);
MailboxQuery[] mbqa = new MailboxQuery[1] { mbq };
smSearchMailbox.SearchQueries = mbqa;
smSearchMailbox.PageSize = 1000;
smSearchMailbox.PageDirection = SearchPageDirection.Next;
//Tell Exchange to return Preview Items
smSearchMailbox.ResultType = Microsoft.Exchange.WebServices.Data.SearchResultType.
PreviewOnly;
ServiceResponseCollection<SearchMailboxesResponse> srCol = service.SearchMailboxes(smSearchM
ailbox);
foreach (SearchMailboxesResponse srResponse in srCol)
{
foreach (SearchPreviewItem srPvrItem in srResponse.SearchResult.PreviewItems)
    {
        //Process Item
    }
}
```

Creating Items Using Exchange Web Services

The other major function in an application for which you will use EWS is when creating new content within the Exchange store. The EWS Managed API's object model allows for the easy creation of new objects, as shown in Listing 11.13, Listing 11.14, and Listing 11.15. In Listing 11.13, we will look at how you can send email using EWS. When you send an email via EWS, it's like sending email from within a mail client. You can resolve addresses in the global address list using partial matches, choose to blind copy recipients, attach a file, and also save the message in the Sent Items folder if desired. In Listing 11.14, we look at requesting a read receipt on the message that was sent. Finally, in Listing 11.15, we look at how to create a new mailbox contact. The code used to create contacts is more complex because contacts have a larger number of properties.

LISTING 11.13: Sending a new email with an attachment using the EWS Managed API

```
EmailMessage EmailMessage = new EmailMessage(service);
EmailMessage.Subject = "Mondays Sales Reports";
EmailMessage.ToRecipients.Add("recipient@exchange-d3.com");
EmailMessage.Body = "Please see the following attached reports";
EmailMessage.Attachments.AddFileAttachment(@"c:\report\MondayReport.csv");
EmailMessage.SendAndSaveCopy();
```

LISTING 11.14: Additional code to ask for a read receipt on the email in Listing 11.13

```
EmailMessage.IsReadReceiptRequested = true;
EmailMessage.IsDeliveryReceiptRequested = true;
```

LISTING 11.15: Creating a new contact using the EWS Managed API

```
Contact contact = new Contact(service);
contact.GivenName = "Bob";
contact.Surname = "Smith";
contact.FileAsMapping = FileAsMapping.SurnameCommaGivenName;
contact.DisplayName = "Bob Smith";
contact.CompanyName = "exchange-d3";
contact.PhoneNumbers[PhoneNumberKey.BusinessPhone] = "612-555-0110";
EmailAddress CntEmailAddress = new EmailAddress("BSmith@exchange-d3.com");
contact.EmailAddresses[EmailAddressKey.EmailAddress1] = CntEmailAddress;

// Specify the Business Address.
PhysicalAddressEntry paEntry1 = new PhysicalAddressEntry();
paEntry1.Street = "123 Main Street";
paEntry1.City = "London";
paEntry1.State = "ZZ";
paEntry1.PostalCode = "02002";
paEntry1.CountryOrRegion = "United Kingdom";
contact.PhysicalAddresses[PhysicalAddressKey.Business] = paEntry1;
contact.Save(WellKnownFolderName.Contacts);
```

Some contact properties aren't definable using the standard EWS strongly typed objects. Thus, if you wish to set these properties, you must use the extended property for each particular property. An example of this is shown in Listing 11.16.

LISTING 11.16: Setting the Gender property on a contact

```
var propType = MapiPropertyType.Short;
var propTag = 0x3A4D;
var pidTagGender = new ExtendedPropertyDefinition(propTag, propType);
contact.SetExtendedProperty(pidTagGender, 2);
```

Other common objects that you may want to create programmatically are appointments and meeting requests. For instance, you want to add a specific company event or holiday to all of your users' calendars. Meetings and appointments are created the same way in EWS with the exception that meeting requests include attendees. Also, when you call the `Appointment` class's Save method, you specify in the method's overload those attendees to whom you want the Meeting Request objects sent. Listing 11.17 details how to create meeting requests, and Listing 11.18 shows you how to set a recurring meeting. Finally, Listing 11.19 shows how to create a Task object.

LISTING 11.17:   Creating a meeting request or appointment

```
Appointment apt = new Appointment(service);
apt.Subject = "Coffee";
apt.StartTimeZone = TimeZoneInfo.Local;
apt.Start = new DateTime(2012, 12, 24, 11, 0, 0);
apt.End = apt.Start.AddHours(1);
apt.EndTimeZone = apt.StartTimeZone;
apt.RequiredAttendees.Add("user@exchange-d3.com");
apt.Save(SendInvitationsMode.SendToAllAndSaveCopy);
```

LISTING 11.18:   Setting a recurring meeting

```
DayOfTheWeek[] days = new DayOfTheWeek[] { DayOfTheWeek.Monday };
apt.Recurrence = new Recurrence.WeeklyPattern(appoint.Start.Date, 1, days);
apt.Recurrence.StartDate = appoint.Start.Date;
```

LISTING 11.19:   Creating a task request

```
Task task = new Task(service);
task.Subject = "World peace";
task.DueDate = new DateTime(2013,1,1,12,0,0);
task.Body = "Archive world peace";
task.Save(WellKnownFolderName.Tasks);
```

The EWS Managed API has object classes to cater to the most commonly-used Exchange item types such as email, calendar, contacts, and appointments. However, for other item types such as notes and journal entries, no strongly typed object is available in EWS. To create one of these item types when there is no corresponding strongly typed object in EWS, use the `EmailMessage` class (`MessageType` in WSDL proxy code) and then modify the `ItemClass` property. For all of the other properties of that particular object, you need to use the corresponding extended property. Listing 11.20 shows you how to create Exchange rich item types like sticky notes.

LISTING 11.20: Creating other Exchange rich item types like sticky notes

```
EmailMessage sn = new EmailMessage(service);
sn.ItemClass = "IPM.StickyNote";
Guid guid = new Guid("0006200E-0000-0000-C000-000000000046");

var Ptype = MapiPropertyType.Integer;
var clr = 0x8B00; //Colour Prop Tag
var wdt = 0x8B02; //Width Prop Tag
var hgt = 0x8B03; //Height Prop Tag
var lft = 0x8B04; //Left Prop Tag
var Top = 0x8B05; //Top Prop Tag
String BodyText = "Test Body of to Note";
var BodyType = Microsoft.Exchange.WebServices.Data.BodyType.Text;

sn.SetExtendedProperty(new ExtendedPropertyDefinition(guid,clr,Ptype),3);
sn.SetExtendedProperty(new ExtendedPropertyDefinition(guid,wdt,Ptype),200);
sn.SetExtendedProperty(new ExtendedPropertyDefinition(guid,hgt,Ptype),166);
sn.SetExtendedProperty(new ExtendedPropertyDefinition(guid,lft,Ptype),200);
sn.SetExtendedProperty(new ExtendedPropertyDefinition(guid,Top,Ptype),200);
sn.Subject = "Test Note";
sn.Body = new MessageBody(BodyType,BodyText);
sn.Save(WellKnownFolderName.Notes);
```

Other EWS features

With each new version of Exchange, more and more functionality is being added into EWS. What follows are additional tasks for which EWS is useful. Of course, EWS is a very large topic, so naturally we haven't covered all of it here. Nonetheless, we hope that we have provided you with a good general understanding of EWS.

OUT-OF-OFFICE SETTINGS

EWS provides operations to set and get both the OOF status and OOF messages for a particular user. EWS also plays a part in allowing other users to view the OOF status of a group of users using MailTips operations, which are discussed in the next section. Listing 11.21 shows you how to get a user's OOF notification.

LISTING 11.21 How to get a user's OOF status using the EWS Managed API

```
string Mailbox = "user@exchange-d3.com";
OofSettings OofUserSettings = service.GetUserOofSettings(Mailbox);
Console.WriteLine("OOF Status : " + OofUserSettings.State.ToString());
```

Listing 11.22 shows you how to set a user's OOF status using the EWS Managed API. You should always get the current OOF setting for a user before submitting your modifications.

LISTING 11.22: How to set a user's OOF status using the EWS Managed API

```
String Mailbox = "user@exchange-d3.com";
var OOFState = Microsoft.Exchange.WebServices.Data.OofState.Enabled;
OofSettings OofUserSettings = service.GetUserOofSettings(Mailbox);
OofUserSettings.State = OOFState;
service.SetUserOofSettings(Mailbox, OofUserSettings);
```

MAILTIPS

MailTips are a relatively new feature of Exchange, introduced in Exchange 2010. They provide the ability to access and present information to a user before they send a message based on the parameters of the message they are about to send. For instance, before a message is sent, you can use MailTips to determine the Out-of-Office status for a particular recipient. They can also be used to flag issues to users before they click Send, thus cutting down on the proliferation of nuisance or accidentally sent email. There are currently no methods available in the EWS Managed API to take advantage of the MailTip operations, but you can use the WSDL strongly typed proxy objects. Listing 11.23 shows you how you can get the Out-of-Office status of a particular user using a MailTip operation.

LISTING 11.23: Getting a user's Out-of-Office status using a MailTip

```
ExchangeServiceBinding esb = new ExchangeServiceBinding();
esb.Credentials = new System.Net.NetworkCredential("uname","password");
esb.Url = service.Url.ToString();
esb.RequestServerVersionValue = new RequestServerVersion();
esb.RequestServerVersionValue.Version = ExchangeVersionType.Exchange2010_SP1;
GetMessageTrackingReportRequestType gmt = new GetMessageTrackingReportRequestType();
GetMailTipsType gmType = new GetMailTipsType();
gmType.MailTipsRequested = new MailTipTypes();
gmType.MailTipsRequested = MailTipTypes.OutOfOfficeMessage;
gmType.Recipients = new EmailAddressType[1];
EmailAddressType rcip = new EmailAddressType();
rcip.EmailAddress = "fsmith@exchange-d3.onmicrosoft.com";
gmType.Recipients[0] = rcip;
EmailAddressType sendAs = new EmailAddressType();
sendAs.EmailAddress = "fsmith@exchange-d3.onmicrosoft.com";
gmType.SendingAs = sendAs;
```

```
GetMailTipsResponseMessageType gmResponse = esb.GetMailTips(gmType);
if (gmResponse.ResponseClass == ResponseClassType.Success)
{
    if (gmResponse.ResponseMessages[0].MailTips.OutOfOffice.ReplyBody.Message != "")
    {
        //User Out
        Console.WriteLine(gmResponse.ResponseMessages[0].MailTips.OutOfOffice.ReplyBody.
Message);
    }
    else
    {
        //user In
    }

}
```

FreeBusy Time

FreeBusy lookups can be used in a number of different ways in Exchange to build different types of application features. For instance, an In/Out board could show which staff members are currently in a meeting and those who are available. The same idea can also be applied to resources or meeting rooms to show availability across a large number of resources, without the need to query each calendar separately.

The GetUserAvailiblity operation in EWS is what allows you to obtain the FreeBusy information for a user. There are two different levels of information returned from this operation. The first, and least informative, option is pure FreeBusy information. This essentially shows the user's availability in different time slots. If the querying user has the appropriate rights, the second option is a full representation of what the user is doing, covering not only the contents of various time slots but also the subject and location details of any scheduled appointments. Listing 11.24 shows you how to retrieve the FreeBusy information for multiple users.

LISTING 11.24: Using EWS to get the FreeBusy status of multiple users

```
//Set the Start and End time to get the FreeBusy Time for this example the time period for
the next 24 hours is used
DateTime StartTime = DateTime.Parse(DateTime.Now.ToString("yyyy-MM-dd 0:00"));
DateTime EndTime = StartTime.AddDays(1);
TimeWindow tmTimeWindow = new TimeWindow(StartTime,EndTime);
//Tell EWS that we want to get the Detailed FreeBusy status
AvailabilityOptions aoOptions = new AvailabilityOptions();
aoOptions.RequestedFreeBusyView = Microsoft.Exchange.WebServices.Data.FreeBusyViewType.
Detailed;
aoOptions.MeetingDuration = 30;
//Tell EWS which users we want FreeBusy for
List<AttendeeInfo> atAttendeeList = new List<AttendeeInfo>();
atAttendeeList.Add(new AttendeeInfo("user1@exchange-d3.com"));
atAttendeeList.Add(new AttendeeInfo("user2@exchange-d3.com"));
```

```
GetUserAvailabilityResults avResponse = service.
GetUserAvailability(atAttendeeList,tmTimeWindow,AvailabilityData.FreeBusy,aoOptions);
Int32 atnCnt = 0;
foreach(AttendeeAvailability avail in avResponse.AttendeesAvailability) {
    Console.WriteLine(atAttendeeList[atnCnt].SmtpAddress);
    foreach (Microsoft.Exchange.WebServices.Data.CalendarEvent calendarItem in avail.
CalendarEvents)
  {
    Console.WriteLine("Free/busy status: " + calendarItem.FreeBusyStatus);
    Console.WriteLine("Start time: " + calendarItem.StartTime);
    Console.WriteLine("End time: " + calendarItem.EndTime);
    Console.WriteLine();
  }
   atnCnt++;
}
```

DELEGATE OPERATIONS

The final example of the application of EWS shows that you can perform all of the delegate permission operations that are available within Outlook. For example, you can enumerate the delegates on a mailbox using the code shown in Listing 11.25.

LISTING 11.25: Enumerating the delegates on a mailbox

```
Mailbox dgDelegateMailbox = new Mailbox("user@exchange-d3.com");
DelegateInformation dgInfo = service.GetDelegates(dgDelegateMailbox,true);
foreach (DelegateUserResponse dgUser in dgInfo.DelegateUserResponses) {
    Console.WriteLine(dgUser.DelegateUser.UserId.DisplayName);
    Console.WriteLine(dgUser.DelegateUser.Permissions.CalendarFolderPermissionLevel);
}
```

Listing 11.26 shows you how to add a new delegate. It is important to note in this example that you should obtain the existing user delegate setting for MeetingRequestDeliveryScope, which specifies how meeting-related messages are handled between the delegate and the delegator's mailbox:

LISTING 11.26: How to add a new delegate

```
String Mailbox = "user@exchange-d3.com";
var CalendarPermissions = DelegateFolderPermissionLevel.Editor;
DelegateInformation dgInfo = service.GetDelegates(Mailbox,true);
//Create a New Delegate
DelegateUser newDel = new DelegateUser("user@exchange-d3.com");
//Set the Calendar Permission to Editor for this user
newDel.Permissions.CalendarFolderPermissionLevel = CalendarPermissions;
//This delegate won't receive meeting Invites for the delegator
```

```
newDel.ReceiveCopiesOfMeetingMessages = false;
newDel.ViewPrivateItems = true;
//Post the request to the server
service.AddDelegates(Mailbox,dgInfo.MeetingRequestsDeliveryScope,newDel);
```

Migrating a CDO 1.2 VBS Script to a PowerShell EWS Managed API Script

Now that you have learned how to use EWS to create Exchange-based applications, in this section we will work with a real-world example of taking a script that was written in VBS using the CDO 1.2 library and converting it to use PowerShell and the EWS Managed API. Recall from earlier in this chapter that in Exchange Server 2013 the available APIs are changing, with libraries like CDO 1.2 being deemphasized and MAPI needing to be encapsulated in RPC over HTTPS.

The following VBS script is one that we wrote a while ago that logs onto a mailbox using CDO 1.2, uses a MAPI filter to find contacts with photos, and then exports those photos to a directory.

Connecting to the Target Exchange Mailbox

The first section of the CDO script creates a dynamic MAPI profile from the mailbox and mailbox server name variables passed in from the command line. Following are the lines of VBS code:

```
snServername = wscript.arguments(0)
mbMailboxName = wscript.arguments(1)
set csCDOSession = CreateObject("MAPI.Session")
pfProfile = snServername & vbLf & mbMailboxName
csCDOSession.Logon "","",False,True,0,True, pfProfile
```

In EWS, you don't need a MAPI profile—all you need is the CAS URL for EWS. Thus, instead of passing in the server name of the Mailbox server, Autodiscover is used to get the CAS URL. In EWS/PowerShell, the following code would establish a connection to a CAS server using the currently logged-on credentials. This achieves the same thing as the CDO 1.2 code:

```
$MailboxName = $args[0]
Add-Type -Path  "c:\EWS API\2.0\Microsoft.Exchange.WebServices.dll"
$ExchangeVersion = [Microsoft.Exchange.WebServices.Data.ExchangeVersion]::Exchange2010_SP2
$service = New-Object Microsoft.Exchange.WebServices.Data.ExchangeService($ExchangeVersion)
$service.UseDefaultCredentials = $true
$service.AutodiscoverUrl($MailboxName,{$true})
```

Establishing a Connection to the Mailbox's Contacts Folder

The next section of the script will establish a connection to the mailbox's Contacts folder. In CDO 1.2, the following code achieves this:

```
Public Const CdoDefaultFolderContacts = 5
set cntFolder = csCDOSession.getdefaultfolder(CdoDefaultFolderContacts)
```

In EWS, the following code uses the `WellKnownFolderName` enumeration to connect to the Contacts folder:

```
$cntFld = [Microsoft.Exchange.WebServices.Data.WellKnownFolderName]::Contacts
$folderid= new-object Microsoft.Exchange.WebServices.Data.FolderId($cntFld,$MailboxName)
$Contacts = [Microsoft.Exchange.WebServices.Data.Folder]::Bind($service,$folderid)
```

Filtering the Contents of the Contacts Folder for Those That Contain a Photo

The third section of the script filters the contents of the Contacts folder to just those that contain a photo. In CDO 1.2, it does this by creating a MAPI filter on an extended MAPI property, as shown here:

```
set cfContactscol = cntFolder.messages
set ofConFilter = cfContactscol.Filter
guid = "0420060000000000C000000000000046"
Set cfContFltFld1 = ofConFilter.Fields.Add("0x8015",vbBoolean,true,guid)
```

In EWS, a search filter is used to limit the items returned by the FindItems operation to just those with attachments, as shown in the following code:

```
$pidTagHasAttachments = new-object Microsoft.Exchange.WebServices.Data.ExtendedPropertyDefi
nition(0x0E1B, [Microsoft.Exchange.WebServices.Data.MapiPropertyType]::Boolean)
$sfItemSearchFilter = new-object Microsoft.Exchange.WebServices.Data.SearchFilter+IsEqualTo
($pidTagHasAttachments, $true)
$ivItemView =  New-Object Microsoft.Exchange.WebServices.Data.ItemView(1000)
$fiItems = $null
do{
    $fiItems = $service.FindItems($Contacts.Id,$sfItemSearchFilter,$ivItemView)
    $ivItemView.Offset += $fiItems.Items.Count
}while($fiItems.MoreAvailable -eq $true)
```

Downloading the Contact Photo Attachment

The fourth section of the script downloads the contact photo attachment. In CDO 1.2, the following code is used to loop though the filtered message collection:

```
Set objFSO = CreateObject("Scripting.FileSystemObject")
For Each ctContact In cfContactscol
   Set collAttachments = ctContact.Attachments
     For Each atAttachment In collAttachments
       If atAttachment.name = "ContactPicture.jpg" Then
         strTempFile = objFSO.GetTempName
         strTempFile = Replace(".tmp",".jpg")
         atAttachment.WriteToFile("c:\contactpictures\" & strTempFile)
        wscript.echo "Exported Picture to : " &  strTempFile
       End if
     next
   Next
```

To do the same thing in the EWS Managed API, first you need to call the LoadPropertiesFromItems method, which will perform a batch GetItem request that will retrieve the details of the attachments on an item. Once this has been completed, the results of the FindItems operation can be enumerated and the attachments can be downloaded to a local directory.

```
do{
$fiItems = $service.FindItems($Contacts.Id,$ivItemView)
//Create Property Set and define the properties you wish to load
$psPropset= new-object Microsoft.Exchange.WebServices.Data.PropertySet([Microsoft.Exchange.
WebServices.Data.BasePropertySet]::FirstClassProperties)
//LoadPropertiesForItems will do a batch GetItems request for the Item Collection
 [Void]$service.LoadPropertiesForItems($fiItems,$psPropset)
 foreach($Item in $fiItems.Items){
 if($Item.Attachments.Count -gt 0){
    #Varible to hold the download directory
    $downloadDirectory = "c:\temp\contactpictures"
    #Loop through and download each attachment using the Attachment Name
    foreach($attach in $Item.Attachments){
       if($attach.IsContactPhoto -eq $true){
          "Found on Item : " + $Item.Subject
          $attach.Load()
          $fiFile = new-object System.IO.FileStream(($downloadDirectory + "\" + $item.
Subject + "-" + $attach.Name.ToString()),[System.IO.FileMode]::Create)
          $fiFile.Write($attach.Content, 0, $attach.Content.Length)
          $fiFile.Close()
          }
      }
   }
 }
$ivItemView.Offset += $fiItems.Items.Count
}while($fiItems.MoreAvailable -eq $true)
```

Mail Apps for Outlook and the Outlook Web App

An exciting new feature in Exchange 2013 is *mail apps* for Outlook, which replaces both add-ins for Outlook and OWA web forms. This feature allows you to build customized applications with a consistent user interface across Outlook and OWA. This was very difficult to achieve in previous versions of Exchange. Currently, this feature is still in its infancy, so there is a limited subset of functionality at RTM. However, as service packs are released, the feature set is expected to grow toward parity with what is available via Outlook add-ins today. Outlook mail apps are only supported in Outlook 2013 and the Exchange 2013 Outlook Web App. For older versions of Outlook you still need to use Office add-ins to provide customization. If you currently have a custom Office add-in for Outlook, this will still be supported in Outlook 2013. However, any custom Outlook web forms that you have in Exchange 2007 or Exchange 2010 will need to be migrated to a mail app to run with the Exchange 2013 OWA.

How Mail Apps Work

Mail apps display within a special application box in the currently viewed Outlook item, such as an email message, meeting request, meeting response, meeting cancellation, or appointment. Figure 11.2 shows the Bing Maps app displayed within a message in OWA.

FIGURE 11.2

The Bing Maps app showing in-line with a message in OWA

This app is activated when an address is detected within a message. A mail app can be identified and activated based on certain strings, referred to as *entities*, in the subject and body of the current Outlook 2013 or OWA item. These entities can include addresses, contacts, email addresses, meeting suggestions, phone numbers, task suggestions, and URLs.

Mail apps can call third-party web services, as shown in Figure 11.2, which uses the Bing Maps web service. They can also use EWS to access more information on the current item or other items that are stored within an Exchange mailbox. Mail apps have *activation rules* that control when they are displayed in messages. For IT professionals, you can think of these activation rules like the Inbox rules that have been around in Exchange since its inception. An activation rule can mean that an app is shown only when mail is received from certain users, with specific text in the subject or body, or is of a particular item type.

Mail apps are built on top of the new Office apps customization framework introduced in Office 2013. Apps can be published to the Office store, Exchange catalog, or other web server. If they are published to the Office store, they can be sold or provided free to a worldwide audience. A permissions framework controls what an app can do, and certain applications can be installed and enabled only by administrators. The ability for users to install and enable third-party mail apps can also be controlled via policies.

A mail app consists of an HTML web page and its associated JavaScript files that are hosted inside the email client. Three email clients offer support for mail apps in Exchange: Outlook 2013, Outlook Web App (OWA), and the Outlook Mobile Web App (Exchange 2013 only). How mail apps execute at runtime differs, depending on the email client you're using. For example, with the Outlook desktop client, the app web page is hosted "out of process" inside a web browser control. *Out of process* means that the app doesn't run within the Outlook process space. Instead, it runs within a web browser control inside Outlook's apps for the Office runtime process. The advantage of doing it this way is that it provides security and performance isolation for the app's code, which stops a malfunctioning app that affects the operation of Outlook. The app for Office runtime translates the JavaScript API calls and events from the mail app's code into native calls, and it is also responsible for rendering the app's output inside any Exchange item that meets the app's activation criteria. How the application renders and the size of the application box are also controllable using the application's manifest file.

A mail app is installed using the XML manifest file for that particular app, which defines various settings for the mail app. The XML manifest for a mail app contains the following information:

◆ A unique GUID that identifies the application and the app's display and icon names.

◆ Details of the application provider and version number.

◆ Activation rules that determine under what conditions the apps will be shown.

◆ Scopes of support for the application and the location of the app's HTML file for different platform types. This lets you have separate application files and size settings depending on platform type, that is, desktop, tablet, or mobile form factors.

◆ The permissions that the mail app requires.

All of the files associated with a mail app need to be hosted on a web server that is accessible by the Exchange 2013 CAS role server.

JavaScript API for Office

One of the critical components for mail apps is the JavaScript API for Office, which includes objects, methods, properties, events, and enumerations that can be used in mail apps in Outlook 2013. A mail app's HTML file should reference this file from the Microsoft Content Delivery Network (CDN), accessible at

```
https://appsforoffice.microsoft.com/lib/1.0/hosted/office.js
```

Or you can host this file along with your application. For example, your mail application's HTML file would include the following line to load the Office JavaScript API:

```
<script src="https://appsforoffice.microsoft.com/lib/1.0/hosted/office.js" type="text/
javascript"></script>
```

Permission Levels in Mail Apps

A three-tiered permission model is used within mail apps that determines what resources a particular mail app can access, what the app is capable of doing, and under what conditions the app will execute. The permission level is configured in the application's manifest file, and if it's not specified, the `Restricted` permission level is applied. Table 11.3 outlines the three permission levels.

TABLE 11.3: Mail app permission levels

PERMISSION LEVEL	PERMISSION DETAILS
Restricted	Activation rules restricted to a specific `ItemClass` or only a limited set of properties (phone number, address, or URL) from the subject or body of the current item
	Limited access to the Office JavaScript API objects and methods
	No access to Exchange Web Services
ReadItem	Reads all properties of the current item
	No access to Exchange Web Services
	Can create and access custom properties set only by the mail app on an item
	Can use all of the well-known entities or regular expressions in activation rules
	Uses all of the Office JavaScript API methods except `mailbox.makeEWS RequestAsync`
ReadWriteMailbox	Reads and writes all properties of any item in the user's mailbox
	Sends an item from the user's mailbox
	Can use all of the well-known entities or regular expressions in activation rules
	Uses all of the EWS operations allowed in the Office JavaScript API

Using Exchange Web Services within Mail Apps

To use Exchange Web Services within a mail app, the application must first request the ReadWriteMailbox permission in the application's manifest file. To make an EWS request, the makeEWSRequestAsync method of the Mailbox class in the JavaScript API for Office is used. As the name implies, the request is made asynchronously and a callback is used to deal with the results. Currently, only a subset of the available EWS operations can be used within mail apps. If you try to use a restricted operation, an error will be returned. Table 11.4 lists the available EWS operations in mail apps.

TABLE 11.4: EWS operations available in mail apps

TYPE	OPERATIONS
Item	GetItem, CopyItem, CreateItem, MovieItem, SendItem, UpdateItem
Folder	CreateFolder, GetFolder, UpdateFolder
Search	FindConversation, FindFolder, FindItem
Other	MarkAsJunk

Getting Started with a Mail App

The Exchange development center hosts a number of mail app samples to get you started. As a primer, we suggest, "How to: Create your first mail app for Outlook by using a text editor," which can be found at: `http://msdn.microsoft.com/en-us/library/fp161148.aspx`. This takes you through a fully working example of a mail app.

Installing a Mail App

Installing your mail app is a rather straightforward process. Depending on the permissions required by the application, mail apps can be installed by the user via EAC in Outlook or OWA. Apps that require `readItem` or `ReadWriteMailbox permissions` need to be installed by an administrator via the EAC or the EMS using the `New-App` cmdlet, as shown here:

```
New-App -URL:"http://<fully-qualified URL">
```

Mail apps can also be installed from the Microsoft store by users, but these apps can only specify the `Restricted` permission set.

Best Practices When Writing EWS Code

We will now consider some of the best practices for writing EWS code. The first thing to remember is that EWS operations are just normal web requests/responses. This means that the requests can be run both asynchronously and concurrently in most instances. Thus, this provides a strong framework on which to build high-performance code. When you are architecting your code, try to keep this in mind and resist the urge to write your code in an overly synchronous manner, that is, one where you need continually to go back to the server to retrieve more information.

Here a few tips to follow to keep your EWS code lean and mean:

◆ Learn to use the `LoadPropertiesFromItems` method in the EWS Managed API (or batch `GetItems` in proxy code) if you need to process attachments and recipients on a large number of messages. Wherever you can, avoid doing a `Load`, `Bind`, or `GetItem` inside of a loop, because this will be costly in terms of performance for your code.

◆ Always use paging in your search operations. The EWS Managed API enforces this, but if you're using proxy code or raw SOAP, then you should implement this yourself. By default, throttling will restrict the total number of items an Exchange Server will return to 1,000. Thus, not using and checking paging results means that your application may not process all of the items you expect.

◆ When you're making requests that are binding, or using any of the FindItems or FindFolder operations, you can reduce the size and amount of properties Exchange Web Services returns by defining only those that you need in your application using the `PropertySet` object and method overloads in the Managed API.

If you're seeking to integrate searches to Exchange from SharePoint 2013, look into using token authentication, which will avoid the necessity of prompting for user credentials. Also, eDiscovery allows you standardize on using KQL to query both Exchange and SharePoint.

Exchange, the Microsoft Stack, and Other Third-Party Products

We have spent most of this chapter examining how you can extend Exchange by creating various add-on solutions using Exchange's APIs. There are, however, a wide variety of products already available that will enable you to extend the functionality of Exchange or, at the very least, with which Exchange can integrate in some way. Such products may thus provide solutions that fully meet your or your customer's requirements.

In this last section of the chapter, we will touch on some of the thought processes required when integrating Exchange both with other Microsoft products (SharePoint, Lync, and so forth) and non-Microsoft add-ons.

Broadly speaking, integration with other products implies either installing something on the Exchange Server or getting Exchange to "talk" to another system. There has long been a rule that you don't install third-party software on your Exchange Servers unless it is absolutely unavoidable. The thought process here is that anything running on Exchange could possibly have a negative impact. Though this is true, well-written code should not cause problems. Therefore, it is important to work with reputable Independent Software Vendors (ISVs) and perform adequate testing beforehand. All of this adds a level of complexity to your solution. In many cases, however, it is justifiable in order to meet the business requirements.

Whether installing code on the Exchange Server, or having Exchange talk to another system, you must always bear in mind the additional load on the Exchange Server. For many extensions, this will be minimal. However, for projects like Lync integration (or, for that matter, integration with a third-party telephone system), where Exchange will provide voicemail capabilities, this load could be significant. At this point, we'll refer you back to Chapter 2, "Exchange Design Fundamentals," where we covered sizing.

Other than the need to size the Exchange system correctly, integration must also take into consideration security aspects. Does the third-party system require access to relay mail? Could that system be easily compromised? What safeguards should be put in place? All of these questions must be considered, and often the answer comes down to a combination of careful restrictions, such as opening up only the access required and backed up by proper auditing. We covered such concepts in depth in Chapter 8, "Securing Exchange."

Summary

Exchange has been designed as a foundation to build upon and to provide services (such as mail and fax transport) to other systems. It is this capability that has allowed Exchange to thrive in the marketplace and to support a large variety of customer requirements. When integrating with Exchange, if you make sure to consider the sizing, security, and stability of your code, you should have a great experience.

Chapter 12

Exchange Clients

One the reasons behind the success of Exchange Server is that it supports many client types. It is possible to connect to an Exchange mailbox from pretty much any operating system. The experience provided by clients varies so dramatically that end users may not even realize that they are using an Exchange Server.

A great example of this took place on a university campus in the United Kingdom. The university had migrated their messaging service to Microsoft Live@edu. The Live@edu service was basically Exchange Server 2010 hosted in the cloud. The university students were provided instructions on how to connect to the new service when using Outlook for either Windows or Mac and also for Linux clients using IMAP. After the migration, a computer science class was overheard talking about how good the new mail service was now that it was running on Unix. They had no idea that they were connecting their open source Linux workstations into a Microsoft Exchange Server, but they were impressed with the service all the same.

There are downsides to this flexibility, however. Not all clients have the same resource usage requirements, and so it can be difficult to project your server sizing numbers with precision if you do not have detailed client inventory data. Additionally, many clients that can connect to Exchange are produced by third-party suppliers or are open source. This means that there is a greater chance of bugs or unpredictable behavior among the clients that impact the Exchange service that you have deployed.

This chapter will address ways in which clients differ and how they may impact your design and deployment approach for Exchange Server 2013. We will also discuss some enhanced features in Exchange 2013 that help protect your Exchange 2013 servers from rogue clients.

Types of Exchange Client

There are a huge number of different email clients that can connect to Exchange Server. This is due to Exchange providing support for standards-based email protocols, such as *Post Office Protocol (POP3)* and *Internet Message Access Protocol (IMAP)*, in addition to Microsoft's proprietary *Messaging Application Programming Interface (MAPI)*. There are also several open source implementations of MAPI, such as OpenMapi, MAPI4Linux, and libmapi, which allow open source email clients to connect to Exchange Servers directly via MAPI.

Because of the number of client types, most design teams group them together based on their protocols.

Messaging Application Programming Interface (MAPI/RPC)

MAPI has been around in one form or another since 1991. Initially, it was used as the protocol for the MS PC Mail product. It was later developed into extended MAPI and used within Exchange Server.

OUTLOOK DOES NOT ONLY USE MAPI

From a client perspective, Outlook is the most common MAPI client used with Exchange Server. Nevertheless, just because Outlook is in use does not guarantee that it is connecting via MAPI, especially in open environments such as universities. Remember that Outlook supports other protocols that can be used to connect to Exchange Server, including IMAP and POP3, and with Outlook 2013, even Exchange Active Sync is supported, which allows it to connect to Outlook .com. Although Outlook does not necessarily imply a MAPI connection, a MAPI connection usually implies Outlook since it is the only MAPI client that is supported by Microsoft for connecting to Exchange Server.

It is worth defining MAPI at this point and how it has changed in Exchange Server 2013. At its core, the Messaging Application Programming Interface is a Remote Procedure Call (RPC) protocol that provides a very rich interface to your Exchange mailbox. One of the main differences between MAPI and Internet standards-based protocols, such as POP3 and IMAP, is that MAPI requires high-speed network connectivity and multiple TCP ports in order to connect. This is in contrast to POP3 and IMAP, which were designed to operate over unreliable Internet connections and through firewalls.

MAPI is still used in Exchange 2013. However, it has been encapsulated within an HTTPS tunnel. *HTTPS* is a secure version of the World Wide Web protocol (HTTP), which is encrypted with a certificate. Encapsulating MAPI within HTTPS was done to simplify the authentication and connectivity model within Exchange 2013. It is important to remember that MAPI is still alive and well, and that it is merely hidden within an HTTPS connection.

This type of MAPI connection is known as *Outlook Anywhere* in Exchange terminology. Outlook Anywhere was available in previous versions of Exchange, where it was mainly used to allow Outlook clients to connect over the Internet to Exchange Servers via MAPI encapsulated within an HTTPS tunnel.

Exchange Web Services

Exchange Web Services (EWS) has been the recommended application programming interface (API) for Exchange Server since Exchange Server 2007. EWS is a web-based protocol that communicates over HTTPS with Exchange Server. The most common user-based EWS clients are on Apple OS X. Apple OS X 10.6+ includes a native mail client, called *Mail*, which supports EWS connections, and Microsoft Office 2011 for Mac includes Outlook 2011, which also uses EWS to connect to Exchange. Prior to Outlook 2011 for Mac, Microsoft provided Entourage 2008 Web Services Edition, which also supported EWS.

From a client perspective, EWS provides a very similar set of features to MAPI. It is not as efficient as MAPI over the network, however, and so it can often appear to take longer to send or receive email on an EWS client than for Outlook connected via MAPI.

EWS is not restricted to end-user client use, though, and it is also frequently used by applications that require mailbox access. The move to EWS for application integration with Exchange has increased dramatically since Microsoft made Office 365, which runs Exchange in the cloud, available. This is because the recommended API into this service for applications is EWS. Some applications also use POP3 and IMAP4 for application integration. This has prompted developers to rewrite many applications that had previously used the Common Data Objects (CDO) API to use EWS instead.

POP/IMAP

The Post Office Protocol was first defined in 1984, and it became ubiquitous as the standard email protocol in the early days of the Internet. Virtually every email client supported POP, largely since it was extremely simple, lightweight, and very reliable. The current implementation of POP is known as POP3, which was defined via RFC 1081 in 1988. POP3 is still in use today, and Exchange 2013 supports it.

The Internet Message Access Protocol was first defined in 1986 as the Interim Mail Access Protocol, before eventually being renamed to Internet Message Access Protocol Version 4 in 1990. IMAP4 was an attempt to improve on POP3 and provide a richer client experience, including the following features:

◆ Ability to leave messages on the server

◆ Multicomputer access

◆ Power to synchronize multiple folders (including sent items)

◆ Ability to work offline

◆ Improved error handling

Since POP3 and IMAP4 are totally unrelated protocols, why do we often group the clients together? The answer here relates more to client commonality than to the individual protocol used. For instance, most clients that support POP3 also support IMAP4. These clients are typically not Active Directory domain-joined and also typically connect over the Internet.

Another use of both POP3 and IMAP4 is for application integration with Exchange Server. POP3 and IMAP4 are extremely simple protocols to use, and so many developers use them when they need to read or write data to an Exchange mailbox.

By far the biggest problem with both POP3 and IMAP4 is the tendency for clients and application developers to send credentials in clear text over an unencrypted connection. Both of these protocols can be secured via the use of encryption certificates. The credentials will still be sent in clear text over an encrypted tunnel, but are protected by the tunnel encryption. Be mindful, though, that not all clients support the secure version of each protocol, and many applications that were developed to use POP3 or IMAP4 are old and may require an upgrade to function securely. In Office 365, only encrypted POP3 and IMAP4 are supported.

ENABLING POP3 AND IMAP4 IN EXCHANGE SERVER 2013

By default, both POP3 and IMAP4 are disabled in Exchange Server 2013. To enable POP3 and IMAP4, you must start the appropriate services on your Exchange 2013 servers. One change from previous versions of Exchange Server is that there are now two services for each protocol.

To enable POP3, run the following PowerShell cmdlets as an administrator:

```
Set-service msExchangePOP3 -startuptype automatic
Set-service msExchangePOP3BE -startuptype automatic
Start-service msExchangePOP3
Start-service msExchangePOP3BE
```

To enable IMAP4, run the following PowerShell cmdlets as an administrator:

```
Set-service msExchangeIMAP4 -startuptype automatic
Set-service msExchangeIMAP4BE -startuptype automatic
Start-service msExchangeIMAP4
Start-service msExchangeIMAP4BE
```

Note that the Backend service (POP3BE/IMAP4BE) will exist on Mailbox roles and the normal protocol service will exist on Client Access Servers. If you have installed both Mailbox and Client Access on the same server, both services will be present.

Web Browsers

In Exchange terms, web browsers are basically users of the Outlook Web App (OWA). It is often useful to discuss browser-based mail clients because of the huge number of web browsers in use in your organization and Exchange Server 2013's varying support of them. We will address browser support later in this chapter.

Browser-based mail clients are becoming more and more popular, largely due to the flexibility and rich feature set that OWA provides combined with operating system independence and the pervasive nature of web browsers. Fundamentally, each release of OWA has attempted to imitate the look and feel of the most current Outlook client. For Exchange Server 2013, this means that OWA looks very similar to Outlook 2013.

By far the most beneficial aspect to browser-based mail clients is that they require no configuration whatsoever. The end user just needs to know the correct URL for the web-based client and to enter their username and password to be provided with a feature-rich experience. The actual features offered vary depending on the browser and operating system, but for the most part, even the poorest OWA experience is far better than using a POP3 or IMAP4 client. This is because, although you may be able to connect a feature-rich client such as Outlook 2013 to Exchange Server 2013 via POP3, many of the rich client features will be disabled, such as availability information and the global address list.

OWA does have limitations, however. Among the most notable restrictions are that performance can suffer over a poor network connection and a reduced set of notifications is available because of browser constraints. Nevertheless, roaming or occasional email users will find OWA perfectly acceptable and sometimes prefer it to an installed desktop application. OWA in

Exchange Server 2013 also supports offline mode with some browsers, which means that OWA can cater to even more user scenarios. Even though OWA provides a feature-rich experience, power email users often prefer to use a rich client, such as Outlook connected via MAPI or Outlook Anywhere, because of its better performance and ability to work with local data files (.pst).

SPELL-CHECK IN OWA

By far the biggest cause of irritation in the Exchange Server 2013 OWA is the removal of spell-check from the application and its reliance on the web browser to provide this feature. Luckily, most operating systems support a web browser that provides spell-check natively. One word of caution here is that Internet Explorer 9 on Windows 7 does not provide spell-check, so Windows 7 users will need to upgrade to Internet Explorer 10, Google Chrome, or Firefox to regain the spell-check feature in OWA 2013.

Exchange ActiveSync

Exchange ActiveSync (EAS) is an email protocol, just like MAPI, except it is primarily used in mobile clients, such as smartphones or tablets. Consequently, it is optimized for low-bandwidth and high-latency scenarios, such as over packet-switching radio data networks. The protocol also provides specific functions for mobile devices, such as being able to wipe the device remotely and to control aspects of the mobile device via security policies.

A complete list of policies that can be configured via the ActiveSync protocol can be found here:

```
http://technet.microsoft.com/en-us/library/bb123783.aspx
```

EAS is one of the most misunderstood protocols for Exchange. Many believe that Microsoft sells EAS and provides third-party manufacturers a finished mobile email product. This is partially true in that Microsoft does sell a license to use the EAS protocol. Microsoft does not, however, provide a finished email client as part of this license. Each EAS licensee is afforded access to the EAS protocol specification and a license to sell devices that use this protocol.

At the time of writing, there are 52 licensees of the EAS protocol, including Apple, Nokia, Google, Sony, Samsung, and HTC to name just a few. The EAS licensee may develop their mobile client in any way they wish. Accordingly, though virtually every mobile device on the market supports EAS, each device is likely to offer a different implementation of the protocol and may support only a subset of its features.

This results in a double-edged sword for EAS. It is an outstanding protocol for connecting mobile devices to Exchange Server. Most mobile devices provide rudimentary support for autodiscover, which makes the initial configuration very simple and enables the devices to provide a rich user experience via EAS. However, not all devices support every EAS feature, and most devices have their own idiosyncrasies, which range from not fully supporting autodiscover to causing backend Exchange Server issues.

Microsoft attempted to resolve this problem by launching the Exchange ActiveSync Logo Program. This program is defined as follows:

> *The Microsoft Exchange ActiveSync Program for mobile email devices that connect to Exchange Server and Exchange Online ensures that customers and IT pros have seamless experiences with setup, support, and use of qualified devices. Only products that meet Exchange ActiveSync Logo Program requirements will be listed.*
>
> *http://technet.microsoft.com/en-us/exchange/gg187968.aspx*

Initially, this seemed to be a great idea. After the initial enthusiasm passed, however, few vendors actually submitted devices. The website for this program today lists Apple iOS 4.3 and Microsoft Windows Phone 7.5, neither of which are current platforms; Google has not submitted anything.

Apple iOS 6.2 was released in February 2013, and this caused Exchange servers to generate huge quantities of additional transaction logs. Apple fixed this with 6.2.1 shortly afterward. Back in June 2010, Apple released iOS 4, which caused severe performance issues when it connected to an Exchange server. Apple eventually issued iOS 4.0.1, which fixed the problem.

We mention these specific events because it is important to remember that the type of client device may not only impact the end-user experience but may also affect the Exchange service itself. Apple is not the only vendor to produce a buggy EAS client (and they won't be the last). However, because of the sheer number of their devices on the market, they are one of the most important.

Collaboration Data Objects

During Exchange design projects, it is easy to slip into a frame of mind where you think only about end-user mailboxes. You imagine your Exchange servers being deployed and providing a great new service to end users. However, it is extremely rare to find an Exchange deployment that does not also have some form of application integration.

Application integration occurs when another program or service needs to use the Exchange service. This integration could be as simple as sending or receiving email to something more exotic such as managing field agents' calendars based on a booking application service. Regardless of the function required, the most common mechanism used to access Exchange Server programmatically is via the *Collaboration Data Objects (CDO)* model. Despite this model being deprecated in Exchange 2007 in favor of Exchange Web Services, it is still very common today.

At its core, CDO exposes the MAPI protocol to programming languages via the Component Object Model (COM). Back when it was introduced (in Exchange 4.0 and called OLE Messaging), this was useful because many applications were written in Visual Basic, and could not use the MAPI C++ libraries directly.

A number of high-profile applications use CDO, such as BlackBerry Enterprise Server (BES), Good Messaging for Enterprise, and Enterprise Vault. We mention this since Exchange Server 2013 will be the last version of Exchange to support CDO; the next version of Exchange Server will not provide a CDO library. This means that all future Exchange application integration will move over to Exchange Web Services or POP3/IMAP4.

Since Exchange 2013 still supports CDO, two points are worth mentioning: First, CDO for Exchange Server 2013 is not available at the time of this writing. Second, vendors will be required to update their applications to use the Exchange 2013 version of CDO because of the change in MAPI connectivity; that is, Exchange 2013 enforces HTTPS Outlook Anywhere client connections only. Accordingly, it is highly recommended that you speak to your software vendors to obtain a product support roadmap for Exchange Server 2013. Be warned that it may take them longer than normal to provide an update given these changes to CDO and MAPI.

MAPI INTERNALS BLOG

Stephen Griffin is a Microsoft employee who maintains a blog dedicated to MAPI and CDO development. If you need to delve more deeply into this area, we strongly recommend spending some time reading through his excellent material.

    http://blogs.msdn.com/b/stephen_griffin

Why Does Client Choice Matter?

For all but browser clients, the client type that is deployed defines the end-user experience. It is not unusual for Exchange Server migrations to occur and for end users not even to notice that they have been migrated since their experience remains virtually the same.

While not a hard-and-fast rule, the Exchange Server software typically provides benefits in terms of service availability and reductions in operation and deployment costs. Client software generally provides improvements in the end-user experience. The obvious exception to this is Outlook Web App browser clients, because they, along with mailbox quota limits, change with each version of Exchange deployed. It is very common for Exchange upgrades to bring about larger mailbox sizes. It is also just as common, however, for end users not to notice this additional space.

To achieve good Exchange design, it is vital to bring client choice into the design process and consider the client as part of the overall service being developed. After all, the client is a fundamental piece of the solution.

User Experience

User experience is the term used to describe how a user perceives the service or application that they are using. Thus it is a somewhat subjective value where individuals may rate their experience differently. From an Exchange client perspective, this means that everyone may not have the same user experience with the same client. For example, one user may be satisfied with a super-lightweight client such as Eudora because of its simplicity and speed, whereas another user requires features found only in Outlook 2013 for Windows.

Real World Scenario

CLIENT RESPONSIVENESS IS NOT ALWAYS AN ISSUE WITH EXCHANGE

Client responsiveness is another feature that is often missed during Exchange service design. We witnessed a great example of this type of omission from a customer who had deployed Exchange Server 2010 successfully. They had increased mailbox quota sizes from 100 MB to 5 GB by moving to Exchange Native Data Protection and low-cost, locally attached storage. The project was thought to be a great success by all metrics. Nevertheless, we were asked to help this customer less than 12 months after their migration because "Exchange was slow" and, despite their best efforts, they were unable to determine the reason why. After a short analysis, we concluded that Exchange was actually performing very well, even though the end users were complaining of poor performance. Further analysis indicated that most of the users who were complaining were using laptops with 5.4K RPM hard disk drives and an old version of an antivirus software program. The combination of additional disk I/O caused by the larger Outlook cache file (.ost), slow hard disk drives, and an overly aggressive antivirus software configuration was causing delays of 3–5 minutes for Outlook to open, and client responsiveness was terrible in general. The customer replaced the older laptops, upgraded the hard drives in the newer models, and updated the antivirus software across the board. The resulting change in user experience was extraordinary without making any changes to the customer's Exchange implementation.

This example is applicable for customers moving to Exchange Online in Office 365. This service provides a 25 GB mailbox for a very low price point. In versions prior to Outlook 2013, the cached .ost file would generally settle on being roughly twice the mailbox size. In the previous case, that would mean that Outlook 2010 would require roughly 50 GB of local disk space on the client machine to cache a full 25 GB mailbox. Outlook 2013 contains two features to help with this issue: First, the .ost file structure has been engineered for improved compression to avoid file growth over time. Second, you can control the age of items that are stored in the local cache via a slider within Outlook.

Smaller Ultrabook-style laptops are now very popular. Their solid-state drives (SSD), however, often have a relatively small capacity—128 GB is commonplace. This means that an end user may run out of physical disk capacity on their laptop before they reach their mailbox quota, which is indeed a very poor user experience!

Supportability

Supportability can be split into two areas. The first is manufacturer support, such as Microsoft providing support for Outlook. The second area is the ability of support personal to operate and troubleshoot the product, such as the local help desk staff's ability to troubleshoot Outlook connectivity issues. For the purposes of this section, we will concentrate on manufacturer support, since the help desk support function is unique to each environment.

OUTLOOK

Outlook has been the primary quality client for Exchange Server since Outlook 97. Every new release of Microsoft Office includes an updated version of Outlook that makes the best use of the latest Exchange Server features. This development cycle has made Outlook the most common email client in use in business today by far.

Nonetheless, with each new release of Outlook, the testing matrix for Exchange has grown. To combat this problem, the Exchange team made the decision starting with Exchange 2007 to discontinue support for older versions of Outlook. For example, support for Outlook 2000 was discontinued with Exchange Server 2007, and support for Outlook 2002 was dropped in Exchange Server 2010. This meant that it was necessary to know which client versions were installed in an organization and which client versions were supported for the version of Exchange that you were deploying. For Exchange Server 2013, the following versions of Outlook are supported:

- Outlook 2013

- Outlook 2010 SP1 + April 2012 CU

- Outlook 2007 SP3 + July 2012 CU

- Entourage 2008 for Mac, Web Services Edition

- Outlook for Mac 2011

The most notable absence from this list is Outlook 2003. This version is still fairly common. Therefore, as part of your Exchange 2013 deployment planning, you should include client inventory and potentially a client upgrade program to remediate unsupported Outlook 2003 clients.

Let's move on to one of the most difficult problems to solve. Some customers have invested significant time and money in Excel and Word macro development. Legacy macros were written in *Visual Basic for Applications (VBA)*. VBA was enhanced with each new version of Office and other Microsoft applications. This can sometimes place Exchange projects in sticky situations where customers need to upgrade the Outlook client for Exchange support. Moreover, upgrading Outlook generally means upgrading the entire Microsoft Office system, and this falls right into the critical path of the Exchange design and deployment project.

There are a couple of options available for solving the Outlook upgrade problem. First, it is possible to install a newer version of Outlook next to an older version of Office. Outlook 2007 with Office 2003, for example, allows a customer with an old desktop installation to migrate to Exchange Server 2013 without having to upgrade the entire Office suite at the same time. This does have its downsides, however. For example, Outlook uses the installed version of Word for various enhanced editing functions. Mixing versions of Outlook and Word results in the loss of automatic spell-check in the Outlook editor, though manual spell-check is still available.

Another option is to use Outlook Web App instead of Outlook. The problem with OWA is that it does not provide the same feature set or user experience as Outlook connected via MAPI or Outlook Anywhere. Most notably in OWA in Exchange 2013, you cannot access public folders or use S/MIME certificates. In addition, there are the usual problems of not being able to access .pst files. Nonetheless, for some users, this may represent a better option than running a different version of Outlook and Office on the same system. Of course, the ideal solution is when the customer upgrades to Office 2013 and has their macros rewritten as necessary.

OUTLOOK WEB APP

Browser support is slightly more complex in Exchange Server 2013 than in previous versions due to the introduction of OWA Offline Access and the removal of spell-check from OWA, relying instead on browser-based spell-checking. All of this along with varying browser behavior depending on operating system makes for a number of situations. Table 12.1 shows the relationships among browser, client, and OWA features in Exchange Server 2013.

TABLE 12.1: OWA feature availability by operating system and browser:

BROWSER	WINDOWS XP	WINDOWS VISTA	WINDOWS 7	WINDOWS 8	MAC OS X 10.5	MAC OS X 10.6+	LINUX
Internet Explorer 7	Good	N/A	N/A	N/A	N/A	N/A	N/A
Internet Explorer 8	Good	Good	Good	N/A	N/A	N/A	N/A
Internet Explorer 9	N/A	Best	Best	N/A	N/A	N/A	N/A
Internet Explorer 10+	N/A	N/A	Best + Offline	Best + Offline	N/A	N/A	N/A
Firefox 12+	Good	Good	Best	Best	Best	Best	Best
Safari 5.1+	Good + Offline	Good + Offline	Good + Offline	Good + Offline	N/A	Best + Offline	N/A
Chrome 18+	Good + Offline	Good + Offline	Best + Offline	Best + Offline	Best + Offline	Best + Offline	Best + Offline

N/A = Not applicable

Best = All options are available.

Good = Most options are available.

+ Offline = OWA Offline Access is available.

POP/IMAP

There is no specific Exchange support statement for POP3 and IMAP4 clients from Microsoft. The only thing regarding these clients that you need to be aware of is that, by default, both are disabled in Exchange Server 2013. To enable POP3, you must start the Microsoft Exchange POP3 service and the Microsoft Exchange POP3 Backend service. To enable IMAP4, you must enable the Microsoft Exchange IMAP4 service and the Microsoft Exchange IMAP4 Backend service. For individual client support, contact the vendor of that client.

EXCHANGE ACTIVESYNC DEVICES

The EAS protocol version is linked to the Exchange Server version. The latest release of EAS at the time of this writing is version 14.1, which was last updated in Exchange Server 2010 SP1. Exchange Server 2013 and Exchange Server 2010 SP1 both use EAS 14. This means that any EAS clients that were supported in Exchange Server 2010 SP1 are also supported in Exchange Server 2013.

By far the biggest problem with EAS clients is determining just how many EAS features are implemented on each device. The most comprehensive listing of EAS feature implementation by client is found at the following address. Nonetheless, some important client devices, such as Windows Phone 8 and later Apple iOS versions, are missing from this list:

```
http://en.wikipedia.org/wiki/Comparison_of_Exchange_ActiveSync_Clients
```

To offer any valid level of assurance that certain devices will provide specific features given the random behavior of EAS devices, it is imperative that you test them explicitly to be sure.

CDO and MAPI

As we have discussed, many third-party systems connect via CDO and MAPI. We also noted that Exchange Server 2013 would require a new version of CDO to connect. What we did not mention was that manufacturers will often specify a preferred version of CDO for each version of their product and Exchange Server to ensure the best level of service.

We suggest that you ask your vendor to recommend a version of CDO to use in these circumstances. They will know best which problems they have tested for that other customers have experienced. Never assume that simply using the latest version of CDO will provide the best experience.

Regulatory Compliance

Compliance is a term often used during Exchange design and deployment projects. *Regulatory compliance* is basically the data control processes that an organization must follow in order to conform to the necessary laws and regulations that govern its business.

Compliance legislation varies by country. In the United States, the Sarbanes-Oxley Act of 2002 (SOX) is the legislation cited most often that impacts Exchange. In the United Kingdom, the Data Protection Act of 1998 applies to every organization. In Canada, the Keeping the Promise for a Strong Economy Act (known as C-SOX) of 2002 applies.

These pieces of legislation have many areas in common. Most enforce rules for data retention, confidentiality, and the release of information. It is also worth noting that many organizations will add their own compliance polices to maintain reputational integrity and to secure sensitive data. These policies may state that the end user's device must be company owned or that certain data on mobile devices must be encrypted.

It is important to understand what legislative compliance requirements apply for each customer and where the design will meet them; that is, on the Exchange server side or client side. Many of the legislative compliance requirements can be met by using journaling at the server side. *Journaling* keeps a digital record of every email communication between users, both inside and outside the organization. The client is generally not aware of this process, and even if the client deletes content, it will remain in the journal repository until such time that it is deleted.

Organization Security Compliance

For organizational compliance requirements such as protecting against data leakage, the issues become more complicated. For example, many organizations wish to control where their data is stored and accessed. This control may include statements such as "mobile devices must have a passcode," "mobile devices must be encrypted," or "only company-provided devices are allowed to connect to the company email system." Such controls often provide the largest hurdles to design teams.

We have already discussed EAS and that although the protocol includes many security policies, the vendor of the device chooses how these policies are implemented. This means that some devices may report that they have met all of the security policy requirements when in fact they have not. This was very common in early Android devices, although most devices today are pretty good in this regard. Additionally, controls to prove that a device is indeed company owned may bring with them complex and expensive dependencies, such as IPSec deployments or certificate-based authentication.

Organizations may even enforce *two-factor authentication (2FA)* for system access. 2FA indicates the control of system access by requiring two bits of authentication data. For example, your username and password plus a security token or smartcard is two-factor authentication. A 2FA system is perceived as being more secure than a single-factor scheme, such as a simple username and password security system, but it obviously brings with it more complexity. Most significant from an Exchange client perspective, many common clients, such as Outlook, do not support 2FA particularly well, if at all.

Given all of this doom and gloom, how should you best meet these security requirements while simultaneously not incurring a huge expense or making system access too difficult for end users? The most common answer to this question is to use *information rights management (IRM)*. IRM works by digitally encrypting and controlling end-user rights at the time the document or message is created. These controls allow variations in end-user permissions such as read-only, do not forward, block copy and paste, and disable print. The end user must authenticate to the IRM service, which in turn will provide the information required to decrypt the message and enforce the granted rights. Using IRM provides many benefits, both internally and externally. From an Exchange client perspective, the most important benefit is that as long as your client is capable of viewing the IRM protected documents, you no longer need to provide client-side access controls.

As a general rule, do not attempt to control data leakage via perimeter controls and device access solutions. Use an IRM product instead, such as Active Directory Rights Management Services from Microsoft.

Performing a Client Inventory

At the beginning of a project, we typically ask for a list of client types that must be supported by the end solution. There are generally two responses to this question: Either the customer responds quickly and confidently with such a list (accurate or not) or we get a look that tells us no one has considered this question previously.

Since we now recognize the importance of client choice, it should come as no surprise that we strongly recommend that you try to determine which client types are used on the existing service before you attempt to design a new one. This recommendation is equally applicable if you are moving to Exchange Online, which is part of Office 365. Client type has a dramatic impact on network and other system resources. If you cannot reasonably assess the client types/versions that will use the service, it could prove to be very difficult to ensure that the service meets all of its requirements.

Messaging API (MAPI/RPC)

By far the easiest way to determine the types of MAPI clients that are connected to a system is via the Exchange Client Monitor (ExMon). While this tool has not yet been released for Exchange Server 2013, at the present time the most important use for it is on an existing Exchange service to get a better understanding of client types within the environment to help with the Exchange 2013 design.

ExMon is a great tool, but it is known to crash frequently. If it does indeed crash, the background ETL trace should continue to run. You can see this by looking for the state of the Exchange Event Trace via logman, an example of which is shown in Figure 12.1. *Logman* is a command-line tool that manages performance counter and event trace log collections on both remote and local systems.

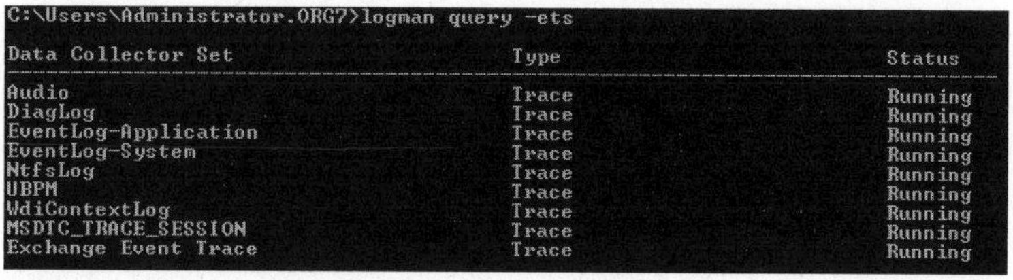

FIGURE 12.1

Logman query results for ExMon trace

```
C:\Users\Administrator.ORG7>logman query -ets

Data Collector Set                           Type                   Status
--------------------------------------------------------------------------------
Audio                                        Trace                  Running
DiagLog                                      Trace                  Running
EventLog-Application                         Trace                  Running
EventLog-System                              Trace                  Running
NtfsLog                                      Trace                  Running
UBPM                                         Trace                  Running
WdiContextLog                                Trace                  Running
MSDTC_TRACE_SESSION                          Trace                  Running
Exchange Event Trace                         Trace                  Running
```

If the Exchange Event Trace shows a status of Running, the trace file is still being created and will stop logging when it reaches 512 MB. If you want to stop the trace before then, you can do so via the following command:

```
logman stop "Exchange Event Trace" -ets command
```

By default, the ETL trace file will be stored in the default directory C:\Program Files (x86)\Exchange User Monitor. To open the ETL file, simply drag it over the ExMon.exe file in File Explorer. It is beyond the scope of this section to walk through the ExMon output in detail, but it is explained quite well in the following TechNet article:

http://technet.microsoft.com/en-us/library/bb508855(EXCHG.65).aspx

For the purposes of client inventory, it is recommended that you run a few traces during a workday and then export that data to a .csv file for analysis within Excel. The aim of this process is to determine which Outlook client versions are currently in use so that you can ensure that your new Exchange 2013 solution will work with them or that they can be identified and upgraded.

LINUX MAPI CLIENTS

A word of warning here about Linux MAPI implementations: The Linux MAPI library allows Linux mail clients, such as Evolution, to connect to Exchange 2007 and Exchange 2010 via MAPI. These clients usually report in ExMon as version 12.0.6206.1000, which is the same as Outlook 2007. The problem with this procedure is that Exchange 2013 does not work with any current Linux MAPI implementation, and so all of these Linux MAPI clients will fail to connect if you migrate them over to Exchange Server 2013 without first reconfiguring them back to IMAP4 or POP3. You first must identity them, however, which is tricky since you can't tell them apart from Outlook 2007. If you have a significant population of Linux users, it's probably a good idea to notify them of this issue prior to migration.

Web Clients (EWS, EAS, and OWA)

Exchange Server uses the standard-issue Internet Information Server (IIS) to serve web requests, both HTTP and secure HTTPS. There is no easy way to see how many of each version of the web client requests are being made to Exchange Server. This information, however, is tucked away in the IIS logs.

Log Parser is by far the best tool for analyzing text logs generated via IIS. There is a great write-up of this tool specifically for Exchange on the Exchange Team Blog:

```
http://blogs.technet.com/b/exchange/archive/2007/09/12/3403903.aspx
```

We recommend spending some time analyzing the data from your Exchange Server IIS logs and grouping the results into device categories. This will help you to quantify the relative size of each device group and allow you to understand the importance of each device type and version. See the end of this section for a link to some scripts to help with this.

POP3 and IMAP4

Since neither POP3 nor IMAP4 has changed recently, it is unlikely that you will need to know the precise client versions deployed for your design. One thing you do need to know is how many POP3 and IMAP4 clients there are in the organization, because potentially you may not need to support POP3 or IMAP4 clients at all.

The easiest way to understand POP3 and IMAP4 usage within an existing Exchange environment is to log some Exchange performance counters over a period of time. We recommend logging the following performance counters every 15 minutes for a couple of weeks:

◆ \MSExchangeIMap4\Active SSL Connections

◆ \MSExchangeImap4\Current Connections

◆ \MSExchangePop3\Active SSL Connections

◆ \MSExchangePop3\Connections Current

Once you have a better understanding of the scale of POP3 and IMAP4 usage, you can then decide if you need to take things further. If there is significant usage in the user population, then you should include POP3 and IMAP4 appropriately in your design. If you are dealing with a very small community of users who rely on these protocols, this may be a good time to move them over to an alternative protocol, such as OWA or EWS.

To enable protocol logging, use the following commands:

```
Set-PopSettings -Server "CAS1" -ProtocolLogEnabled $true -LogFileLocation "E:\POP3Logs"
Set-ImapSettings -Server "CAS1" -ProtocolLogEnabled $true -LogFileLocation "E:\IMAPLogs"
```

WARNING IMAP4 and POP3 protocol logging can consume considerable disk space on heavily used servers. Make sure that you specify a log file location with plenty of space, and remember to disable protocol logging when you have finished.

Analyzing these logs should provide sufficient information about the users who are authenticating to the mailboxes and also the client device IP addresses. Such information should be sufficient to locate the individual users and have a conversation with them about their client usage.

Here is a short example from a POP3 protocol log. This log shows both the client IP address and username that was used for authentication.

```
2013-03-12T15:11:40.765Z,0000000000000002,2,192.168.15.101:110,192.168.15.100:51632,,5,20,
5,user,jenson@org7.lab,R=ok
```

When performing this process, it is important to remember that the fewer client types and protocol mechanisms that your Exchange design needs to support, the simpler it will be. Additionally, it reduces the attack surface of the solution, which is always a good thing.

Scripting

All of this log file analysis is great. But if you have lots of Exchange Servers, or you are just not comfortable with LogParser, then there is still some hope. Our friend Steve Goodman has created a couple of scripts that will analyze your IIS logs and generate a nice report.

The scripts can be found here:

```
http://www.stevieg.org/2011/04/how-to-get-info-about-your-activesync-ews-and-
webdav-clients-before-migrating-to-exchange-2010/
```

Design Considerations

As we have discussed, clients offer a varying range of features and thus they have a varied range of requirements and dependencies. Client choice can be both a solution to a design requirement and a design requirement in their own right. An example of this might be that a customer has deployed Outlook 2007 and for some reason cannot upgrade. Thus Outlook 2007 becomes a design constraint; that is, regardless of any other requirements, the solution must support Outlook 2007. In contrast, consider a customer who has a widespread use case that is satisfied only by a new feature within Outlook 2013. Then the use of Outlook 2013 becomes a design decision that satisfies a requirement.

Supportability

Supportability of the client is clearly important, but it is often not viewed strategically. In an ideal world, the version of Outlook and Exchange should be from the same release wave. This would mean that a customer would pair Outlook 2010 and Exchange 2010 or Outlook 2013 and Exchange 2013. One reason for this suggestion is that these products were developed together and will provide the best feature set and end-user experience. Additionally, the support life cycle is likely to be well matched in that both client and server will be at the same support life cycle phase.

As mentioned previously, Outlook 2003 is not supported with Exchange Server 2013. Many customers currently use Outlook 2003 with Exchange Server 2010. If you spend some time on support forums, you will see that many customers are experiencing performance problems with this configuration, especially if Outlook is in online mode. Switching to Outlook cached mode or changing the MSExchangeRPC polling interval on the Exchange 2010 server can help, but be aware that if you have a significant mismatch in client release version and Exchange release version, you may run into difficult-to-resolve problems.

As a general rule, the best design is the most common one. We often have discussions with customers about "the art of the possible." However, the reality is that, for most customers, you should deploy a solution that is based on common components and software. The main benefit of this is that whenever an update is released, it is highly likely that someone on the technical adoption program shares a similar environment, and so bugs will be caught before you get the update.

The bottom line is that when making decisions about client versions, you do not want to be the exclusive user of a specific client version with Exchange Server 2013. Stick to the well-trodden path to avoid problems. Also remember that clients have support life cycles as well. As an example, Outlook 2010 was first released in July 2010. It is in mainstream support until October 2015 with extended support running until October 2020. *Extended support* means that the product receives critical security fixes only and that there will be no feature development and limited updates.

You can check Microsoft client version support at the following address:

```
http://support.microsoft.com/gp/lifeselectindex
```

Although Outlook is most likely to be the primary interface between end users and an Exchange service, do not forget about browser support for the Outlook Web App and Exchange Administration Center (EAC). As mentioned previously, browser support has changed with Exchange 2013. Many customers still have older browsers installed, such as Internet Explorer 7, which are not supported in Exchange Server 2013. Also make sure that the customer's browser will support any features that you need to provide in OWA. This is especially important if you intend to make use of new features such as OWA offline mode.

Security

Security is a broad topic and is covered in detail in Chapter 8, "Securing Exchange." From a client perspective we are usually interested in the areas of connection encryption, data encryption, and authentication.

CONNECTION ENCRYPTION

Connection encryption is the use of encryption technology to secure communication between two or more computers. Typically, an encrypted connection will make use of Public Key Infrastructure (PKI) to issue certificates, which are used to encrypt and decrypt data.

Clients create network connections to the server, typically over TCP/IP. One of the most common requests from security teams is to ensure that all client traffic is encrypted when passing over untrusted networks such as the Internet. When making design decisions, it is important to consider how your clients will meet these requirements. For example, some POP3 and IMAP4 clients can only create an encrypted secure sockets layer (SSL) connection if the encryption certificate has the uniform resource locator (URL) name at the top of the list of subject alternate names (SAN), or it is the only name on the certificate. Many design teams do not consider this when planning their certificates, and they end up having to request a new certificate just for POP3 and IMAP4 clients. Our advice is to ensure that you analyze encrypted client connectivity in your design test lab to ensure that your proposed certificate and name spaces will work with your clients.

DATA ENCRYPTION

Data encryption refers to encrypting data sent between computers; that is, rather than encrypt all communications as with connection encryption, only the data that needs to be securely transmitted is encrypted. This is often used in combination with connection encryption to provide a robust and secure communications mechanism. Typically, the certificates used to create the secure sockets layer connection encryption and the email body encryption will be different, and so an individual would need to breach both layers of encryption and get both certificates before they could read the contents of the email message.

There are many ways to encrypt message contents, ranging from simple password protection of a Microsoft Office document or compressed Zip file to encrypting the entire message body with secure MIME (S/MIME). Attaching an encrypted attachment to the message only protects the attachment. Thus if someone is able to intercept the email message, they are still able to view the message body and any text that is in it. S/MIME encrypts the entire message body, and so it protects both the attachment(s) and message content. Not all clients, however, support S/MIME, whereas virtually all clients allow an encrypted attachment to be sent.

Additional levels of security can be provided through information rights management (IRM). But not all clients support IRM, and those that do often provide varying IRM feature levels. Again, our recommendation here is that your design test lab include an implementation of your proposed IRM solution so that you can validate client behavior.

AUTHENTICATION

Authentication is the process of identifying yourself to the messaging service so that it knows to which mailbox to provide you access. Unfortunately, network authentication credentials suffer from exactly the same problems as real-world credentials; that is, if an ill-intentioned individual gains access to them, that individual can impersonate the user to whom the credentials apply and access their data.

The simplest form of authentication is providing a username and password in plain text to the server. As discussed earlier, this was very common with early Internet protocols, such as POP3 and IMAP4. Most enterprise customers, however, do not relish the prospect of their user-name and password being sent unencrypted over a network for someone to view with a freely downloadable application, such as Wireshark or Microsoft's Network Monitor.

To protect plain-text credentials from being viewed via a network monitor, you can encrypt the network connection via secure sockets layer (SSL), as discussed in the "Connection Encryption" section. This process works by using certificates to establish an encrypted connection prior to sending the credentials. This does not prevent an ill-intentioned person from capturing the credentials from the network, but it makes what they manage to capture a lot less useful by encrypting it with the same level of security that online commerce companies and banks use to secure their transactions. It's a bit like stealing a safe but not being able to get at what's inside. This mechanism is used in many scenarios, such as Outlook Anywhere where MAPI is used to connect to Exchange via SSL, and also for secure POP3 (POP3S) and secure IMAP4 (IMAP4S).

Many organizations are concerned not only with the identity of the end user but also with the identity of the device. This brings with it a separate set of challenges, especially for mobile devices. A common solution to this requirement is to use *certificate-based authentication*. This process uses a certificate to prove identity. For mobile devices, this certificate replaces the requirement for a password (with the exception of first configuration). The connection between the device and the server is encrypted and then the certificate is sent to the Exchange server as proof of identity. This solution is very robust, but it does require that the organization have a well-deployed PKI and the ability to deploy certificates to both end users and mobile devices.

Client Performance

Design teams are typically concerned with two aspects of client performance. First, they are concerned with the performance of the client itself from the end-user perspective. This makes up a huge part of the user experience, and it should not be overlooked. Microsoft was very cognizant of this fact during the development of Windows 7 and Office 2010, and these design principles were carried forward to Windows 8 and Office 2013. If the client performance is perceived to be slow by the end user, it doesn't matter what you did with the Exchange service—the perception is simply that "Exchange is slow."

Second, the client choice has a performance impact on Exchange Server. Some clients, such as MAPI or POP3, are extremely light when it comes to using Exchange system resources, while others are much heavier, such as Outlook Web App or IMAP4. Table 12.2 was derived from a fantastic white paper released by Microsoft for Exchange Server 2010. It compares client types and their resource usage in Exchange Server 2010. This data is not yet available for Exchange Server 2013, but it is included here for comparison purposes between the client types and to highlight the differences that client choice can have on server resource usage.

TABLE 12.2: CPU usage for Exchange 2010 Client Access role

CLIENT	CPU (MHz/USER)
Exchange ActiveSync (delta)	1.60
Exchange Web Services (Entourage)	0.71
IMAP4	0.86
Outlook	0.35
Outlook Anywhere	0.80
Outlook Web App	0.86
Outlook Web App in Exchange 2010 SP1	1.17
POP3	0.33

http://technet.microsoft.com/en-us/library/ff803560(v=EXCHG.141).aspx

Outlook provides some useful information that helps you determine the source of performance problems. The Outlook Connection Status dialog, as shown in Figure 12.2, can be viewed either by starting Outlook using the /rpcdiag switch or by Ctrl+right-clicking the Outlook icon in the taskbar. This dialog reveals details about each logical connection to your Exchange Server, including RPC response latency information.

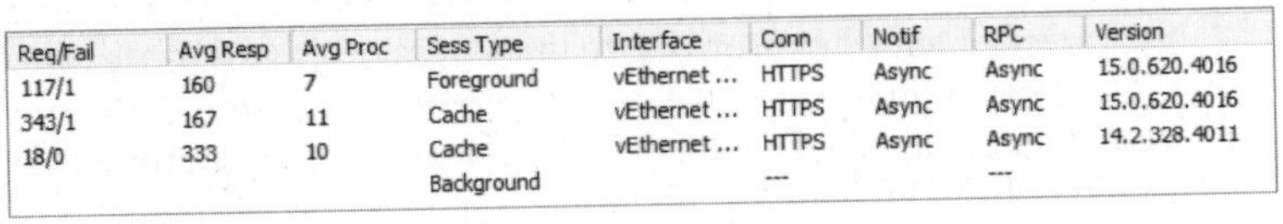

FIGURE 12.2
Outlook
Connection Status
dialog

Req/Fail	Avg Resp	Avg Proc	Sess Type	Interface	Conn	Notif	RPC	Version
117/1	160	7	Foreground	vEthernet ...	HTTPS	Async	Async	15.0.620.4016
343/1	167	11	Cache	vEthernet ...	HTTPS	Async	Async	15.0.620.4016
18/0	333	10	Cache	vEthernet ...	HTTPS	Async	Async	14.2.328.4011
			Background		---		---	

There are three columns of interest here: Avg Resp, Avg Proc, and Version. *Avg Resp* is the average response time from the server, including network latency. *Avg Proc* is the time that Exchange spent processing the requests. *Version* is the version of the Exchange server that processed the request.

Figure 12.2 shows an example from my mailbox, which is connected to Exchange 2013 in Office 365. I am located in England, and my mailbox is hosted in North America. You begin by finding the line with the highest Req/Fail value and then pick the values for Avg Resp (167 ms) and Avg Proc (11 ms). These values tell you that Exchange has dealt with my requests on average in 11 ms. If you subtract this value from the Avg Resp value of 167 ms (167 ms - 11 ms = 156 ms), you can see that the network latency between Exchange and me is 156 ms on average. This is extremely useful when you are trying to determine if a poor user experience is caused by Exchange Server or by the network connection. If Avg Proc is less than 50, Avg Resp is less than 200, and the client is still experiencing poor performance, then the most likely cause is the client device itself.

Network Usage

Network usage for clients became a hot topic with Exchange Server 2010 and even more so with Microsoft Office 365. Exchange 2010 moved the client connection point to the Client Access Server, and that meant that, for the first time, most customers had to use a load balancer with Exchange Server. Load balancers are required to spread the client workload evenly across multiple Exchange Client Access Servers. They also handle directing clients to a functioning Exchange Client Access Server in the event of a server failure. To scale a load balancer effectively, you need to know how much network bandwidth it will need to handle at peak time. This is the same for Exchange Server 2013, although you can now use a layer 4 load balancer. However, you will still need to know how much bandwidth it will need to handle before you purchase it.

Cloud deployments on Microsoft Office 365 bring with them a similar challenge. Your design needs to define how much network capacity will be required to connect the clients to the service via the Internet. Since network capacity often has to be purchased in advance and can also have long lead times, it is extremely important to get this scaling right to avoid poor client experience or buying too fast an Internet connection. Yes, although you may believe that there is no such thing as "too fast an Internet connection," remember that you are responsible for the budget and thus you need to determine the difference between too fast (very expensive) and too slow (poor user experience).

The easiest way to determine your client bandwidth usage is via the Exchange Client Network Bandwidth Calculator, available at the following address:

http://gallery.technet.microsoft.com/office/Exchange-Client-Network-8af1bf00

This calculator allows you to model various user profile and client type combinations. This calculator also accounts for time zones to accommodate users in different geographic locations and in different time zones so that they can share the same Internet connection or load balancer.

Figure 12.3 shows a bandwidth prediction made by the calculator. You can see that the prediction is not a simple curve—it is based on morning and afternoon logon peaks. In this example, which is for 53,000 light Outlook Anywhere 2010 users, the calculator predicts that the peak network usage will be 69.12 Mbits/sec at around 14:30 (2:30 p.m.). Knowing not only the peak value but also the usage curve is extremely important for network capacity planning since network links are frequently shared with other services. To plan adequately, the network team needs to know the quiet times as well as the peak times.

At the time of this writing, the Bandwidth Calculator has not been updated for Exchange Server 2013. It also does not include third-party clients such as BlackBerry OS, Good for Enterprise clients, or Apple iOS because of constraints enforced in the end-user license agreement for those devices. The biggest omission in the current beta is that it does not provide data for POP3 and IMAP4. But since the author of the calculator is also the author of this chapter, we can say with some certainty that both POP3 and IMAP4 will be added in the next version.

FIGURE 12.3
Network bandwidth
prediction

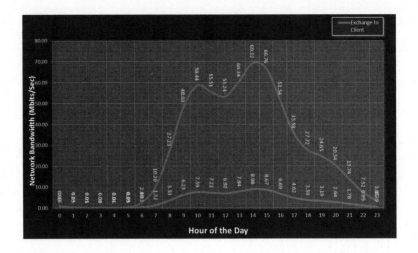

Exchange 2013 User Throttling

User throttling was introduced in Exchange Server 2010. The fundamental idea behind *user throttling* in Exchange Server is to prevent users from consuming more than their fair share of system resources. This is intended to prevent a denial-of-service attack and to promote fairness. If one user is using more than their fair share of resources, then they may experience a poor user experience. However, the rest of the users on the system will be protected from their misuse because of user throttling.

One question that we are often asked when discussing client scaling with customers is why didn't user throttling protect Exchange from the iOS bug in Apple iOS 6? (iOS 6 shipped with a bug in the way the client handled recurring meetings, which caused a continuous synchronization loop.) The answer is that user throttling in Exchange Server 2010 was intended to protect the system from a small subset of users monopolizing system resources. If a large number of users set out to monopolize system resources, the system just gets busier and busier until throttling simply cannot protect it any further.

User throttling in Exchange Server 2010 tracked three parameters: PercentTimeInCAS, PercentTimeInAD, and PercentTimeInMailboxRPC. When a user needed to be "backed off," Exchange Server 2010 would issue a delay or deny access to the user, depending on the protocol in use. This often led to a very poor experience and potentially even an error being displayed on the client device. Our observations with Exchange 2010 suggest that the resource usage limits were possibly set too high and the back-off penalties were too severe. This meant that clients that hit the throttling limit were likely to have a poor user experience, but also that the throttling process did not protect the Exchange Server from misuse as well as it should have.

Exchange Server 2013 improves user throttling in a number of ways. First, it simply tracks the amount of time that a user spends in the server, that is, processing time. Second, the model for resource utilization is based on a token bucket. This model works like a monthly salary; that is, you are given some resources on a schedule and, if you use all of your resources too quickly, the system will begin to throttle your connection until your next "paycheck" when you will get some more resources. This model allows for client bursts to take place quickly and without penalty, but it will still control overuse by rogue clients. Third, the delays applied by the user-throttling process are now much finer (micro-delays). The delay applied to the user increases proportionally to the deficit of the user, namely, the larger the resource overuse, the larger the delay. Once the user reaches the CutOffBalance, Exchange Server will begin to reject the user's requests. However, the client would have to be performing very badly to reach this point.

Summary

As you have seen in this chapter, Exchange Server clients vary considerably. The reality of most deployments is that your primary client will be some version of Outlook, and this is where you should focus your efforts. Ultimately, you must make sure that the most common client receives the desired user experience. In addition to Outlook, Exchange Server ActiveSync is almost a given for most deployments because of the pervasive use of EAS in mobile devices such as Apple's iPad, Microsoft's Surface tablet, and a variety of smartphones. BlackBerry devices are still relatively common, but our experience is that most organizations are looking to phase out this infrastructure.

Remember that the clients in use may need to be upgraded or replaced to support a new version of Exchange Server. Exchange Server 2013 does not support Outlook 2003, and so any installations of this version will need to be upgraded before beginning a migration to Exchange Server 2013. Although an Exchange Server upgrade can often be transparent to end users, if you need to replace or upgrade their mail client, it will indeed be noticed and not always positively. Our advice here is not to underestimate how big a job it can be to upgrade Microsoft Office or Outlook in a large enterprise. These projects can take years to complete, so be realistic in your Exchange planning schedules if you are planning this type of upgrade.

By far the most difficult client-related task when upgrading Exchange is identifying and managing application clients such as those based on MAPI CDO and Exchange Web Services. Not only is it difficult to identify mail-enabled applications, but they also often require upgrades between Exchange versions. Our advice here is to perform a client inventory by looking at the POP3, IMAP4, and IIS logs in addition to running some client tracing with ExMon. This inventory process should identify the different types of clients using the current system and help to highlight which ones will require upgrades.

Client performance makes up a huge part of the user experience. Client performance is dependent on the performance of every link in the chain, from the end-user device right through to the disk spindles that store the mailbox data. Poor performance in any of these areas is likely to lead to a poor user experience, which is what you are trying to avoid in your design process by scaling your Exchange servers effectively and validating with Jetstress. But don't forget the end-user client machines and network performance. It is surprisingly common to see customers complain of poor Exchange performance only to find out that the cause is actually the network or something awry on the end-user device.

Above all, we hope that this chapter has helped you to view clients as a part of your Exchange design process and not just as an afterthought. Throughout the design process, remember that the user experience provided by your solution is primarily determined by the type and behavior of the client that they use.

Chapter 13

Planning Your Deployment

Deploying any version of Exchange for the first time can be a daunting task. Each version of Exchange has architectural considerations that are different from previous versions. Prerequisites may even change between service packs as well as best practices relating to both the deployment and operation of Exchange.

Understanding what makes Exchange 2013 different from other versions of Exchange is critical to rolling it out successfully.

We have emphasized the importance of trying and verifying processes in a controlled lab setting in this book. In this chapter, we wish to emphasize this point once again. Never deploy Exchange 2013 in your live infrastructure without first installing and understanding the subtleties of Exchange 2013 in your lab environment.

Exchange 2013 Information Resources

As in other parts of the book, we will refer in this chapter to external documentation, such as the Exchange 2013 installation checklist found at:

`http://technet.microsoft.com/en-us/library/ff805042.aspx`

Unless you're deploying a single Exchange 2013 server in your lab, you will find that there is more to consider than installing the prerequisites and running setup. The references to external documentation are quite necessary, because the requirements or practices for deploying Exchange vary from time to time. This chapter is not meant to replace the Exchange Server 2013 Deployment Assistant found at `http://technet.microsoft.com/exdeploy2013`. It is meant to augment the assistant with additional processes and best practices.

NOTE   We suggest that you become familiar with the architectural concepts introduced in Chapter 3, "Exchange Architectural Concepts," as a starting point to learn about the differences between Exchange versions.

Required Documentation

Very few deployments are as simple as deciding to install Exchange 2013, downloading the latest Cumulative Update (CU), and running setup. Even a single server hosting a few mailboxes requires a minimum amount of planning.

Irrespective of whether you have one or dozens of servers to install, your minimum pre-deployment checklist should be similar to the following:

- Design document signed off and accepted

- Hardware allocated (physical or virtual)

- Storage allocated

- Exchange 2013 prerequisites understood and met, including the mitigation of any deployment blockers

- The correct Exchange 2013 CU or service pack applicable as per the design document downloaded

- Third-party certificates obtained as per design document

- Coexistence prerequisites deployed (if required)

- Migration plan documented (if required)

- Permissions obtained required to install Exchange

Preparing Active Directory

The minimum Active Directory requirements to deploy Exchange 2013 are as follows:

- Windows 2003 SP2 or higher global catalog servers and domain controllers in each Active Directory site hosting Exchange 2013 servers

- Writable domain controllers in each Active Directory site hosting Exchange 2013 servers

- Windows Server 2003 domain functional level and forest functional level or higher

Planning for the changes that need to be made to Active Directory is essential. The setup process as well as the prerequisite service packs for earlier versions of Exchange may extend the Active Directory schema, which, depending on the size of your Active Directory, may impact replication. Active Directory replication must be completed before the first Exchange 2013 server can be introduced into the domain. Active Directory preparation occurs when installing the first Exchange 2013 server via any setup method. Nevertheless, a number of organizations prefer to introduce Active Directory changes by the team responsible for Active Directory, not the team responsible for Exchange.

Extending the Schema

As with earlier versions of Exchange, Active Directory schema extension may be done as part of installing the first Exchange server or as a separate step via the command line, specifically setup /PrepareSchema or setup /ps. The account used to run setup must be part of the Schema Admins group and the Enterprise Admins group. Setup must be run on a 64-bit machine that is in the same domain and the same Active Directory site as the schema master. For example, if the schema master is in the root domain of your forest, then you would run setup in the root domain.

Note that the schema extension process is included in the next step of preparing Active Directory, as well as in installing Exchange via the GUI.

Creating or Updating the Exchange Organization

This step updates and/or creates the required objects in the Active Directory configuration container, which stores most of Exchange 2013's configuration information.

Note that for the following command line, the parameters in square brackets are optional. If a previous version of Exchange exists in the forest, then the `OrganizationName` may be omitted. From a command line run

```
setup /PrepareAD [/OrganizationName:<organization name>]
```
or
```
setup /p [/on:<organization name>].
```

As with the schema extensions, these commands will require Active Directory replication to complete.

The account used to run setup must be part of the Enterprise Admins group. As with the previous step, setup must be run on a 64-bit machine that is in the same domain and the same Active Directory site as the schema master. The machine must be able to contact all domain controllers in the forest on port 389.

Preparing or Updating Active Directory Domains

This step updates domains for Exchange 2013 or, if necessary, it creates the required objects for Exchange 2013. You must prepare every domain into which Exchange 2013 will be installed. If this command is run in a child domain, then replication from the other two commands must finish or setup will fail.

NOTE   `setup /PrepareAD` prepares the local domain. That is, if `setup /PrepareAD` is run in the forest root domain, then this domain is prepared and does not require `setup /PrepareDomain` to be run within it.

From a command line, run `setup /PrepareDomain` or `setup /pd` to prepare the local domain in which you are running setup.

Run `setup /PrepareDomain:<FQDN>` where `<FQDN>` is the fully qualified domain name of a specific domain to be prepared.

Run `setup /PrepareAllDomains` or `setup /pad` to prepare all domains in the forest.

The account used to run setup must be part of the Enterprise Admins group to run `setup /PrepareAllDomains`. In order to run `setup /PrepareAD`, the account must be part of the Domain Admins group. As with the previous step, setup must be run on a 64-bit machine.

Designing a Rollout Process

At this point in the chapter, we assume that in order to become familiar with Exchange 2013, your first install will occur in a lab in the virtual environment of your choice. As we called out in Chapter 2, "Exchange Design Fundamentals," your virtual environment for both lab and production should be listed in the Server Virtualization Validation Program found at:

```
http://www.windowsservercatalog.com/svvp.aspx?svvppage=svvp.htm
```

In order to design a rollout process, you need to decide if your deployments will be interactive (that is, an administrator installing Exchange 2013 via the GUI or the command line), or if the process will be unattended and entirely scripted. In order to make this and other rollout decisions, you need to build and test your process in a lab that is representative of your live environment.

The ultimate purpose of the lab beyond becoming familiar with Exchange is to roll out Exchange 2013 for the first time as per the design. This allows administrators to familiarize themselves with the new product, as well as generate the operational documentation that may be required, such as build guides, administrative and helpdesk documentation, and so forth.

Once you have gained familiarity with Exchange 2013, you may then design a rollout process to suit the organization's needs. Such needs may vary along a spectrum from running the setup process on every machine manually, to building a scripted process that starts with a non-domain-joined machine, or to a fully configured Exchange 2013 server.

Installing into an Existing Organization

When deploying a newer version of Exchange into an existing organization, it is customary to redirect incoming client requests to Exchange servers with the newest version of Exchange. The newest version tends to be shipped with the logic for redirection and coexistence with previous versions of Exchange.

NOTE When you install Exchange 2013 for the first time, make sure that you install both the Mailbox server and Client Access server roles. These roles can be combined as a single Exchange server role. Otherwise, the Exchange 2013 Management Tools will be unable to connect.

When installing Exchange 2013 into an existing Exchange 2010 or Exchange 2007 organization, the following need to be considered:

◆ Both Exchange 2007 and Exchange 2010 require the activation of Outlook Anywhere on all Client Access servers, irrespective of whether they are Internet facing or not. Exchange 2013 will be unable to proxy and/or redirect client requests without Outlook Anywhere enabled on previous versions of Exchange. In the case of Outlook clients, their only access protocol is Outlook Anywhere.

◆ Exchange 2010 Edge servers must be upgraded to Exchange 2010 SP3, and the Edge subscription must be redone in order to support Exchange 2013, because Exchange 2013 did not ship with a version of the Edge Transport role specifically updated for Exchange 2013.

◆ Exchange 2010 does not require a legacy address space in order for Exchange 2013 to proxy down version requests, but Exchange 2007 does require a legacy address space.

A *legacy name space* is a combination of DNS records pointing to legacy Exchange 2007 Client Access Servers and the addition of the legacy name to the Subject Alternative Name (SAN) certificate. This establishes the lower version of Exchange as the legacy version. The updated certificate is then installed on all Exchange 2007 Client Access Servers, since all servers are required to have Outlook Anywhere enabled and all web URLs require updating to reflect the legacy name space.

SMTP Considerations for Existing Organizations

Exchange 2007, Exchange 2010, and Exchange 2013 are all capable of accepting email from the Internet and routing to the correct mailboxes; however, there is much to consider besides Internet-based mail flow when considering SMTP mail flow interaction for an organization.

MX records are DNS records that define the email delivery location for a given domain. MX records will need to be updated to point to the Exchange 2013 servers during the migration. Considering the complexity of the organization, this may occur at the 50 percent mark of user migration, or it may occur after all mailbox migrations have been completed.

Incoming Internet email is one of the considerations as is outgoing mail flow. Exchange 2013 servers may be added to existing send connectors, or they may have dedicated send connectors created, in order to route outgoing mail by version of Exchange. Send connectors may reflect external as well as internal SMTP name spaces for which Exchange may route email. You need to consider the mail flow via Exchange to these systems when planning for mail flow cutover.

The greatest point of complexity in the migration, however, is not Internet mail flow but rather interorganizational mail flow, which includes down-level versions of Exchange, journaling, other application integration such as SharePoint, and devices including multifunction devices that relay via the older version of Exchange.

Finding and documenting the various elements that send mail via Exchange can be a considerable and daunting task, unless updated configuration documentation exists. Consider enabling verbose logging on the receive connectors used to accept mail from devices for a period of time in order to assist with device discovery.

Many devices in the enterprise may need to have their configuration changed to reflect new destination IP addresses for the newer Exchange servers.

Certificate Considerations

Starting with Exchange 2007, Exchange administrators were required to be familiar with the process of creating SAN certificates or wildcard certificates. While the new Certificate Wizard in Exchange 2013 certainly makes certificate creation easier, the following considerations still apply:

◆ The number of certificates has a direct impact on the complexity of your Exchange 2013 deployment. Use as few certificates as possible. SAN certificates, which consolidate all name spaces onto a single certificate, are preferred over individual certificates.

◆ Wildcard certificates are supported and pose no higher security risk than SAN certificates.

◆ Split DNS, that is, the use of the same DNS host names for both external and internal usage, is still a recommended practice.

◆ Do not include server names in the certificate. Use load-balanced names for both internal and external access, even if a downstream site contains a single server.

Choosing a Load Balancer

Exchange 2013 provides more load-balancing choices than any previous version of Exchange. The fact remains, though, that some form of load balancing is required in order to ensure that traffic is distributed evenly among CAS servers in the local site.

Exchange 2013 CAS no longer requires affinity for client connections, which allows load balancing to occur at Layer 4 as opposed to Layer 7. At Layer 4, the load balancer is unaware of the application for which it is load balancing; it load balances toward a pool of IP addresses and a port, for example, TCP 443.

At Layer 7, the load balancer is aware of the application it is load balancing, and it is configured toward the target URL, for example, /owa, /ews, and so on.

At Layer 4, load balancers are able to direct significantly more traffic than at Layer 7, since the processing overhead is vastly reduced. Application health, however, is very difficult to track. A Layer 7 device may be able to inject a synthetic transaction toward OWA and adjust its load-balancing profile based on the response. Typically, at Layer 4, a load balancer can track whether TCP port 443 is responding.

At Layer 4, you are faced with choices not available to you in previous versions of Exchange, specifically using DNS round robin as a load-balancing mechanism. *DNS round robin* returns a list of IP addresses to the requesting client. The client is then able to try each address in turn for a response. A modern HTTP-based client has fault tolerance and retry behavior built into it that allows you to add DNS round robin as a valid choice to your list of potential load balancers. While DNS round robin is a supported choice, it should not be considered except for very small or lab deployments, since it is not service aware. It will continue to balance requests to CAS servers that are down or out of service.

A simple Layer 4 load balancer will distribute incoming requests among all available servers, with respect to the availability of TCP port 443. DNS round robin distributes requests to all CAS servers defined in DNS, irrespective of their status. Together with DNS round robin, a device at this layer offers a single, unified name space with speed and simplicity.

Moving up the functionality scale, load balancers offer per-protocol availability (OWA, EWS, SMTP, and so forth) as well as the ability to define one name space (OWA, ActiveSync, EWS, SMTP) per protocol.

At the top of the scale, load balancers are able to offer all of the previously mentioned features as well as SSL bridging and a single, unified name space. Exchange 2013 no longer supports SSL offloading at the load balancer. Exchange 2013 supports SSL bridging, where the connection is terminated at the load balancer and then re-encrypted toward the Exchange 2013 CAS server.

The downside is that, at this level, considerable networking skills are required in order to configure and maintain the load balancer.

Making the Choice

Choosing a load balancer for Exchange 2013 depends entirely on the level of service required by the business. Most organizations will benefit from some level of load balancing, one level up from DNS round robin. While DNS round robin is a viable alternative for very small or lab implementations, it does not offer the level of service required to meet a stringent SLA.

Since Exchange 2013 offers Managed Availability, which tracks which CAS servers are able to answer requests and redirects them to the healthiest node, Layer 4 devices with the ability to check on the health of a CAS server based on protocols such as OWA will normally meet most availability requirements.

At the top end of the scale, SSL offloading and other high-end features are not in as much demand as in previous versions, since modern Exchange servers tend to be less processor bound.

Starting with the availability requirement for each site, you must weigh the risks against the costs and benefits of each load-balancing choice level. Some sites may deploy DNS round robin, whereas larger datacenters may benefit from medium-level Layer 4 devices or even high-level Layer 7 devices.

Although there is no one-size-fits-all answer for this choice, a number of vendors have certified devices for use with Exchange 2013 with a range of virtual and physical devices from which you may choose.

Deploying Operating System-Based Antivirus Programs

Operating system-based antivirus programs will not protect against email-based worms or Trojans. However, they do offer a greater level of protection of the host itself. Very few environments are secure enough to run without any operating system-based antivirus software. In our opinion, operating system-based antivirus software must be configured correctly, or an outage or data loss will inevitably occur. The few customers who are unable to set and maintain the correct exclusions for Exchange 2013 in their environments should not be using antivirus protection because of the risk presented to Exchange and Exchange-based data.

Operating system-based antivirus software intercepts and inspects file-level activity, among other things, such as preventing communication via network ports, which is deemed unsafe. An incorrectly configured operating system-based antivirus product may break Exchange and/or cause data loss by deleting or quarantining an Exchange log file before it has been written to a local database or shipped to a remote database in the case of a database availability group (DAG). In some cases, antivirus products have been known to edit an Exchange database directly in order to remove what was considered to be a virus, thereby rendering the Exchange database unusable and causing an outage.

In our experience, operating system-based antivirus products have occasionally interfered with Exchange, even when explicit exclusions have been set. Therefore, you should approach this setup with caution. This does not mean, however, that we are recommending that operating system-based antivirus programs should not be deployed. We are recommending that they should be deployed strictly in accordance with the guidelines set out in the TechNet article "Anti-Virus Software in the Operating System on Exchange Servers," which specifies the recommended directory exclusions, process exclusions, and filename extension exclusions:

```
http://technet.microsoft.com/en-us/library/bb332342(v=exchg.150).aspx
```

While troubleshooting an issue with Exchange such that it is unable to execute a particular task that it should be able to perform, you may want to uninstall the operating system-based antivirus product completely and reboot the Exchange server in order to ascertain if the issue is removed or resolved.

Firewalls and Exchange

Per the guidance provided for previous versions, Exchange 2013 should not be firewalled or segmented away from other Exchange servers or any Active Directory domain controllers to which it may need to connect. Because of the distributed nature of Active Directory, this includes Active Directory domain controllers in other Active Directory sites. Some customers insist on placing firewalls between Exchange servers; however, these need to be configured with a rule allowing "ANY/ANY" port and protocol communication between Exchange 2013 servers and any Active Directory domain controller in the forest.

While significant documentation exists for those ports and protocols that Exchange 2013 and earlier versions use, this documentation should not be confused with a guide for configuring firewalls that could separate Exchange servers from each other.

Exchange client subnets, however, may be firewalled from Exchange servers. The port and protocol segmentation required for load balancing effectively supplies a rule of thumb for firewalling Exchange clients from Exchange servers. Depending on your client configuration, the list of allowable protocols between Exchange clients and servers includes the following:

HTTPS Exchange web services, Outlook Address Book downloads, Outlook Anywhere, Active Sync, and so on

SIP Unified Communications

SMTP Email submission via SMTP clients

POP Email retrieval

IMAP Email retrieval

Publishing Exchange to the Internet

Pre-authenticating gained popularity with products such as Microsoft Forefront Threat Management Gateway (TMG) and Microsoft Unified Access Gateway (UAG). However, with the announcement by Microsoft that no further development will take place on Forefront Threat Management Gateway and that the product would no longer be available for purchase as of December 2012, many Exchange customers were left wondering what they should do. For customers with existing TMG installations, updated guidance is available that demonstrates how to publish Exchange 2013 securely. Publishing Exchange 2013 via TMG is fully supported and greatly extends the usable lifespan of TMG, up to the end of the support life cycle. Customers who have deployed UAG can publish Exchange 2013 as of UAG Service Pack 3. Several firewall vendors offer reverse-proxy functionality, allowing Exchange 2013 and other services to be published securely to the Internet.

A number of load-balancing vendors now offer pre-authentication as part of their suite of products for load balancing Exchange. While this method of publishing Exchange is popular, it is not required in order to publish Exchange 2013 securely to the Internet.

Microsoft supports publishing client ports via a load balancer directly to the Internet without any intermediary authentication of client traffic, as evidenced by the Microsoft on-premises deployment of Exchange as well as Exchange Online.

Preparing Clients

The largest change for email clients in Exchange 2013 is the use of Outlook Anywhere as the only method of connectivity for Outlook clients. Outlook 2007, Outlook 2010, and Outlook 2013 are supported email clients, but Outlook 2007 and 2010 require updates before Exchange 2013 can be introduced. Outlook versions prior to Outlook 2007 are not supported.

Apple-based clients are required to upgrade to an email client with support for Exchange web services, such as Entourage 2008 Web Services Edition or Outlook for Mac 2011. Apple-based email clients that require DAV, such as Entourage 2008 and Entourage 2004, are no longer supported.

In summary, the following is the list of supported clients for Exchange 2013 with required patches:

- Outlook 2013

- Outlook 2010 SP1 with April 2012 Cumulative Update (or later)

- Outlook 2007 SP3 with July 2012 Cumulative Update (or later)

- Entourage 2008 for Mac, Web Services Edition

- Outlook for Mac 2011

- Clients that use the ActiveSync protocol

Preproduction Load Testing

The Exchange Load Generator (LoadGen) and Microsoft Jetstress are tools designed to stress test Exchange 2013 as valid for deployment.

In Chapter 5, "Designing a Successful Exchange Storage Solution," we described how Jetstress validates the storage deployed with Exchange as fit or unfit for production.

LoadGen creates load on a preproduction Exchange system by simulating different types of users. Email is sent and received to generate a user-defined load pattern, the result of which is then interpreted in order to validate that a deployment matches the sizing stipulated in the Exchange design as well as that the Exchange deployment is fit for production. Note that LoadGen is not supported to run in production.

Both LoadGen and Jetstress are useful in your pre-deployment testing, but only Jetstress should be considered mandatory before commissioning Exchange.

User Acceptance Testing

Before Exchange is considered "live," a number of tests are normally conducted. These include mail-flow testing, database-failover testing, and Exchange server failover testing in the case of high-availability deployments. Nevertheless, the final and arguably most important test mechanism is pilot users. A small group of pilot users is selected in order to validate the desired functionality of the Exchange 2013 implementation. These users' mailboxes are first moved to the system, and they are required to use the email system as they would under normal circumstances. This type of testing is generally referred to as *user acceptance testing*, and it is common practice when adopting a new system.

If no modifications to Exchange are required, this pool of users is widened to a larger and larger audience until the "all clear" is given to migrate the remainder of the user population.

These steps help validate and correct any flaws in the design and/or implementation of Exchange.

Summary

Deploying Exchange for the first time, or for the nth time, requires a certain amount of rigor and process to be applied. Correct interpretation of the design and subsequent planning are part of the process. While implementing and while still in preproduction, design validation using Jetstress is an essential step. Besides testing Exchange functionality, consider adding user acceptance testing as part of your acceptance procedures for signing off the Exchange implementation.

Chapter 14

Migrating to Exchange 2013

Exchange migrations are just like any other type of solution deployment: They require practical planning to ensure success. This chapter outlines some of the more important aspects for migration planning and some common problems that you may experience in the field.

According to Gartner, around 20 percent of small IT projects fail. This number increases to 28 percent for large ($1 million+) IT projects. One of the benefits of working for a large consulting organization is that we get to see both good and bad examples of migration projects. We will discuss these observations in order to help you learn from our experiences.

Before delving into migration design, it is worth spending a bit of time discussing the different types of Exchange migrations and the terminology involved in each.

Inter-Org Migrations

An *inter-org migration* refers to migrations between different Exchange organizations. By definition, an Exchange organization is also a single Active Directory forest, and so frequently the terms *cross-forest* migration and *inter-org migration* are used interchangeably.

Inter-org migrations are often the cause of most problems for migration teams. The primary reason for this is that the very nature of an inter-org migration involves a second Active Directory forest and a second Exchange organization. Having multiple directories and Exchange organizations often means that there will be a requirement for cross-organization collaboration; that is, users in one organization sharing information with users in another organization. This scenario brings with it complexity, and we all know that complexity is something we can usually do without.

The following items are very likely to impact an inter-org migration:

Outlook Client Reconfiguration

Outlook client reconfiguration is always a requirement when you migrate a mailbox. If the mailbox remains within the same Exchange organization, however, then Outlook will receive an *ecWrongServer* response back from the original Exchange Server, which will prompt Outlook to determine the new location of the mailbox. This process happens automatically, and the end-user experience is best described as seamless.

If the mailbox move is to a new Exchange organization, then the redirection process is more complex. There are generally two approaches to this. The first (and best) approach is to configure autodiscover to return the correct RPC client access endpoint in the new Exchange organization. The second approach is to use Outlook profile files (PRF) to force the client to update. The PRF method requires that a script or some other mechanism act on the client machine. The script detects when the user's mailbox has been migrated and then imports a preconfigured PRF file with a valid destination in the target Exchange organization. Outlook will then connect and determine its actual server connection endpoint. Even though we have reconfigured our Outlook client, we now have another potential problem: How is the client going to authenticate to the new mailbox? Our source user logon account had rights over the old mailbox, but it doesn't necessarily have rights over the new, migrated mailbox. The migration process in an inter-org migration must ensure that the account that the user is going use to log on with post-migration still has the access rights to log on to the mailbox.

Availability Data Sharing

Availability data sharing is somewhat taken for granted in most organizations. The ability to see whether someone is free or busy when trying to arrange a meeting, for example, is a critical service for many business users. Historically, system public folders provided this service, but since Exchange Server 2007 and Outlook 2007, availability data is provided by *Exchange Web Services (EWS)* instead. The *Availability service (AS)* will proxy availability requests between the two forests and send back the data to the calling client. This assumes, however, that the client access servers have been configured correctly in each Exchange organization and that all dependencies are in place, including certificates, network connectivity, name resolution, and Global Address List Synchronization. The bottom line is that it is possible to provide a pretty seamless cross-organization availability experience, but that solution brings additional complexity.

Global Address List Synchronization

The Global Address List (GAL) is a directory of all mail-enabled objects within the organization. It allows end users to pick from a directory rather than having to remember individual email addresses. The problem arises when you have multiple Exchange organizations that want to have a common shared *global address list (GAL)*. This requires a process for synchronizing entries within the GAL across the forests while maintaining all required attributes. Microsoft's *Forefront Identity Manager 2010 (FIM2010)* has a GALSync component *management agent (MA)* that provides this functionality. However, this is another added level of complexity that requires designing, testing, and deploying prior to any migration work taking place.

The freely available GALSync MA in FIM2010 has some limitations, but most notably it will only create a mail-contact object in its default configuration. A mail-contact object type is perfectly acceptable for maintaining a common GAL across multiple Exchange organizations, but it is limited in a migration scenario due to it not being possible to log on to a mail-contact object. Typically, it is more useful to customize FIM to generate a mail-enabled user instead. Handily, the Exchange product group has provided some sample code that does exactly this, and it is available for download at the following URL:

```
http://technet.microsoft.com/en-us/library/ee861124(v=exchg.141).aspx
```

Public Folder Data Synchronization

Public folder data synchronization is also often a migration requirement. Organizations have used public folders for many years, and they maintain a mix of high-priority workflow data and unstructured data stored across their public folder databases. The biggest problem with inter-org migration of public folder data is that the free *Inter-Organization Replication (IORepl) tool* is limited in functionality and receives limited support from Microsoft. It was updated to support Exchange 2010, but there are no indications currently that it will be updated for Exchange Server 2013. It does a fairly good job of synchronizing folder data between Exchange organizations. There are issues with folder permissions, however, and many organizations have problems with performance. Also, since this tool is not currently supported in Exchange Server 2013, it will require Exchange Server 2010 with a legacy public folder database in the target forest to make it work. In addition, the other end must be Exchange Server 2003.

There are rumors that Microsoft will eventually provide a solution for legacy public folder migration directly to Exchange Server 2013; however, there are no defined timelines available nor is it clear if any solution would include Exchange Server 2003.

If this all sounds like too much complexity, then you have two options: Either move the public folder data to another service (SharePoint, for example, or Exchange 2013 site mailboxes) or look for third-party public folder migration tools. Obviously, none of these routes are very appealing, which is why most migration teams groan whenever public folders are mentioned. By far best approach for inter-org public folder data migration is to avoid it entirely. Try to classify your public folder data as "old and unused," "move to alternative technology," or "stuck in public folders." Ideally, you are looking to remove or relocate everything prior to the main migration. If you have to deal with inter-org public folder data migration, test it thoroughly in a lab beforehand and validate the deployment in a production environment before migrating any mailboxes. Also, make sure that you have a way to monitor the success of ongoing public folder data replication, because IORepl has a tendency to stop working of its own accord. Public folder migration is discussed in more detail later in this chapter.

NOTE   Quest has announced that v9.x of its Migration Manager product will provide support for legacy to modern public folders in Exchange 2013.

Mail Flow

Maintaining mail delivery during an inter-org migration is not always a simple task. The most common problem that you need to solve is that both Exchange organizations will be sharing the same primary SMTP name space, for example, exchange-d3.com. When you move a mailbox from one organization to the other, you need to ensure that mail delivery is maintained both prior, during, and after the mailbox move. To achieve this, there are several dependencies:

- ♦ All SMTP addresses must be migrated from the source to the target mailbox.

- ♦ The legacyExchangeDN attribute from the source mailbox must be added as an X500 proxy address on the target mailbox.

- ♦ Each Exchange organization must have a unique mail routing domain.

WHAT IS LEGACYEXCHANGEDN?

LegacyExchangeDN is an Active Directory attribute that has been around since Exchange 2000. Its original purpose was to store the Exchange 5.5 obj-dist-name attribute after migrations from Exchange 5.5 to Exchange 2000. Even in a native Exchange 2013 deployment, the legacyExchangeDN attribute is still populated. This may seem unnecessary, but both the Exchange mail routing categorizer, which is responsible for delivering mail, and Outlook use the legacyExchangeDN attribute.

When you send an email to someone within your organization using Outlook, it stores the recipients by their legacyExchangeDN. This makes the job of the Exchange routing categorizer easier since it can perform a lookup of the recipient directly and thus speeds up the routing process.

Outlook also uses the legacyExchangeDN within its local nickname cache. The impact of this is that the legacyExchangeDN attribute becomes a vital part of email delivery within all Exchange environments. Whenever a mail-enabled object must have its legacyExchangeDN attribute changed—for example, if it is migrated to another Exchange organization—it is vital that its original legacyExchangeDN attribute be maintained by storing it as an X500 proxy address in the Active Directory proxyAddresses attribute. If the legacyExchangeDN attribute is not retained, people who try to reply to previously received emails from the user will receive a non-delivery report (NDR) stating that the mailbox cannot be found.

SMTP addresses on a mailbox are used for mail delivery, and thus it is vital to maintain any valid addresses on the mailbox during its migration. The legacyExchangeDN is also used for mail delivery. Adding the legacyExchangeDN attribute as an X500 proxy address post-migration helps to prevent delivery failures. For example, someone hitting Reply to an email rather than picking an address from the global address list or typing in the SMTP address manually causes Outlook to attempt to deliver the email based on its previously cached information for that user, the legacyExchangeDN. If a mailbox is migrated without the legacyExchangeDN in its X500 proxy address list and someone replies to a previously received email, then Exchange will not be able to identify the correct target mailbox for delivery, and delivery will fail. Luckily, a PowerShell script that ships with Exchange Server 2013 called Prepare-MoveRequest.ps1 handles this. This script is so important for inter-org migrations that we will cover it later in this chapter.

Mailbox Permissions

Mailbox permissions refers to any permissions that govern access over the mailbox itself, such as full mailbox rights, send-as, receive-as, and any of the folder-level delegate permissions. Historically, it has been difficult to migrate these permissions between Exchange organizations using native Exchange tools. With Exchange Server 2010 and later, it is possible to migrate all of the mailbox permissions and delegate access rights as long as the target environment is correctly prepared using the Prepare-MoveRequest.ps1 script. This script ensures that all of the necessary attributes are copied from the source object to the target object to enable Exchange to remap the permissions once the mailbox migration is performed.

Mobile Device Reconfiguration

Mobile device reconfiguration is one of the trickier aspects of an inter-org migration. Fundamentally, there is no easy solution for all mobile devices, and each mobile platform will need to be addressed in its own way. Research in Motion has the Enterprise Transporter that can move BlackBerry devices between domains relatively seamlessly. Good For Enterprise (GFE) has no known way of doing so without the end user erasing and re-creating the device relationship. ActiveSync devices, such as Android, Apple iOS, and Windows Phone, can all use autodiscover. Not all mobile devices, however, will follow autodiscover redirection requests to the new target forest, and some will need to be reconfigured manually.

The bottom line is that migrating mobile devices between forests is difficult. It will require a significant amount of time to discuss the issues involved with your mobile device vendors and to test the proposed solutions in your lab environment. Since we cannot provide an easy solution here, our best advice is not to skimp on mobile device migration testing, because the impact on mobile device email service is one of the most common problems of a migration. Implementing mobile device infrastructure in a migration test lab can be complex and costly, but the time spent getting this aspect of your migration right will more than pay itself back in the long run.

External URL Publishing

External URL publishing, or publishing an Exchange organization, can be a tricky subject even when you only need to consider a single Exchange organization. It becomes much more so during an inter-org migration when you need to account for multiple organizations. The problem in this case is that Exchange is not aware of the correct URLs to provide to users who have been migrated. For example, User1 is trying to access OWA, which is published on the external URL `https://mail.exchange-d3.com/owa` that proxies HTTPS requests back to `server1`
`.forest1.com`. After the migration, however, forest1 no longer has a mailbox for User1, and so when the user tries to access OWA, an error message is received. The most common approach for resolving this issue is to notify users about a new URL to access OWA post-migration, such as `https://owa.exchange-d3.com/owa`. This information can be delivered via an email message after the mailbox is successfully moved. This approach is relatively trivial from a design perspective, and it lessens user frustration through a simple and effective communication.

Exchange Application Integration

Exchange application integration is a minefield of a topic in its own right. During an inter-org migration, this is one area that cannot be rushed, and it often remains an ongoing issue long after the majority of mailboxes have been migrated to the new platform. The reason that application integration is so difficult is that there are a number of ways that an application or service can integrate with Exchange: SMTP, MAPI client and Collaboration Data Objects (CDO), WebDAV, IMAP/POP, or Exchange Web Services. Some applications will have gone through a formal project-delivery process, and thus they will be a known quantity. Others, however, may not have gone through such a process and may have taken advantage of the Exchange 2003 open SMTP relay to send messages, or they may be using normal user mailboxes via CDO, and so forth.

The first problem is discovering each and every application that is relying on the messaging system, understanding how it connects, and taking into account how it will be affected by the migration. Some may be easy to migrate, while others may require a total application upgrade. The key to making this part of the inter-org migration successful is good communication with the business units, analyzing server logs (SMTP and IIS), using Microsoft Exchange Server User Monitor (ExMon), and creating a register of each service—who owns it, how it connects to Exchange, if it uses a mailbox, and what is required to migrate the service to the new platform.

Be warned, however, this is a tedious and time-consuming task, which if not done properly can turn an otherwise excellent migration into a disaster. We have all worked migrations where this process alone has caused an Exchange migration project to be viewed as a failure.

Offline Address Book

Outlook clients in cached mode use an *offline address book (OAB)* to allow offline access to the global address list. Once Outlook has downloaded an OAB, it will use that by default to query the Exchange infrastructure directly for directory information. This is a great efficiency, and it provides a better user experience while reducing the server workload. It is a problem, however, when you migrate mailboxes between Exchange organizations. Although the global address list looks similar from an end-user perspective in two Exchange organizations that have GALSync configured, the actual attribute data for message delivery is quite different. This means that a migrated user will be performing directory lookups against the wrong GAL post-migration. For this reason, it is necessary to delete the OAB files from Outlook after the mailbox has been migrated. Typically, you delete the OAB file in the same client-side script that imports the PRF file, as noted previously. The downside is that after every user mailbox is migrated, a full OAB download will be required. Depending on the size of the OAB file, you may need to take this additional network traffic into account when you are planning your migration schedule.

Distribution Groups

Distribution lists (DL), or *distribution groups (DG)*, are used heavily in most organizations. Essentially, a distribution group is a way to send a single email to a group of individuals. The problem with DG migration is that it must result in a delivery to the same users, even halfway through a migration. If you think about this for a minute, this means that you either need to update the DG membership constantly as each mailbox is migrated, or you need to leave all of the DGs in the source environment until the end of the migration, when they can be migrated in one step. There are third-party software tools that can help. The most common approach is to create empty DLs in the target environments and then place a single hidden contact within the DL that has the target address of the source DL. This has the effect of correctly displaying the DL in the global address list, but it defers expansion and delivery back to the source environment where the membership is correct. As each mailbox is migrated, the moving process will leave behind a mail-enabled user in the source environment who is a member of the same groups as before the migration. Once all of the mailboxes have been migrated, the DGs can then be migrated and the membership can be updated in the target organization. Although there are various ways of achieving this, most migration teams tend to use PowerShell or the Active Directory Migration Tool (ADMT) for this task. It is important to note here that ADMT does not migrate Exchange attributes, such as `proxyAddresses`, so there is also some post-migration processing work that may be required if this route is taken. The trick to getting this right is the same as always: Test thoroughly in your migration test environment before migrating any distribution lists.

Intra-Org Migrations

In an *intra-org migration* the migration takes place within the same Exchange organization. In other words, multiple Exchange Server versions coexist within the same Active Directory.

This is by far the most straightforward of Exchange migrations because it involves many fewer complexities than an inter-org migration.

With Exchange version coexistence in mind, it must be noted that Exchange Server 2013 cannot coexist in the same Active Directory forest with Exchange Server 2003 or earlier versions. We will cover options for migrating from unsupported legacy environments later in this chapter, but for now it's worth noting that you cannot simply install Exchange 2013 next to Exchange 2003 and move the mailboxes over.

Regarding Exchange 2007 and Exchange 2010 coexisting with Exchange Server 2013, during an intra-org migration you essentially install Exchange 2013 into the existing environment and then move the mailbox from one Exchange Server to another, though running different versions of Exchange. This happens all the time in most Exchange organizations, and it is a well-understood process.

The potential problem areas we identified for inter-org migration remain considerations with an intra-org migration as well. They are far less likely, however, to cause problems since the majority work well once you have deployed Exchange 2013 in coexistence with an older version.

Outlook Client Reconfiguration

Outlook client reconfiguration is provided via the MAPI protocol. Autodiscover is provided natively within an Exchange organization.

Availability Data Sharing

Availability data sharing again occurs natively when you have multiple versions of Exchange installed in the same organization. Some planning is required to ensure that autodiscover and the Availability services are properly configured, but from a migration perspective, end users should not notice any significant impact as their mailboxes are migrated from one version of Exchange to another.

Global Address List Synchronization

The global address list remains the same before and after migration. However, it may now be supplied from a different server.

Public Folder Data Synchronization

Public folder data synchronization becomes public folder migration and becomes slightly less problematic. However, with Exchange 2013 and modern public folders, things become more interesting. Exchange 2013 introduces a totally new implementation of public folders, and although they look the same to the end user, they actually function completely differently from an administrative perspective. We will discuss this further later in this chapter.

Mail Flow and Mailbox Permissions

Mail flow and mailbox permissions "just work" when migrating between Exchange Servers in the same organization. Assuming that the Exchange 2013 infrastructure has been deployed correctly, the mailbox migration will maintain all previous email addresses and permissions throughout the move. Additionally, since the legacyExchangeDN of the mailbox remains the same, there is no need to modify any proxy addresses during the migration.

Mobile Device Reconfiguration

Again, mobile devices vary in their behavior. However, the majority of mobile devices support mailbox moves within the same Exchange organization with little or no impact on the end user. BlackBerry and Good for Enterprise require a specific minimum version to support Exchange Server 2013. At the time of this writing, BlackBerry requires BES 5.0 SP4, and Good for Enterprise has not yet provided a definite release date, but they have confirmed that they are developing support for Exchange 2013. ActiveSync devices such as those from Apple, Google, Microsoft, and others all support mailbox moves natively within the same organization.

External URL Publishing

External publishing needs to be moved over to the newest version of Exchange within the organization prior to a migration being initiated. But once the infrastructure has been correctly configured, an end user can connect to the same URLs initially and rely on Exchange to connect them to the correct server after authentication.

Exchange Application Integration

Application integration remains largely as tedious and manual a process as it does with an inter-org migration. As Exchange has evolved, the methods and APIs used for application integration have changed. The older the application, the more likely it is that problems will be present after migration to Exchange Server 2013. The key to mitigating these is the same as with inter-org migration: good communication with the business units, analyzing server logs (SMTP and IIS), using Microsoft Exchange Server User Monitor (ExMon), and creating a register of each service—who owns it, how it connects to Exchange, if it uses a mailbox, and what is required to migrate the service to the new platform.

Offline Address Book

The offline address book (OAB) is likely to change publishing location, and the server that generates it will change after Exchange 2013 has been installed. Nothing specific, however, is required post-mailbox migration. Outlook will take care of updating the OAB file via its normal incremental update mechanism, and no additional action is required.

Distribution Groups

Normal distribution groups (DG) do not have to be migrated during an intra-org migration. Dynamic distribution groups, however, may need to have their LDAP search filters upgraded to OPATH filters. The change from LDAP to OPATH was introduced with Exchange 2007, because of PowerShell's use of OPATH filtering. This means that, for an Exchange 2013 migration, it is very likely that this has already been done. Nevertheless, in case it hasn't, it is worth verifying this after the installation of Exchange Server 2013.

Moving Mailboxes

Moving mailboxes and data is probably the most critical part of any migration. Any mistakes made here will almost certainly result in a meeting where you are asked to explain your actions, which everyone would prefer to avoid.

We have witnessed some painfully difficult scenarios over the years where mailbox data migrations went wrong. For example, take the scenario where a Lotus Domino migration to

Exchange 2007 mixed up the source and the target mailbox data. The result was that some users logged on the morning after the migration only to be presented with someone else's mailbox and calendar data.

Another scenario occurred when a migration team decided to migrate only the last 30 days' worth of email and no calendar data but hadn't informed the business of this. While the IT team viewed this as a successful migration since it met all of *their* requirements, the business units held a somewhat different viewpoint. The bottom line is that end users are rightfully very protective of their data, and there will be quite an uproar if any of it goes missing, whether intentionally or not.

Mailbox Replication Service

For Exchange-to-Exchange migrations, moving mailbox data is handled by the *Mailbox Replication Service (MRS)*. The MRS was introduced in Exchange Server 2010, and it brought with it some extremely useful benefits over the legacy approach for moving mailboxes:

◆ Mailbox moves are now asynchronous, and they are performed by the MRS.

◆ Mailboxes can be kept online during the move process.

◆ The items in a mailbox's Recoverable Items folder are moved with the mailbox if the source mailbox is on Exchange Server 2010.

◆ As soon as the mailbox move begins, content indexing starts to scan the mailbox so that fast searching is available on completion of the move.

◆ You can configure throttling for each MRS instance, each mailbox database, or each mailbox server.

◆ Remote mailbox moves work over the Internet by way of the Microsoft Exchange Mailbox Replication Proxy (MRSProxy) service.

◆ MRSProxy helps to simplify migration over firewalls because of fewer ports being required.

◆ Mailbox moves can be managed from any Exchange 2013 Server within the organization.

◆ Mailbox content doesn't move through an administrative computer.

◆ The mailbox's move history is maintained in the mailbox.

Exchange Server 2013 incorporates MRS from Exchange Server 2010 and adds the following improvements:

◆ The ability to move multiple mailboxes in large batches.

◆ Email notification during a move with reporting.

◆ Automatic retry and automatic prioritization of moves.

◆ Primary and personal archive mailboxes can be moved together or separately.

◆ An option for manual move request finalization that allows you to review your move before you complete it.

◆ Periodic incremental syncs to update migration changes.

◆ Migration endpoints for cross-forest or remote moves.

At its heart, the MRS is a mailbox move-queuing service. It takes requests to move a mailbox from a source to its destination and then processes each request on the administrator's behalf.

One of the most important things to remember is that the mailbox data is not routed via the administrator's management console, as it was in Exchange 2007 and prior. The actual mailbox data movement is controlled via an instance of the Exchange 2013 Mailbox role in the target AD site. This means that you can generate a move request for a mailbox between two databases in Hong Kong from a PowerShell session in London, and the migration data will remain within Hong Kong.

Here is a link to a great post on the Exchange Team Blog that talks in some detail about how MRS in Exchange Server 2010 works:

http://blogs.technet.com/b/exchange/archive/2010/07/19/3410438.aspx

Although Exchange Server 2013 has made improvements, the fundamental mechanics of moving a mailbox via MRS remain the same. This article is highly recommended in order to obtain a working understanding of MRS prior to beginning your migration planning.

Preparing for Inter-Org Mailbox Moves

We have already discussed inter-org migration considerations. This section is intended to take a look at what you need to do to prepare your target user objects to get them ready for migration. Before MRS can move a mailbox into another forest, there must be a mail-enabled target object in the target forest with matching attributes. A list of mandatory attributes is provided in Table 14.1.

TABLE 14.1:   Mandatory attributes for a cross-forest move

MAIL USER'S ACTIVE DIRECTORY ATTRIBUTES	ACTION
displayName	Copy the corresponding attribute of the source mailbox or generate a new value.
Mail	Directly copy the corresponding attribute of the source mailbox.
mailNickname	Copy the corresponding attribute of the source mailbox or generate a new value.
msExchArchiveGUID and msExchArchiveName	Directly copy the corresponding attribute of the source mailbox. Attributes are available only if the source mailbox is Exchange 2010.
msExchMailboxGUID	Directly copy the corresponding attribute of the source mailbox.
msExchRecipientDisplayType	-2147483642 (decimal) //equivalent to 0x80000006 (hex).
msExchRecipientTypeDetails	128 (decimal) /0x80 (hex).
msExchUserCulture	Directly copy the corresponding attribute of the source mailbox.

(continues)

TABLE 14.1:   Mandatory attributes for a cross-forest move   (*CONTINUED*)

MAIL USER'S ACTIVE DIRECTORY ATTRIBUTES	ACTION
msExchVersion	44220983382016 (decimal).
cn	Copy the corresponding attribute of the source mailbox or generate a new value.
proxyAddresses	Copy the source mailbox's proxyAddresses attribute. Additionally, copy the source mailbox's legacyExchangeDN as an X500 address in the proxyAddresses attribute of the target mail user.
sAMAccountName	Copy the corresponding attribute of the source mailbox or generate a new value. Ensure that the value is unique within the target forest domain to which the target mail user belongs.
targetAddress	Set this to an SMTP address in the proxyAddresses attribute of the source mailbox. This SMTP address must belong to the authoritative domain of the source forest.
userAccountControl	Constant: 514 //equivalent to 0x202, ACCOUNTDISABLE | NORMAL_ACCOUNT.
userPrincipalName	Copy the corresponding attribute of the source mailbox or generate a new value. Because the mail user is logon disabled, this userPrincipalName isn't used.

Note: The proxy addresses of the source mailbox user must contain an SMTP address that matches the authoritative domain of the target forest. This allows the New-MoveRequest cmdlet to select the target address of the source mail-enabled user correctly (converted from the source mailbox user after the mailbox move request is complete) to ensure that mail routing is still functional.

These mandatory attributes can be managed in two ways. The first is via the Forefront Identity Manager 2010 (FIM 2010), which can be configured to synchronize between the source and the target environments in such a way as to support MRS mailbox moves. The necessary code and configuration information for this approach can be found here:

http://technet.microsoft.com/en-us/library/ee861124.aspx

If you do not have FIM 2010 available, then there is an alternative method that works just as well. The Exchange team provides a PowerShell script called prepare-moveequest.ps1. This script is installed as part of every Exchange Server 2013 installation in the C:\Program Files \Microsoft\Exchange Server\V15\Scripts folder. This script has been the cornerstone of many migration projects since it was introduced in Exchange Server 2010. The script is capable of creating and updating user objects in the target forest, and it ensures that they are ready for a cross-forest mailbox move with all of the mandatory attributes in place.

Use of this script is detailed here:

http://technet.microsoft.com/en-us/library/ee861103.aspx

Storage Capacity

Storage capacity within the target Exchange infrastructure is a predictable, though frequently overlooked, consideration during a migration. There are two areas to consider.

Mailbox Database Volume Size

Mailbox database Volume size is simply how large your mailbox databases will become when you migrate your mailboxes into them. Rather than attempting to plan for this specifically during the migration, it is better to plan your target environment adequately to accommodate all of your mailboxes at their maximum quota size during the design phase. It's easiest to use the Exchange Mailbox Server Role Requirements Calculator to help you with this since it provides the best approximation of the size required to store each mailbox in your environment. Your completed design should specify a limit on the number of mailboxes at the maximum quota size that can safely fit into each mailbox database. As you are planning your migration, you must ensure that no target mailbox database exceeds the design target. Additionally, it is recommended that you validate the predictions at around 25 percent migration complete in order to ensure that the database sizes agree with those predicted during the design phase. Do not be tempted to do this validation check too early since Exchange mailbox databases contain an amount of whitespace that may make things look worse than they are.

Transaction Log Volume Size

Transaction log Volume size has been a problem for Exchange migrations since the very beginning of Exchange. The main problem is that transaction logs record all changes made to the mailbox database, including the data that was added or modified. This is done so that, in the event of a mailbox database problem, the transaction logs can be used to replay changes from the last full backup and bring the database back to a consistently healthy state. This has always been a great feature of Exchange, and it has saved many an administrator's bacon when things have gone awry. It also means that if you move a 1 GB mailbox from the source environment to the target environment, you need to account for the space to hold both the mailbox data in the mailbox database and the transaction logs. So while transaction logs are indeed great, they are also something you need to watch carefully during a migration.

As a general rule of thumb, the size of transaction log data generated on the target database will be roughly equal to the size of the mailbox data being moved. We generally advise adding 10–20 percent headroom when calculating this to account for variations. You should also try to leave the log drives with a minimum of 25 percent free space after each daily migration batch. This may seem like an overly conservative approach. If you do run out of transaction log space, however, then the mailbox database will dismount, and you know what happens next. Thus, all things considered, it's better to migrate conservatively and work upward rather than begin with a tidal wave of mailbox migrations, only to begin day two of your migration in the IT director's office explaining why the new super-highly available Exchange solution was offline after only half a day in production. (Yes, this really happened to one of our more zealous customers.)

Having said all of this about storage capacity during a migration, make no mistake that failing to account for it adequately is a very easy trap we have all fallen into at some point in our careers. All it takes is a failed backup or someone accidentally scheduling in a few too many or too large mailboxes, and you too can run into this scenario. Our best guidance here is to define a plan of action to bring service back online quickly after a transaction log volume has filled up, and make sure that your support teams know what to do if it does occur. Monitoring and alerting can sometimes help here, but typically the rate of change during the migration is very fast, and so, by the time someone has been contacted because of a log volume running low on space, it is generally too late.

Content Indexing

Content indexing (CI) in Exchange has evolved greatly over the years. CI is the process by which the content of a mailbox is stored to improve its searchability. As mailbox sizes have grown over the years, so too has the difficulty in finding what you are looking for. Maintaining a content index allows you to search against mailbox contents based on keywords. Initially, it was very resource-intensive and it provided a fairly poor experience, so most customers chose not to enable it. Exchange 2007 brought with it a much better CI implementation, which was retained in Exchange Server 2010. This new implementation of CI was enabled by default since it was more efficient. However, the downside of having CI enabled permanently was a fairly dramatic increase in CPU utilization during mailbox migrations. With Exchange 2007 and Exchange 2010, a newly migrated mailbox is scheduled for indexing once it has been successfully migrated. This means that during a typical migration window, the migration processes are fighting with the CI processes for system resources. This can dramatically reduce migration throughput.

Exchange Server 2013 introduced a totally new CI mechanism based on the Microsoft FAST Search technology. Furthermore, mailbox migration data is now indexed as it is added rather than post-mailbox migration. The idea here is to ensure that the CI is as up to date as possible if the user logs on directly after a mailbox migration. Initial lab testing suggests that Exchange Server 2013 is throttling index generation during migrations, and disabling CI during your migration window may no longer have any significant benefit.

Modern Public Folder Data Migration

Public folders have been complicating Exchange migration projects since they were first introduced in 1996. Exchange 2013 brings some benefits as well as some problems in this area. These problems include the following:

◆ The Inter-Organization Replication (IORepl) tool is unsupported in Exchange Server 2013.

◆ Modern public folders are now stored in mailbox databases, and so the old replication mechanism is gone, replaced with continuous replication within a database availability group.

◆ The final process of modern public folder migration is a big-bang process, i.e., all public folders must be switched over from legacy to modern at the same time. This means that either legacy public folders or modern public folders are being accessed but never both. For example, you need to pick a time during the migration where all public folder content will be served from Exchange Server 2013.

If you remember back to the section on inter-org migrations, we mentioned that migrating public folder data between organizations relied on either the IORepl tool or a third-party solution. The free IORepl tool required one end of the connector to be Exchange 2003 and the other to be Exchange 2007 or Exchange Server 2010 SP1. Since this tool is no longer being updated, if you need to migrate public folder data cross-forest, you have the choices listed in Table 14.2 available to you. Migrating intra-org within the same forest requires yet a different process, which is unique to modern public folders. This process is discussed later in this section.

TABLE 14.2: Migrating public folders

SOURCE VERSION	MIGRATION TYPE	NATIVE TOOL STEPS
Exchange 2003	Inter-org (cross-forest)	◆ Ensure Exchange Server 2010 SP3 is present in Exchange 2013 environment and that Exchange 2013 has CU1 installed. ◆ Configure the public folder database and hierarchy on Exchange 2010 Server. ◆ Migrate all public folder data to Exchange 2010 Server. ◆ Complete mailbox migration to Exchange Server 2013 (via inter-org migration through Exchange 2010). ◆ Perform the same public folder migration as for the intra-org scenario in Exchange Server 2010.
Exchange 2007	Inter-org (cross-forest)	◆ Requires third-party toolset.
Exchange 2010	Inter-org (cross-forest)	◆ Requires third-party toolset.
Exchange 2003	Intra-org (same forest)	◆ Unsupported.
Exchange 2007	Intra-org (same forest)	◆ Migrate all mailboxes to Exchange 2013. ◆ Analyze the public folder hierarchy to determine the correct quantity of public folder mailboxes (`PublicFolderToMailbox MapGenerator.ps1`). ◆ Create Exchange 2013 public folder mailboxes in HoldForMigration mode, which is a special mode for modern public folders that hides them from end users until they are fully migrated and ready for use. ◆ Create the background public folder migration request. ◆ Finalize the migration request.
Exchange 2010	Intra-org (same forest)	◆ Migrate all mailboxes to Exchange 2013. ◆ Analyze the public folder hierarchy to determine the correct quantity of public folder mailboxes (`PublicFolderToMailbox MapGenerator.ps1`). ◆ Create Exchange 2013 public folder mailboxes in HoldForMigration mode. ◆ Create the background public folder migration request. ◆ Finalize the migration request*.

Once the migration request has been finalized, it cannot be reversed.

Interestingly, it is possible to migrate public folder data from Exchange 2003, Exchange 2007, and Exchange Server 2010 directly to a new Office 365 Exchange Online tenant that will provide 1 TB worth of modern public folder data storage space for every tenant. We discussed this in detail in Chapter 7, "Hybrid Configuration."

If you are performing an intra-org migration within the same forest, the change from legacy to modern public folders is significant. It will require some design investment to ensure good distribution and usage of public folder mailboxes.

Intra-Org Migration to Exchange Server 2013

The intra-org migration path from Exchange 2007 or Exchange 2010 is as follows:

1. Move all mailboxes from legacy to Exchange Server 2013.

   This step is required since once public folders have been migrated to Exchange Server 2013, they will not be viewable via legacy mailboxes.

2. Export public folder statistics (`Export Export-PublicFolderStatistics.ps1`).

   This script will create the folder name to folder size file, which is used in step 3 to determine how many modern public folder mailboxes will be required.

3. Generate the public folder to mailbox mapping file (`PublicFolderToMailboxMapGenerator.ps1`).

   This script reads the CSV file generated in step 2, and it attempts to distribute public folders evenly across public folder mailboxes.

3. Create public folder mailboxes in HoldForMigration mode.

   This step creates all public folder mailboxes in Exchange 2013 as defined within the CSV file export via `PublicFoldertoMailboxMapGenerator.ps1`. Each public folder mailbox must be created with `HoldForMigration:$true`.

4. Begin public folder migration (`new-publicfoldermigrationrequest`).

   This process begins the background data migration. Clients remain connected to legacy public folders during this stage. Progress can be viewed via the `Get-PublicFolderMigrationRequestStatistics` cmdlet.

5. Lock Exchange 2010 public folders that are ready for finalization.

   This process prevents access to public folders until the migration is finalized. This step logs all users off from public folder access, and they cannot reconnect until the migration is finalized.

6. Finalize public folder migration.

   This stage syncs any final changes from the source to the destination, and it brings the public folders back online.

This process is explained in more detail here:

`http://technet.microsoft.com/en-us/library/jj150486%28EXCHG.150%29.aspx`

In summary, if you need to migrate public folder data cross-forest from Exchange 2007 or 2010 to Exchange Server 2013, you are going to need to talk to a third-party vendor. Quest and

Binary Tree both have mature and established toolsets that can deal with this scenario. If you are migrating from Exchange 2003 to Exchange 2013, you can use IORepl, but an Exchange Server 2010 SP3 public folder database is required in your Exchange 2013 environment for this to work. Alternatively, you may talk to Quest or Binary Tree and avoid dealing with IORepl and Exchange 2010 in your Exchange 2013 environment.

If you are migrating public folder data intra-org within the same forest from Exchange 2007 or Exchange 2010 to Exchange Server 2013, you need to migrate all of your mailboxes first and then perform the modern public folder cutover migration process as detailed previously.

Foreign Systems

Migrations from non-Exchange systems represent fewer and fewer migration projects nowadays. Exchange Server has been an extremely successful product over the last decade, and the majority of our work these days is migrating Exchange to Exchange. This trend has led to a somewhat specialized community catering migrations to Exchange from non-Exchange platforms. These foreign systems are best classified as follows:

◆ Lotus Notes/Domino

◆ Novel GroupWise

◆ Other IMAP-based solutions

Let's discuss some of the options and challenges of migrating from each of these systems.

Lotus Notes

Lotus Notes has been around since 1989, and despite changing the server software name in 1996 to Domino 4.5, Powered by Notes, most IT teams still casually refer to it as Lotus Notes. Notes is an interesting service to migrate to Exchange. Although both Exchange and Notes provide an email service, Notes also provides a rich application and database-programming platform while Exchange does not. It is debatable, however, that for most organizations, Exchange provides a better platform for email and collaboration. Migration of email from Lotus Notes to Exchange is a relatively well-understood process, and although there are no longer freely available native migration tools, both Quest and Binary Tree offer specific migration tools for the migration process to Exchange Server 2013. Both toolsets deal with this process from end to end, including planning, scheduling, coexistence, and data migration. However, there are still some common issues when coexisting between Lotus Notes and Exchange:

Mail and Calendar Interoperability   Attachments in meeting requests frequently disappear, and recurring meetings may not be migrated correctly. Also, obtaining reliable availability data across the messaging platforms can be unpredictable.

Special Content   Both the Notes and Outlook clients can sometimes create content that the other cannot understand. This can vary from unusual rendering of HTML messages in the Notes client to Notes active content getting lost when viewed in Outlook.

Broken Links   The Notes client can include links to other Notes databases or documents. During the migration these links sometimes cannot be converted, and so they do not work post-migration.

End-User Experience   This is one issue not to be underestimated. End users who have been using the Lotus Notes client over the last 15 years will often take a significant amount of time to become accustomed to Outlook. Be sure to provide as much online training, tips and tricks, and so on for the user community pre- and post-migration.

Performance   Migrations from Lotus Notes to Exchange are often much slower than native Exchange-to-Exchange migrations due to the demands of converting the data. It is possible to migrate from Lotus Notes quickly, but it often requires a significant investment in migration infrastructure.

Outlook Deployment   Making sure that Outlook is deployed prior to migration from Lotus Notes is vital. Although this may be obvious, we have all seen cases where a user's mail file has been migrated successfully from Lotus Notes to Exchange, and the next morning when the end user logs on to their desktop, they learn that they do not have Outlook installed or it's the wrong version of the program, which of course diminishes the user experience. It is easy to assume that Outlook is part of Microsoft Office, but many organizations customize the deployment. Thus, you should verify not only that all machines have Outlook installed, but that it is the right version of Outlook for your needs. This means Outlook 2007 SP3 or greater for Exchange Server 2013.

Having taken care of the email portion of the migration, all that remains are the Lotus Notes applications. There are many vendors that claim to have a solution for this and that offer a tool that will analyze your Lotus Notes applications and determine the correct migration approach. They can even tell you which are used or unused.

This can be very useful and surely reduces some of the migration burden. However, application migration can take many years to complete, especially for heavily used and complex applications. Some can be migrated easily or deleted. What remains, however, is often very difficult to migrate. We advise that you decouple your Lotus Notes email migration project from your Lotus Notes application migration project. It is usually possible to migrate most Lotus Notes mailboxes without migrating a single Lotus Notes application. The end user will require access to both Outlook and the Lotus Notes client until all Lotus Notes applications have been migrated or replaced.

The bottom line for Lotus Notes migrations is that email is relatively easy to migrate, assuming that you plan correctly and use a robust migration toolset. Application migration, however, is usually very complex, and unless you have a trivial set of Lotus Notes applications, do not fall for the application migration toolset hype—it's usually a long and slow process to get rid of those Lotus Notes applications.

Novell GroupWise

Novell GroupWise has a similar migration and coexistence story to Lotus Notes, and the same pitfalls and warnings apply. Quest has the most comprehensive toolset available for GroupWise migrations.

Other IMAP

Many alterative mail systems exist. Most of these mail systems provide IMAP integration that can be used to migrate mailbox data. However, these systems often pose additional problems including the following:

◆ *Password sync between IMAP mail host and Exchange*—Once the mail has been migrated, you need to ensure that the end user knows how to access the new service, including knowing the right password. Some migration teams will set a known password on the new account, while others may try to synchronize the password from the source platform to the target if they can find a way to do so.

◆ *Directory synchronization*—If the source platform has a rich directory full of people's names, job functions, telephone numbers, and so on, it is highly beneficial to try to synchronize that over to Exchange. The format and attribute names, however, are almost certainly going to be different and will require manual mapping of fields and potentially some data cleaning to get a good result.

◆ *End-user client reconfiguration*—Once the mail content has been moved, you then need to reconfigure the email client to connect to the Exchange system rather than the legacy system. Most IMAP clients require manual reconfiguration.

Unfortunately, there is no simple solution for all of these systems since they vary widely. Some run on Windows servers and integrate with Active Directory, but most are Unix/Linux-based and have totally separate account and password information.

Back with Exchange Server 2007, Microsoft published the Microsoft Transporter Suite that would migrate from IMAP to Exchange Server 2007. This suite was dropped for Exchange Server 2010, however, and there is no expectation that Microsoft will provide anything similar for Exchange Server 2013. This means that you will need to engage with a third-party vendor to obtain migration tools for this scenario. At the time of this writing, the only tool we are comfortable recommending for this type of migration is Transend Migrator.

Legacy Exchange Migrations

This section covers migrations from older versions of Exchange Server with no direct migration path. In the case of Exchange Server 2013, this means Exchange 2003 or older. There are still many deployments of Exchange 2003 in the business world, and so there will be many migration project teams that need to deal with this problem.

Before we dig in to some solutions, let's confront the real problem: There is no way to migrate directly from Exchange Server 2003 to Exchange Server 2013. This includes inter- and intra-org migrations. If you attempt to install Exchange Server 2013 into an existing Exchange organization with any Exchange Server 2003 servers remaining, Exchange setup will block the installation. If you attempt a cross-forest mailbox move from Exchange Server 2003 to Exchange Server 2013, MRS will tell you that you are attempting to move a mailbox from an unsupported Exchange version. Clearly this is a problem if you are still in Exchange Server 2003, so let's review some of your options.

Version-to-Version Upgrade

This process is exactly as it sounds. You cannot migrate directly from Exchange Server 2003 to Exchange Server 2013, but you can migrate from Exchange Server 2003 to Exchange Server 2010 and then from Exchange Server 2010 to Exchange Server 2013. For most organizations, this is a particularly painful migration path. It is, however, the one that the Exchange product group recommends if you wish to migrate to Exchange 2013 from Exchange Server 2003.

The migration process is made more difficult by the requirement that you remove all traces of Exchange Server 2003 before installing the first Exchange Server 2013 infrastructure into the organization. On the plus side, once you have all of your mailboxes running in Exchange Server 2010, the mailbox move to Exchange Server 2013 can be performed online, thus reducing the migration time somewhat.

Double-Hop Inter-Org Migration

Because of pressure from customers who did not wish to migrate from version to version, the double-hop inter-org migration approach was conceived. This approach relies on a resource forest with both Exchange Server 2010 and Exchange Server 2013 installed. Mailboxes are first migrated cross-forest from Exchange 2003 to Exchange 2010 and then immediately on to Exchange Server 2013. This method allows for mailboxes to be migrated to Exchange Server 2013 before Exchange Server 2003 has been totally decommissioned, and it requires only a small deployment of Exchange Server 2010 in the target forest. There are some downsides, however:

◆ It is an inter-org migration, and this brings with it the complexities discussed earlier in this chapter, such as having multiple Exchange orgs, GALSync, complex mail routing, and client redirection post-migration.

◆ Each mailbox must be migrated twice during each migration window, reducing migration speed.

◆ It enforces a resource forest model that increases complexity, especially if you wish to deploy a hybrid solution with Office 365 at a later date.

Migrating to Office 365

Office 365 provides *Exchange Online*, which is Exchange Server 2013. It also provides a way to migrate from Exchange Server 2003 directly to Office 365 via MRS over the Internet. This migration process is similar to the one used for an inter-org migration. However, the Office 365 platform provides most of the tool and coexistence software for enterprise customers free of charge.

We discussed hybrid deployments in Chapter 7, "Hybrid Configuration." However, for most customers who wish to take advantage of Exchange Server 2013, and who are currently running on Exchange Server 2003, moving to Office 365 is the easiest and most cost-effective way to achieve this at the current time.

Migrating to Exchange Server 2010

Sometimes our advice to customers running Exchange Server 2003 who must remain on-premises due to legislation or other constraints is to migrate to Exchange Server 2010 as a strategic platform. This may seem like unusual advice, but Exchange Server 2010 has proven to be a very solid platform and delivers huge improvements over Exchange Server 2003. For some Exchange 2003 customers, Exchange 2010 represents a better target platform than Exchange 2013 because of its easier migration path, and yet it still provides a very low total cost of ownership (TCO), including the ability to coexist with Office 365 in a hybrid environment.

The migration tools and process are well defined, and there are many skilled resources in the market with expertise in these types of migrations. All major third-party integrators have solutions for Exchange 2010, and the product remains in mainstream support until 2015 and extended support until 2020.

Common Migration Problems

This section provides some insights into problems that we have observed during migration projects and some possible ways to help you avoid them. All successful Exchange migration projects should be able to react well to unexpected events. As a mentor of mine used to say, "Expect failure." He was right—any project that cannot deal with setbacks is destined to failure. However, our experience shows that "forewarned is forearmed," and a little upfront planning can save you a world of pain down the line.

Failure to Get Business Support

Exchange migrations are very public projects. Most if not all employees of an organization will be customers of the Exchange service. This means that if there are any problems during the migration, there is a strong possibility that you will affect someone's working day negatively.

Frequently migration project teams use the term "seamless" to describe a mailbox migration. Although it may be possible to migrate the majority of mailboxes in an organization without them noticing, there are often times when this is not the case. Things can get interesting, especially if you have not taken the time to engage directly with the business area that is experiencing the problem.

IT project teams sometimes have a tendency to plan and act within a bubble. Exchange migrations are often a good example of this behavior. Since the migration project team does not need any technical assistance with the Exchange mailbox migration, the migration is tested, planned, and executed without engaging with the business at all. Although this can work sometimes, it is our experience that something usually goes wrong that could have been avoided by consulting the business unit beforehand.

Working with business area representatives prior to a mailbox migration and discussing their needs and use of the service can pay huge dividends in the event of problems down the line. This is especially true if contact is made in person by the migration project team. This type of engagement is extremely common in smaller environments. However, as the organizations with which you are dealing get larger and larger, it becomes harder to achieve. Nevertheless, it is in these larger environments where the payback is the greatest. If the project team has a personal relationship and contact point with the business area where disruptions may occur, then that issue is far less likely to be escalated, and it can be dealt with at a project level. Being able to deal with problems at the ground level rather than having them escalated to senior management is without doubt a huge benefit.

Once a business area feels undervalued and insignificant, they can make life extremely difficult. We have seen Exchange migration projects put on hold for six months because a single business area was unhappy about their mailboxes being migrated without being consulted beforehand. When we became involved and made contact with representatives from the particular business area, they had no complaint with the migration process itself. Rather, their main complaint was about the potential risk to service and lack of consultation beforehand. This relationship took a long time to mend, and the whole thing could have been avoided by a simple meeting between the parties beforehand.

Although not always necessary, our advice is to make contact with key business representatives, present them with details about the proposed migration process, schedule dates, and the expected user experience, and ask them for feedback. Determine how they would prefer to be kept informed of progress on the migration project, and ask if they want to be involved in the migration design and testing signoff. Experience shows that, once involved, the business representatives are generally very helpful and truly want the project to be successful.

Insufficient Planning

"Failing to plan is planning to fail" is a commonly quoted expression when it comes to project and design planning. Certainly, it is good advice to do adequate up-front planning, but what exactly is involved and why is it so important?

As it is for most projects, planning is vital for Exchange migration. However, by far the most important aspect of this is being practical. Many migration projects have a plan that looks just great on paper or when projected on a sparkly Gantt chart. When it comes down to implementing that plan, however, things often begin to unravel. This is not a failure to plan—it's because the plan itself is a failure. The tendency is for technical resources to try to work around a mess of a plan in order to get the job done. Sometimes this is successful, while at other times it's not. When it is unsuccessful, it can be extremely difficult to figure out exactly what has happened and to get back on track.

Our advice is to avoid very complex planning charts and keep migration planning as simple and practical as possible. Try to create a visual representation of the plan that can be presented to business areas and the project team. Most good project managers will maintain a complex Gantt chart for their own sanity, but this rarely is presented to or published for the business areas. Ideally, the plan should include all phases of the project, including the design, testing, piloting, and business area migration schedules.

Build slack into the schedule between phases to accommodate unexpected issues and to provide the design teams with adequate time to rethink and resolve issues appropriately. One of the most common mistakes we've observed is poor migration design decisions that were made because of rushing the design phase. Exchange migration design can be very complex, especially in large organizations.

Do not fall into the trap of thinking everything will work just fine because you purchased an expensive migration tool. It may simplify the migration process, but you still need to plan, design, and test your solution to ensure success.

Incorrect End-User Expectations

Different organizations maintain different relationships between the IT department and their end users. For some organizations, IT will go to great lengths to make the life of the end user as simple as possible—even if it means spending colossal amounts of time and money to avoid the user having to perform mundane tasks. Other organizations pursue a different path, and they embrace programs such as allowing end users to use their own devices and welcoming end-user interaction during a migration project.

While there is no right or wrong here, it is important that you understand the organization's expectations before you begin a migration project. If the end users who will undergo migration have been pampered by IT in the past, and the migration process that you intend to deploy requires them to perform manual tasks, you may expect that this plan will not be well received. Likewise, if the users being migrated are used to performing manual tasks, then you should not over-design the migration process.

Be aware of both the implicit and explicit expectations of the end user, and design your migration solution accordingly. Over-designing can lead to unnecessary expense and complexity, whereas under-designing may lead to an unacceptable experience for the end user.

Seamless vs. Velocity

You will need to determine whether your plan is focused on migrating everyone as quickly as possible to the new platform in order to minimize the impact of coexistence issues, or if end users will migrate slowly and in batches in order to minimize disruption. This issue is not as important with an intra-org migration, but it becomes extremely relevant for inter-org and foreign system migrations, where coexistence problems are very likely.

Many organizations have attempted to identify end-user relationships via delegate permission mappings and organization charts in an effort to migrate mailboxes in batches. The aim here is to reduce the likelihood of two users who share mailbox data frequently from being migrated at different times and thus experiencing disruption if they are migrated independently. The outcome of such attempts has always been fruitless in our experience. The problem is that the delegate permission relationships are highly complex in nature, and it is impossible to determine if they are in active use or not. For example, this may occur when a user has granted a colleague access to her calendar in a former role. The user now has a different role, but the old delegate relationship still exists along with new delegate permissions. How do you know which permissions are in use and which are not? Likewise, attempting to group users by department, physical location, or project is unsuccessful since these factors are not boundaries for data sharing.

As a general rule, attempting to group users together is rarely successful, and it often results in a complex migration scheduling process that leads to uneven batches of mailboxes to migrate. The only exception to this is for shared mailboxes, where it can be very useful to migrate the shared mailbox and everyone who has access to it at the same time.

Our recommendation for both foreign and inter-org migrations is to migrate as quickly as possible after a successful pilot has been performed. Provide an emergency "quick migration" process to migrate users who have problems accessing a previously migrated mailbox; that is, add them to that night's migration schedule.

The golden rule for migrations is never to migrate users backward; always migrate them forward. For example, if you migrated someone's mailbox inter-org but not their personal assistant's mailbox, the assistant may lose access to that mailbox after it was migrated. The first course of action here is to migrate the assistant over as quickly as possible, either via a support process that would move it immediately or add the assistant mailbox to the next migration batch to minimize disruption.

The aim is to migrate everyone as quickly as possible by maximizing every minute of the available migration window. This approach will cause some temporary disruption, but it generally provides the best overall experience. Attempting to avoid end-user disruption entirely during an inter-org or foreign system migration is generally an exercise in futility in any sizeable organization.

Application Integration

IT experts have often frowned on migrating to a new version of Exchange early in its release cycle. Many insist on never deploying a Microsoft product prior to its first service pack, believing the initial release will surely be full of bugs. The reality is somewhat different these days: Exchange Server 2010 had over 20 million hosted mailboxes running at the time it was made generally available, and it was proven to be a high quality piece of software very early on.

Exchange Server 2013 is a major new product release. This means that it has many more areas of significant development than Exchange 2010. Nevertheless, the same engineering quality processes have been used during its deployment, and it has been tested and operated within Office 365 by customers in the *Technical Adoption Program* and internally at Microsoft during its development phase.

Unfortunately, the quality of the Exchange release is not the only concern. Most organizations rely on third-party applications that must integrate with their Exchange infrastructure. These systems provide mobile device access, fax integration, customer records management, archiving and compliance, antivirus and message hygiene, and so forth. The bottom line is that a messaging infrastructure will typically rely on many vendors and software products, not just Exchange Server. When a new version of Exchange is released, the vendors of each of these supplemental products potentially will be at different phases of their own product release cycle and may not have a version of their product that supports the version of Exchange Server that you are deploying.

Our recommendation is to perform an early discovery operation and make sure that all of your dependent services and applications support Exchange Server 2013. Most vendors will share their planned product development roadmaps with existing customers and, in many cases, will work with customers to run and test pre-release software. For many organizations, it is a valuable process to be able to deploy early and potentially provide feedback for products in development.

Compliance

Many organizations operate in areas that have operating standards defined by a governing body. These standards often dictate rules defining how data should be kept and for how long and, potentially, in which country the data must remain. Exchange migrations must be designed to meet these requirements before, during, and after the mailbox is migrated.

Our advice is to get clear guidance on these compliance requirements and design a migration solution with them in mind. There is no more certain way to shut down a migration project than to discover a breach in data compliance. Some organizations may even be in danger of losing their operating license if they are found to be in breach of their compliance standards. Once you have a migration process designed, take the time to speak with the IT risk and compliance teams and get their input about whether it is going to meet their compliance requirements.

Migration Improvements in Exchange 2013

Exchange Server 2013 builds on the Mailbox Replication Service used in Exchange Server 2010 and provides a few new features to help with mailbox migrations. Some of these new features are described next.

Batch Moves

A *migration batch* is a group of mailboxes that is moved in one batch. With Exchange Server 2010, this approach was commonly achieved by scheduling a move request with the `-batchname` and `-suspend` options. These requests would then be started at the same time via the `resume-moverequest` cmdlet.

The `new-migrationbatch` cmdlet in Exchange Server 2013 provides this ability and retrieves the mailboxes to add to each batch from a predefined CSV file.

The new cmdlet features and examples are detailed at

`http://technet.microsoft.com/en-us/library/jj219166`

Although this new feature is hardly groundbreaking, it does simplify the creation of batch migrations via PowerShell.

Migration Endpoints

Migration endpoints are designed to simplify remote mailbox moves, such as those made during an inter-org or hybrid cloud migration. Each endpoint defines specific requirements to move mailboxes to that target environment, such as the type of mailbox move, the remote servername, and the credentials to use.

In Exchange Server 2010, these items had to be specified on each move request. By storing them as migration endpoints in Exchange Server 2013, they need only be defined once, and then each migration batch simply has to reference the name of the migration endpoint to determine the right location and credentials to use to move the mailbox.

Again, this was achievable in Exchange 2010 via PowerShell and saving credentials. The new-MigrationEndpoint cmdlet, however, makes this whole process much simpler and easier to manage.

Detailed information for the new-MigrationEndpoint cmdlet can be found here:

```
http://technet.microsoft.com/en-us/library/jj218611
```

Summary

Migrations can be monster projects that run for many years, while others are short and sweet. This chapter covered the most important aspects of a migration project, but it should be viewed merely as a starting point for your planning and not a complete reference on migration.

It is a relatively straightforward process to migrate to Exchange Server 2013 if you are running Exchange Server 2007 or Exchange Server 2010. The golden rules for this type of intra-org migration are to communicate with the business effectively, understand your application integration remediation steps, deploy your Exchange 2013 environment in coexistence according to Microsoft's recommended guidelines, and perform good quality testing prior to migration.

Legacy Exchange Server migrations, for example, Exchange 5.5, Exchange 2000, and Exchange 2003, require a more complex solution. Most of these environments will require a third-party migration solution due to the lack of continued support from Microsoft. Exchange Server 2003 customers wishing to migrate to Exchange Server 2013 should strongly consider Office 365, with Exchange Server 2010 on-premises being the next best alternative. If you must migrate from Exchange Server 2003 to Exchange Server 2013 on-premises, you will need to follow an involved migration path or speak to Quest or Binary Tree.

Foreign system migrations, such as Lotus Notes and Novell GroupWise, will require third-party tools for success. Again, Quest and Binary Tree have solutions available that are proven and reliable.

Chapter 15

Operating and Monitoring Exchange Server 2013

Why monitor and report on your Exchange service? Exchange monitoring, reporting, and alerting are fundamentally about one thing—keeping your messaging infrastructure running sufficiently to meet your service availability targets. Given this fact, it often surprises us that project teams will go to great lengths designing highly available clustered solutions, with overly complex redundant components, and then assume that installing an operations-monitoring product with its out-of-box configuration will be sufficient to keep things running.

Predictably, this approach rarely results in a great experience, and instead it tends to swamp the operations teams with initially interesting though largely irrelevant alerts that eventually get disabled to reduce "noise." These environments inevitably end up having an expensive monitoring solution installed with most of its alerts disabled. The main form of service alerting then comes from the most accurate barometer of Exchange service problems—the end users.

This is clearly an extreme scenario. Hopefully, though, it highlights a couple of points:

◆ Monitoring Exchange should be about the service it provides to its customers, not just miniscule variations in disk latency counters.

◆ If you are going to deploy an expensive monitoring solution and then ignore most of the alerts, you might as well have ignored the built-in product alerting system in the first place.

◆ Not every failure needs fixing immediately.

The final point here is worthy of a little more discussion. Quite often in enterprise environments with 24x7 operations teams, a server failure, or blue screen, will result in someone being paged to come and fix it. Obviously, this may be necessary in some cases. However, if your Exchange 2013 infrastructure has multiple database copies, and the service workload has not been interrupted significantly, then paging an expensive resource to come by and resolve a problem that does not demand immediate attention makes no sense. The difficult decision for an operations team is how to assess the actual impact of a specific failure.

Unless the Exchange design team has provided specific guidance for alerting, then the operations teams will often end up applying the same logic used for the previous system to the newly deployed service. This may or may not be appropriate, and the risk is that the operations teams may not be able to make best use of the new platform.

We will make reference to and give examples of how the Microsoft Exchange team operates the Office 365 service at extreme scale (many millions of mailboxes). As you read through this chapter, above all remember that the primary goal of service monitoring, reporting, and alerting is to maintain the level of service defined for *your* messaging service and *your* end users. Also remember that things fail—it's a normal part of running a service. Making intelligent decisions when dealing with failure is what separates great operations teams from the rest.

While preparing this chapter, we were lucky enough to spend some time with Matt Gossage, principal program manager lead in the Exchange product group, who was responsible for running Office 365. Matt made one thing crystal clear to us—you should *expect failures* within your service. Failure is a normal part of running a service at scale; the way in which you deal with these failures is the important part.

Monitoring

Historically, Exchange monitoring was performed via an external monitoring solution such as System Center Operations Manager (SCOM) or SolarWinds. These types of applications gather information from the service such as performance data, event logs, mail delivery metrics, and so on. Then they store that data in a database for analysis. Following that, the monitoring solution takes action based on the recorded data. For example, SCOM has a collection of Health Manifests that can trigger when a service is not running or if a performance counter is outside acceptable thresholds.

The problem with these types of applications is that they require fine-tuning for most deployments. Even for the Exchange Online part of Office 365, the SCOM deployment requires heavy customization to meet the operating requirements.

The root cause of this monitoring problem is simple. Albert Einstein said it the best: "Not everything that can be counted counts, and not everything that counts can be counted." What this means is that just because we can alert on how many milliseconds an operation took to complete, it doesn't necessarily mean that we should. Likewise, what is important is how the system is perceived to be meeting the demands of its end users. Recording how long an I/O operation took to complete is simple. Likewise, it's simple to define some thresholds and take action if they are exceeded. However, what if the threshold was exceeded and the end-user experience was just fine? How can we monitor the experience provided to the customers of our messaging service?

The truth is that a quality monitoring solution will require as much effort to design as the underlying service that it is monitoring. Not only will it monitor easy-to-harvest system data from event logs, performance counters, and message tracking logs, but it will also simulate user requests from outside the organization to observe how the system is performing from a user perspective. The solution should also be able to take action to fix common scenarios, such as failing over workload from an unhealthy DAG node to a healthy alternative.

Two important things to remember while reading this chapter are these:

◆ Change the way you think about monitoring. The name of the game is no longer just about sending alerts for individual performance counters or isolated critical system events—it's about maintaining service and keeping things running when you potentially have several places that could run the same workload.

◆ It is impossible to achieve a highly available service in the absence of a thoughtful and appropriately deployed monitoring solution. Although some may disagree, installing Gartner's monitoring product of the week and hoping for the best is unlikely to result in long-term success.

We will discuss some of the fundamental changes in Exchange 2013 that address these shifting requirements later in this chapter. We will also discuss how the Office 365 team approaches service operations.

Alerting

Alerting is what a monitoring solution does when something unusual has occurred. Historically, monitoring solutions ship with a database of thresholds for events and performance counters that, if exceeded, will result in some form of notification being dispatched: a Simple Network Management Protocol (SNMP) trap or an email, an SMS message, or a combination of both. The expectation is that a human being will eventually be tasked with resolving whatever anomaly is present.

As IT systems have evolved and have become ever more complex, so too have the systems designed to monitor and produce alerts on them. The bottom line is that it is a waste of time and effort to page an expensive on-call resource to fix something that is not directly affecting service. More significantly, the risk of human error increases dramatically when complex infrastructure is resolved under pressure by on-call resources.

One way to approach the issue of when to contact such resources is to consider service impact as a part of the alert. This can be complicated, however, and so it generally will require human involvement. (For example, it may not be an Exchange problem that has taken down service.) As a general rule, there are three types of failure in an Exchange 2013 system:

- Non-service-affecting failure

- Service-affecting failure

- Data corruption event

In the case of a *non-service-affecting failure*, the resolution will vary depending on what exactly has failed. If you have a DAG and other high-availability features, a single server failure or storage chassis failure could fall into in this category. If you have four copies of the data spread across four DAG nodes and one node fails, you still have three left, and so there is no real requirement to summon on-call resources. Instead, the failure should be investigated and resolved by the normal operations teams during normal working hours.

Service-affecting failures are significant in that there are end users without service. This is a no brainer—on-call resources should be mobilized, but "who you gonna call?" as the trio from *Ghostbusters* would say. Some of the worst cases we have worked on with Exchange systems had their root cause in a disaster recovery event where resolution was first attempted by the wrong resource and hence was done incorrectly. The single most important aspect of a service-affecting failure is to get the right resource to the right place as quickly as possible. It also helps if there is a set of predetermined scenarios readily available to resolve predictable problems, such as database reseeds or DAG node rebuilds.

Data corruption events are the worst type of alert, and they should be treated with the highest priority (so-called red alerts). There are various kinds of potential data corruption within Exchange, and all should be treated immediately. However, by far the worst is something called a *lost flush*. A *lost flush* occurs when Exchange thinks it has written data to the disk, but that data never got there—despite the operating system receiving confirmation that it did. Exchange attempts to detect these issues, and it will raise an alert if it detects one. Our guidance is to treat data corruption events with the highest possible priority—even if they are not affecting service. Have a remediation plan for data corruption and make sure that your team is drilled in its use. If a lost flush is detected, remove the suspect storage hardware from service immediately—do not put it back into production until the root cause is identified and resolved.

Reporting

Reporting covers a myriad of things, such as notifying customers, the business of system availability metrics, or system usage capacity reports showing availability headroom and trending.

Types of System Availability

It sometimes surprises design teams that there are two types of system availability: one that is presented to the business and one that is used within IT.

Business availability is generally a straightforward statement of system availability. That is, it is a statement of the availability of the system over a specific duration. Downtime during system maintenance windows and so forth is considered to be unavailable time. Sometimes, this value is actually calculated manually based on incident records and is not generated by system availability monitoring software.

IT availability data is usually more detailed, and it will take scheduled system maintenance windows into account. Typically, this data will be generated via a system monitoring application, and it will indicate periods of service outage and downtime during maintenance as available—even though, strictly speaking, the system was down.

Most system monitoring tools offer the ability to generate IT availability data, and the reports and charts that are produced are tailored to the IT audience; that is, they consist of relatively technical, jargon-rich information. On the other hand, business availability reports tend to be jargon free and simply state the system availability number for the month.

Trending

Trending is the taking of historical observations and using that data to predict the future. As anyone who has tried to predict the future knows, it's not often easy or accurate. Some things, however, are easier to predict than others, while, generally speaking, the farther into the future we wish to predict, the more imprecise things become.

Thirty years ago, weather forecasts were mostly inaccurate. In 2012, the Met Office (the United Kingdom's national weather service) ranked their five-day predictions to be as accurate as their 24-hour predictions were 30 years ago. This increase in prediction accuracy is mostly attributed to having precise historical data and more extensive observations from around the globe to work with.

The same logic applies when you are trying to make predictions about your Exchange infrastructure—the more information you have available, the more accurately you can predict what will happen next. Storage capacity usage is a common example. Imagine that you had capacity data for 100 mailboxes over the last six weeks compared to data for 10,000 mailboxes over the last six years. The smaller sample size will yield a less accurate picture of growth within the organization, especially if it was taken during a holiday period or during a particularly busy time. Moreover, a few of the 100 mailboxes may be especially heavy users, skewing the average. Having a significant historical data size available plus a representative sample size on which to base prediction trends is vital. There are various statistical methods for determining minimum sample sizes for a population. For Exchange trending, however, we recommend taking the simplest approach possible and recording trending data for as many users as you possibly can.

The next step is to know what kind of information is available that you should trend. As a general rule, the following are areas that benefit most from some form of trending:

- Storage capacity

- Network utilization

- System resources

- Service usage

- Failure events

Storage capacity trending is obviously not unique to Exchange. However, Exchange does bring with it some interesting nuances. Exchange storage capacity trending is made up of various subcategories, including the following:

- Mailbox databases

- Transaction logs

- Content index

- Transport queues

- Tracking and protocol logs

MAILBOX DATABASES TRENDING

It is important to understand that Exchange databases are not just made up of mailbox data; that is, there is other "stuff" in the database including database indexes (a structure to speed up data access), white space (empty pages that can be used to write data), and items that have been deleted that nonetheless are retained. Also, Exchange will never regain used storage space— even if the data inside the database shrinks. For instance, if you moved half of the mailboxes from one database to another, the source mailbox database would remain the same size, even once all of the deleted items have been purged. This is important since it means that there are many factors that can influence the size of mailbox databases. For example, some mailboxes may be moved from database to database leaving behind white space. This white space exists within the database, and it is not reclaimed from the disk. Thus, the actual storage capacity used on the disk remains the same. However, when new data is written to the database, Exchange will try to make use of the white space before extending the size on disk. This behavior can lead to unusual storage capacity data reports on Exchange Servers, and it is another reason why it's useful to have as much historical data available as possible. Short-term capacity trending for Exchange databases is usually meaningless. Try to get at least 12 months' worth of "steady state" capacity data before trying to predict storage capacity trends for Exchange.

TRANSACTION LOG TRENDING

Transaction log capacity trending may not initially seem like an interesting metric for trending. However, this metric provides two interesting pieces of information. First, the log generation rate is a very good way to observe the rate of change within the database, and second, if we know how many logs are generated per hour, it tells us how long we can potentially go without a sustained database copy outage (or backup if native data protection is not being used). Customers who have deployed a multicopy native data protection DAG often miss the second point; that is, they are relying on Exchange database copies and also potentially lagged copies rather than taking backups. They will then configure *Continuous Replication Circular Logging (CRCL)* to truncate the transaction log files automatically once they have been successfully copied, inspected on lagged copies, and replayed on all other nonlagged database copies. The key here is that the transaction log files do not get truncated unless they have been copied, inspected, and replayed on all other database copies. If you have a situation where you have four database copies and one is in a failed state, then the transaction log drives on *all* of the other database copies will begin to fill up. If this is left unchecked, the database will dismount. Therefore, having good trending data for your transaction log generation rate will govern how long the support teams have to resolve database problems before they affect service. Quite often, this value will have been predicted during the design phase but never checked or validated in production. Furthermore, the rate of transaction log file generation can change from service pack to service pack. This situation affected many customers when they deployed Exchange Server 2007 SP1, which radically increased the number of transaction logs generated.

TIP   The easiest way to gather transaction log file generation data is from a lagged copy, since these are persisted for 24 hours or more.

CONTENT INDEX TRENDING

The *content index (CI)* has changed significantly in Exchange 2013. The content index provides the ability to search mailbox data more quickly and effectively by creating a keyword index for each item stored within the Exchange database. In previous versions, there was a rough rule of thumb that said to account for 10 percent of the mailbox database for CI data. This guidance has changed for Exchange Server 2013 and CI database is now roughly 20% as large as the Mailbox Database. From our lab environment observations, the new CI database in Exchange 2013 appears to be roughly 7 percent as large as the mailbox database that it is indexing. It is not generally required to record or trend the CI space usage explicitly, but be aware that it exists in the same folder as the mailbox database and it requires additional space.

MESSAGE QUEUE TRENDING

Although there is no longer a specific transport role for Exchange Server 2013, the old Transport role has simply been incorporated into the Mailbox role. Message delivery is now a combination of the Front End Transport service on the Client Access role and the Transport service on the Mailbox role. This means that there is still a `mail.que` database on every Exchange 2013 Mailbox server but no `mail.que` on the Client Access Server unless it is collocated with the Mailbox role. The transport queue holds email messages that are queued for delivery or that Exchange is retaining as part of the new Safety Net feature. Because of this feature, most organizations will store the `mail.que` on a dedicated LUN. Trending storage capacity for the message queue database is nontrivial since, like the mailbox database file, it does not shrink as data is removed. From a trending perspective, it is sufficient to monitor the storage capacity required for this database file. It is rare, however, to see problems caused by a lack of space for the transport database because of the large size of today's hard drives and the relatively small size of the database.

WARNING   Watch out for the transport queue database growing in the event of a failure that impacts message delivery. This will cause the database to grow—potentially very quickly—and even once the fault has been resolved, the database file will not shrink. Our advice in this scenario is to ensure that you have a process in place to shrink the `mail.que` file after an event that causes an exceptionally large number of messages to be queued.

Because of Safety Net data being stored within the database, the recommended way to remove white space is to perform an offline defragmentation via the `eseutil /d` command. This will require taking the transport server offline for the duration of the process. If you have multiple Exchange Servers within the AD site, however, it is possible to take one offline and defragment the databases one at a time until they are all back to a normal size without affecting message delivery.

TRACKING/PROTOCOL LOG TRENDING

Message tracking logs are text files that contain routing and delivery information for every message that was handled by the Exchange Server. These files are used to track messages throughout the organization. The longer the files are retained, and the more messages your organization processes, then the greater the amount of space that will be required.

We have seen cases where a monitoring solution has been deployed that increased the duration for which message tracking logs were kept. The customer had not changed the location for the tracking logs, and they were still on the system drive when, a few weeks later, the customer's systems began running out of space. (Luckily, their monitoring system spotted this before it affected the system.) The bottom line is that even though these files are not especially large, they are stored within the default installation path unless moved and thus could potentially cause a problem down the line. Trending the storage space required over time is useful, although not typically vital.

NETWORK UTILIZATION TRENDING

Network utilization trending data has always been a critical resource for Exchange. It is becoming more and more important, however, as organizations look to consolidate datacenter locations and synchronize data between them to improve resilience to failure scenarios. The most important thing about network usage trending is to be aware of the data direction. Most network links are full duplex; this means that they can transfer data in both directions at the same time, although not necessarily at the same speed.

Network links may be synchronous (same speed, both ways) or asynchronous (faster one way than the other). This is an important differentiation since when we are planning and trending network usage, we need to specify in which direction the data is moving, for example, from Server1 to Server2 or from load balancer to client. By far the two most important areas of Exchange network utilization are from Exchange to the end user and replication traffic between DAG nodes.

End-user network traffic is typically asynchronous, with much more data passing from the Exchange service to the client than vice versa. If there is insufficient network capacity to meet end-user requirements, then network latency will increase. *Latency* is a value that expresses how long network data packets take to pass between hosts. As network latency increases, the end-user experience will begin to slow down due to data and operations taking longer to perform. We will discuss this in more detail in Chapter 12, "Exchange Clients." However, from a monitoring perspective, it is vital to record and trend network utilization information, especially for the Exchange Online part of Office 365 or consolidated environments.

DAG replication traffic is generated to keep database copies up to date and their associated CI. Database replication traffic is very asynchronous, and it occurs almost entirely between the active database copy and the replica copies. If the network link used for this replication traffic is insufficient, latency will rise, and this may lead to a delay in transaction logs being copied to replicas. This could be important since the delay in copying transaction log files between database copies increases the *recovery point objective (RPO)*. RPO is a value stating how much data you are prepared to lose in the event of a failure within your service. Obviously, if a failure occurs and the replica copy is 100 log files behind the active copy, then you have lost at least 100 MB of data on that database. Monitoring network links used for replication and attempting to trend capacity usage changes during the day can help prevent unexpected data loss during a failure.

Many organizations already have some form of enterprise network link-monitoring software. Not all of these programs, however, will perform trending of the usage patterns. The *Multi Router Traffic Grapher (MRTG)* provides the most common data by far. This is partly because it is free and partly because it uses Simple Network Management Protocol (SNMP) to query routers, switches, and load balancers, so it's a relatively straightforward process to get the data you need. MRTG displays this data in real time and historically in chart format. However, it will not show predicted future trends, and thus this will have to be performed manually.

Figure 15.1 shows sample output from MRTG taken from my home broadband router. (None of my customers wanted to share their link data!) You can see from the chart that there are periods of 100 percent link utilization. In my case, this is usually for synchronizing data to SkyDrive or downloading ISO files from MSDN. In an enterprise environment, this could easily be a scheduled backup occurring or perhaps someone reseeding an Exchange database across the network. Short periods of 100 percent utilization on a network link are relatively normal. However, those periods should be relatively short and ideally infrequent during the work day.

FIGURE 15.1
Sample network utilization graph from MRTG

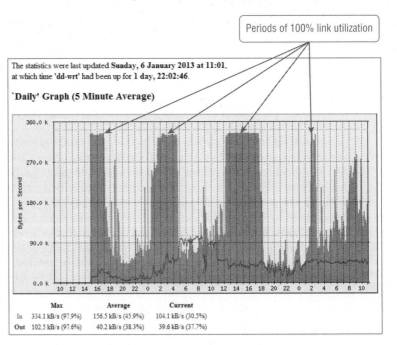

Monitoring and trending network usage are relatively easy, but they're only half the story. As mentioned earlier, network latency tends to have the most dramatic effect on data throughput and client experience.

Network latency is usually expressed as *round-trip time (RTT)* in milliseconds. It is common for network teams to monitor link latency within their datacenters between switches and routers. Nonetheless, it is not always common for this data to be used for future trend prediction.

System resource trending is the process of recording how servers within the Exchange service are using their critical system resources such as the processor, memory, and disk. Additionally, it is often useful to trend some key Exchange performance counters such as RPC Averaged Latency. RPC Averaged Latency is a very special counter for Exchange, since it essentially shows the average time taken for Exchange to satisfy the previous 1024 RPC packets. We highly recommend trending the `MSExchange RpcClientAccess\RPC Averaged Latency` value for all servers within your Exchange 2013 service.

Many teams perform this type of trending simply by recording performance monitor counters via the standard Performance Monitor tool included with Windows. Other customers prefer to use a third-party tool to do this. The most important thing about resource trending as opposed to alerting is that you are trying to predict *when* the system will begin to trigger alert thresholds. We will examine how to use Excel to generate future predictions later in this chapter.

Service usage trending is performed by recording historical information about *how* the service was used and then attempting to predict future growth patterns. This may include the number of active users on the system, the number of messages processed, the number of TCP connections, or Exchange performance counters such as RPC Operations/sec. Service usage trending is primarily used to justify changes in system performance behavior.

Imagine a scenario where the RPC Averaged Latency during the workday has gradually increased from 5 ms to 10 ms over a three-month period. Although this is useful information, you need to determine what is causing this change. Do you have more users on the system? Are the users working harder (increase in RPC Operations/sec)? Have you reached a system bottleneck (system resource exhaustion, processor, disk, memory, and so on)?

The job of service usage data is to help you understand what the customers of the service are doing, when they do it, and how their behavior impacts the performance of your Exchange service.

Recording failure occurrence is something that most organizations do as a matter of course, largely due to the mass introduction of the *Information Technology Infrastructure Library (ITIL)*, which also recommends trending of problems. Defining how to deal with such problems is outside the scope of this chapter. From a trending perspective, however, you are interested in when the problem occurred, how significant it was, whether it is happening regularly, and whether we can do anything to stop it from happening again. Remember the advice from Matt Gossage at the beginning of this chapter; that is, expect failure, because you will never be able to design the perfect system. Instead of attempting to stop all problems from ever occurring, consider designing the system to tolerate failure without affecting the service availability—especially if it is easier to do this than to fix the root cause.

Matt also provided one additional piece of advice, and that was to evaluate data corruption events seriously and quickly. Exchange 2010 introduced *ESE lost flush detection*. This is a form of logical data corruption that could impact all database copies, and these events should trigger the highest possible level of alerting and receive immediate attention. Any event that results in database corruption should be considered an extreme high priority. You must work to understand, resolve, and take action on such events immediately and to prevent them from occurring in the future.

USING EXCEL TO PREDICT TRENDS

We have talked about some interesting things to record and trend so far, but we have not discussed how to perform trending. Our favorite way to deal with trending is by using Excel. Ideally, this process should be completed roughly every three months, although some organizations do this on an annual basis only. The process begins with collecting the data and then converting it into a usable format. The potential sources of data are too varied to discuss here. Nevertheless, you'll eventually want something that you can import into Excel, ideally in a comma-separated value (CSV) format.

Once the data is in Excel, you can plot it against time and then use one of the Excel trend-line functions. Excel provides six options: Exponential, Linear, Logarithmic, Polynomial, Power, and Moving Average. Our advice is to begin by adding Linear trending to your chart and then experiment with the other options to find the best fit.

Figure 15.2 illustrates our recommended approach to trending. This example shows the disk LUN capacity data for a mailbox database. In this example, the customer wanted to know when their database LUNs would reach 65 percent capacity in order to allow them sufficient time to commission more storage. The chart shows two sets of data, an initial prediction based on 12 months of historical data and another prediction based on 24 months of historical data. A trend was identified and a prediction date derived for when the LUN would reach 65 percent capacity.

FIGURE 15.2

Example trend
chart in Excel

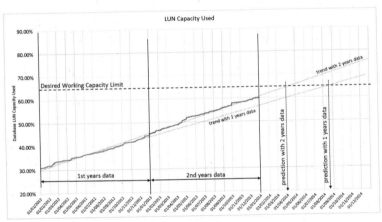

Initially, the historical data was plotted against the date axis and then a linear trend line was added. In this case, a linear prediction fits our data very well. We then drew a line at 65 percent capacity and looked to see where the trend line crossed the 65 percent capacity line. If we draw a line directly down to the date axis, this will give us a predicted date when the LUN will reach 65 percent capacity.

Figure 15.2 shows clearly that our prediction may change as more data is analyzed. This is why it is important to reevaluate your trending predictions regularly. We recommend that you update trending predictions quarterly.

As stated previously, though, the farther into the future the prediction looks, the less accurate it is likely to be. Likewise, the more historical data you have, the more likely the prediction is going to be accurate.

As a general rule, do not attempt to predict any farther into the future than the amount of historical data you have. That is, if you have 12 months' worth of data, only predict 12 months into the future. Attempting to apply a relatively short historical sample to predict well into the future is little more than guesswork and is unlikely to be accurate.

Inventory

Maintaining a list of hardware and software components that make up your Exchange service is extremely useful. Patching and maintaining an Exchange service can be complex, especially at scale. In the past, we have seen organizations that believed that *all* of their Exchange Servers were at a specific patch level, only to discover that some were not when we verified them physically. This problem only gets worse once you begin to include operating system patches, hardware drivers, and, potentially, even things such as hardware load balancer operating systems. All of these things can impact the service and the way the components interact with each other.

By far the best way to approach inventory management is to use a script or tool to do it for you. Luckily, Exchange 2013 has PowerShell, which makes it easy to find this kind of information. There are even some freely available scripts that you can download, which will provide a rich set of data. Steve Goodman wrote our favorite example of an Exchange inventory script, and it is available for free at the following URL:

```
http://www.stevieg.org/2013/01/exchange-environment-report-v1-5-6/
```

At the time of this writing, version 1.5.6 is listed on Steve's blog.

Figure 15.3 shows a sample output of this script. The script provides most of the critical information that an Exchange team will require to operate their service successfully.

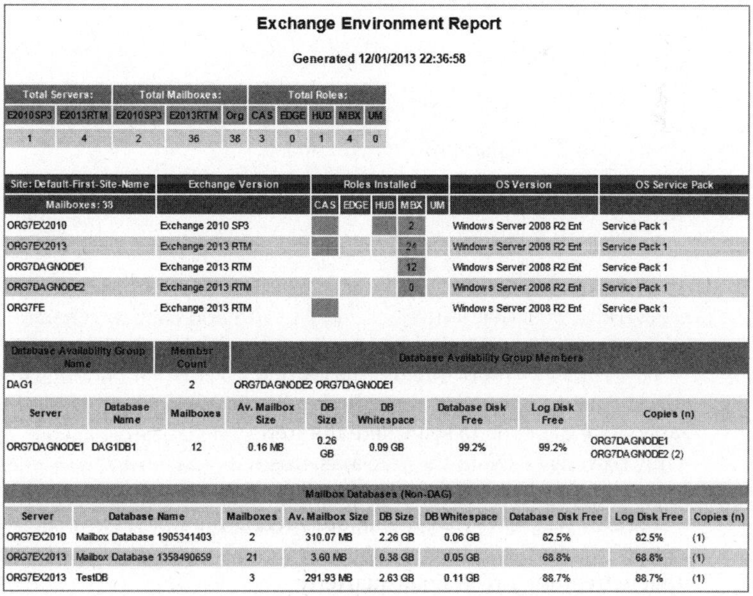

Exchange Environment Report

Generated 12/01/2013 22:36:58

Total Servers:		Total Mailboxes:			Total Roles:				
E2010SP3	E2013RTM	E2010SP3	E2013RTM	Org	CAS	EDGE	HUB	MBX	UM
1	4	2	36	38	3	0	1	4	0

Site: Default-First-Site-Name	Exchange Version	Roles Installed					OS Version	OS Service Pack
Mailboxes: 38		CAS	EDGE	HUB	MBX	UM		
ORG7EX2010	Exchange 2010 SP3				2		Windows Server 2008 R2 Ent	Service Pack 1
ORG7EX2013	Exchange 2013 RTM				24		Windows Server 2008 R2 Ent	Service Pack 1
ORG7DAGNODE1	Exchange 2013 RTM				12		Windows Server 2008 R2 Ent	Service Pack 1
ORG7DAGNODE2	Exchange 2013 RTM				0		Windows Server 2008 R2 Ent	Service Pack 1
ORG7FE	Exchange 2013 RTM						Windows Server 2008 R2 Ent	Service Pack 1

Database Availability Group Name	Member Count	Database Availability Group Members
DAG1	2	ORG7DAGNODE2 ORG7DAGNODE1

Server	Database Name	Mailboxes	Av. Mailbox Size	DB Size	DB Whitespace	Database Disk Free	Log Disk Free	Copies (n)
ORG7DAGNODE1	DAG1DB1	12	0.16 MB	0.26 GB	0.09 GB	99.2%	99.2%	ORG7DAGNODE1 ORG7DAGNODE2 (2)

Mailbox Databases (Non-DAG)

Server	Database Name	Mailboxes	Av. Mailbox Size	DB Size	DB Whitespace	Database Disk Free	Log Disk Free	Copies (n)
ORG7EX2010	Mailbox Database 1905341403	2	310.07 MB	2.26 GB	0.06 GB	82.5%	82.5%	(1)
ORG7EX2013	Mailbox Database 1358490659	21	3.60 MB	0.38 GB	0.05 GB	68.8%	68.8%	(1)
ORG7EX2013	TestDB	3	291.93 MB	2.63 GB	0.11 GB	88.7%	88.7%	(1)

FIGURE 15.3 Example Exchange Environment Report

We recommend keeping track of the following core information about your Exchange platform:

Organization information

◆ Organization name

◆ Versions of Exchange installed

◆ Number of servers installed

◆ Number of mailboxes in total

◆ Ad-site topology

Per-server information

◆ Operating system

◆ Exchange roles installed

◆ Exchange version and patches

◆ Mailbox databases per server

◆ Network card device driver and firmware

◆ Host bus adapter/RAID controller device driver and firmware

◆ Version of storport installed

◆ Build date

DAG and database information

◆ Database availability groups

◆ Database availability group membership

◆ Number of mailboxes per database

◆ Mailboxes in each database availability group

◆ Database/log LUN capacity usage

The free script provides an amazing starting point for this information. It does not gather everything, but what it does gather is useful and easy to generate. It also shows what is possible natively with PowerShell.

For many enterprise organizations, a free script will not meet their requirements adequately. Connecting to their corporate inventory system may be a part of the production handover process, but it may still be useful for the Exchange operations teams to maintain their own specific data about their service, since it will be more readily available and easier to modify if additional information is required. It is not unusual to see multiple inventory systems in use in large enterprises due to different teams requiring different information. For example, IT leadership may be interested in server numbers, costs, and licensing but probably not the device driver for the RAID controller in use on mailbox servers.

Our recommendation is to give Steve's free PowerShell script a test run, modify and update it as appropriate, and schedule it to update the HTML daily.

Monitoring Enhancements in Exchange 2013

Exchange 2013 is the first version of Exchange to be written since the Exchange product group became responsible for Exchange Online within the Office 365 platform. This is not often discussed outside of Microsoft. However, there is no denying that having Exchange developers and program managers called out to resolve faults within Office 365 has dramatically affected the direction that Exchange 2013 has developed. The benefits of running Office 365 are obvious when you look at a few new features in Exchange 2013.

Managed Availability

Managed Availability (MA) is a total shift in approach for Exchange. At its core, MA is a native health monitoring and recovery system. Historically, Exchange has provided a number of performance counters and application events that described how the system was performing. It was then the job of some other program or utility to analyze that information and do something with it. In Exchange 2013, this has been taken to a whole new level. Exchange MA is not only aware of how the system is behaving from both a performance and health perspective, but it also has predefined recovery actions that it can trigger to attempt to resolve any issues itself.

Exchange is now aware of itself in three ways:

♦ Availability

♦ Latency

♦ Errors

These items together define the health of the Exchange Server.

The MA service is made up of three main processes:

♦ Probe engine

♦ Monitor

♦ Responder engine

The *probe engine* is responsible for gathering data about the running of Exchange Server. This data is then passed to the monitor, which applies a set of logic to determine system health. If the system is found to be unhealthy, the responder engine will use its own logic to determine the correct recovery action to take at the time of the event.

Like most things, the monitors can be queried via PowerShell and have the following values: Healthy or Unhealthy (Degraded, Disabled, Unavailable, or Repairing). Once a monitor has entered an unhealthy state, a responder will take recovery action. This action will depend on the event and also on how many previous times it attempted to recover from it. The recovery action may be as simple as terminating and restarting a service, or it may be as significant as forcibly terminating a server.

One of the best sources of information on Managed Availability is Ross Smith IV's and Greg ("The Father of Modern Exchange HA") Thiel's blog post:

```
http://blogs.technet.com/b/exchange/archive/2012/09/21/lessons-from-the-
datacenter-managed-availability.aspx
```

When this feature was first presented to the messaging community, many people commented that there would be no need for Exchange operations teams or third-party monitoring solutions.

This was nonsense, obviously, but Managed Availability is likely to reduce the frequency of someone being summoned to deal with an easily rectifiable problem. If Exchange experiences a failure that MA cannot resolve, then in all likelihood the resolution process will require a skilled third-party support resource.

VIEWING SERVER HEALTH

Managed Availability brings with it a record of server health. To view the health information for a single server, run the following PowerShell command, replacing the server name with that of your own server.

```
Get-ServerHealth -Server org7ex2013 | Get-HealthReport
```

Figure 15.4 shows an example from one of our lab machines. Some unhealthy monitors are highlighted.

FIGURE 15.4

Sample health report output

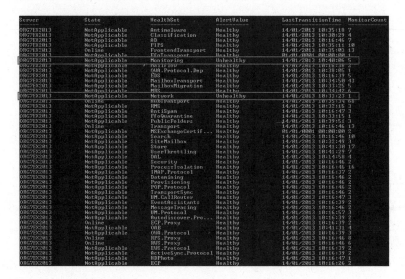

We can tweak this command a bit to show the unhealthy monitors:

```
Get-ServerHealth -Server org7ex2013 | Get-HealthReport | where { $_.alertvalue -eq
"Unhealthy" }
```

Figure 15.5 shows the output of this command, listing the unhealthy monitors for this server. In this example, you can see that we have a problem with the Monitoring and Network healthsets, but it doesn't give us any more information.

FIGURE 15.5

Unhealthy monitor example

Server	State	HealthSet	AlertValue	LastTransitionTime	MonitorCount
ORG7EX2013	NotApplicable	Monitoring	Unhealthy	14/01/2013 10:40:06	5
ORG7EX2013	NotApplicable	Network	Unhealthy	14/01/2013 10:33:23	1

To get more information, you need to pipe the previous command to format-list (fl).

```
Get-ServerHealth -Server org7ex2013 | Get-HealthReport | where { $_.alertvalue -eq
"Unhealthy" } | fl
```

Figure 15.6 shows the detailed output of our failed health monitors. You can see from this that we have a number of problems with system resources:

FIGURE 15.6

Monitor detail example

```
MonitorCount          : 5
Entries:
{MaintenanceFailureMonitor, ProcessIsolation/PrivateWorkingSetWarningThresholdExceeded,
ProcessIsolation/ProcessProcessorTimeErrorThresholdExceeded,
ProcessIsolation/PrivateWorkingSetWarningThresholdExceeded,
ProcessIsolation/ProcessProcessorTimeErrorThresholdExceeded}
```

Remember that this is a lab system, and so it has less than the minimum recommended system resources available. Thus, it would be a surprise if Managed Availability reported it as healthy. The report also shows us that this particular monitor has been triggered five times previously.

The second event is from the Network healthset, and its entries suggest that we have a problem with this server's DNS host record. The MonitorCount of 1 suggests that this is the first time that this problem has occurred:

```
MonitorCount          : 1
Entries:
{Network DnsHostRecordMonitor}
```

Hopefully, this brief walkthrough has highlighted the monitoring enhancement possibilities of Exchange Server 2013. For some environments, it may be possible to use Managed Availability and PowerShell to create an adequate monitoring and alerting system. Obviously, this is not to say that you will never need an additional solution for Exchange 2013. Nevertheless, many organizations will be able to operate without one for Exchange 2013.

Workload Management

Workload Management (WLM) is another new process within Exchange 2013 that aims to reduce the workload on the operations staff. The primary goal of WLM is to prioritize user experience over system tasks. WLM is also responsible for stopping a single "bad" client from overconsuming system resources.

Before we discuss what WLM does, we need to address what system resources actually are and how we think about them. System resources represent things like processor capacity, physical memory, or storage IOPS. Historically, these tended to be reported by percentage utilized; that is, how much of your system is actively at work at a given time. The tendency here is for teams to view low percentage utilized as good and high percentage utilized as bad. This behavior is understandable to some degree, since having a low percentage utilization of core system resources is likely to mean that your end users are experiencing good performance.

In recent years, however, there has been an increasing focus on service running costs. Thus, having systems running in the single-digit percentage utilization range represents a large amount of wasted resources. Ideally, you want to make full use of your system resources without impacting end-user performance. This is partly what WLM tries to do.

What Is Workload Management?

Workload Management (WLM) means trying to optimize resource utilization while at the same time preserving the end-user experience. It does this via the following processes:

◆ Intelligent prioritization of work

◆ Resource monitoring

◆ Traffic shaping

WLM is aware of how Exchange Server is managing its end-user requests by monitoring performance counters. It is then able to schedule background system tasks to use the space resources available. If these system tasks begin to impact end-user performance, then they are throttled back until they do not, or it may potentially delay these tasks from running until the system has more resources available. This is a simple but very ingenious way of removing the requirement to plan and schedule things like maintenance tasks. An important point to remember here is that background database maintenance, a process that performs physical database integrity checking, is never throttled, regardless of system resource usage.

The impact of WLM on operations is interesting. For example, consider moving mailboxes. A mailbox move is subject to system WLM, and so it will be throttled back if it impacts end-user experience. This means that you could perform mailbox moves during the day knowing that WLM would protect service performance. The mailbox moves may take a little longer than if you performed them during off hours, but since they can happen online, end users may not even notice.

Also, think about our trending and resource planning. If WLM is making use of system resources for background tasks, then this will impact how your system resource trending patterns will look; that is, they may appear as more highly utilized than with Exchange 2010 across the workday. However, the huge spikes in nightly maintenance tasks will not be apparent. The concept of trending system resources is still vital for Exchange 2013. Jeff Mealiffe, the program manager responsible for Exchange performance and sizing, often refers to this as "smoothing peaks and filling in the valleys." The workload remains the same, however, because WLM is just spreading it out more evenly.

WLM also introduces an improved end-user throttling system to prevent monopolization of system resources. The idea behind this is to promote fair use of Exchange Server resources for all users. Exchange Server 2010 introduced user throttling, and Exchange Server 2013 takes this further by providing better resource utilization tracking, using shorter client back-off delays, and the introduction of a token bucket.

From a deployment perspective, it is worth noting that if you are deploying in coexistence with Exchange Server 2010, mailboxes hosted on 2010 servers will use the 2010 policies, while mailboxes migrated to Exchange 2013 will make use of the newer policies.

Our recommendation for throttling policies remains the same in Exchange 2013 as it did in Exchange 2010: Leave the default global policy at its default values, and create and apply a new policy for system mailboxes where required.

Summary

This chapter walked you through some of the more interesting aspects of monitoring, reporting, alerting, trending, and operating an Exchange service. One of the challenges of writing this material is that Exchange is operated in such a wide variety of environments that what is important to one organization is irrelevant to another.

Hopefully, we have managed to convey the more important aspects of this topic for design teams; that is, design your solution with operations in mind. When you are making your design decisions, think of how those decisions may affect operations and support teams. The cost to operate and manage an Exchange service is usually an order of magnitude higher than the cost of designing and installing it in the first place.

Alerting should have some intelligence built in. Just because something has stopped working does not necessarily mean that you need to summon an on-call resource immediately, especially if the service is highly available and the end users are unaffected.

The goal of trending is to head off problems before they occur. It may take a little manipulation in Excel or the purchase of a third-party product, but being able to predict accurately when your system will run out of core resources is a vital competence for most IT shops.

Above all else, go and talk to the operations teams that will be responsible for running your designs, and make sure that you understand their requirements. It is generally much easier to hand a service over to production when the operations teams are included in the design and testing process. Don't forget that operations teams are also customers of your design.

Index

Note to the Reader: Throughout this index **boldfaced** page numbers indicate primary discussions of a topic. *Italicized* page numbers indicate illustrations.